The Individual in Cultural Adaptation

THE INDIVIDUAL IN CULTURAL ADAPTATION

A Study of Four East African Peoples

BY ROBERT B. EDGERTON

With an Introduction and Epilogue by
Walter Goldschmidt

A contribution to the Studies in Culture and Ecology
Edited by Walter Goldschmidt

UNIVERSITY OF CALIFORNIA PRESS

Berkeley   Los Angeles   London   1971

University of California Press
Berkeley and Los Angeles, California
University of California Press, Ltd.
London, England
Copyright © 1971 by The Regents of the University of California
ISBN: 0–520–01730–7
Library of Congress Catalog Card Number: 73–117948
Designed by Sandy Jo Greenberg
Printed in the United States of America

To Ceel

Foreword

THE INDIVIDUAL IN CULTURAL ADAPTATION by Dr. Robert B. Edgerton is a contribution to the Culture and Ecology in East Africa Project. It is thus one part of a larger collaborative effort designed to study the adaptive processes of change in culture, society, and individual behavior. The research team, consisting of five anthropologists and a geographer, did fieldwork in East Africa in 1961–1962 under grants from the National Science Foundation and the National Institute of Mental Health under the auspices of the University of California, Los Angeles.

The broad purpose of the project was to determine whether alterations took place in institutionalized behavior, in customary procedures both of ceremonial and everyday life, in cultural values, and in patterns of individual behavior in response to altered economic circumstances under aboriginal conditions. The general strategy of the research program was to study four tribes, each of which had sectors devoted largely or wholly to pastoral pursuits and other sectors devoted to hoe farming, and to examine through questionnaires, tests, and the usual anthropological methods of intimate observation and the questioning of informants, the social, cultural, and behavioral attributes of two communities (one pastoral and one farming) in each of the four tribes. Information on the geographical circumstances, the resource potential, and the man-land relationships in the four tribal areas was obtained by the geographer. An anthropologist obtained the social and cultural data for each tribe. Dr. Edgerton elicited responses to a battery of questions and tests from a sample of men and women in each of the eight communities being studied. It is this aspect of the project which is the subject of the present work.

The full research will be reported in a projected set of monographs by the research team. The projected substantive volumes, aside from a summary and theoretical one, are as follows:

Francis P. Conant, *The Pokot People*
Walter Goldschmidt, *The Culture and Behavior of the Sebei*
Symmes C. Oliver, *The Kamba of Kenya*
Philip W. Porter, *The Ecology and Environment of East Africa*
Edgar V. Winans, *Hehe Local Neighborhoods*

W. G.

Preface

In the wake of a somewhat belated liberation from the belief that social solidarity and functional integration constituted the essential characteristics of social living, some social scientists are coming to reject social order altogether and are seeing in its stead an increasingly unbounded social universe in which change and diversity are the paramount features. Man, who was once the conscientious conservator of culture, is now in danger of becoming a changeling, as whimsical as the vagaries of the situation or his reinforcement schedule.

Although this extreme position will probably prove to be no more than a temporary access of enthusiasm, it does contain some truths. Change and diversity *are* ubiquitous aspects of human conduct and human culture, and these facts *are* too seldom taken seriously by those who formulate or follow theory in the social sciences. It is surely a critical task of anthropology to record ambiguity, diversity, and change in rules, in attitudes, and in behavior, for all of these are to be found in any human community. Nevertheless, social order and cultural consistency are also facts of human existence, everywhere. The goal of the research reported in the following pages is to make a contribution toward an understanding of the processes by which human diversity becomes orderly and change becomes predictable.

Specifically, we examine the thesis that the environment exerts causal force over its human inhabitants, and that man's thoughts, feelings, and actions will for the most part be a response to his environment. Furthermore, we look specifically to the economy and to technology, and to those institutions deriving from them, for the most fundamental causal domain of the environment. In this search for regularities of sociocultural process, we can hardly shrink from questions of determinism, but we must be clear about what we mean by this term. We mean it in a probabilistic sense. Just as we must qualify statements of causal regularity by saying "in the long run" and "given a sufficient number of cases," we must also add to our probabilistic formulas that not all individuals in our population aggregates will change in the same way.

Therefore we clearly dissociate ourselves from the assumptions of homogeneity characterizing the formulations of Sumner, White, or Kroeber. For example, we could never endorse—even in less baroque language—what Kroeber wrote of the role of individual variability in cultural evolution: "A geologist could as usefully set himself the task of explaining the size and shape of each pebble in a gravel bed. We are but such stones."[1] Or this of individual innovation: "When a tide sets one way for fifty years, men float with it, or thread their course across it; those who breast the vast stream condemn themselves in advance to futility of accomplishment."[2] Kroeber's view of man helpless before the tidal wave of culture is as medieval as the view that the product of successful adaptation is an immutable social order. It has long been obvious that diversity, ambiguity, and change are present in any social order, no matter how "organized" or "well adapted" its institutions may be. A large and rapidly growing body of research attests to the omnipresence of variability in human behavior, beliefs, motives, and feelings, of ambiguity in man's cultural prescriptions and proscriptions, and of change in social institutions. This research also reports acts of individual innovation which have resulted in substantial changes in social organization or culture.[3]

That man is not a passive recipient of his environment but is instead an active reactor against it may reduce our ability to predict how his behavior will relate to specific environmental conditions. Our predictive abilities are also lessened by the fact that environments differ in their degree of coercive force over individuals. Some physical environments—arctic areas, deserts, tropical forests—are highly coercive in the limits they set upon human utilization of them. Of course, other environments are far less coercive in that they permit a wide range of economic adaptation even within simple technological systems. Similarly, sociocultural environments differ in their coercive force. Some, like many religious orders, may be highly intolerant of ambiguity or innovation; others, like some academic institutions, may be quite tolerant. However, as yet we know far too little about the relationship between the limits of physi-

1. Kroeber (1919), pp. 262–263.
2. Kroeber (1919), p. 261.
3. For various introductions to questions of variability and innovation, see Barnett (1953), Goodman (1967), Spuhler (1967).

cal environments for economic exploitation and the development of flexible or restrictive sociocultural control systems.[4]

What is more, if we accord man a common nature, and if we also admit that all social systems have many similarities, then we must expect to find a common core in the psychological relationship of *any* population to *any* environment. We must assume, therefore, that psychological differences between populations are likely to be less great than are the uniformities. Nevertheless these differences *can* be expected to form modal patterns that differentiate population aggregates, even though we reject a conception of man as a passive recipient of environmental influence, even though we see man as a striving, changing, complex, and variable system, and even though we are properly skeptical of all notions of homogeneity in personality.

Our perspective is that of ecology and our focus is upon the individual as he is engaged in coping with his environment. We examine the similarities and differences of farmers and pastoralists in four East African tribes. We are concerned with ecological adaptation; but we are aware that all change is a product of individual action, and we are therefore attuned to individuals with their aspirations, their joys and fears, and their complex, contradictory perceptions of themselves and their lives.

An elderly Kamba man once said to me: "A man is like a river. You can see what direction the water takes, but you cannot tell what is beneath the surface." We shall endeavor to see beneath the surface of life in these four East African tribes but we shall be satisfied if we succeed in describing the direction that these people—farmers and pastoralists—have taken in fashioning their lives.

This monograph reports the findings from one aspect of the Culture and Ecology in East Africa Project, directed by Walter Goldschmidt. This research has been a cooperative enterprise from the initial planning stage, through the field research from July 1961 to September 1962, to the present day. My research in particular could not have been conducted without the continual help of my colleagues: Francis Conant, Chad Oliver, Phil Porter, Bud Winans, and Wally Goldschmidt. To each of them I offer my thanks, not only for their generous cooperation, but for their friendship. It is to them that this monograph owes its greatest debt, for nothing that I attempted in the field could have succeeded without their assistance.

4. Cf. Bidney (1963), Goodman (1967), Lee (1959).

For their help in Africa, I am especially grateful to Yovan Chemtai, Thomas Aperit, Simeon Kioko, John Kalolo, and Ruth Yudelowitz. For their help with various aspects of the coding and analysis of the data presented in this monograph, I thank David Boyd, Lois Crawford, Karl Eggert, Carol Gaspari, Jerry Habush, Jerry and Susan Jacobs, Kay Kataoka, and Fred Prinz. For their help in preparing the manuscript, I am indebted to Juanita Baiz, Brenda Bassham, and Carol Camus. Mary Schaeffer has my gratitude for her labors over this manuscript, from the roughest field notes to the finished product. For their comments on various portions of this monograph, I thank John G. Kennedy, Craig MacAndrew, William B. Rodgers, all my colleagues in the project, and Cecile M. Edgerton.

The Culture and Ecology in East Africa Project was sponsored by the University of California, Los Angeles, and supported by a United States Public Health Service grant, MH-04097, from the National Institute of Mental Health. I have received additional support from the California Department of Mental Hygiene, Exploratory Research Grant 63-2-31. Computing assistance was obtained from the Health Sciences Computing Facility, UCLA, sponsored by NIH Grant FR-3. I also wish to acknowledge the assistance of the Social Science Research Institute (NIMH Grant MH 09243) at the University of Hawaii in the preparation of this manuscript.

The African people whose lives I entered, however briefly, in this research deserve my sincere thanks. Many men and women among the Hehe, Kamba, Pokot, and Sebei answered my questions with care and consideration. If the roles are one day reversed, I shall try to do as well.

To Walter Goldschmidt, who conceived and directed this project, my last word of gratitude is due. My debt to him as a scholar is obvious; my debt to him as a man is equally great.

Contents

Introduction:

THE THEORY OF
CULTURAL ADAPTATION

By Walter Goldschmidt

THE INDIVIDUAL IN CULTURAL ADAPTATION is the detailed analysis of the attitudes, values, and personality attributes of four East African peoples. It is a particularly crucial part of a research program designed to demonstrate the process of cultural adaptation. It is my responsibility to set forth the broader context within which Robert Edgerton's study was executed, to give the theoretical orientation of our common enterprise, and to place this book within that framework.

In very general terms, the Culture and Ecology Project was perceived as a means of illuminating the process of cultural evolution. It is a study, if you will, in the microevolution of culture. The four tribes selected for analysis each had sectors with primary emphasis on farming and other sectors with primary emphasis on pastoralism. The focus of our attention has been to record the differences between these sectors and to discover whether such internal variances demonstrated consistent patterns of adaptation in accord with a general theoretical construct of the relationship between the manner in which a livelihood is secured and the patterned aspects of interpersonal relationships and the behavior, values, and attitudes of the personnel.

The research was prosecuted by a team of six scholars: four ethnographers, each of whom recorded the social behavior in two communities (one predominantly farming, the other predominantly pastoral) in one of the tribes; a geographer who examined the environmental base and studied the economic relations of man to the land in all four tribes; and Edgerton, whose work consisted primarily of securing responses to a battery of questionnaires and tests from sample populations of each of the eight communities under investigation.

It can readily be seen that we have attempted to preserve the holistic approach that characterizes anthropological study while at the same time taking cognizance of internal variation and individual behavior, and have therefore used statistical treatment whenever possible and appropriate. The holistic approach was necessary, for our

1

ultimate interest lies in the manner in which culture (i.e., the general pattern of group behavior and perceptions) is shaped by external circumstances.

The strategy of our research led us to a plan in which social and cultural patterns of each tribe would be the subject of individual monographic treatment, while the comparisons of attitudes and values, based on the data recorded in the field by Edgerton (as well as the analysis of the cultural geographer), would be presented in comparative terms. The former would deal with what may best be called institutionalized adaptations, while the present work focuses on individual adaptations. Since the comparison of individual behavior has been completed and is here being offered well in advance of the ethnographic studies, and since it contributes a major basis for our general conclusions, it seems appropriate to include in this volume a summary of the theoretical position out of which the work emanates and something of the history of the project itself.

The Culture and Ecology Research Project was formulated just after I had completed *Man's Way*. That book was one of the expressions in the late fifties of the reformulation of evolutionary theory in anthropology. This new development of evolutionary thought, though it owed much to the dogged insistences of Leslie White and to the more systematic and ecological theories of Julian Steward, was nevertheless a break with the older schematic kind of evolutionism. In my mind, evolution (in terms of the grand scheme of development from simple to complex) increasingly came to be seen as but an epiphenomenon, as the perhaps inevitable but nevertheless secondary product of forces that were more immediate and realistic and which should be amenable to empirical demonstrations if not actually to proof. A similar set of ideas obviously infused the students of White, particularly as expressed by Sahlins and Service in their *Evolution and Culture* (1960), where they make the distinction between general and specific evolution. Specific evolution, to use their term for the moment, was simply the process of adaptation, of *cultural* adaptation. We must, therefore, examine the theoretical assumptions that underlie the idea that there is an adaptive process in culture, and how this relates to the general theory of cultural evolution, as well as to the work before us.

Man, like every other animal, must obtain food and shelter and must reproduce and nurture his young in order to sustain life. Like many other animals, he does this in the context of social groups. Unlike other animals, in massive degree if not in kind, his means of exploiting his environment is based on learned techniques rather than on innate patterns of action, and he uses for these purposes tools and instruments rather than actual parts of his body. In short and simple terms, he meets these exigencies through culture, and culture is to be seen as an instrumentality.

But whatever one's definition of culture may be, it is certainly more than merely the tools and techniques of living; it includes the institutions of social relationships, the beliefs, values, and shared sentiments of a population. Implicit in a theory of cultural ecology, these aspects of culture (or, at the very least, some of them) must also be seen as instrumentalities. Such a thesis is neither new nor self-evident. It is, again implicitly, recognized in functional theory, though here the purposes of institutions are seen to be merely those of self-maintenance. Ecologic theory places a greater demand on the instrumental character of institutional behavior, which is seen to relate not merely to self-maintenance, but to external (environmental) conditions of the social system as well. And in order to make such a program of explanation viable, it is necessary to formulate a more coherent set of ideas about man as an individual, as well as about society as a system and culture as a patterning of behavior. Here we can but outline the central elements of such a set of ideas.

Man's livelihood depends upon his continued collaboration, both in the production of food and other necessities of life and in the nurture of the young; thus there is a functional commitment to some kind of institutional form for the preservation of collaborative activities. Institutional forms are necessary, first because man is not genetically preprogrammed for such collaboration but develops it through the inculcation of behavioral sets in the process of growing up; that is, through learned behavior. They are necessary further, in our view, because man *is* preprogrammed for self-maintenance as an individual, and his individual impulses must be restrained or channeled into socially useful modes. Self-maintenance in man, however, is not merely the gratification of his appetitive behavior, though it includes this; it is more importantly the gratification of his ego, and this aspect of man must be fully and explicitly taken into account in any effort to formulate a theory of society. I take this "need for positive affect," as I formulated the concept in *Man's Way*, to be characteristic of the human animal, and the basic mechanism for both the maintenance of society and the continuity of culture.

Man is also programmed to deal with symbols, not only in his utterances, where this quality is thoroughly recognized, but in all aspects of his behavior. Thus the individual is not to himself merely a bundle of impulses that must be satisfied or restrained, but also a symbolic entity whose fate is his chief concern. But symbols, including the symbol of the self, are not, like appetitive behavior, simply products of biological chemistry; they are by their very nature taken from the environment of a symbol-using and symbol-sharing community. The symbolic self, the fate of which the individual endeavors to control, is therefore a product of the culture in which the individual is operant, as well as the actions the individual has himself taken. Community consensus regarding the desirable conduct of life, generally referred to as cultural values, provides a template for conduct by which the individual measures his self-esteem. In a theory of cultural adaptation, the elements that enter into this model are relevant to the activities necessary under a particular set of economic conditions. That is, the ego rewards, offered in the form of esteem or status, are made available to those whose performance is meaningful in the socioeconomic situation under which the people live.

Personal self-motivation is potentially disruptive to that level of social harmony necessary for the maintenance of a viable community. A social system must provide motivation that channels these self-oriented impulses so as to minimize this disruptive potential. Or, to put the matter in positive terms, it must capture these impulses so as to make possible the collaborative efforts necessary for maintenance of the community. The most powerful weapon for bringing this about is the establishment of a personal identification of the individual with some larger social entity, so that his ego needs are fulfilled by events that advance this larger social group. The form and character that such groups will take on should, in terms of this theoretical position, be relevant to the explicit requirements of the situation in which the community finds itself, that is, to the ecologic circumstances under which the community is operant. Such social units can be formed on a variety of bases, but as ethnographic literature demonstrates, they are most commonly built upon the sentiments of kinship.

The concept of ecology carries with it the notion of a relationship between a biological entity, in our instance a tribe or community, with an external environment. The community must derive its support from the environment and must protect itself from the dangers that inhere in it; the ecological perspective concerns itself with the formulation of patterns of behavior by means of which these two categories of action are undertaken. In other animals this takes place

4

primarily through genetic elements that control the structure, physiology, and behavior of the life forms. In man, as we have already noted, this involves a change in learned behavior—the technical apparatus and knowledge that he possesses and the systems of collaborative action among the members of the community. A theory of cultural ecology postulates that, as the external situation varies, the effective instrumentation in the form of tools and techniques also varies and the requirements for effective human collaboration are altered, and that, therefore, it is possible and often necessary for *institutions* to take on different forms and hence for *individual behavior* to change in conformity, if it is to be appropriate to the new situation. Or, to put the matter so that it has particular relevance to the general progress of evolutionary development, when and as new techniques for effectively exploiting the environment are discovered or invented, the ecological relationships of the community and its environment are altered, making possible and perhaps necessary the development of new institutional forms and requiring alteration of propriety in individual behavior, attitudes, and values. Of course, neither the invention of a new device nor the "invention" of a new institution is a self-evident matter, and social systems are not notably characterized by perfect systems of environmental exploitation nor by perfectly developed institutional patterns, for the fitness of the cultural repertoire depends in no small degree upon the creative imagination of the personnel to find solutions to their problems, as well as upon other more difficult considerations which need not be brought forward here. Yet, in the evolutionary perspective, it is ultimately those cultures that most nearly meet these needs that will survive.

This, then, in barest outline, is the theoretical construct of the relationship between technology, institution, and personal behavior that underlies a general theory of cultural ecology. Specifically, our interest has been to test this adaptive process in a natural laboratory. Two earlier research experiences led me to the plan of the project. In 1944, I had made a detailed comparison of two communities in which I endeavored to show that the means by which the environment was being utilized (essentially the difference between family farms and corporate farming) had a chain of sociocultural consequences (Goldschmidt, 1944). I felt, therefore, that a holistic comparison could be fruitful as well as feasible.

In 1954 I engaged in research among the Sebei of Uganda, and my East African experience led me to recognize that aspects of tribal economic life provided a natural laboratory setting for testing this adaptive process. The Sebei were clearly an ethnic unit, united by the recognition of the primacy of a single prophet for the several constituent tribes. Yet they were quite variant in the subtler aspects of culture. Indeed, I soon discovered that the Sebei themselves recognized these differences (often expressed in prejudicial remarks about the people from other sectors of Sebeiland). Such evidences led me to believe that in important ways the Sebei differed internally, and that these differences could reasonably be attributed to the different kinds of economic life modes that characterized the diverse sectors of the population. At that time anthropologists were still unquestioningly speaking of tribes as social entities, assuming the homogeneity of tribal cultures (as frequently they continue to do). It was clear that homogeneity did not characterize the Sebei, a point amply confirmed in this volume, and such internal differences could be seen in other African tribes. It was the recognition of this situation that led to the central idea that underlies the Culture and Ecology Project, namely, that a shift from pastoralism to farming, or vice versa, had profound effects on the patterned behavior of a people.

My first effort to investigate such differentiation was initiated in conjunction with Edgar V. Winans, a participant in this project, with whom I had worked out a dissertation research plan to analyze the Arusha, the settled Masai of Tanganyika, with specific reference to the adaptation of Masai culture to farming life. But our interest there had been anticipated by Philip Gulliver, who was just then engaged in the field research that led to his *Social Control in an African Society* (which gives us much insight into the very processes that are the subject of this project), so that Winans's plans had to be altered.

I had also long been impressed with the essentially ecological analysis by Frank Secoy (1953) who, in his brilliant monograph on Great Plains history, showed how the horse, the fur trade, and the gun altered the intertribal relationships, as well as the relation of man to the land, and required shifts in patterns of institutional behavior to meet the exigencies of the new situation. Symmes C. Oliver (1962), one of my students and a member of the Culture and Ecology research team, further examined this ecological adjustment, showing evidence both of the continuation of older cultural forms and the emergence of adaptive institutions necessary for Plains life of the nineteenth century.

By 1959 Winans had returned from the Shambala and was teaching at the Riverside campus of the University of California, and

Edgerton and Oliver were completing their doctoral work. Edgerton, trained in psychology as well as in anthropology, helped to develop and had tested the values instrument (which, with modifications and adaptations, became part of the battery of tests used in his research on the project) as his doctoral dissertation (Edgerton, 1960; Goldschmidt and Edgerton, 1961). These three worked with me to formulate the basic design and research strategy, and we continued our discussions throughout the academic year 1960–61, having received some preliminary funding from the National Science Foundation. In the fall of 1960, Francis P. Conant, who had made ecological investigations in Africa, joined our team and our discussions; and in the spring of 1961, Philip W. Porter, whose studies in West Africa were clearly relevant to our interests, filled out our complement of staff and rapidly added sophistication not only to the environmental end of our investigation but to our understanding of the man-land relationship so crucial to our study.

As already indicated, we worked out a research plan in which an ethnographer studied the culture and institutional behavior of one tribe, concentrating his attention on two communities within the tribal boundaries that would be representative of the farming and pastoral sectors, respectively. His work, in addition to standard ethnographic techniques, involved the accumulation of certain consistent data from a sample population, basically the sample utilized by Edgerton in his comparative work on all four tribes. An analysis of the environmental characteristics, the methods by which the resources were exploited, and some measure of environmental potential under native technological competence formed the task of the geographer. Fundamentally, our test was one in which, in a manner that has precedent if not tradition, we converted space into time.

We chose to study four peoples, believing that this was the most that could be undertaken with the concepts and ideas we had in mind, and the fewest that would provide a satisfactory "sample" of such instances. Furthermore, we felt it was absolutely necessary to have these instances within reach of one another; that is, broadly speaking within one culture area and, if possible (for administrative reasons), within one modern state. Ultimately we chose to work with the Hehe of Tanzania, the Kamba and Pokot of Kenya, and the Sebei in Uganda.

Now it should be stated that the contrast between pure hoe farming and pure pastoralism is as clear and massive a contrast as one is apt to find in the operations of tribal economies. That is, if we con-

trast a pattern of life activities in which people engage in hoe farming and have no livestock with one in which people are caring for
cattle, sheep, and goats but do no farming whatsoever, we arrive at
contrastive forms of activity that are about as "far apart" in the demands they make on human behavior as we are apt to come upon
when dealing with self-sufficient, noncommercial forms of economy.
Perhaps a shift from hunting to agriculture, or from one of these to a
fishing economy, would be as dramatic, but such instances are rare
and even more difficult to research. It is fortunate that the contrastive
qualities inherent in the pure economies are so pervasive, for the fact
of the matter is that we did not find such pure dichotomies in any of
our tribes; indeed, while the "most pastoral" community was actually
entirely dependent upon its livestock, the "most farming" community
(in a different tribe) was not entirely devoid of any livestock whatsoever, though the animals that were owned were not by any means
setting the life habits of the people. This is, of course, one of the imperfections of our "laboratory situation," rather than our research
design, and one that has caused us not only additional labor but considerable agony as well—as is clearly shown in the substance of this
volume.

A comparative analysis of the type that we are engaged in in the
Culture and Ecology Project involves us in the concept of ideal types;
and before we discuss the more specific elements of the types we had
in mind, it is necessary to explore the nature of pastoralism and farming or, more particularly for our purposes, hoe farming or horticul-
ture.

Pastoralism is widespread, being found on three continents of
the Old World and, if we accept the development of native economies
built on the horse and sheep in the Americas, both continents of the
New World. But there are important differentia with respect to the
forms pastoralism takes: the animals may be largely capital equipment rather than sustenance, as was the horse among the Plains Indians and the camel among many peoples of North Africa and South-
west Asia; the form of integration of pastoral peoples with farmers
varies widely, from complete independence (separate tribes or na-
tions) to subservience of the pastoralists to a dominant farming community, as is true in parts of modern Europe; dominance of pastoralists over farming communities of slaves or subordinate classes, as
among the Watutsi; and various forms of symbiotic mutual dependence of the pastoral and the agricultural communities. Furthermore,

many people who can best be described as pastoralists (i.e., peoples whose life mode is dominated by the needs of their animals) also engaged in varying degrees of farming operations, as is true among the Navaho and the Turkana.

Pastoralism also varies with the kind of animals under domestication, for the needs and habits of cattle are not the same as those of sheep and goats, or of reindeer or llamas. It is not necessary here to go into the differential demands these diverse animals make, but merely to take cognizance of the fact that there are variations and that insofar as these are salient, they have implications for any model that we may build. It goes without saying that our model is directly concerned with that form of pastoralism in which there is a primary dependence on cattle, but significant secondary dependence on goats and sheep; furthermore, that these are consumable goods, however much they are also capital or measures of prestige. We might also take note of the fact that our pastoralists are unmounted, for it is reasonable to believe that the increment in mobility that derives from riding animals would have important potentials for altering the institutions of society. Our ideal type of pastoral economy, then, is one in which unmounted herders maintain cattle as a primary objective, augmented by sheep and goats to the degree that this appears feasible, heavily dependent for their personal welfare on these animals which they must, therefore, husband as best they can.

If pastoralism is far from a constant, it is clear that farming allows for even greater variation. Even when we limit ourselves to the cultivation of plants without the use of plow and draft animals, we readily recognize there is diversity in crop, with the particular demands each makes of its cultivators, and the length of fallow between successive land uses, not to mention the ratio of yield to labor input and the probability level of crop failure, all of which have direct consequences for the character that social life can assume. Consider merely the difference between grains grown under the technological competences of aboriginal Africa, with its limited use of irrigation and fertilization, and the cultivation of plantains in the same region. Not only does the latter yield substantially greater amounts of edible food per acre and per unit input of labor, but it does so year after year, for the plantain is a "permanent" crop, sustaining its diligent cultivator year in and year out for two or more generations. Grains, on the other hand, not only yield less food (though of a higher quality) per acre and per unit of labor, but also under native African cultivation techniques can be sown on the same land for no more than two or

9

three years, after which the land must be fallowed for a period of time, variably in accordance with local conditions. These factors make for quite different man-land relationships and have their implications for the forms that social life will take. Winans (1965) in his analysis of the Hehe for the Culture and Ecology Project has discovered no fewer than five basic land-use adjustments within modern Uhehe, four of which are predominantly agricultural and each of which directly influences the character of the interpersonal relationships in the respective areas.

Realistically, the farming in East Africa before Westernization strongly affected procedures was one of hoe farming on small plots, the primary crops being either maize, millet, sorghum, or plantains; we made the assumption that circumstances and techniques made possible relatively short fallow periods, so that land was more or less in continuous use, for where land is abandoned between one use and another, the farm communities do not have that stability that provides so essential a contrast to pastoralism. This situation did obtain in varying degrees among the four tribes studied, though otherwise there was considerable variation, with plantains the major crop among the farming Sebei, maize the major one among the farming Hehe and Kamba, and finger millet among the farming Pokot, though in each instance there were other crops of importance. Cultivation techniques also differed.

It is reasonable to assume that some modes of economy are more "demanding," that is, more delimiting on the character of social behavior, than are others. Just as we may say that the demands on a ballerina for muscle control not only differ from those on a bricklayer but are also more exacting, we may reasonably assert that the limits set by one economic form may not only differ from those of others but may be more explicitly defined. To take an obvious anthropological example, an arctic environment places greater limitations on the potential forms a culture may take than does a tropical one. It is reasonable to believe that pastoralism places narrower limits on potentially viable social forms than does hoe farming. There is in fact empirical evidence for this belief, for while in nearly all pastoral societies the animals are under masculine control and the social organization is patri-oriented, among hoe farmers there is by no means so consistent a pattern. The data presented in this volume further corroborate this supposition, for as Edgerton demonstrates, a clearer and more consistent pattern of behavior emerges for the pastoralists of the four tribes than for the farmers. It is perhaps worth noting that

Leonard Doob, who had engaged in extensive psychological research in Africa and who graciously served as a consultant while we were formulating our research plans, anticipated this conclusion, saying: "Herders may have more consistency in psychological traits or in value traits throughout a battery of tests than do farmers. Thus though horticulturists may differ greatly from herders on the whole, they may be less consistent among themselves."

There are some further details of our research situation that deserve consideration. The most important of these has to do with the degree to which our actual research situation failed to conform with the ideal pattern we had used as the basis for our hypotheses. In none of the four tribes examined was there that clear distinction between pastoralists and farmers to which the model makes reference. Indeed, only by contrasting the Pokot pastoralists with the Sebei or Hehe farmers do we get close to the limits of the range between the two modes of economy; all others are better characterized as mixed economies. We were not so innocent as to have been unaware of this possibility, though we had expected to find a somewhat closer approximation to our models than we did. We had also thought it would be possible to formulate a rather clear index by means of which we could range the eight communities between the polar extremes, and in chapter 10 Edgerton discusses this effort. It is quite clear that the several measures we used failed to meet this objective. One measure that would have been the most fruitful is the proportion of labor time devoted to farming and to pastoral pursuits. Indeed, the logic of our position suggests that this is the single most important operative factor in the differentiation, for we argue directly from the tasks imposed to many of the elements of behavior and attributes of personality. We did not develop such an index, for to gain a quantifiable measure of such an allocation of work time was clearly beyond our resources. Any reasonable measurement would have had to take an age and sex distributed sample from each population over a year-long cycle of activity.

But I am now convinced that the search for a linear index was destined to fail because the "intermediate" forms of ecologic adaptation do not range themselves in a simple bipolar series; that is, the divergence from the pure form of pastoralism is not merely toward a pure form of farming, but is a particular ecological adaptation of its own, with its own peculiar qualities and its own inner dynamic. Thus Hehe pastoralism was leavened by, of all things, a pattern of irrigated farming, a kind of farming that requires a high rate of interaction and tends to create stable communities, even though the herds may be far more significant to the economy than the farm produce, and though men may be away for long periods of time with their stock. In the Sebei pastoral community, on the other hand, a pattern of farming with ox-drawn plows was rapidly growing in an area pioneered fifty years earlier by a few herdsmen. The Kamba farmers did not operate cattle camps, but they did place their "savings" in livestock which were taken care of either by sons or by others at a long distance from the community. It is important to realize that these communities each made a unique ecological adaptation and each form of adaptation had its own particular influence upon the character of social life and personal behavior. This does not undermine either the theoretical presupposition with which we entered into the research nor the validity of our findings. On the contrary, the fact that certain pervasive features of the model contrast are demonstrable, despite the imperfection of our laboratory situation, suggests that the forces at work are indeed salient and effective determinants of behavior. Nor should we be apologetic for the limitations imposed upon us by this situation; these are the inevitable conditions under which the anthropologist must work.

Another element in our field situation which had potentially disruptive effects on our results was the fact that each of the tribes had long been subjected to Western influences. Our interest was essentially in adaptation to *native* economic forms, yet we were studying people who had in varying degrees adopted European practices and had altered their patterns of life to the new context provided by colonial governance. Furthermore, it was not reasonable to assume that farmers and pastoralists should have been affected by these external influences to a like degree, but that the farmer would (as our data subsequently reaffirm) be much more subject to them. We anticipated this problem and endeavored to correct for it in diverse ways: by selecting communities relatively uninfluenced by modern developments; by keeping the farming and pastoral communities within each tribe at a similar level of acculturation; and by formulating an "index of acculturation" with which to measure the degree to which individuals had been subjected to Western influences. Edgerton found that there were no significant correlations between the degree of individual acculturation and the responses to his tests, and that therefore the differential behavior and personality attributes he analyzes here cannot be viewed as a product of acculturative influences. To be sure, the acculturation of a tribe or a community is not merely the sum of the measures of individual Westernization, and the communities have been altered by the European presence. But it is reasonable to assume that in the degree to which it is present, Western influence has tended to mute and obscure ecologically adaptive differentials rather than to account for those we found, to lessen rather than heighten the processes we were seeking to analyze.

It is proper to make explicit three basic assumptions in our thesis. We made the initial assumption that a people with a common name represents a population of common historic background (perhaps with external accretions) or, more simply, that each tribe shares a basic culture. The differences between the communities of pastoralists and farmers are thus seen as the result of a shift from the common tradition on the part of one or both of these sectors. It is in this sense that we are translating spatial variations into a temporal sequence in order to arrive at a social process. The longer the time of separation and the more complete the isolation between sectors, the greater would be the expected level of cultural differentiation. However, the very fact that each of our four societies regarded itself as a single people indicates that neither could the length of time be very great nor could the degree of isolation be absolute. This points up two aspects of our research design that must be fully appreciated: (1) we are dealing with short-run changes rather than with what might be called anthropological time, and (2) the interactions between the two sectors of each tribe are mutually "contaminating." Both serve to minimize the differential; we are indeed dealing with *micro*evolutionary phenomena.

A second assumption is that a people will tend to develop those techniques for the exploitation of the environment which prove the most fruitful in terms of population maintenance, within the limits of the repertoire of technical knowledge available to them. This assumption clearly evokes a concept of rational actors, at least with respect to those elements of behavior which can clearly be seen by the people themselves to have a direct payoff in terms of sustenance. (It does not require that every individual will act with such rationality nor at all times, nor that there are no areas of tradition which survive in the face of more rewarding "rational" alternatives.) There is sufficient evidence in the details of our investigation to indicate that this assumption is quite valid and that, in fact, such a rationalizing factor operates rather quickly and efficiently in establishing patterns of land use suited to local conditions. The evidence for such an adaptive process among the Hehe, taking place within a century, has already been noted. That all aspects of institutional life do not display so clear a pattern of adaptive behavior will surprise no one, least of all ourselves. In some areas of sentiment, notably emotional attachment to cattle, there clearly is resistance to change.

The statement, "within the limits of the repertoire of techniques available to them," has reference to the fact that any people is apt to know about more technical information than they will be using at any one time. They know, for instance, some of the practices of their neighbors, which they either do not care to employ or which for ecological reasons do not serve them. While we cannot expect a people to invent or discover whatever might be useful to their purposes, we can expect them to take over the use of such practices when circumstances manifestly make them effective, as the Sebei adopted the plantain in some not very remote prehistoric period from their Bantu neighbors. On the other hand, the Sebei did not adopt the irrigation system known to the Pokot and Marakwet, though surely they must have known of its existence. Whether their failure to adopt irrigation relates to some ecologic condition, to the unwillingness to invest so great an amount of labor, to institutional incapacity, or to a lack of specific knowledge in engineering such a system, I do not know. We can say that plantain cultivation was in the technological repertoire of all Sebei, whether they actually engaged in its cultivation or not; we cannot be so certain with respect to irrigation works, and we can clearly say that the ox-drawn plow was not within that repertoire until Europeans brought it.

Since, assuming the repertoire of technology to be a constant, the effective exploitation of the land depends on the character of the environment, our analysis treats these environmental factors as the "independent variable" and the exploitation of that environment as the dependent one. However, since our primary concern is with nontechnological attributes of culture, it is perhaps better to consider the mode of economic exploitation as an "intermediate variable," leaving institutions and behavior as the "dependent variable." It was precisely because of this logical construct that we needed to have a detailed knowledge of the physical environment and the degree to which the people were efficiently exploiting it, within the limits of the repertoire of techniques available to them, and therefore to include a geographer on the research team.

As we anticipated, pastoralism dominates in areas of relative aridity and farming in areas of relatively greater moisture; in East

Africa, the former on the relatively low-lying plains and the latter in the uplands or mountainsides. The pastoralists, therefore, live in areas where both mobility and the danger from marauding neighbors are greater. While no two environments are exactly alike, and while many of the other characteristics of the environment have potential consequences for the economies of their inhabitants, this is certainly the basic and most pervasive environmental differential from the standpoint of cultural adaptation.

Our third assumption, already alluded to, is that the mode of environmental exploitation has pervasive effects on all other aspects of culture. This involves a view of a sociocultural milieu as an interlocking system in which there are chains of cause and effect of such a character that when one element is significantly altered it has direct or indirect repercussions on other parts of the system. Such alteration is produced by an "external event," such as removal to a new environment or the adoption of new elements in the technology, or both. (Other kinds of external events could be posited, such as a new ideological movement impinging on the population, or the infusion of a militaristic group, for example, the Ngoni invasion of Central Africa. However, our analysis is concerned with the repercussion of an *economic* change.) Disregarding feedback loops and other complications, we can generalize such an analysis in the following diagram (see p. 16).

During the planning phase we developed a series of specific hypotheses regarding both institutional and behavioral characteristics we would expect to differ between pastoralists and farmers, to which attention should be given. These were constructed in terms of the theoretical position already outlined, and in terms of ideal types of the two forms of economy. For reasons indicated, we felt that the model for pastoralists was clearer than for farmers, and we tended to formulate our thinking in terms of shifts from pastoralism to farming, but without the assumption that this was necessarily the historic sequence of events. We preserved various working papers from our extensive discussions, and it is from these that I draw some of the anticipated variances in culture and behavior.

The first and most important comparison has to do with the relation of man to the land. In essence, the keeping of cattle requires of the herdsman a high degree of mobility, requires it of him and also makes it possible, for the obverse of this is seen in farming communities where an individual can leave the community only by abandoning his capital (which is in the form of land), while the pas-

15

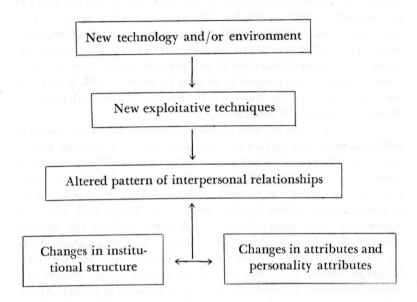

toralist's capital can be moved with him. We are convinced that this very clear and very obvious difference has many far-reaching consequences.

This differential has direct institutional consequences with respect to land rights: in pastoral societies individual private control of grazing land and other natural resources creates major diseconomies, and we would not expect such ownership of grassland. Farmers, on the other hand, must usually make an investment in the land they use, and to the degree that they do so, require assurance of access to it. Individual farmers, therefore, normally have such assured rights, though these may be institutionalized variantly.

This situation, in turn, permits mobility to the pastoralists and deters it among farmers, for the cattleman's capital can be moved with him while the farmer loses his investment and the basis for his security if he leaves the community. We anticipated that this would have far-reaching influences on behavior, for the pastoralists could move away from a situation where hostilities developed, while the farmer had to live with his neighbors no matter what social strains characterized the relationship. Thus, for instance, we expected that the pastoralists would be more "acting out" in their interpersonal relationships, more ready to express anger and to take direct action, while the farmers

16

would suppress their negative emotions and restrain their actions. A further consequence of this, we thought, would be that the farmers would be more secretive in their behavior, use indirect means of expressing their hostility, and that therefore the incidence and emphasis on the use of witchcraft and sorcery would be greater.

Another line of thought is related to the kind of work each engages in. It is a fact of comparative ethnography that large animals kept by pastoralists are handled by the men, and we believe this relates basically to the difficulties and dangers inherent in the pastoral pursuits. I think also there are other more subtle factors at work; that large stock has an effect on the psychological orientation of the population, quickening a kind of "masculinity" which is reinforced by the demands made upon the men in herding them. Comparable forces are not at work in farming communities; the work is often in the hands of women or shared by them; it is characterized by drudgery rather than danger, by hard work and long hours rather than by hardships and deprivation; nor does it heighten the differentiation of the sexes either by separation in work routine or by physical separation.

We think there is a further consequence of the difference in work routine in that the pastoralist is required to make far more independent and meaningful decisions than the farmer, and in these he must calculate more uncertain variables. The cogency of his decision-making ability is apt to be the basis of his success. He is also more apt to be alone when he makes these decisions, relying less on either tradition or community support in arriving at them. Farmers do make decisions as to what and when to plant, but this is a limited choice and tends to be set by custom. These elements require the pastoralist to be more independent-minded, more given to taking risks, and hence to have a greater capacity to act. A consequence of the recurrent need for decision making, we anticipated, would be a greater reliance on divination but a less fatalistic view of events.

While warfare is certainly not limited to pastoral societies, the nature of military threat is apt to be quite different in the two economies, and the institutional needs should likewise be different. Pastoral warfare consists of the constant possibility of an imminent raid by which the cattleman may lose his wealth and his life if he is not on the alert. This constant preparation for military action has as a natural counterpart the readiness to engage in aggressive action as well. The essence of such warfare is speed and mobility. Farmers are more apt—especially in acephalous societies—to engage in defensive warfare. This differentiation has both institutional and personality consequences.

On the institutional side, we anticipate that the farmers must be organized on a community basis for mutual defense, while pastoralists need a means of articulating a dispersed population (for which either the age-grade or the segmentary lineage system functions admirably). Together with the masculine control of wealth, the military pattern was also seen as supportive of patri-oriented social systems, while farmers' activities were not so determinative.

With respect to personality, we anticipated two major consequences. The first is further support of the acting-out pattern of behavior already noted. The second is the support of a syndrome that can best be phrased as a masculine sexiness, a concern with the body and its adornment, sexual aggressiveness, and *machismo*. The kind of work the men do in each society is influential to this attitude as well, for the pastoralist must be ready for action, suffer physical hardship and deprivation, but he spends his time in a kind of enforced idleness even when at work. This is particularly true of the young men. We did not see in farming activities, whether in the demands of their warfare or their work routine, any support for such an orientation, but rather a contrary one.

In our planning for the research we also felt that the nature of the capital on which the two economies are based would have consequences for the systems of social status, as well as the means for status advancement. If we contrast cattle to land as the basic capital resource, we may characterize the former as being relatively volatile in the sense that size of holdings is subject to gross fluctuations. Furthermore, the increase in size of one man's herd does not, or at least does not appear to, lead to the decrease in that of another member of the community, whereas land acquisition tends to be either a withdrawal from a limited public store or taken directly from another member of the community. Also, the increase in livestock holdings is apt to be more directly related to the qualities of the husbandman than is the increase in landholdings. The pastoralists' status system was therefore seen as more likely to be based on assumptions of achievement than ascription, as a manifestation of personal qualities (whether skill or luck or mana) of the owner rather than as a consequence of some external definition of his social position. It was also thought that social mobility would be greater among pastoralists than among farmers, or at least that status would be perceived as being more mobile. We saw these elements as reenforcing more egalitarianism, a heightened individuation of behavior among pastoralists, as against the heightened importance of office and inherited position among the farmers.

Closely associated with this aspect of social organization is the handling of legal disputes. Under the conditions of mobility, both geographic and social, that characterizes pastoral communities, we anticipated that the kin group would be the jural unit upon which the ultimate sanction of law enforcement rested, adjudicated either by resort to vendetta, wergild, or both. Though farmers may also have this form of legal action, they are more apt to have formalized courts, allocating jural decision to a neutral third party representative of the community. Indeed, the continued close proximity of people within farming communities creates a pressure for the establishment of some internal mechanism for regular noncombative settlement of disputes, and I have elsewhere (Goldschmidt, 1967a) shown that the Sebei did develop a limited form of community law with the advent of settled agriculture.

Notice has already been taken of some aspects of religious activities that flow from the economic differences. A greater emphasis upon witchcraft should be found among farmers, as they must restrain their open expressions of hostility and yet cannot escape the objects of such hostility. The use of divination would be more important to pastoralists, because they have a greater need for decision making. Fatalistic attitudes should prevail among farmers, who have less power to act when faced with a threat from nature. Rituals (and other social gatherings) would be expected to place greater emphasis upon the individual (rites of passage) in the pastoral communities where the youth must be socialized to independence, but more emphasis on the community (rites of intensification) in farming areas, where they must be socialized to interdependence.

These, then, are the kinds of differentiating social characteristics that we developed in the course of formulating our plan of research. In view of the short time involved and the continuing interaction between the sectors of the peoples under study, we did not expect to find clear-cut institutionalized expressions of these differences, but only tendencies toward the formation of the patterns that our models called for. At the time these ideas were being formulated, we were breaking away from the generally accepted notion of the cultural fixity of primitive people which has dominated anthropological thought from its inception. We were not then denying the reality of the construct culture, nor do we do so now. We expected behavior to be conservative, that there would be resistance to change and evidence of "irrational" and nonadaptive behavior. In the substance of this volume, consideration is given to the continuity and consistency of cultural attributes in the face of ecological adaptation, and if there is any surprise to us in this it is that these are not more pronounced, despite the fact that we concentrated our attention on those aspects of behavior we anticipated would be more responsive to change.

In this context, a word might be said about the Bumetyek, a group of originally Bantu-speaking Bagwere who moved eastward to Mount Elgon perhaps a century ago and became a part of Sebei though retaining some of their ethnic identity. They all speak Sebei, both the men and women undergo the Sebei ritual of circumcision, and, though they retain Lugwere as their domestic language, they minimize their cultural separateness. They live in a farming sector of Sebeiland, and are not intensively concerned with livestock. What is striking about these Bagwere, however, is that in subtle but expressive ways they retain qualities of their older culture. This was brought firmly to my attention when I chanced upon a minor ceremonial—one shared with the Sebei, though perhaps also it was an old Bagwere custom—and observed their sinuous dancing and relaxed comport-ment, so very unlike the rigid and controlled dancing with which I had become familiar. It was this experience that led me to suggest that Edgerton obtain some protocols from among them, in addition to the regular controlled samples from the four tribes. That the Bumetyek display patterns quite unlike the Sebei, despite their efforts to identify as Sebei, is made clear by the results of this special in-vestigation.

In final analysis, despite cultural consistencies and institution-alization of action, behavior is a matter of individual acts, and what the anthropologist observes is the actions and the expressions of so many individuals. While the consistency among them is inculcated by the accepted ideas of the community as to the appropriate forms of behavior and the reinforced expressions of belief, each individual must ultimately come to terms with the existing establishment in a form that is personal and idiosyncratic. Culture change is the center of our interest, and such change is seen as taking place through indi-vidual acts of disaffection with established wisdom and individual acceptance of new forms of thought and action. This forces us to ex-amine the behavior of individuals in the social system, in particular their personalities, sentiments, expressed attitudes and personal val-ues, and it is this aspect of life that is the subject of investigation in *The Individual in Cultural Adaptation.*

It seems appropriate, therefore, to conclude this discussion of our anticipations by summarizing those that pertain to the character-istics of the individual, though we have anticipated many of them in the preceding discussion.

In the area of expressed values we anticipated that pastoralists would recognize: (1) militaristic virtues such as bravery, readiness to take direct action, capacity to endure hardships and pain; (2) decision-making ability; (3) sexual prowess, including sexuality, concern with physical beauty, and a concern with the body, its ornamentation, and display; and (4) a sense of "face." We expected values to receive sym-bolic expression in possession of cattle and in bodily decoration.

Farmers' central values would center around: (1) manipulative skills, particularly verbal ones; (2) industriousness; (3) relative sexual chastity and fidelity; and (4) qualities of outward amiability rather than preservation of face. Status would be symbolized by land owner-ship, quality of the house and household goods, and perhaps by mul-tiple wives, though we doubted that this last item would be differ-entiating.

On many attitudes and relationships we expected a differential emphasis, rather than sharp differentiation. We expected that pastor-alists would display more paternal role dominance; that they would engage in more extramarital sexual rationships, that among them the co-wives would not display as much mutual hostility and antagonism, that they would focus more on youth status as against farmers' greater interest in the mature years, and that they would be less anxious to have children, and would prefer sons to daughters.

In the realm of personality traits our expectations were quite clear. We anticipated that pastoralists would be more "acting out," would be more independent, would show more direct aggression, would generally be more able to express their emotions. By contrast, we expected the farmers to suppress their emotionality, to be more hostile in interpersonal relationships but unable to express such senti-ments through direct action. We expected that they would, therefore, be more devious and more given to witchcraft as a means of handling their aggressive feelings. We were not certain whether the greater free-dom of expression among the pastoralists or the greater restraint among the farmers would lead to greater impulsivity of action, but the findings clearly indicate that such impulsivity is associated with con-straints.

An examination of Edgerton's conclusions makes it clear that the general pattern of our expectations has been realized. Though the differences he has demonstrated as existing between the pastoralists and the farmers have not been great in magnitude, they are statistically significant, internally consistent, and, moreover, clearly consistent with the conceptual model we developed on the basis of our general theoretical orientation. There were, to be sure, some surprises and some discrepancies, all of which are clearly indicated in the text; but on the whole we believe that our picture has been confirmed, and that they are supportive to our general theory regarding the adaptive character of culture. The data on the institutional aspects of the differentiation are yet to be analyzed; the evidence of the adaptation of individual behavior, values, and attitudes is presented in this volume.

Procedures and Methods: Collection and Coding of the Data 1

In accepting an invitation to participate in the Culture and Ecology in East Africa Project, I accepted a mandate to devise means for discovering and recording variations in values, attitudes, and personality attributes within and between pastoral and farming populations in four East African tribes. This mandate carried with it formidable conceptual and methodological challenges. Many of these are described in later chapters. This chapter introduces the methodological considerations that gave direction to my research within the project, and reviews the procedures and methods employed in the collection of data.

A detailed report of the assumptions, procedures, and methods of this study is called for not only to avoid the common practice of partial and imprecise recording of field procedures (one that obscures much that is of methodological significance), but also because a principle is at issue. I believe that it is improper to report anthropological findings without reporting the processes of discovery which led to these findings. We cannot simply presume that all ethnographic findings are alike the product of a standard and acceptable conduct of inquiry; much less can we remain silent about these procedures when the research inquiry departs from the ethnographic "field study" tradition. The present study is such a departure, for although the cross-cultural comparison of values, attitudes, and personality attributes is not without both illustrious and excellent antecedents, the trail that pioneering researchers have left is neither wide nor well marked, especially when one attempts to follow it through tribal Africa.

The following account of the research undertaken in this project may be useful to those with an interest in the comparative study of peoples' beliefs and feelings, but the primary purpose of this chapter is not the enlightenment of specialists in the cross-cultural study of values or personality. For that purpose a far more detailed account would be required. This chapter is intended to serve a dual purpose, as a cautionary note to those so unwary that they would attempt similar research without thorough preparation, and as an essential aid to those wishing to understand and evaluate the findings presented in succeeding chapters.

THE DECISION TO MEASURE

In our view of ecology, any human society was seen as a social and cultural system, existing in a continuing process of interaction with its physical and social environment. We assumed that the components of this system were complexly organized, with human beliefs and feelings being as much a part of the system as technology and features of social organization. Our presumption, then, was not that values, attitudes, and personality attributes were epiphenomena of the essential social and cultural processes that stood at the core of an ecosystem, but rather that they were part and parcel of the system itself. Indeed, since ecosystems are but models that purport to reflect or clarify the organized nature of human living, it is difficult to imagine that values (beliefs regarding what is proper), attitudes (dispositions, preferences, opinions, and the like), and personality attributes (largely unreflective patterns of thought and emotion that activate and characterize individual behavior) could be anything other than essential components of that system.

This is not the place for an excursion into ecological theory. I want only to clarify our concern with values, attitudes, and personality. As I have noted, these matters received special attention in our research design not because they were thought to be "special" or epiphenomenal features of ecological adjustment, but rather because we believed that such matters were important, and because their systematic comparative study required specialized procedures that could not easily be utilized by each resident ethnographer. What is more, given the necessity to make comparisons among eight separate populations within four different tribes, the study of such phenomena required both freedom of movement and a concerted research focus.

As Walter Goldschmidt has shown in his introduction to this research, many of our anticipations about the nature of the variation between pastoralists and farmers were focused upon values, attitudes, and personality characteristics. Over the course of many planning sessions, a large number of hypotheses—or, to be more candid, guesses —were formulated. Over the months of discussion that preceded our field investigation, these generally worded hypotheses varied in number and in content, but a core of these expectations remained as a consensus of our thought.

These and related anticipations were never precisely worded as hypotheses for formal test within hypothetico-deductive procedure. They remained throughout as general orientations around which I was to assemble data and in relation to which the ethnographers would, insofar as possible, direct their attention. As orientations they were useful, indeed necessary, because they provided foci around which investigation could center. Phrased as formal hypotheses, they might well have constricted inquiry. Our interest in this research lay in a broad range of possible differences between populations. Therefore, unless the theoretical and conceptual apparatus behind this project were so sensitive and refined that we could be certain we knew all the important questions to be asked, to have explored only those questions specific to certain hypotheses would have incurred a great risk of overlooking important issues. That is, as David Bakan (1968) has recently argued, an overreliance upon specific hypotheses can blind the investigator to *unanticipated* differences. In this study, it was simply impossible to anticipate all the meaningful differences that might obtain between "pastoralists" and "farmers," so it was decided to attempt to discover as many unanticipated differences as possible. Consequently, our "hypotheses" served primarily as orientations, and data collection was permitted to range over a wide array of questions in an effort to discover important differences between farmers and pastoralists.

However, our goal was not confined to discovery; we also wished to document our findings in such a way that they would easily be understood and evaluated, and thus confirmed or disconfirmed. Therefore, prior to any decision on the selection of data-gathering techniques, we had to determine upon the degree of precision of measurement we would seek. That we were obliged to measure was obvious, for the data sought had be maximally comparable if the intertribal evaluations we intended were to be successful. Hence, objectivity was an essential goal.

One means to objectivity is quantification. As Abraham Kaplan (1964) has pointed out, what we mean by objectivity is intersubjectivity, and intersubjectivity can be achieved—and often is—without benefit of numerals. Yet, counting is undeniably useful, perhaps even imperative, when objectivity in large-scale comparisons is the goal. The assignment of numbers to data not only provides a standard language of comparison, but also permits the use of modern statistical techniques of description and analysis.

For these reasons, the decision to measure was made, but without any commitment to the illusion that numerical data are "hard" data whereas data that are not quantified remain "soft." The distinction between hard and soft data, I believe, is an illusion, one that often collides with other illusions in behavioral science to leave all too many confusions in the semantic wreckage. What was sought here were techniques of collecting data that would *efficiently produce valid information*.[1] To assign numbers to such data *may* improve both precision and efficiency, but it need not do either.

With this commitment to precision, it was fundamental that any data collection techniques employed would have to rest upon a foundation of probability sampling. The details of the sampling philosophy and procedure are presented later in this chapter. For now, it is enough to say that all considerations of data collection and measurement were predicated upon the availability of a large number of informants selected by probability sampling methods.

Because of my belief in the value of observation, every effort was made to locate observational techniques that were both objective and practical. As Heyns and Lippitt (1954), White (1951), and others had pointed out well before this research was begun, techniques for objective observational data collection do exist, and one need only devise appropriate categories by which observed behavior is to be rated to assure the feasibility of measurement. Such measurement systems have varied from the mechanical sophistication of Chapple (1942, 1953), Bales (1950), and Matarazzo et al. (1956), through the ingenious and systematic judgmental systems of Barker and Wright (1954) and Harris (1964) to the simple approaches used by Gellert (1955) and Whiting and Whiting (1960).

From these and other studies it was obvious that values, attitudes, feelings, and personality attributes could be inferred from observable behavior. Surely ethnographers do so routinely, as does each

1. See Kaplan (1964) and Zelditch (1962).

one of us in everyday life. The problem, however, lay in locating a technique whereby I, as a lone observer, could arrange to view relevant interaction among a large number of people in eight distinct populations, and observe the same interactions in each place under comparable conditions. That is, the problem was not so much a matter of special techniques as it was one of special circumstances.

Therefore, although I decided to make as many comparable observations as possible in each site, I concluded that nothing short of an immense research staff, formidably equipped with training, sensitivity, skill, and photorecording equipment, provided with time in abundance, and blessed with almost perfect rapport, could hope to make precise and comparable findings by observational techniques alone. To have attempted comprehensive, objective observation of the varied interactions among many individuals in eight separate areas within the resources and design of this project would have been a lunatic enterprise.

Nonobservational techniques of eliciting data consist of one or another variant on the theme of, "If you want to know, ask." These techniques ask questions of informants, either directly or through pictorial or manipulable stimuli as in the psychological or projective methods; and, as the crude saying implies, they assume that people can and will answer your questions. The design of this research made a reliance upon interviewing mandatory. The decision was not made lightly. No one in this research project suffered under the illusion that "words are deeds in miniature." Quite the contrary. Indeed, I endorse heartily Irwin Deutscher's (1966) indictment of social scientists for their unreflective choice to study words, not deeds. I take Deutscher's broadside to be well aimed and long overdue. I agree that, in our collective study of verbal behavior, social scientists have opted for neatness and precision of measurement, and thus for convenience, not for behavioral reality in all of its contradictory complexity. Yet I must nonetheless defend this decision for the study of words, precisely on the grounds that it *was* a means to neatness and precision of measurement. I believe that our comparative design left us no choice but to interview, and to concentrate our comparative analysis upon the words thus elicited.

I must also take issue with Deutscher's conclusion that, in all our long concentration upon the study of verbal behavior, we have yet to show that there is any necessary, or even predictable, relationship between what men say and what they do (1966, p. 247). I agree that many efforts to demonstrate such relationships have been un-

27

successful, but I conclude, as does the social psychologist Milton Ro-keach, that such efforts often betray faulty research design, and that some studies *have* shown that how men behave can be predicted from their attitudes, values, and beliefs (Rokeach, 1968). To take such a position is not to assume any simple or invariant relationship between words and deeds; nothing could be more absurd or easily contradicted by research, or by commonsense. Neither do I wish to give the impression that I believe that attitudes or values necessarily have causal priority over behavior; I believe that attitude change *can* bring about behavioral change, but in general, and given sufficient time, it is more reasonable to assume that, as men adapt to environments, their behavior, their thoughts, their feelings, and their beliefs change more or less together, with behavior, if anything, having primacy. But even if attitudes and values lag behind adaptive behavior change, as we know that they often do, it is nonetheless reasonable and important to study attitudes and values as indices of ecological change.

CONSTRUCTING THE INTERVIEW BATTERY

Techniques of interviewing have been reviewed by Hyman (1954), Paul (1953), Campbell (1955), Richardson et al. (1965), and many others. Most of these formalized question-asking techniques can be placed in one of these three classes: (1) interview schedules, (2) projective tests, (3) multiple inventory tests of personality or attitudes. Anthropological interviewing has tended to be informal, concentrating upon intensive questioning of "key" informants. Survey research methods involving the brief and relatively impersonal use of interview schedules with large numbers of strangers have been shown to possess some predictive validity in the West, yet they are rarely employed in anthropological research with non-Western and nonliterate populations. In a few instances, as with Streib's work among the Navaho (1952), and that of Leighton et al. (1963) in Nigeria, survey interview methods have been successfully employed.[2] Yet such methods are apparently still regarded as novel. For example, Leighton et al. (1963, p. 269) described their work as follows: "The present study broke new ground by indicating that it is possible to ask a systematic sample of Yoruba people questions about integration and cultural change which will yield responses leading to quantitatively significant

2. For a review of survey techniques in anthropology, see Bennett and Thaiss (1967).

information about the group." This work by Leighton and his associates was not published in time to be of any influence in planning the Culture and Ecology Project.

The multiple inventory tests of personality or attitudes have proven to be very little adaptable to cross-cultural use, but the so-called projective tests have been widely used.[3] Among the projective techniques to which I gave serious consideration as being potentially useful for this study were: the Thematic Apperception Test (TAT), Rorschach, Holtzman Inkblot Test, Draw-a-Picture Test, Mosaic Test, Kennedy and Lasswell Test of Self-Image, Four-picture Test, Caligor 8-card Redrawing, Osgood's Semantic Differential, Baron's Rorschach Variation, Pfister Pyramid, Stewart's Ring Puzzle, Stewart's Emotional Response Test, Flanagan's Critical Incident Technique, word association, doll play, storytelling, the Make-a-Picture Story Test, the Bavelas Test of Moral Ideology, and Biesheuvel's "conversations attitude inventory."

Although the utilization of projective interviewing techniques in Africa had been quite limited prior to 1960 when my search for available materials was underway, there were some useful suggestions to be found in the published literature. For example, I was influenced by Simon Biesheuvel's studies of attitudes in South Africa (1958), Gustav Jahoda's work with children in West Africa (1958), S. G. Lee's application of the TAT among the Zulu (1953), André Ombredane's research with the TAT in the Congo (1954), and Mary Lystad's study of the paintings of Ghanaian children (1960). Of particular influence were the work of Leonard Doob on the psychology of acculturation in East Africa (1960), Edward Sherwood's revision of the TAT for use among the Swazi (1957), and Maria Leblanc's extensive psychological research, especially involving the TAT, in Katanga (1960).

In evaluating the many available techniques, three considerations were dominant: (1) efficiency, (2) relevance, (3) diversity. The first consideration was efficiency, to be calculated primarily in terms of the time required for the technique's proper utilization. Because it would be necessary to employ a probability sample requiring that certain specified individuals be interviewed, much time would be lost seeking and waiting for reluctant or missing individuals. Consequently, the time available for actual interviewing would be substantially reduced. Moreover, it would be necessary to interview a substantial number of persons—in all, over 500. Finally, in determin-

3. See, for example, Anderson and Anderson (1956), Hallowell (1956), Henry and Spiro (1953), and Lindzey (1961).

ing an optimal length for each interview, it would be necessary to take into account, on one hand, the necessary minimum of questions and eliciting stimuli, and on the other hand, the endurance of the respondent and the investigator. Second, the task had to be a relevant one for the respondent. A meaningless question or an absurdly foreign stimulus could both waste time and distract or alienate the respondent. Third, I felt that no single technique had so demonstrated its virtue that it should serve as the foundation of the inquiry. On the contrary, I believed that in order to tap as many facets of the respondent's structure of values, attitudes, and personality as possible, a diverse set of eliciting materials should be employed.[4]

PREPARING THE INITIAL INTERVIEW BATTERY

Based upon the literature, consultations, repeated conferences with Walter Goldschmidt, and my own practical experience, I chose to submit the following techniques to pretesting in East Africa: (1) questions of both a multiple choice and open-ended character directed toward values, attitudes, and feelings, (2) a modification of the Rorschach technique, (3) a picture test of values, (4) a form of storytelling, (5) 35mm color slides as entertainment and as projective stimuli, and (6) a variation of doll play, called "cattle play." A review of these materials and their success during the pretest is a necessary prelude to a discussion of the considerations involved in the construction of the final interview battery.

THE QUESTIONS

Some of the pretest questions were general and open-ended, for example, "If you could have anything you wanted, what would you choose?" Others offered multiple choices, for example, "Is it more important for a man to be a good speaker, a hard worker, a good warrior, or a friendly man?" Some were complicated and conjectural: "Suppose that a man had a nice herd of cattle, but one day three

---

4. During 1959 and 1960, I consulted a number of persons experienced in the cross-cultural application of projective testing or survey research. For suggestions offered, I am grateful to William Caudill, Jules Henry, John Honigmann, Harold Schneider, Melford Spiro, J. W. M. Whiting, and Edward Winter. Of particular help were David Aberle, Leonard Doob, and Philip Gulliver. Of course, none of these persons bears responsibility for the decisions that were made.

healthy young cows died. How would he decide what to do?" Others were relatively simple: "What should be done with an infant who cries all the time?"

The form of the questions was varied widely in order to determine the type of question that would most effectively elicit response. The content of the questions was varied as well in an effort to detect both potentially rich subject matters and dangerously sensitive ones. For example, personal questions—"What would *you* do . . . ?"—were contrasted with impersonal ones—"What would *a man* do . . . ?" All questions were original; none was knowingly borrowed from existing schedules or inventories.

THE RORSCHACH

The Holtzman Inkblot Test has many methodological advantages over the Rorschach as traditionally constituted; however, I thought that there would be insufficient time in the planned interviews to use all, or a substantial number, of the 45 Holtzman cards. Furthermore, I was reluctant to abandon the Rorschach because of the possibility of comparing its results with those of the many Rorschach studies already conducted among non-Western peoples. At that time (1961) the new Holtzman blots had not been used cross-culturally to any substantial degree. Also, I had received formal training in the Rorschach from Klopfer and thus felt that I might better evaluate it as a technique than I might the quite dissimilar Holtzman Test.

The major unresolved question regarding the Rorschach was not whether tribal Africans could respond to it—ample evidence existed that nonliterate, non-Western people could respond to the blots—but rather what would be the most complex level of usage at which it would be effective.

THE PICTURE TEST OF VALUES

The picture test of values, developed by Goldschmidt and Edgerton (1961) and experimented with on the Menomini and Navaho Indian reservations,[5] is a modification of the TAT. Unlike the TAT, which seeks "projective" responses to ambiguous stimulus pictures, this approach attempts to build specific, clear contrasts in values

5. A report of the Menomini experiment is available (Edgerton, 1960, and Goldschmidt and Edgerton, 1961) ; the Navaho research is, as yet, unpublished.

into a single picture. The subject then responds primarily in terms of values, rather than with psychodynamically revealing projections. This technique does not entirely avoid the "projective" level of response, however, as it asks the respondent both what *is* happening in the picture and what *ought* to happen, and thus secondarily seeks responses of a psychologically revealing nature.[6]

STORYTELLING

The storytelling technique asks either individuals or groups of individuals to tell a story regarding a particular subject. Various stories were to be asked for. Respondents were to be asked to "tell a story about" such subjects as: "a good man," "a bad man," "something that made you very happy recently," "something that annoyed you very much," "a legal case that you particularly remember," and so on. Also, after Flanagan (1954), a variation of the "critical incident technique" was to be tried. The questions here took this form: "Can you recall being praised (criticized) lately? Tell me about it." Throughout, the informant was to be asked not to tell traditional tales, or folklore, but to describe actual people he knew or events he had witnessed.

35MM COLOR SLIDES

The respondent was presented with a varied selection of color slides seen through a slide viewer to entertain him and encourage him to continue the interview, as well as to evoke responses to be systematically recorded.[7] The content of the slides was to be men, women, cattle, landscapes, and abstract art. In some instances, informants would be asked to express preferences between certain slides.

"CATTLE PLAY"

"Cattle play" combines elements of "structured doll play" as used by Lynn and Lynn (1959) and the Make-a-Picture-Story Test as conceived by Shneidman (1947). This technique involves placing carved wooden figures—cattle, men, women, and children—in different relationships against a standardized background. Each respon-

---

6. For a recent review of such picture techniques, see Spindler and Spindler (1965).

7. I am grateful to Leonard Dobb for his suggestion that such an approach, similar to the one used in his own East African research, might prove useful.

dent is presented with the figures in a particular relationship and is asked to explain, as in a TAT, what is happening, what brought it about, and what the outcome will be. The informant is then asked to put the figures in some sort of order of his own choosing before answering once again the same sorts of questions.

After the technical questions regarding the selection and utilization of techniques of data collection were asked and, in greater or lesser degree, answered, one large and perplexing question remained: Could it be done? Surprisingly, to me at least, many fieldworkers experienced in Africa thought that it could, although they usually added the caveat that they personally would not care for the headaches that the doing of it would entail. A few were frank to say that the project was not practical, that comparable, measurable findings on so large a scale could not realistically be hoped for under fieldwork conditions as they existed in East Africa in 1961–62.

It would be less than honest for me to say that fieldwork was begun with complete confidence. My previous experience with similar research in modern American, Mexican-American, and American Indian settings had made me painfully aware of the problems that could, and usually did, arise. I approached the data collection phase of my part of the Culture and Ecology Project sincerely dubious that I could in fact collect the data on the scale necessary with the precision required. My colleagues, despite some nervousness regarding what was for them, even more than for me, an experimental form of field research, were nonetheless considerably more sanguine than I, or at least so they appeared.

Almost forty years ago, Percy Bridgman remarked that the best method any scientist had was "doing his damndest." [8] Fortunately, before I was compelled to do my "damndest," I was able to employ the insurance policy of any behavioral scientist—the pretest.

PRETESTING

Thorough pretesting was unquestionably essential to the successful conduct of this research. Materials had to be prepared, techniques tried, motivational tactics explored, and the entire content and form of the approach worked out. In all, fourteen months were to be spent in field research. That at least three of these fourteen months were

8. Bridgman (1927).

allotted to preparations and pretesting is an indication of the importance assigned to this initial phase of the research. Once the final data collection was begun, the process would necessarily be completed in a once-and-forever fashion. There could be no second trial.

The first ten days after arrival in Nairobi, Kenya, on July 1, 1961, were occupied by general preparations involving official contacts and the acquisition of vehicles, equipment, and supplies. Next, pretest materials had to be prepared: colored slides had to be taken or purchased, values pictures drawn, and the "cattle play" objects had to be designed and carved. These tasks were completed on schedule only because we had allowed ample time for excessive and inexplicable delay. For example, after a person described as the "best artist available" to draw the values pictures had been located, it took five days for him to produce a sketch. The sketch, to speak charitably, was completely unacceptable, bearing no resemblance whatever to the scene I had asked for. After this delay another artist agreed to draw the pictures and did so with relative dispatch. Even though his pictures all portrayed Africans who looked rather like hydrocephalic Masai, it was too late to look further and these pictures were used for the pretesting.

It was possible to purchase both human and animal figures carved in wood by Kamba artists for the tourist market. Some of these carvings were quite suitable for the proposed "cattle play"; but, unfortunately, carvings of cattle are not greatly sought after by tourists (who tend to favor more exotic beasts), so these had to be carved to order. Since these East African carving are restricted to a limited number of designs, it was difficult to locate someone who would accept a commission to carve cattle; but after considerable delay, I did obtain two reasonably recognizable cows and an ox. The preparation of 35-mm color slides appeared to go well until it was discovered that the camera I had used to take the pictures had malfunctioned. When it was repaired, some photos had to be retaken and other scenes were purchased in Nairobi.

The first use of the assembled questions and visual stimulus materials (hereafter to be referred to as the "interview battery" or simply "interview") was made with some twenty African college students in Nairobi, and later, twelve more students in Kampala, Uganda. These educated young men and women responded easily to all parts of the interview but expressed displeasure with the crudely drawn values pictures. Next, over twenty-five African employees of a large hospital in Nairobi were interviewed. These persons, again both male and female, were nonliterate and only moderately acculturated.

Finally, eleven Masai, all male, were interviewed under less than ideal conditions in the Kajiado area. As warfare had only recently subsided between these Masai and their Kamba neighbors, many Masai were still quite agitated. Yet after the experience with urban Africans, I wanted to see the reaction of unacculturated, pastoral people before beginning formal pretesting. The Masai were less than enthusiastic about the interviews—for example, none was willing to sit through the complete two-hour interview—but their response was at least sufficient to demonstrate that even through indifferent interpretation, the questions and visual stimuli could be made intelligible to them with a minimum of preparation. This was especially encouraging in regard to the visual stimuli.

These initial pretesting efforts were carried out with little preparation on my part in mastery of the interview, with poor motivation on the part of the respondents (e.g., some were paid, most were not), without any concern for sampling, and under most irregular and undesirable interviewing conditions (e.g., some interviews were in bars, some in classrooms, some in hotel rooms, some in automobiles, some while walking along behind a herd of cattle, and some in the open air with a bemused audience in attendance). Still, the experience gave me some skill in the use of the interview materials, provided some insights into the techniques being used, and made me aware of many of the problems that needed to be examined closely in the more careful pretesting that would follow.

It was my intention to conduct about a one-week pretest with each of the four tribes in the study. As Walter Goldschmidt had previously worked with the Sebei (in 1954) and had by this time once again established himself among the Sebei on Mount Elgon, he was obviously best able of the ethnographers to help me with a pretest at this early date. The Sebei pretesting was to begin the first week in August, but after a 450-mile drive from Nairobi to Mbale, Uganda, I was forced to remain in a hotel at the foot of Mount Elgon for four days while "unseasonal"rains made a quagmire of the only road up the mountain. When the rains intensified instead of subsiding on the fifth day and weather forecasts called for a continued deluge, I decided to return the 450 miles to Nairobi and begin pretesting with the Kamba. After this experience, I always expected the worst possible weather, and often got it. Yet I subsequently allowed adequate time to meet a schedule that involved the ethnographers and me in a series of meetings that had to be scheduled long in advance.

Although Chad Oliver, who was at work with the Kamba in Kenya, was still in the process of setting up camp, he generously gave me every assistance he could. The Kamba pretest stretched over nine days, and although the sampling and interviewing conditions were not carefully controlled, over fifteen men and women in farming as well as pastoral areas were interviewed. To avoid possible respondent contamination, these interviews were all completed in areas distant from those to be chosen for the final study.

Following four days in Nairobi spent in futile search of an artist to redraw the values pictures, the Sebei pretesting began. Here, too, the areas in which final interviewing was to be done were avoided. Walter Goldschmidt's prior acquaintance with the Sebei made it possible to interview persons of both sexes and varied ages during a one-week period. Eleven people were interviewed in the Kapchorwa area and another eight were contacted in widely scattered places on the mountain. The continuing heavy rains rendered inaccessible the flooded pastoral areas on the plains below.

The pretest was not extended to the Pokot and Hehe. Francis Conant had not yet begun his research with the Pokot so no pretest there was practical, and because of my bout with malaria and the distance to the Hehe (1,000 miles by largely unmetaled road from the Sebei), it was decided that a pretest there would not be feasible.

Fortunately, one of each of the two language pairs (Pokot and Sebei—Kalenjin; Hehe and Kamba—Bantu) had been pretested. And the pretesting, although abbreviated, had been extremely helpful. A host of problems had been discovered and many answers had been found. For example, translation problems had been clarified. Words such as "insult," "assault," "curse," and "abuse"—all importantly differentiated in the questions asked—had been translated in Sebei by a single general term, and the Kamba had found difficulty separating "should" from "must" until more careful translation was provided. Other problems in the use of interpreters for such interviewing were also clarified. I was able to work out a shorthand system of writing to replace tape-recording, and a number of motivational tactics and interview settings were tried out. Most important, it was possible to determine which techniques were effective in eliciting response, what the content of these techniques should be, and, finally, how long the interview might last without exhausting the informant.

Following these pretesting efforts, a summary of the results was prepared and presented to the assembled staff of the project at a conference at Malindi, Kenya, in September, 1961. Here, each staff member considered my pretesting experience in relation to the final interview battery I proposed to them. The comments of Francis Conant (Pokot) and Edgar Winans (Hehe), with whom I had not worked in a pretest, were especially important. Preparations for the actual interviewing procedure were also agreed upon at this time.

It was agreed that each ethnographer was to provide a translation of my final interview schedule by going from English to the native language and back into English as often as was necessary to produce an impeccably equivalent translation. Each ethnographer was also to hire an interpreter and provide him with the initial training and experience necessary before I began actual work in that tribal area. Of course, the ethnographer was responsible for developing rapport and establishing good research relations. Also, forms containing much ancillary material on each person whom I was to interview had to be filled out by the ethnographer. These points are considered later in more detail, but I should say here that all the ethnographers and the geographer, Philip Porter, worked wonders in achieving efficient and congenial cooperation.

After the Malindi staff meeting, I was most fortunate to find Miss Ruth Yudelowitz, a talented artist from Nairobi.[9] The general content of the values pictures had been decided during the pretest and at the Malindi conference. Now, with the help of Walter and Gale Goldschmidt, we were able to portray the desired scenes in a manner most likely to be meaningful to the African respondents. Miss Yudelowitz's long experience in drawing for nonliterate East African populations, coupled with her obvious talent, made collaboration with her a pleasure.

Each of the final nine pictures was to be drawn so that it would have as nearly as possible the same stimulus value in all four tribes and all eight interviewing sites. It was clear that in order to accomplish this, it would be necessary to make minor changes in the pictures for each of the four tribes but not, we thought, for the two sectors within each tribe. Consequently, each picture was redrawn four times in order to provide a Sebei, Pokot, Kamba, and Hehe version of the same picture. Minor changes in material culture and physical environment were necessary but, of course, the basic content of the pictures remained the same. In this assignment, Miss Yudelowitz, with the assistance of the ethnographers who quickly provided her with

9. My indebtedness to Miss Yudelowitz is great. Appreciation is also expressed for the cooperation of her employer, Mr. Richards, of the East African Literature Bureau.

photographs of required tribal scenes and materials, succeeded beyond my expectations. The reader may judge for himself the equivalence of the four versions of the same picture by consulting Appendix I. With minor exceptions that will be considered later, I believe that the equivalence of the pictures was excellent.

Miss Yudelowitz's drawings had to be converted from her original pencil to ink so that they might be photocopied for field use. This conversion, in her mind at least, deprived the pictures of some of their "motion" or "feeling." Almost without exception, however, the respondents found them to be quite realistic.

THE FINAL INTERVIEW BATTERY

The various phases of pretesting indicated that some of the techniques used in the pretest were inappropriate or inefficient means of eliciting response. The open-ended interview questions, almost without exception, were easily and appropriately responded to by both men and women. Respondents were able to answer questions such as, "What is the worst thing that can happen to a man?" The answers—"poverty," "death," "impotence," and the like—came easily and were apparently quite meaningful to the respondents. This ease of response to so open-ended a form of question came as a surprise. However, elaborate multiple-choice questions that provided four or more choices were not effective; the respondents said that they could not remember all four choices, and they tended to respond with the third or fourth choice because they did not recall the earlier ones. As a result, I included a larger number of open-ended or general questions than was originally intended, and eliminated multiple-choice questions with more than three choices.

The values pictures were so poorly drawn for the pretest that few valid conclusions regarding them could be reached; nonetheless, it was clear that most people were able to understand the content of the pictures. Their reluctance to respond freely to this content was marked, but it was hoped that with more effectively drawn pictures this reluctance could be overcome. Drawing from our experience with American Indians, we believed that if these pictures were better executed—more realistic and more dramatic—they could yet elicit valuable data.

The Rorschach was, in general, unpopular. People were clearly uneasy about the task and reluctant to associate freely to these ink-

blots. Still there was no doubt whatever that even the least acculturated of Africans (e.g., the Masai) were *able* to respond to the configurations of the inkblots. There were also some suggestive differences in response between the Sebei and the Kamba. It appeared, then,
that with modification, the Rorschach might be made to work.

From the beginning, storytelling, in any form, was a total failure. The alleged African passion for telling stories (Biesheuvel, 1958)
was nowhere in evidence, and later it was discovered that adults, at
least among the Kamba and the Sebei, rarely tell stories or recite folktales, and when they do it is primarily to children. Respondents
clearly regarded me as more than a trifle odd when I asked them to
tell stories, and it was only by asking a specific question involving the
same subject matter that I could persuade them to respond. For example, they would not respond to, "Tell me a story about a very bad
thing that has happened to you," but they would answer the specific
question, "What is the worst thing that can happen to a man?" Storytelling, at least in this context, was out of the question.

The "cattle play" technique evoked nothing but scorn. Consistent with the goal of diversity in task materials, it was originally included to provide an expressive-manipulative task. Unfortunately,
adults simply would not move the figures around when I asked them
to, and even when I presented them with a scene that I had arranged,
they only laughed and said that Europeans were "silly, like children."
Their feeling, freely rendered, was that only children would play such
"games," and to ask adults to do so was ludicrous, if not insulting. In
fact, children in these societies do play with small stones which are
used to represent cattle and, sometimes, people. So thorough was the
adult rejection of this manipulative task that I felt it would be unwise
to attempt to replace it with another set of stimulus materials (e.g.,
mosaics). The technique was counted as a failure, and it was dropped.

The color slides, on the other hand, were an instant success.
The respondents enjoyed looking at these dramatic and appealing
scenes. They were entertained by them and talked freely about what
they saw. The slides both motivated the respondents to continue the
interview and elicited revealing comments from them. The original
set employed in the pretest was so successful that it was retained without alteration.

The final interview consisted of: (1) 85 questions, (2) 10 Rorschach cards, (3) 9 values pictures, and (4) 22 color slides.

The 85 questions that were asked are listed in Appendix II.
They were composed to inquire into most of the critical issues raised

39

by the pastoral model and the hypothesized farming divergence from this model, and are considered in detail in a later chapter.

The Rorschach technique as used in this study varied from standard usage in a number of important ways. It had become apparent in the pretesting that with one or two exceptions the respondents refused to accept the blots as ambiguous stimuli, capable of being seen in as many ways as imagination permits. For them, it was *a* picture of *a* particular thing, the identity of which they were expected to guess. No amount of explanation from me to the contrary was sufficient to disabuse them of this approach to the blots. In an effort to overcome this difficulty and to insure that all respondents were given the same understanding of this perceptual task, the first card was employed as an *instruction card*. Each respondent was shown the first card with these instructions: "I am going to show you some 'designs.' These 'designs' are specially made so that they look like a great many different things. Everyone who looks at these 'designs' sees something different—there is nothing here that you are supposed to see or supposed not to see. I just want you to look at the 'designs' and tell me what they make you think of. For example, in this one [card 1] you might say that it looks like (1) an elephant doing something, (2) a woman just standing there, (3) a cloud drifting by, (4) a skeleton of an animal, (5) mountains or hills sticking up off in the distance." As each of these five concepts was listed, I pointed it out in the blot. These five possible percepts offered a variety of determinants and locations in an effort to convince the respondent that the blots might be seen as many things and not simply as one thing (locations of the concepts within card 1, the instruction card, are shown in Appendix III).

For statistical reasons to be discussed later, and to conserve time in a long interview, only the first response to each blot was to be scored. For this reason, although respondents were permitted more than one response to each blot, they were not encouraged to produce more. Obviously, many respondents learned that only one response was required and responded accordingly. Others, however, produced several responses to each blot.

The "inquiry," which is an essential feature of the ordinary Rorschach procedure, consists of a series of probes composed by the investigator in order fully to understand the response. Since these probes necessarily vary depending upon the investigator, the response, and the blot, problems of statistical comparability arise (cf. Zubin, 1954; Holtzman, 1961). Thus, to maximize the precision of the technique for quantitative analysis and, again, to conserve time, the inquiry was omitted. Doob (1960) reported that, in his use of the Rorschach in East Africa, it was necessary for the inquiry to follow each response rather than occur as a separate section following the conclusion of all ten cards.[10] My pretesting experiences confirmed this view. Consequently, if there were to be an inquiry, there would have to be various and varied probes attached to *each* response, and as a result comparability would be seriously reduced, if not lost altogether. I chose not to compromise consistent comparison in this fashion.

The nine final values pictures (shown in Appendix I) presented what we intended to be the following scenes: (1) a father confronted by a misbehaving and disrespectful son, (2) cattle damaging a farmer's maize field, (3) armed warriors raiding cattle protected only by children, (4) an ill person and a diviner, (5) a man either watching or interceding in a fight between two other men, (6) a man performing an ambiguous act with a child, (7) a woman passing by a partially hidden man, (8) a man viewing what could be construed as a sexual act, (9) a man kicking over a beer pot being used by several other men.

While each picture was designed to confront the respondent with a meaningful and explicit conflict in values, in another sense each was also ambiguous. The values picture technique provides for both psychological "projection" and "cultural" valuation by asking for what *is* happening and what *ought* to happen. Further explanation of the technique as it was used is provided later.

When shown the 35mm color slides, respondents were encouraged to comment freely about each slide; but, in addition to this unsolicited response, some specific questions were asked. These questions and the content of the slides are discussed more fully in the context of the interviewing process.

Each question and visual stimulus included in the interview was reduced to that degree of simplicity required for the least articulate, least acculturated, and least motivated respondent. My purpose was to make comparisons among *eight populations,* and it would have been contrary to this goal to have included materials to which some of the more articulate persons could have responded, but by which others would have been baffled. Hence, the interview is a least common denominator, a simplified set of eliciting devices to which most persons in all eight sites were expected to be able to respond. Therefore, if all respondents could produce relevant answers, however short, the interview would achieve its purpose.

10. Leonard Dobb, personal communication, 1960.

41

Finally, all pretesting experience indicated that even the most appealingly designed interview could not exceed sixty to ninety minutes without fatiguing the respondent beyond the point of diminishing returns. The final interview was designed not to exceed ninety minutes.

THE INTERVIEWING PROCESS

INTERPRETER TRAINING

Before elaborating on the process by which the interpreters were trained, it might be well to review the reasons behind the decision to use interpreters. One alternative to the use of interpreters would have been for me to conduct the interviews in the native language; however, for me to acquire fluency in four African languages was obviously completely out of the question. Another alternative would have been to interview in Swahili, the so-called lingua franca of the area. However, the Pokot and Sebei speak very little Swahili or none at all, and many of the Kamba speak the language poorly. Only the Hehe speak Swahili as anything approximating the intricate and rich language that it can be. Therefore, even to conduct interviews in the simplified "kitchen" or "up-country" Swahili would not have been possible with many of the older respondents or with women. Furthermore, "kitchen" Swahili is an impoverished "baby talk" in which complexity of expression is virtually impossible, and it connotes to many Africans the master-servant relationship of European employer to African employee. By elimination, then, the only acceptable alternative was to interview through interpreters in the native language.

Without doubt, facility in the native language can be of immeasurable importance in the conduct of any field research, as it could have been in this interviewing research. However, it can also be a dangerous snare when, as sometimes happens, the fieldworker comes to rely upon a language that he speaks and understands only imperfectly. I was subject to no such danger, for there was no alternative to the use of interpreters. And, as it turned out, the use of interpreters had some important advantages.

The interpreters were selected, hired, and given initial training and experience by the ethnographers. The ethnographers' judgment in these selections was extraordinary. All four of the interpreters with whom I worked were competent and responsible. Each performed far better than I, or anyone else, had any reason to expect. In part, this excellent performance resulted from the fact that, when I visited each ethnographer to begin interviewing in his area, I was provided with the interpreter best suited for my interviewing, while for this period the ethnographer worked selflessly (sometimes at a distinct advantage) with a second interpreter.

In addition to the training and experience that each interpreter had acquired before beginning to work for me, each was put through my own training procedures. Each man had impressed upon him anew that he was never to summarize but was always to give a complete, literal rendering of *everything* the respondent said. Each man had to learn, often with difficulty, that what seemed to him an irrelevant comment not worthy of translation was to me of utmost interest. None of the four men ever became perfect in this regard but all eventually became acceptable. It was also necessary to caution them against displays of their virtuosity in English; each had an inclination to embellish and elaborate by phrasing the mundane utterance of the respondent in an elegant but less than literal version of his own composition. This practice was not difficult to discourage; each man soon learned that I respected his skill in English and that performances of this kind were unnecessary. It was also important that the interpreter never "lead" or "cue" a respondent by giving anything more than a literal statement of instructions or questions. All four men quickly saw the necessity of this and did very well in avoiding such hints. Although some leading was discovered, it was extremely rare.

The next essential problem was that each interpreter had to become completely confident in his understanding of the interview, his grasp of each instruction and each question, and the translation of each word in the interview. This confidence could come only with experience, so each interpreter was given several days of full-time training and trial interviewing under the same conditions as would occur in the actual interviewing. With repetition, each interpreter became immensely skilled in his knowledge and use of the interview; for example, in a matter of a week or so, each man had memorized virtually all of the instructions and questions in the interview.

Each interpreter began the training by responding to the interview himself in English. Upon completion of the interview all his questions were answered until he had a general understanding of what I expected from him as well as the meaning, but not necessarily the purpose, of each question and visual stimulus. For example, when

43

my Sebei interpreter took the Rorschach himself, he did so with manifest discomfort, although he was able to produce careful and intelli-
gent responses to all ten blots. At the conclusion of the test I asked if
he had trouble with it and he denied that he had. He also denied that
he had experienced any discomfort. Finally I said, "Look, I know
you were acutely uncomfortable. You were squirming around like a
boy about to be circumcised." At this he laughed, somewhat too
loudly, and said that he was afraid to say so to a European, because
Europeans often discouraged any discussion of sex with Africans, but
each blot looked to him like a woman's vulva. I assured him that not
all Europeans were displeased by discussion of sex with Africans, that
Goldschmidt and I, in fact, required that he speak freely of all matters, including sexual ones. I then told him that the blots sometimes
looked like vulvas to Europeans, too, and that, in fact, this perception of the blots was something of a joke among Europeans. As far as
I was able to learn, he had no further reluctance to discuss matters
pertaining to sex.

While the formal training and cross-checking of the interpreter
and his performance did much to develop my confidence, often it was
some unforeseen happening that provided the final conviction that he
and I were sufficiently on the same wavelength to begin the actual
interviewing. For example, my Kamba interpreter Samuel was quite
competent in English, was a dignified gentleman in my eyes, and was
obviously a man of some stature among his people. The training sessions and pretesting seemed to be going well; however, I felt he was
not being completely open with me. Samuel had earlier responded to
me, as to other Europeans, with a fervent: "We're all Christians here.
There is no witchcraft or superstition among my people." After a time
he seemed to conclude that I (and Chad Oliver) meant him and the
Kamba no harm and that we could be, indeed should be, told the
truth. Eventually, Samuel spoke very freely about even the most sensitive areas of Kamba culture.

But in the training period, I sometimes felt that he was not
translating literally and that his failure to do so might indicate that
he was withholding information that he did not feel I should receive.
I could find no way effectively to face this issue until we began to
work on the Rorschach. In administering the fifth card of the test one
day, I was startled to see the respondent burst with laughter, gurgle a
few words, and finally lapse into a prolonged paroxysm of mirth.
Samuel, too, was laughing mightily. When the merriment subsided,
I asked for a translation and Samuel said that the man's words were:

"It is a rabbit." I argued that he must have said something more than that to occasion such a reaction, but Samuel insisted that the man had said only that. I then asked what was so funny if that were all he had said, and was told that, "The rabbit is a funny animal." I wanted to know what was funny about it, but the most I could get in explanation was the declaration that the Kamba think rabbits are exceedingly funny animals.

I next demanded that the respondent repeat his answer to card 5 and I recorded it phonetically. An independent translator confirmed that he had just said what Samuel had reported and no more. Throughout the pretest of the Rorschach I received wild laughter as a response to the fifth card. Each time I transcribed the answer phonetically and each time it was apparent that Samuel was translating correctly. Because of this incident, Samuel and I were able to discuss the necessity for literal translation much more freely. I never was able to find out exactly why the rabbit is such an amusing beast (although it obviously has much to do with the place of the rabbit as a sexual trickster in Kamba and other East African folklore), but I was able to confirm that Samuel knew his job of interpretation and that he was performing it well.

After a minimum of three and a maximum of seven full days of training, each interpreter was ready to begin formal interviewing. Each man performed extremely well, and I am confident that the interview responses were not systematically biased as a result of interpreter effect. Two possible exceptions are these: (1) the responses of the Kamba farmers regarding witchcraft against rich men may have been influenced by the fact that the Kamba interpreter was a relatively wealthy man (this point is problematic, however, and is discussed in a later chapter); (2) among the Hehe, the translation of "a case of suicide" in question 89 was faulty in that it suggested "a legal case" rather than "any instance of" suicide, as was intended; this mistranslation was corrected, but not before all of the Hehe farmers and nine of the pastoralists had been interviewed. This point, too, is discussed later.

The question of the interpreters' prior acquaintance with, or relationship to, the respondents was taken into account. The degree of prior acquaintance or relationship between interpreter and respondent was recorded for each respondent. In general, statistical tests showed no significant differences in response between persons related to the interpreter and persons not related to him. The same was true between persons whom the interpreter knew and those he did not. The one exception involved questions with manifest sexual content. When the interpreter's relationship to a female respondent was one of sexual distance (e.g., the woman was referred to as "mother" or as "daughter"), then she could not be asked direct sexual questions, nor could she directly refer to sexual matters in any of her answers. Fortunately, the number of such relationships (between four and seven) was approximately the same at each interviewing site, so this problem produced no difference in response from site to site.

STANDARDIZING THE INTERVIEWING SITUATION

It is indisputable that the effect of the interviewing situation upon interview responses, as well as upon responses to psychological tests, can be considerable. Anthropologists are acutely aware of the difficulties that surround any attempt to provide acceptable standardized interviewing or testing conditions in non-Western societies. Privacy is breached by children, wives, drunks, and goats; interruptions, including those by the respondents themselves who simply get up and wander off, abound; and two interviews rarely take place under identical conditions, even identical bad conditions. Many anthropologists have assumed that conditions cannot be otherwise and that attempts to impose Western research conditions of standardized interviewing or testing would result in loss of data or alienation of the respondent, or both. Often, I am certain, they have been justified in their pessimism. My own view, however, was that matters not only could be otherwise, but *had* to be, or the comparative research we proposed would achieve little.

By my criteria, each interview had to be conducted in privacy and under closely comparable circumstances. Thus in each of the eight sites where interviewing took place, only one place of interviewing was set up; and in each site, this place was, to a high degree, like every other. Each respondent came to this place to be interviewed or he was not interviewed. Despite strong pressure to pursue reluctant or distant respondents to their homes, this rule was never violated.

The place of interviewing in each of the eight sites was either a tent or a native house. An enclosed interviewing place was necessary to insure privacy, and privacy was strictly maintained. The door of the interviewing place was always left open so that it was possible for passersby to see what was being done but not to overhear the interview or to interrupt it. Each interview was conducted in the presence of only three persons—the investigator, the interpreter, and the respondent. The only exception was for nursing infants who sometimes remained with their mothers during the interview.

In order to avoid undue distraction and to put the respondent at ease, foreign (i.e., European) articles were removed from the place of interviewing. For example, with the Pokot pastoralists, who were not familiar with chairs, no chairs were present during the interviews; I sat on a Pokot-made plank bench, and the respondents sat either on the floor of the hut or upon their own wooden stools.

Obviously, standardization was not without its problems. Some women (or, perhaps I should say, their husbands) disliked the privacy and all that it suggested sexually. Others were suspicious on the grounds that anything private was naturally sinister. In some instances, especially in the pastoral areas, some respondents lived many miles from the place of interviewing. Thus, despite the expense and time involved, it was sometimes necessary to pick up respondents, especially older ones, and transport them by Land Rover portal-to-portal. In addition, heavy rains, great heat, economic duties, illness, threats of enemy raids, ceremonial occasions, and the like sometimes prevented anyone from coming to be interviewed for days at a time. But no compromise with standardization was made. All respondents were interviewed under conditions no less standard and private than those that ordinarily obtain in Western survey research. Indeed, conditions were more uniform than those sometimes encountered in Western household survey research.

PROVIDING MOTIVATION

There were two basic problems in motivating the respondents: first to persuade them to come to me for the interview, and then to persist through it; and, second, to provide them with a common motive for doing so. To a degree, the ethnographers and I were at odds on how best to solve these problems. The ethnographers rightly wanted to avoid any interview payments on my part that might subsequently involve them in a policy of paying for all their ethnographic information. I, on the other hand, wanted to provide sufficient incentive for good interview response even if it meant paying for the interviews. A compromise solution was reached by my offering each of my respondents a "gift" upon completion of the interview, with the clear understanding that due to the special character of this work, I would like to reward them for their cooperation, but that the resident ethnographer would continue his relations with them as before.

The interview procedure began with assurances to the respondents that no harm could come from "talking to me," that I was only

47

interested in learning more about their way of life. My *bona fides* for interest in them inevitably rested upon whatever regard they already had for the resident ethnographer. Fortunately, each ethnographer had established good working relations that I was able to capitalize upon.

As each person in the sample was contacted (either by the interpreter or by another person hired for this person), he was told that I wanted to see him, that it would take "a short time" (sixty to ninety minutes was specified for those few who understood European time), and that following the "talk" he would receive a "gift." But it was made very clear that the entire interview had to be completed or no gift would be received.

The nature of the gift varied slightly from interview site to interview site, but its value was always between two shillings (twenty-eight cents, U.S.) and one shilling, fifty cents (twenty-one cents, U.S.). The fundamental gift was beer, usually native beer, but for those few who preferred it, European beer was also offered. During the interview itself, tobacco (chewing tobacco or East African cigarettes) was available for those who wanted it. So were bottled soft drinks, although few persons were interested in this beverage. For women or Muslims who did not want to drink alcohol or who could not (Kamba women are not permitted to drink alcohol), alternatives such as soap, tea, salt, sugar, beads, and maize meal were available, and were eagerly accepted.

How many respondents saw the "gift" as a true gift rather than a simple payment is not known. I suspect that most saw it as a payment (exchanges in these societies typically carry with them obligations of reciprocity), and that their willingness to be interviewed was in large measure a product of their desire for the gift. So great is the lure of beer in these four societies that men would happily walk great distances to obtain it, and would willingly endure an interview after getting there. That the offering of beer was a potent persuader can best be seen by the rather substantial number of people in most communities who volunteered to be interviewed (and, of course, to receive beer); needless to say, their confusion and chagrin were great when they had to be told that they were not "in the sample," and hence could not be interviewed. For women, the opportunity to acquire maize meal, salt, tea, or sugar was also a substantial inducement.

Thus it is probable that most of the respondents agreed to the interview because of the gift that was offered. This single motivating factor undoubtedly reduced other factors in the motivation of the respondents such as the desire for prestige or fear of pressure; but, of course, such additional motivations could never be ruled out completely. The offering of a gift satisfied the first consideration: it brought people in to be interviewed. Whether or not it completely satisfied the second, to give each respondent the same motive for undergoing the interview, is less certain. Happily, this policy of payment did not notably complicate the work of the ethnographers, who were able to continue their research as they had before I arrived.

SAMPLING: SELECTION OF RESPONDENTS

Justification for the use of sampling procedures in this research should not be necessary. We could not, as so much anthropological research has done, assume the basic homogeneity of our societies. I would insist that to assume the homogeneity of small and simple societies, even in the study of customs, is always misleading, but it cannot even be considered where feelings, attitudes, and personality attributes are concerned.[11] Thus while formal sampling procedures are not considered to be necessary, or feasible, in most anthropological research, this research would in large measure succeed or fail on the quality of its sampling.

The design of this research called for each ethnographer to select a representative pastoral and farming site. To accomplish this, a survey of the entire tribal area was made. This procedure will be described in detail in Philip W. Porter's forthcoming volume on the ecology and environment of East Africa; but, in summary, the survey was accomplished through the use of available governmental and ethnographic records, by taking air photos, and through land reconnaissance by the ethnographers and the geographer. Once the pastoral-farming variation within the tribal area was known, it was possible to select areas of maximal "farmingness" and "pastoralness." A site within each of these areas could then be chosen by more or less random probability techniques. In fact, however, randomness was in part sacrificed to the concerns of: (1) reducing acculturative influences from both Europeans and other African societies, (2) avoiding newly settled or otherwise greatly distributed areas, and (3) finding a place in which it was physically possible to work.

Sites were chosen with great care, and they probably represent a good approximation of each tribe's center of "farmingness" and "pastoralness." Because my findings, even more so than those of the

11. The literature on variability in tribal societies has expanded so rapidly in recent years that no justification for this position should be necessary.

ethnographers, might easily be distorted by acculturative influence, care had to be taken to equalize the degree of acculturation in each site. The extent to which acculturation was controlled is discussed in chapter 6. Newly settled areas or those recently disturbed by governmental action were avoided, and it was feasible to work in all eight sites although some were so remote that it was clear that comfort and accessibility had not been important criteria in their selection.

Sample size was an important question for the sampling design, but the size of the sample necessary for statistical comparison of the interview data to be collected was not easily determined. Estimates of the safe side of small sample considerations range for the most part between a sample number (N) of 20 (Dixon and Massey, 1957) and one of 30 (Guilford, 1956). Both for statistical and common sense reasons it was desirable to avoid a sample that would be statistically "small." Consequently, the high estimate of 30 was accepted as a rule of thumb: in each of the eight sites the minimal number of respondents interviewed would be 30 men and 30 women.

When a "site" consisted of a social-territorial unit (village, neighborhood, local community, etc.) of about this size (30 heads of household), every adult male in the unit was to be interviewed. In all other instances, individuals within the social unit or units were to be sampled randomly. Because the sampling process is of such importance, details of the sampling procedure used in each of the eight sites follow.

Sebei farmers.—Research among Sebei farmers was centered in the neighborhood of Sasur. At the time of my visit, there were 27 heads of household in Sasur. Three of these men left the area before they could be interviewed; the remaining 24 were interviewed. Another eight men were taken on a random probability basis from the contiguous neighborhood of Kamingong, which was formerly a part of Sasur. The wives of these men were also interviewed; but, because the selection of women offers some problems in a polygynous society, it was sometimes necessary to specify which of a man's several wives I wanted to interview. It was easiest to select each male respondent's first wife, but such a sample would have excluded all younger married women. Thus, an age-stratified sample of wives was taken. Because of the need for age stratification, sampling here was systematic rather than random.[12] There was only one known refusal to be interviewed, a woman from Kamingong.

12. For the distinction between these forms of probability sampling, see Blalock (1960a). For a complete discussion, see Kish (1965).

Sebei pastoralists.—There were 39 heads of household in the neighborhood of Kapsirika. Three of these were eliminated: one was blind, one worked out of the area, and one was in prison. Five men, one of whom appeared to be psychotic, refused to be interviewed. Thus 31 of 36 possible men were interviewed. No women were known to refuse to be interviewed; again, with age stratification, 32 wives were chosen systematically to duplicate the actual proportion of wives in various age categories.

Kamba farmers.—Of 51 men resident in the neighborhood of Ngelani at the time of interviewing, 33 were selected randomly. Two of these refused and 31 were interviewed. Three women refused to be interviewed, and 31 women, systematically sampled within age strata, were interviewed.

Kamba pastoralists.—Of 52 male heads of household in the neighborhood of Kilungu, 33 were selected randomly; only one refused to be interviewed, and of him the Kamba had earlier said, "If you need nine men, he is number 10." Thirty-five women were selected randomly without age stratification (the universe of women here was not at all age-skewed); three refused, 32 were interviewed.

Hehe farmers.—The neighborhood of Ngelewala contained 34 heads of household who were Hehe without any intermarriage with other tribes (e.g., Bena, Kinga, Sangu, etc.); of these, five were traveling out of the area at the time of the interviewing. Despite some difficulties, all the remaining 29 men were interviewed. To boost the N over 30, two men who lived on the border of this neighborhood were also interviewed. Their selection was not random. They were recommended by the interpreter as being former residents of the neighborhood. Their responses did not differ from those of the 29 Ngelewala men. There were 36 Hehe women available at the time of my visit; of these 30 were interviewed. Four women were ill, traveling, or legitimately busy and could not be interviewed; two women refused to be interviewed.

Hehe pastoralists.—Thirty-four men from four contiguous villages in Pawaga (Segerere, Magangamatitu, Mikosi, and Majengo) were systematically selected (two out of every three heads of household were taken). Three men refused to be interviewed, and 31 were interviewed. One man attempted to disrupt the interviewing by trying to persuade all women to remain at home; but, after some resulting delay, 31 women were interviewed without any refusals. (I later learned that, by accusing me of conduct that would have made Rasputin blush, this man was attempting to force me to buy his silence.)

Pokot farmers.—The Pokot farmers of Tamkal Valley tended to arrange themselves territorially by lineage membership. Thus to avoid taking only the members of one lineage for the interviews, three social units *(korok)* were sampled (Tirtoi, Kamichich, and Assar).[13] Of the 51 married men in these three units, 35 were selected systematically on the basis of age. Two refused and 33 were interviewed. Thirty-three women were selected, and only one refused to be interviewed.

Pokot pastoralists.—It was not possible to employ probability sampling among the Pokot cattle herders of Masol Location. At the time of my work in this area, the basic demographic survey had not been completed. As a consequence, the parameters of the sometimes mobile Pokot pastoral population within this vast and remote area were largely unknown. Without detailed knowledge of the Pokot pastoral universe, the "sampling" process was necessarily less than precise. With the assistance of several Pokot, a list of 66 married men and 65 married women was drawn up. The names of these persons were simply those of persons known to be located nearby. I then selected every other person on these lists. Because there was considerable confusion regarding duplications in the names of Pokot men in Masol, on a few occasions the wrong man was probably interviewed. A later government census estimated the population of the Location at 1,600, 811 of whom were adults.[14] I interviewed 31 men and 32 women. Conant later collected demographic data concerning 87 men and 146 women. The demographic characteristics of my sample are in no significant way different from those of Conant's larger sample, so perhaps there was, after all, little bias in my "sampling" technique.

Five men and three women refused to be interviewed; but, with one exception, the refusals were based upon physical disability. Cooperation was excellent. Indeed, large numbers of people whom I had not selected presented themselves at the camp to be interviewed.

In summary, although randomness was not achieved in all eight sites, except for the Pokot pastoralists, there was an adequate foundation of systematic sampling. Furthermore, the refusal rate overall was just about 5 percent, with the highest refusal rate within any community being under 8 percent. I have no reason to believe that the sampling procedures produced any systematic bias.

13. Conant (1965).
14. Kenya Government Census, 1963, Government Printing Office, Nairobi, Kenya.

THE CONDUCT OF THE INTERVIEW

The first step in the conduct of the interview was to locate the potential respondents whose names appeared on the list developed through the various sampling procedures. Earlier, the people in the area were made aware of my presence and purpose. Now, the interpreter was sent forth to gather persons whose names had appeared in the sample. Often, he was required to set up appointments one night for the following day; needless to say, not everyone was punctual. Indeed, well over 50 percent of such appointments were not kept. When potential respondents failed to appear, the interpreter, or an assistant hired especially for this purpose, would rush out and try to find someone on the sample list to replace the absentee. As these assistants were hired with less care than the interpreters, not all were reliably diligent. One feckless fellow regularly went in search of beer rather than respondents; another devoted himself to seducing wives whose husbands happened to be away from home when he stopped by. Others, however, were more reliable, and eventually the correct respondents did arrive to be interviewed.

I cannot emphasize too strongly the frustration that was inherent in this situation; often an entire morning or even a full day was spent waiting at the interviewing place for respondents who never appeared. Most of these elusive people eventually made their appearance, as few of them had actually refused to be interviewed. They were simply deflected from their appointment by more important or more appealing affairs. While I waited for someone on the sample list of names to appear, it was frequently necessary to discourage persons not on the list who just happened to stop by without invitation. These people often made good informants on other matters, but they could not be interviewed without violating the sampling design.

When an invited respondent arrived to be interviewed, he or she immediately began the interviewing routine. First, the respondent was invited to come inside the interviewing tent or house and sit down. For no more than two or three minutes, friendly greetings and conversation were exchanged to relax the respondent. Following these introductory remarks, the respondent was told: "Thank you very much for coming to talk to me. I want to ask you about some Sebei [Kamba, Pokot, Hehe] customs and about how the Sebei [Kamba, etc.] feel about things. After my questions are finished, I will be happy to answer any questions you may have about my country."

From the beginning of the interview I had a pen and paper in

53

full view of the respondent who was told that I would write down his answers so I would not forget them. Not a single person objected. I also had before me (and memorized) a phonetic transcript of the native language translation of all instructions and questions to be used in the standard interview. I was therefore usually able to notice any departure from standard terminology; the interpreter knew that I would sometimes correct him as he read the questions from his copy of the same document. As a consequence, the instructions and questions were highly standardized; indeed, the interpreters knew the interview so thoroughly that they were able to maintain a steady flow of questions without seeming to read the transcript of the interview questions at all.

After I offered the respondent cigarettes or native tobacco, I began the actual interview with the values pictures: "First, I want to show you some pictures of things that could happen right here among the Sebei [Kamba, etc.]. Please look at each picture and tell me what you think is happening in the picture. Then I will ask you some questions. For example [picking up picture 1], in this picture you might say that it looks like this man is the father of these three boys. He is telling them something, perhaps he is scolding them. These two boys are listening politely, but this boy refuses to listen. Now, what does it look like to you?"

Following this explanation, the respondent usually gave his own version of the scene, after which I asked what *ought* to happen in the scene. All nine pictures were presented in order, but without any further cues from me concerning the content. After the ninth picture, the respondent was thanked for his answers and told: "That is the last picture I want to show you. Now I would like to ask some questions."

The first sixteen questions followed immediately. After the sixteenth question, approximately a one-minute break for a cigarette or soft drink took place. If the respondent wanted to ask questions at this time, he was asked to defer them until the completion of the interview. No relevant information was exchanged during this or subsequent pauses, and the pauses rarely consumed a full minute.

The Rorschach was then introduced as previously described. Following the *instruction card,* correct Rorschach procedure was followed except for the exclusion of the inquiry.[15] After the Rorschach, questions 17 through 24 were asked.

After question 24, another cigarette was offered and, without

15. Klopfer et al. (1954).

delay, the first color slides, four scenes portraying East African men, were shown. After spontaneous comments were recorded, male respondents were asked which man was best dressed, and women were asked which man was the most handsome.

Questions 25 through 41 were asked next, followed by slides of four East African women. Again, after spontaneous comments about all four slides, the men were asked which woman they liked best and the women were asked which woman was best dressed.

Next were questions 42 through 54, followed by five color slides of French impressionistic paintings. After spontaneous comments about each slide, all respondents were asked which picture they liked the best. Questions 56 through 63 were followed by four slides showing East African cattle. Here, after spontaneous comments, respondents were asked which cattle they thought were best. Another cigarette break followed.

Questions 64 through 75 were followed by five slides of animals —an elephant, a lion, a hyena, a leopard, and a harmless but large sand snake. Following spirited and often horrified comments, respondents were asked which animal shown was the most dangerous.

The interview was concluded with questions 76 through 91. Any questions the respondents might have were now answered. Most had one or two questions about me personally, or why I wanted to know such things. I answered all these questions honestly. The pastoral Pokot, the least acculturated people interviewed, had by far the most questions. They asked about America, particularly about American clans, cattle, warfare, and sex. But many respondents in other tribes, especially the women, were too shy or indifferent to ask any questions at all. Perhaps because of the relief the respondents felt after the termination of the interview, virtually all of the interviews ended on an exchange of thanks and good wishes.

ROLES IN THE INTERVIEW

It is important to describe the roles of the three participants in this interview. The interview was essentially impersonal and might be thought of as taking place under conditions of "nil-rapport." Efforts made to insure that each person I interviewed would be a stranger to me were successful in over 90 percent of the interviews. (As previously mentioned, the degree of prior acquaintance with the respondent was recorded both for the interpreter and for me.) Only two to three minutes were devoted to putting the respondent at ease. What followed was a highly impersonal form of interviewing. For one thing, personal questions were never asked. Questions were couched in terms of the tribe as a whole: For example, "How do the Hehe feel about a poor man?"; never, "How do *you* feel about a poor man?"

In part, this impersonality was thought advisable in order to reduce the respondent's tension regarding personal or private questions, but it was also the result of my desire to find a form of communication that could effectively take place between strangers, because the design of the project insured that most of the persons interviewed would necessarily be total strangers to me. Even in the impersonal form of questioning, respondents regularly revealed themselves as persons, but the pretense that they were talking about others was always present. It should also be borne in mind that not only were the respondents strangers to me, they were unacculturated Africans talking to a "European." Although all had seen Europeans before, few had had much previous contact with them and none was accustomed to exchanging personal information with so elevated and distant a person.[16] And, of course, the use of an interpreter itself efficiently precluded much direct and personal communication. Thus to have attempted to interview on a basis of personal confidence and close rapport would have been impossible. The interview, then, was designed to make the most of an impersonal situation; if strangers had to be interviewed, then the interview would be routinized, and long, rich, personally tinged response would not be expected.

The interpreter was presented to the respondent as a familiar figure, a member of his own tribe, usually known personally at least by reputation, and usually trusted, at least as one African would trust another vis-à-vis a European. As such he could serve as a buffer between the strange and somewhat threatening European and the respondent. In fact, the interpreter did mediate between me and the respondent, and in so doing he was able to maintain the routine flow of questions and answers. This use of the interpreter as a familiar buffer or mediator was made the most of;[17] he sat directly facing the respondent while I made myself inconspicuous; he spoke loudly and I spoke (except in response to a direct question) quietly. It was always clear that all information was for my ears, and in response to my ques-

16. For a discussion of some of the problems involved in such a relationship, see Edgerton (1965).

17. S. G. Lee (1950) in his study of the Zulu employed a similar device even though he was able to speak Zulu. I had not read Lee's paper before deciding upon my own approach.

tions, but the respondents eagerly accepted the fiction that they were speaking directly to the interpreter.

This fiction was especially important in the freedom the respondents thought it gave them to make off-the-record comments. Most informants were plainly anxious early in the interview, and they expressed their anxiety by speaking directly to the interpreter about me or the interview. These comments were not necessarily hostile, although a few were; they were primarily requests for additional information about a particular question or the purpose of the interview itself. Each interpreter was carefully trained to give standard answers to these questions and then without seeming to do so, to translate the question and answer for me. The interpreters became very adept at mollifying the respondent while letting me know what was said without the respondent being the wiser. Proof of this was seen in the fact that respondents continued to make comments of this sort. Such anxious exchanges might go as follows:

> RESPONDENT: I don't know the answer to that question. Help me.
> INTERPRETER: Just give me whatever your true feelings are, I will make everything sound all right.

Or:

> RESPONDENT: Why does this man ask such questions? I am afraid.
> INTERPRETER: Don't worry. He is a good man who will not harm you or any Kamba [Sebei, etc.]. Just tell me what you think and it will be all right.

These confidences apparently helped the respondent to continue responding. In a face-to-face confrontation with me, such exchanges would not have been possible. Indeed, the advantage of the barrier that the interpreter provided between me and the respondent was, in my mind, essential to the interview. Personal communication with so strange a person as a "European" would have been too difficult for most of the respondents without extensive preparation before each interview.

Thus, as much as the interpreter was to be trustworthy, friendly, and familiar, I was to recede into the background. Of course, I was sincerely friendly and harmless; but since I was essentially an unknown quantity to the respondents in all communities, it was the appeal of the interpreter, the ethnographer, and the beer that carried the respondents to, and through, the interview.

FOLLOW-UP VERIFICATION INTERVIEWS

Following the completion of all interviews at a particular site, what I have called follow-up verification interviewing took place. In contrast to the impersonality of the preceding interviews, these talks were highly personal and intensive. As each respondent in the sample was interviewed, he or she was rated as a potentially good "personal" or "key" informant, that is, someone who was thoroughly knowledgeable and very willing to share that knowledge. After completion of the probability sample interviews, a list of five to ten such potentially good informants was made and each was asked to come to see me "as a favor." These interviews took place in privacy, too, but under quite different conditions: food was eaten, confidences were exchanged, and direct personal questions were asked.

The purpose of these follow-up interviews was to explore each question and visual stimulus used in the interview at great length. These "personal" informants were asked to explain their own reactions to each question and *why* they responded as they did. In these talks I was not inconspicuous although, of course, I did use an interpreter. I worked as an ethnographer, pressing each question as far as possible and probing inconsistent or vague answers. I attempted to discover every possible misunderstanding of a question and every possible instance, or at least every general subject area, where information might have been withheld or distorted. After each "personal" informant had been queried about his or her own response, the answers as given by other people were explored. I asked why people might have answered as they did, what it might mean to have said some other thing, and whether or not people had left anything out. Each possible point of misunderstanding, lying, or withholding which might have occurred with any frequency—or misinterpretation on my part—was explored; and as each point was made, behavioral and anecdotal examples were collected.

Each point in the interview battery was covered in detail with each personal informant in an interview that usually lasted (in several sessions) between six and eight hours. In each site, at least four such follow-up verification reviews of all points in the battery were made, two with men and two with women. Any points about which there were conflicting opinions were then pursued still further with other informants. Points that could not be resolved after eight or ten such sessions were regarded as being hopelessly snarled, and had to be left as puzzles. Fortunately, such points were very few, and always trivial.

By means of these intensive follow-up sessions, it was possible to examine frankly the answers given to each point in the interview. These verification interviews were, therefore, invaluable in clarifying and adding depth to what took place in the formal, impersonal interviews. The process did not turn up data suitable for statistical processing, but it did provide a much more complete background against which the data from the survey interviewing might be evaluated and validated. Without these follow-up interviews, the survey interview responses would have remained, as do most survey research data, presumably honest answers to presumably meaningful questions. Because of the follow-up verification interviews, I feel confident in saying that, with rare exceptions, respondents in every one of the eight interviewing sites understood the questions they were being asked, found most of them meaningful, and answered all questions as truthfully and as well as they could.

CODING THE DATA

In the course of reducing interview responses to categories that can be assigned numbers or names, one runs the risk of simplifying and distorting those responses. For some purposes, the utility of highly abstract categories is sufficiently great that the distortion involved is thought to be justified. In this research, however, I felt that it was necessary to hold such distortion to a minimum, and consequently the categories into which the interview responses were to be coded were as concrete as possible, consisting of nominal scales that were typically phrased in the words of the respondents themselves. Such scales attempt to retain the exact meaning of the respondents' words, but as a result they have only nominal properties of measurement. This nominal scale tabulation was the first and most fundamental coding procedure.

Table 1 was chosen at random to illustrate the nature of this nominal coding procedure. It provides all the categories that were used to code all responses to the question, "What is the most important thing for a young woman to know before marriage?"

As table 1 indicates, all the answers given by the respondents in all of the eight interviewing sites could be subsumed under nine categories. There were fifteen persons who did not answer the question, but only nine categories were needed to code all the answers. These nine categories were sufficient to classify the answers to most of

TABLE 1

What Is the Most Important Thing for a Young Woman to Know Before Marriage?

Tribe	(1) How to work hard	(2) How to do housework	(3) How to do farm work	(4) How to be polite, obedient	(5) How to find a husband	(6) How to get wealth	(7) How to care for children	(8) How to avoid promiscuity	(9) How to please men sexually	(10) No answer OR Don't know
Hehe										
Farmers (N = 61)	1	24	7	5	5	14	0	2	1	2
Pastoralists (N = 62)	7	17	16	1	9	5	0	3	0	4
Kamba										
Farmers (N = 62)	5	37	11	6	1	2	0	0	0	0
Pastoralists (N = 64)	8	47	6	1	0	2	0	0	0	0
Pokot										
Farmers (N = 65)	5	28	21	1	3	0	0	0	7	0
Pastoralists (N = 63)	11	30	0	4	9	0	1	0	8	0
Sebei										
Farmers (N = 64)	10	8	14	7	19	0	0	0	1	5
Pastoralists (N = 64)	19	18	4	5	13	0	0	0	1	4

the questions, but some required an "other" category because the answers given included a small number of unusual responses that could not easily be categorized. The number of responses falling into such an "other" category was always minimal. As table 1 illustrates, the categories are phrased in the approximate words of the respondents themselves. There are no abstract categories used; one might, for example, have coded all these responses into the following two categories: economic or moral.

All responses to all eighty-five questions, nine values pictures, and twenty-two slides were categorized into nominal scales by the author. Although this task was extremely time-consuming, requiring months of work, few difficult judgments were required. The responses sorted easily into categories without any feeling on my part that the judgments were arbitrary. However, to confirm my impression of objectivity, two graduate students were employed to repeat this coding process independently both of me and of one another. The three judges' coding of all responses to all questions and pictures in the interview were compared, and in no case was the agreement between the judges less than 0.84, and in well over 75 percent of the cases, it was above 0.90. The magnitude of the interjudge agreement is not surprising in view of the fact that the judges were merely fitting the respondents' answers into categories that closely matched the words actually being categorized. Indeed, most discrepancies among the judges' codings were found to be simple mechanical errors (intending to place the response in one category but inadvertently placing it in another) rather than actual disagreements about the category in which a response correctly belonged.

It was my intention to provide a clear and objective foundation for the comparison of the pastoral and farming interview responses. I believe that this simple tabulation of the responses constitutes such a foundation, one that is adequate as a reliable description of the principal categories into which the responses fell. Undeniably, however, such a categorization of the responses restricts some forms of statistical analysis and, what is more important, it fails to utilize all of the information provided by the respondents. To retrieve this additional information yet to retain a clear and objective set of data categories, a second coding of the data was carried out.

This second coding was a manifest content analysis. As Bernard Berelson (1954, p. 489) has said in his review of content analysis as a research tool: "Content analysis is a research technique for the objective, systematic, and quantitative description of the manifest

61

content of communication." In its simplest form, content analysis involves counting every occurrence of any category of content within a given corpus of material. The technique has been widely used in a variety of forms and with varying degrees of apparent success.[18] As a descriptive device, there is general agreement that content analysis is a reliable, objective technique. Although most uses of content analysis have weaknesses as explanatory techniques,[19] the procedure was a useful one for my purposes.

The first coding operation—the nominal scale tabulation—categorized specific answers to all the questions and pictures in the interview battery; however, it did not tabulate all the irrelevant remarks, anecdotes, explanations, and general comments that most respondents made at places throughout the interview. Such utterances, although not direct answers to the questions or pictorial stimuli, were nonetheless potentially revealing indicators of beliefs, values, attitudes, and emotions, and, consequently, I did not want to ignore them. Neither did I want all the coded data to remain in a simple and specific nominal form when it appeared to be useful to combine certain of these specific categories into more abstract ones. The content analysis, therefore, was intended to tabulate the general comments of the respondents and to combine specific categories into more general ones.

For each of the 505 respondents, all responses given during all portions of the interview were typed onto protocol sheets. This entire protocol—including all casual remarks, explanations, and illustrations, as well as the relevant comments and answers—was examined by the coders. A set of categories was developed, each one of which was related to some important area of anticipated difference between farmers and pastoralists. Each category was defined for the coders, who were instructed to count each occurrence of that category (complete scoring instructions are given in Appendix IV). By this procedure it was possible to derive a measure of the overall emphasis that each respondent gave to certain values or attitudes without being bound to consider only his specific answers to specific questions.

The content analysis categories, including brief definitions were: *adultery* (sexual relations between a married person and anyone who is not a spouse), *affection* (love, tenderness, concern, etc., for another person—excludes explicit physical sexuality), *cattle* (any cattle), *clan* (clan or lineage), *concern with death* (death, burial or serious

18. See: Berelson (1954), de Sola Pool (1959), North (1963), Stone et al. (1966), and White (1967).
19. See Mitchell (1967).

disease thought to lead to death), *conflict avoidance* (valuation of avoidance of intrasocietal disputes or conflicts), *concern with wrongdoing* (explicit concern over the consequences of wrongdoing), *cooperation* (two or more persons in a mutually helpful activity), *depression* (gloominess, sadness, dejection, discouragement, etc.), *desire for friends* (personal wish for, or valuation of, friends), *direct aggression* (any overt physical action that harms another person or his interests within the society), *disrespect for authority* (disregard for, or disvaluation of, political authority—e.g., elders, chiefs, prophets, courts, etc.), *divination* (any divinatory activity, including that of prophets), *fatalism* (man's action said to be inadequate to overcome or prevent misfortune), *fear* (fear, worry or nervousness in any context where the cause is evident except poverty), *fear of poverty* (poverty is or should be feared), *guilt-shame* (either guilt or shame regarding any activity), *hatred* (hatred for other people when *not* accompanied by any kind of aggression), *hostility to opposite sex* (any criticism of, hostility toward, or aggression against the opposite sex), *independence* (any action explicitly described as being an individual decision), *industriousness* (hard work by either sex, mentioned or valued), *insults* (any explicit affront), *jealousy of wealth* (covetousness of another person's wealth), *land* (cultivable land), *litigiousness* (any actual litigation or the desire for it), *physical beauty* (either sex said to be physically attractive), *respect for authority* (respect for any authority —elder, chief, father, husband, etc.), *self-control* (control of impulses, improper desires, disruptive activities, etc., described or valued), *valuation of cattle* (cattle ownership valued), *valuation of independent action* (individual freedom of choice in action valued), *witchcraft* (witchcraft or sorcery in any context). Unless otherwise indicated, the category was scored whenever it was specifically mentioned.

The thirty-one categories listed above, as well as four others, were scored by three judges, the author and two students. Because such scoring must be reliable if it is to be of any value, only those items for which the interjudge agreement was greater than 0.70 were retained. By this criterion, four categories were eliminated. Table 2 gives the interjudge agreement on all categories, including those that were eliminated.

That the agreement among the judges should have been high is not surprising in view of the fact that the judges were carefully trained to make what were, for the most part, nonjudgmental enumerations about manifest content. An example of the scoring process, showing the coding of an actual protocol, is given in Appendix V.

Although the resulting scores are relatively imprecise as sum-
mations of any given individual's existing attitudes, values, or feeling

TABLE 2

INTERJUDGE RELIABILITY OF THE CONTENT ANALYSIS CATEGORIES

Category	Correlation coefficient among the coders
Adultery	.92
Affection	.71
Cattle	.96
Clan	.97
Concern with death	.93
Concern with wrongdoing	.79
Conflict avoidance	.76
Cooperation	.73
Depression	.77
Desire for friends	.89
Direct aggression	.82
Disrespect for authority	.81
Divination	.90
Fatalism	.74
Fear	.71
*Fear of moral violation	.43
Fear of poverty	.89
*Guilt-shame (version 1)	.37
Guilt-shame (version 2)	.74
Hatred	.87
*Hostility	.51
Hostility to opposite sex	.90
Independence	.76
Industriousness	.78
Insults	.82
Jealousy of wealth	.95
Land	.96
Litigiousness	.88
Physical beauty	.78
Respect for authority	.79
Self-control	.72
Valuation of cattle	.95
Valuation of independent action	.82
Witchcraft	.97
*Xenophobia	.58

*Later omitted so that the total number of content analysis categories was 31.

state, when the scores of all individuals in an interviewing site are
converted to mean scores for that site, I believe that these scores provide excellent general indicators of how response tendencies differ

from site to site. However, since different sites provided protocols of differing mean length, some adjustment in mean scores was necessary. Thus, for each site the words per protocol were counted, and each site was given a mean score adjusted for the average number of words in its protocols. This adjustment is approximate at best, but it helped to overcome the inequities imposed by unequal protocol length.[20]

As a result, while minor differences between pastoralists and farmers in their mean scores on any content analysis category cannot be assumed to be significant because of the imprecision of the measurement, the precision of measurement was sufficient to allow the assumption that fairly sizable differences in mean scores probably represent significant differences in response tendencies.

Finally, the Rorschach performance, in addition to being scored in the content analysis, was also coded following the Klopfer system (by the author, by a graduate student in psychology who was trained in this coding system, and by a psychologist who is a specialist in the Rorschach technique). This coding process followed standard Klopfer procedures. A full description of these procedures and scoring criteria is available in Klopfer et al. (1954). More extensive discussion of this coding process is presented in chapter 8.

A REVIEW OF THE DATA

The purpose of this chapter has been to provide a sufficiently detailed introduction to the procedures of data collection and coding to permit the following kinds of evaluations: What kind of confidence do these data warrant? What can we expect them to do well? What are their limitations? Do they serve as they were intended to do, as a means by which farmers and pastoralists can be distinguished with regard to some of their attitudes, values, and personality characteristics?

No doubt each reader will differ in his evaluation of the utility of these data for that purpose. Although it may be argued that I, as one who has so long labored over the collection and analysis of these data, must perforce be an enthusiast whose evaluations are unlikely to be sufficiently critical, it may nonetheless be helpful for me to summarize my own view of the virtues and liabilities of these interview data. Let me be the first to note that this study, in my own eyes, is con-

20. For an example of a similar measurement of "wordage" in anthropological research, see the work of R. Naroll (1962, 1969).

siderably removed from perfection, not only in the best of all possible research worlds, but in the ethnographic world of reality in which the survey was conducted. Yet, assuredly, I did "my damndest" and even after years of reflection, my ideas concerning possible improvements upon these data shift as often as do my memories of the difficulties of this kind of field research. Thus, while I am aware of the weaknesses of this research, I am not convinced that alternatives offered better solutions within the design and resources of the Culture and Ecology Project. So much for my enthusiasm.

The first and most basic criticism of which I am aware concerns this study's reliance upon survey interviewing techniques. All of the complaints commonly directed against survey research data can be applied to this research. I shall not reiterate these charges here, as they are presumably known to everyone.[21] Most such charges are not directly contestable here. I am most concerned with the complaints that such data cannot be "validated"—an ambiguous and complex assertion. In defense against those charges that tend to focus upon the absence of validity checks in survey interviewing, I would say only that the interview data in this study are adequately placed in broader cultural context by the verification interviews I conducted, by my ethnographic observations, and by the extensive ethnographic investigations of the four ethnographers.

A second criticism, this time particular to this research, has to do with my efforts to increase the comparability of the responses by simplifying my eliciting techniques in search of what I have referred to as a lowest common denominator. Although I feel strongly that this decision was correct as a necessary aid to comparability, there can be no doubt that it reduced the complexity and detail of the responses of *some* persons. The alternative, as I have noted, was between complex and detailed response from a minority of the respondents, or a simplified form of response from a majority of the respondents.

Another problem area concerns the impersonal tone of the interview process and the impersonal form of the questions. It is possible that this impersonality induced the respondents to speak in terms of norms and values rather than personal preferences or individual style. Therefore, the interview may have promoted a kind of modal or ideal response pattern. I suspect that this is true. However, for the purposes of this research, a tendency to respond in terms of norms or values

21. For a review, see Crespi (1965), Dollard (1948), Galtung (1967), Glock (1967), Hauck and Steinkamp (1964), Hyman (1955), Phillips (1966), and Schreier (1963).

was exactly what we sought. It is also problematic that a more personal form of interviewing would have elicited personally revealing or idiosyncratic answers from more than a minority of the respondents.

Even should it be agreed that the interview succeeded admirably in provoking answers to the questions at hand, it might still be argued that the wrong questions were asked and the wrong pictures shown. Here, each reader must judge for himself the content of the eliciting materials. In my own view, the interview battery was least adequate in the following three regards. First, I believe, in retrospect, that there were too few questions involving decisions, especially decisions that would have required cooperation. Such questions were tried during the pretest and were poorly responded to; nevertheless, perhaps more effort should have been devoted to devising decision-choice questions that could have elicited response pertaining to cooperation. Second, I feel that the interview gave disproportionate attention to sexual matters in the belief that sexual concerns would serve dramatically to distinguish farmers from pastoralists. Finally, I regret that the interview battery did not include better means of evoking fantasy, either in traditional or personal form.

Mention should also be made of the failure of the interview to achieve the degree of diversity I had originally desired. Diversity of question, task, and visual stimulus was a principal goal in order to tap as great a variety of response potential as possible. For reasons already detailed, many of the proposed parts of the interview were dropped. As a result, the interview consisted only of questions and assorted visual stimuli: all manipulative, expressive, and behavioral tasks were left out. These latter are at best difficult to quantify, or score, and tricky to interpret, so their omission probably increased the objectivity of the interview. Nonetheless, the diversity within the interview was less than originally had been intended.

It might also be contended that the burden I placed upon the interpreters was too heavy. In answer, I feel that the performance of the interpreters within the design of the project was excellent and that the use of an interpreter was a genuine advantage over direct (interview-to-respondent) interviewing. I have outlined the various practices employed to insure the standardization and fidelity of the interpreted interview, yet one might justifiably ask why the additional safeguard of tape-recording was not attempted.

There are several reasons for my decision not to tape-record the interviews. In the first place, the pretesting indicated that a tape recorder was such a novelty that it distracted many respondents and frightened a few. Furthermore, the transportation and maintenance of a tape recorder in rain and heat, while fording flooded rivers and bouncing along rutted, potholed, and nonexistent roads, were challenges I chose not to accept. I refused to be dependent upon the whim of such a tormented machine to operate reliably; should it have failed, irreplaceable data could have been lost.

It would have been delightful to sit serenely during interviews, without the handbreaking task of taking a verbatim transcript, while a tape recorder did the work for me. But even should the machine have operated perfectly, it still would have been a false economy. Were I to have taken time in the field to sit down and transcribe each tape, the time so spent would have severely cut into the time available for actual interviewing. On the other hand, were I to have sent each taped interview away for transcription, no secretary could possibly have understood the fast, clipped, Afro-British accent, the peculiar expressions, and the liberal infusion of local and Swahili terms. As a result, I would have had to transcribe over 500 taped interviews after returning from the field, and, by that time, even I might not have been able to translate some portions of the tapes.

As I was convinced that the interpreters were well trained, and my own "shorthand" was fast and accurate, the only reason for tape-recording would have been to check the accuracy of the interpretation. I made this check during pretesting and I was satisfied that the interpreters were accurate. To have tape-recorded every fifth or so interview as a regular practice would have been impractical, and would in any event have proved little. A bad interpreter could easily be precise while a tape was running, only to become lax again during nonrecorded interviews. To have so spot-checked a good interpreter would only have weakened the trust between us. In short, the failure to tape-record was not an oversight. The tape recorder was rejected, regretfully, as more of a burden than a blessing.

Another problem to be considered is the timing of my visits to the eight interviewing sites. The order of my visits was: Sebei farmers, Kamba farmers, Pokot pastoralists, Sebei pastoralists, Hehe farmers, Hehe pastoralists, Pokot farmers, and Kamba pastoralists. Obviously, the possibility of an "order effect" or "instrument fatigue" influencing my feelings toward the people in the communities, and consequently my conduct of the interview, cannot be discounted altogether. However, the order is generally well scrambled. For example, I did not visit all the farming communities before the pastoral communities or vice versa. Moreover, there were so many extraneous factors that the "order effect" itself seems of minimal importance.[22] Some sites were visited during the rains, others during a dry season; some following harvests, others during periods of food scarcity; in some places a ceremonial of importance was taking place, in others there were no unusual events; some sites were under pressure of the threat of enemy raids, others were not; and there were, undoubtedly, other situational factors entirely unknown to me.

How much and in what ways the interview responses may have been affected by such contingencies is not known, but it is possible that there may have been an effect. For example, the Pokot farmers insisted that during the lean part of the year just before harvest, they are too weak and hungry to engage in their popular pastime of adultery. It was during this part of the year that I interviewed in Tamkal. Did the people talk about adultery less, or more, than they would have at another time of the year? One could argue either side. Where possible, such situational influences are taken into consideration in appraising the findings. Hopefully, the interview was not sensitive to many such influences but that it was not cannot simply be assumed. That the interviews should have been differentially subject to influences of this kind is an obvious flaw in the research design. But East Africa is not a laboratory, and time, distance, and weather were the implacable enemies of any effort to regulate the timing and circumstances of the scheduled visits to each site.

With regard to the coding procedures by which the interview responses were assigned numbers, my own principal concern is that the content analysis scores not be accorded a precision that is not rightfully theirs. These scores are reliable and they are *relatively* precise. In my use of these scores in the analyses of the response patterns, I shall try not to make more of this precision than is warranted.

The criticisms considered here are by no means the only ones of merit: they are merely those that most strongly suggest themselves to me. In conclusion, I believe that the strength of these data is their objectivity and comparability. Our primary goal—indeed, our essential goal—was to collect comparable data from eight distinct populations. In attempting to achieve this goal, a concession had to be made. That concession was in favor of objectivity and comparability, and it produced data that were relatively reduced in complexity, subtlety,

22. See, for example, Campbell (1961).

and personal involvement. That this concession had to be made was unfortunate, but unavoidable. Yet, all data, properly collected, serve as answers to questions. All things considered, I believe that in accord with our assumptions about the distinguishing features of pastoral and farming life, the data of this study effectively serve to answer our questions about the similarities and differences of the eight populations we studied.

An Introduction to the Tribes 2

This chapter consists of brief introductions to some principal social and cultural features of each of the four tribes represented in this research, and brief descriptions of each selected pastoral and farming research site with special emphasis upon relevant aspects of the physical environment and the economy. These introductions and descriptions are written in the present tense, but document conditions as they existed in 1961 and 1962.

From the Hehe in the south to the Sebei in the north, the four tribes studied in this research were spread over a great expanse of East Africa, from the southern highlands of Tanzania to the plains north of Mount Elgon in Uganda. The map shown in figure 1[1] indicates the locations of the Hehe, Kamba, Pokot, and Sebei at the time of our research.

THE HEHE

The Hehe are a Bantu-speaking people who occupy the Iringa area of the southern highlands region of Tanzania. Most of this area is high, rolling country characterized by woodland, grassland, and, in its highest parts, tropical rain forest. The Hehe also occupy the low plains area of the valley of the Great Ruaha River.

The Hehe of today represent an amalgamation of thirty or so small chieftaincies which were united about four generations ago by

1. For all maps and for the geographic and economic data used in this chapter, I am indebted to Dr. Philip Porter, whose forthcoming Culture and Ecology Project monograph deals in detail with the geographic and economic matters I have introduced here.

71

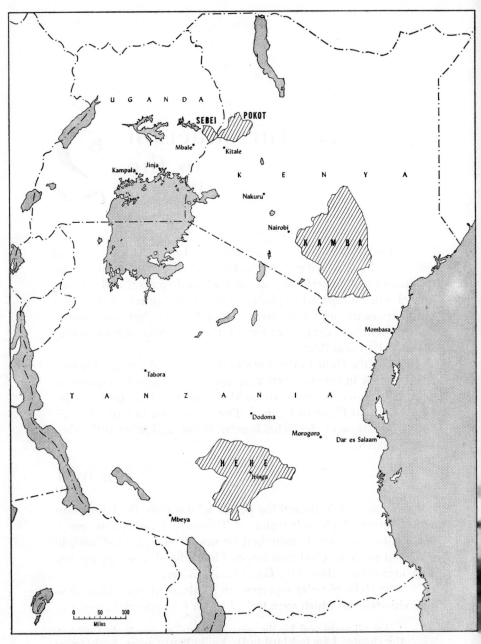

Figure 1. Locations of the Hehe, Kamba, Pokot, and Sebei in East Africa at the time of the Culture and Ecology Project research in 1961 and 1962.

the military and diplomatic successes of Muyugumba and his son Mkwawa. These men extended Hehe dominion over an immense region of south central Tanzania. In the latter part of the nineteenth century, Hehe expansion came into direct conflict with German colonial administration, but it was only after a series of bloody defeats that German military power was finally successful in subduing the Hehe and confining them to their present political boundaries.

The 250,000 Hehe of today practice a mixed economy based upon the cultivation of maize, squash, cassava, beans, millet, and other crops, together with the herding of relatively small numbers of cattle, sheep, and goats. Most Hehe live in dispersed homesteads which are formed into neighborhoods. Each homestead, typically including a male head of household, his wife or wives, and their children, is surrounded by the family's cultivated fields where both men and women work. Some economic activities also involve cooperative work parties.

The Hehe recognize patrilineages and clans, but they also regard descent from them other as important, and thus give recognition to a group (lukolo) composed of the localized members of several patrilineages which possess matrilateral linkages. This group has its importance reinforced by frequent interaction because of the nearness of residence among its members, and the lukolo today appears to be the most important kin group for most kinds of joint action, for example, that accompanying birth, death, litigation, and the like.

The Hehe do not organize themselves into age-sets, and neither do they engage in an elaborate round of initiation ceremonies, although girls do undergo initiation and clitoral excision. The Hehe recognize, and give considerable authority to, a set of headmen, subchiefs, and chiefs (prior to German conquest, the Hehe Kingdom established a similar set of offices). These authorities have power in matters of litigation and in the inheritance of land.

Despite their illustrious military past, the Hehe of today are not organized for military action, nor do they engage in more than occasional, locally limited, skirmishes along their border with pastoral neighbors. Although there has been considerable Muslim influence upon the Hehe, most Hehe maintain their own religious belief and practices, among which ancestors occupy a place of central importance.

The modern Hehe are neither remote from Western influence, nor highly Westernized. Acculturative influence within Hehe territory is quite uneven: some areas have been much influenced by cash

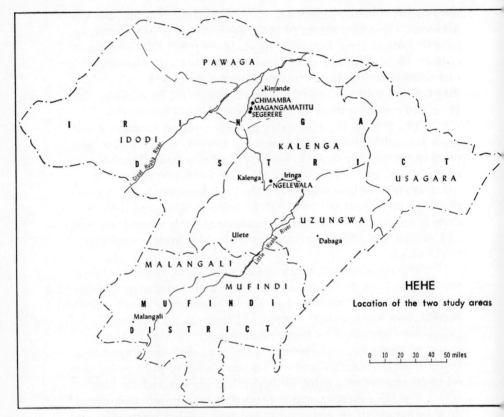

Figure 2. Locations of the Hehe pastoral and farming study sites.

economy and education, while others have been left largely untouched
by these factors.[2]

The locations of the pastoral and farming study sites within
Uhehe are shown in figure 2.

THE HEHE FARMING SITE (NGELEWALA)

The farming neighborhood of Ngelewala is situated some six
to seven miles to the southeast of the administrative center of Iringa,
near the center of the traditional Hehe Kingdom. Ngelewala is small,

2. For information concerning the Hehe, I am grateful to E. V.
Winans. For additional description of the Hehe, see Brown and Hutt
(1935), Nigmann (1908), Winans and Edgerton (1964), and Winans
(1965). To simplify presentation, I have omitted the prefixes when
discussing the Hehe, Kamba, and other Bantu peoples.

covering only about one square mile. Located in the cool highlands, it is green and heavily overgrown with vegetation in the rainy seasons, but between the rains it is brown and dry. Its fields are separated by hedges and by stands of large trees, and so heavy is this growth of crops, shrubs, and trees at the peak of the growing season that in some places the houses of the Hehe of Ngelewala are all but obscured. Yet the houses are not easily obscured for they are massive, square, *tembe*-type houses with thick walls and heavy roofs. The houses are L- or U-shaped, and sometimes enclose a central courtyard. Of the 300 people in Ngelewala, some are employed in wage work outside the neighborhood, but most are occupied with their crops near their houses.

Precipitation in Ngelewala is adequate to produce one crop without much risk (it rained 30.6 inches the year of our research), but double cropping is not possible because of its seasonal distribution. The Hehe cultivate many crops in addition to maize, which is most important. They plant finger millet, bulrush millet, beans, cassava, sweet potatoes, groundnuts, and other lesser crops. In Ngelewala, there are 1.7 acres in crop per capita. Each acre is estimated to produce an average yield of 755 pounds of edible food, an annual production of 1,284 pounds of food per person.

That the people of Ngelewala are successful farmers is indeed fortunate for they are quite poor in livestock. Only 18 percent of the heads of household own any cattle whatever; and, all told, the 276 people of Ngelewala own only 268 cattle, 19 goats, and no sheep. Hence, they are relatively little involved with livestock and derive little of their sustenance from their animals. Philip Porter, the project's geographer, in rating the farming and pastoral orientation of each site, considered Ngelewala to be second among the eight study sites in its dependence upon farming.

Ngelewala is blessed with a benign climate and few virulent health problems. There are no dangerous animals in the area and few poisonous reptiles or insects. What is more, there is no threat of attack by neighboring tribes.

THE HEHE PASTORAL SITE (PAWAGA)

Pawaga lies far below Ngelewala, several hours by difficult, four-wheel drive road down a rugged escarpment to the north of the highland zone in which the people of Ngelewala live. Located in the low basin of the Ruaha River, this area is a stark contrast to Ngelewala. The land is flat, covered by acacia scrub and thicket, and sprinkled with the spoor of the rhinoceros, elephant, lion, and hyena that so freely roam through it.

The people of Pawaga, unlike those of Ngelewala, are clustered together into villages. These small villages are strung out adjacent to the Little Ruaha River. Most of the houses of Pawaga are smaller and less substantial than those of the farmers in the highlands. We studied the four villages of Segerere, Magangamatitu, Mikosi, and Majengo, which together control some 31 square miles and include about 200 people. Pawaga is oppressively hot and dry, with vegetation sparse except for the fields concentrated along the irrigated canals drawn from the Little Ruaha.

Rainfall in Pawaga is scant (13.7 inches in the unusually wet year of our research), and from May through November there is often no rain at all. In this arid land little agriculture is possible if it must depend upon precipitation. Thus the people of Pawaga irrigate, taking water from the river that cuts across the area, and capturing runoff in ponds where they plant maize and millet. Their principal irrigated crop is wet rice. Although only a few acres of land can be sufficiently watered (0.7 per capita), these few acres are productive, yielding 1,145 pounds of food per acre, more than the cultivated land of Ngelewala yields. But there are so few acres that can be irrigated that only 802 pounds of food per capita are produced (compared with 1,284 pounds in Ngelewala).

Although the people of Pawaga grow moderate quantities of agricultural produce, they also engage in regular hunting and fishing, both of which are important subsistence activities. And, unlike Ngelewala, Pawaga is a land of livestock. In this area with only about half the population of Ngelewala, there are close to 1,500 cattle, over 700 goats, and over 600 sheep. Forty-seven percent of the heads of household in Pawaga own cattle, as opposed to 18 percent in Ngelewala. Thus while Pawaga does depend upon cultivation for much of its subsistence, it is greatly involved with livestock, without which its people probably could not subsist.

The area is far more involved with pastoral life than is Ngelewala, and it is far more dangerous. It is troubled by all the epidemic and endemic diseases of lowland East Africa, and the many reptiles and large animals of the area are a constant menace. In addition, cattle theft, sometimes by armed raiders from neighboring tribes, is a continual threat.

THE KAMBA

The Bantu-speaking Kamba occupy a large area of southeastern Kenya. Their territory is divided into two administrative districts, Machakos and Kitui, which correspond closely to a long-standing tribal division recognized by the Kamba. Of the more than 800,000 Kamba, close to 550,000 live in Machakos. When the Kamba were first contacted by Europeans, they were occupying their present territory, having successfully maintained themselves against the military pressures of their neighbors, principally the Galla to the north and east and the Masai to the west and south. Moving first into the hills of Machakos and later across the Athi River into Kitui, the Kamba probably occupied their present territory sometime before 1700.

Throughout their territory, the Kamba practice a mixed economy, planting maize, millet, sorghum, and some cash crops, as well as keeping livestock. The Kamba live in scattered homesteads, composed of the usual polygynous family group. The Kamba recognize patrilineages and clans, with the clan assuming great importance to them as a corporate entity with legal and economic obligations. Territorial groups are also important. In addition to the tribe and the two districts, the Kamba are organized by the *utui* ("neighborhood") which is highly autonomous, the *thome* (a subdivision of an *utui*), and the *kibalo* (a grouping of adjoining neighborhoods). Of these, the principal unit is the neighborhood, which is governed by a council of elders.

Beyond the very limited authority of their local councils of elders, the Kamba recognize little authority, having no formal judicial, military, or religious offices except those imposed by colonial government. Their legal action is conducted in council or very rarely by the collective action of neighbors. Their religious activities are largely unorganized, with ceremonies (except those of initiation but including those involving sacrifices at the sacred tree) being variously and sometimes indifferently performed. One important activity involves the diagnostic and curing skills of certain practitioners who treat victims of witchcraft. An important feature of Kamba legal procedure involves the *kithitu*, a widespread and greatly respected oath. Boys and girls both undergo several ceremonies of initiation into age categories. These ceremonies include formalized dancing, circumcision, and various kinds of instruction. Although the Kamba do not

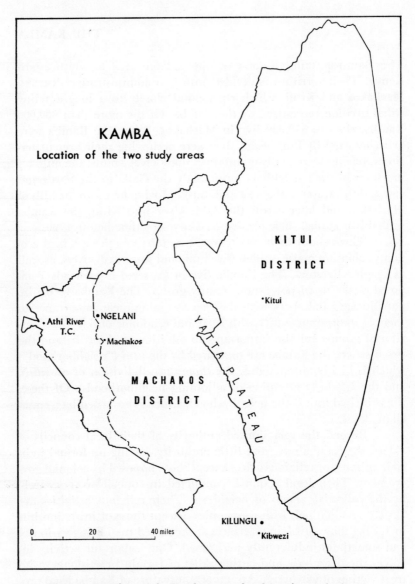

Figure 3. Locations of the Kamba pastoral and farming study sites.

possess a complex age-set system, all men pass through three age categories: warrior, married man, and elder.

As recently as 1961 the Kamba of Machakos were engaged in a

brief but large-scale combat with the Masai. In this warfare, as in pre-British conflicts, the Kamba lacked formal military organization or leadership. Both offensively and defensively, warfare was largely left to the talents of individual young men of the warrior category.

Although the Kamba who remain with the tribal area are usually not highly acculturated by East African standards, wage work has taken large numbers of young Kamba into the cities and towns of East Africa.[3]

The locations of the Kamba pastoral and farming study sites are shown in figure 3.

THE KAMBA FARMING SITE (NGELANI)

The neighborhood of Ngelani is located in the softly molded hills a few miles from the administrative center of Machakos. Most of the neighborhood lies between 5,500 and 6,500 feet, in cool wind-swept hills. Ngelani extends over less than three square miles atop the hills and down the slopes of this hill mass. Its small area is covered by fields, sisal hedges, and paths, with the houses of the Kamba scattered here and there next to the fields of green and brown. But this small area is the permanent home of 1,543 persons, a density of more than 500 persons per square mile. The crowding and the shortage of land in Ngelani is one of its most conspicuous features. Almost all land is cultivated, and people are everywhere.

The Kamba of Ngelani cultivate maize and a great many other crops, but there are so many humans in this small neighborhood that the number of acres in cultivation is less than the number of mouths to feed (0.87 acre per capita). The people of Ngelani use manure and the plow in their agriculture, and they have sufficiently reliable rainfall for two crop seasons. Their estimated average yield per acre is 1,167 pounds of edible food; this provides about 1,000 pounds of edible food per capita.

The people of Ngelani also keep substantial numbers of livestock. Estimating livestock ownership in Ngelani is difficult because the people are evasive, and most of the stock is kept many miles away on the plains of Mitaboni; but it is estimated that there were over 1,100 livestock units (a unit consists of one adult cow, bull, or heifer,

3. For information concerning the Kamba, I am grateful to S. C. Oliver. For additional description of the Kamba, see Dundas (1913), Hobley (1910), Jacobs (1961), Lindblom (1920), Mbiti (1966), Middleton (1953), Ndeti (1967), and Oliver (1965).

or five sheep, goats, or calves), or 2.59 units of livestock per person. Thus, while the people of Ngelani are intensive farmers, as are many Kamba, they also own sizable herds of livestock.

Ngelani is little troubled by diseases, dangerous animals, or snakes. It is far removed from the cattle raids of the Masai and is not threatened by warfare of any sort. Instead, it is troubled by crowding —by its own population. Consequently, most of the young men of Ngelani have sought long-term wage work outside the area.

THE KAMBA PASTORAL SITE (KILUNGU)

The neighborhood of Kilungu is more than one hundred miles to the east and south of Ngelani. It occupies nine square miles of flat land between the Athi River and the Uganda railroad. Kilungu is 3,000 feet lower in elevation than Ngelani, and it is hot and dry. Although Kilungu is more than three times as large as Ngelani, its population is much less, only 675 persons, or 75 persons per square mile. Thus, where Ngelani was, above all else, crowded, Kilungu is seemingly empty and desolate, its houses often hidden by dense thorn thickets, its people seldom noticeable.

The people of Kilungu farm, planting a bewildering variety of crops (maize, sorghum, millet, and castor beans being but a few of the more prominent ones) in large, haphazardly cleared and tended fields. They cultivate more than four acres per capita, yet the yield per acre is almost nonexistent, an average of 100 pounds of edible food (compared with more than 1,100 pounds in Ngelani). In part, this low yield is the result of the light and irregular rains that make even a single crop season a risky matter. Although it rained 25 inches during the year of our research, this was an unusually wet year, and even in this wet year there were five consecutive dry months. But the people of Kilungu are also indifferent farmers, making little use of the plow, and showing little apparent interest in improving the size or productivity of their holdings.

People in Kilungu make extensive use of the honey taken from a great many individually owned beehives, but their greatest economic involvement is with livestock. The much smaller population of Kilungu possesses 1,406 units of livestock (compared with 1,139 units in Ngelani), or an average of more than 4 units of stock per person. What is more, unlike the people of Ngelani who graze most of their stock far from the area where they live and work, the stock of Kilungu are kept in kraals and are grazed and watered in Kilungu. The Kamba of Kilungu make very little use of the permanent waters of the Kibwezi River for irrigation; however, they drive their cattle to the river to drink, and it is around the needs of these animals that the activities of most of the people of Kilungu center.

Kilungu also differs from Ngelani by being a dangerous place. It suffers from endemic diseases that kill adults as well as children. Although the Masai have not raided into the neighborhood of Kilungu itself, they have often raided nearby, and the people of Kilungu must reckon with cattle raiding, and resulting combat, as an ever-present possibility. The poisoned arrows of game poachers are another constant—and lethal—threat, especially to men who are checking their beehives. Kilungu is not far from a large game preserve, and its inhabitants must also contend with rhinoceros, lion, and buffalo, with many lives being lost to these animals and to snakes. Thus, the men carry their bows and poisoned arrows when they leave their homesteads, and all the people are wary.

Although Kilungu is somewhat less acculturated than Ngelani, it too has lost many of its young men to wage work in distant cities.

THE POKOT

The Pokot, sometimes referred to as the Suk, are a Nandi- or Kalenjin-speaking people who occupy a remote area of western Kenya and eastern Uganda. In all, there are probably 100,000 Pokot, almost 60,000 of whom occupy West Pokot district of Kenya, the area in which our research was located. Of these 60,000 Pokot, at least two-thirds occupy the district's highlands and valley slopes, and the remainder occupy the lowland plains where they subsist as pastoralists.

European knowledge of the existence of the Pokot dates back to 1854, but the first European to report a visit to them was Joseph Thomson in 1883. The Pokot cattle herds were decimated by the general rinderpest epidemics of the late 1800's, and raiding between the Pokot and the Turkana was widespread until the British launched military expeditions against the Turkana between 1914 and 1917. Since that time, the Pokot and their herds have increased.

The highland Pokot use a network of irrigation canals in the cultivation of finger millet, sorghum, and maize. These farmers also keep livestock, but in far fewer numbers than the lowland pastoralists who herd cattle, sheep, goats, and donkeys. The lowland Pokot seldom attempt any cultivation; however, they do maintain economic exchange relationships (produce of their stock for grain), and this ex-

81

change plus intermarriage and a set of ritual events link the farmers and pastoralists together in a common social and cultural system. What is more, the highland and lowland economic zones are linked by an interchangeability of personnel. Not only are wives exchanged, but visits are often exchanged, and men may move back and forth between the two environments, spending some years in one before taking up residence in the other.

The Pokot live in dispersed homesteads in the highland areas and in temporary kraals in the lowlands. In both areas they are strongly patrilineal, with shallow segmentary lineages and exogamous clans. The family is ideally polygynous, and serves as the fundamental economic unit, either in the cultivation of their fields or in the care of their stock. In addition to the family and consanguineal kin groups, the Pokot recognize territorial groupings called *korok* which delimit both physical and social relationships. *Korok* define certain significant environmental features including waterway demarcations, but they are also the social units from which councils are drawn and cooperative labor is recruited. Consanguineal, affinal, and territorial groupings are overlain by associations derived from circumcision groups, formalized age-sets, and stock exchange partnerships.

Both farmers and herders exchange livestock as bridewealth. A man's own requirements for stock, plus those of his kinsmen and the demands of his stock associates and age-mates, obligate him to demand as many animals as possible during negotiations for the marriage of a daughter. Conflicting claims to livestock cut across generations, age-sets, circumcision groups, and ties of kinship and locality.

The Pokot are influenced by prophets, whose importance continues to be related to their success in predicting the outcome of cattle raids, the location of good pasture, and the timing and nature of crops to be planted. Pokot social unity is enhanced by their age-sets which have continuing ceremonial, economic, and military significance, and by a cycle of ritual activities which brings together farmers and pastoralists.

Cattle raiding, particularly involving the Turkana and the Karamojong, continues, although large-scale raiding is now rare. Such military actions strike against the pastoral Pokot, but both the highland Pokot and the pastoral Pokot organize offensive raids.

The Pokot are as yet little affected by the acculturative influences of the West. Although they are more or less effectively under police control, they alone among the four tribes in this research sel-

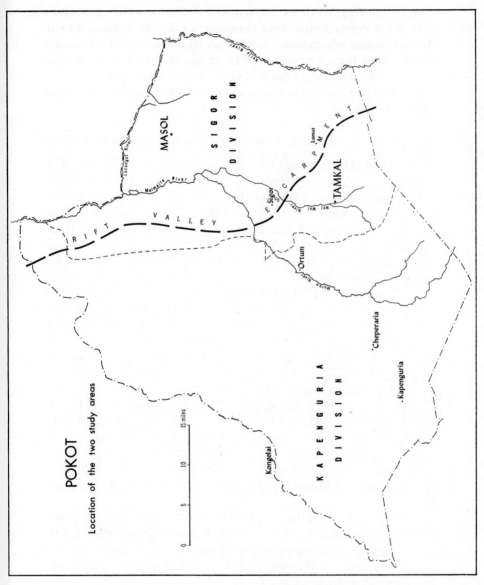

Figure 4. Locations
of the Pokot
pastoral and
farming study sites.

dom adopt Western dress, preferring to wear the traditional dress. Men often wear nothing more than a cape over the shoulders; their decoration and ornamentation, particularly of the head, is elaborate. Women wear leather wraparound skirts, but their breasts are usually bare. Like the men, the women are elaborately ornamented.[4]

Figure 4 shows the locations of the Pokot pastoral and farming study sites.

THE POKOT FARMING SITE (TAMKAL)

Tamkal is the name of a valley on the edge of the Gregory Rift Valley in the Pokot highlands. The valley is about twelve miles in length, and rests some 4,000 feet above sea level. The valley floor and the steep-sided walls that rise several thousand feet above it are the sites of homesteads and fields. Research was centered in the three *korok* of Tirtoi, Kamichich, and Asar, which covered about five square miles and contained some 1,220 people, a density of 244 persons per square mile.

The valley and the mountain peaks that loom above it are green with natural vegetation and cultivated fields, the air is cool, and rain showers are frequent. Yet there is enough precipitation for a reliable single crop season only if supplemental irrigation is employed, and several irrigation canals are in use. It is estimated that a second crop would be successful in only four out of ten years. The Pokot of Tamkal cultivate finger millet and sorghum, and while they have recently come to plant maize, it is still rather unpopular. It is estimated that they have only 1.1 acres in crop per capita, with each acre yielding an average of 825 pounds of edible food. This amounts to only 907 pounds of edible food per capita, which is, compared to the other farming sites, a low output. It is also estimated that they have only 1.35 units of livestock per person, again only a moderate number.

Thus, although the people of Tamkal strongly identify themselves as cattle owners and desperately hope to increase their herds, their principal subsistence comes from their fields. Yet their fields are barely adequate, for they are a poor people whose lean seasons are frequent and difficult.

Although there is some danger from pneumonia, adders, and

4. For information concerning the Pokot, I am grateful to F. C. Conant. For additional description of the Pokot, see Barton (1921), Beech (1911), Conant (1965, 1966), Edgerton and Conant (1964), Peristiany (1951, 1954), Schneider (1953, 1957, 1959, 1967).

leopards, residents of the Tamkal Valley are little threatened by disease, insects, and reptiles, and some of its residents have never seen the large wild animals that live on the plains below. The area is also safely removed from the raids of the Turkana and other neighboring tribes.

THE POKOT PASTORAL SITE (MASOL)

Masol is a Location covering some 600 square miles and containing about 1,600 Pokot, half of whom are adults. Research in Masol was centered in three *korok* (Arror, Katawun, and Kakalmong) at the foot of the Masol Hills, in the north central portion of this plains area, 25 miles from Tamkal in an area close to the territory of the Turkana. The area is remote, and access to it (possible by vehicle only during the dry season) requires that several rivers be forded and areas of tsetse fly be traversed. Some parts of Masol are cut by streams, and precipitation during the period of the research was unusually heavy (25 inches), yet cultivation throughout the area is extremely difficult and is rarely attempted.

The Pokot of Masol are pastoralists who herd large numbers of cattle, sheep, and goats and also possess smaller numbers of donkeys and an occasional camel. Accurate enumerations of the livestock in this area are difficult, but it was estimated that there are at least five livestock units per capita in Masol.

Despite the imposition of a grazing scheme by the administration (one that divides the western part of the area into four large blocks to be grazed over by prearranged plan), the Pokot of Masol continue to be mobile. They establish their thornbush kraals in large clusters when the rains permit many people and animals to be together, but when the dry season comes, families disperse with their herds.

As the Pokot pastoralists move with their herds, they must consider the availability of water, grass, and forage, as well as the threat of raids by the Turkana and the Karamojong. But these pastoralists are also dependent upon grain obtained from highland farming Pokot in exchange for products of their herds. Thus, their movements must also take into consideration the availability of grain from the mountains, or more recently, from trading posts.

Life in Masol is concentrated upon the herds, particularly upon the cattle, whose beauty and beautification is a constant subject of interest. Stock management is the center of attention for all the

Pokot of Masol. Men, women, and children all have responsibilities to the herds—to plan their care, to milk them, to guard them. Men go heavily armed, carrying long, thin-handled spears, as well as sticks and knives. Stock must be defended against humans and predatory animals alike, and in an area where everything—enemies, animals, weather, and disease—is so uncertain, men devote themselves to continual planning for the welfare of their herds, and to frequent divination to determine the most propitious course of action.

Life in Masol is periled by disease—tsetse-borne disease for cattle, smallpox, encephalitis, dysentery, malaria, and tracoma for humans. Wild animals, especially the many buffalo in the area, take a toll of human life, as do snakes. And death by an enemy's spear, although no longer a common occurrence, is never to be discounted.

THE SEBEI

The Sebei, like the Pokot, speak a Nandi or Kalenjin language. They occupy the northern and northwestern slopes of Mount Elgon in eastern Uganda and also some of the plains area at the northern foot of the mountain, a massive volcanic cone. Most of the approximately 35,000 Sebei live on the escarpment zone of the mountain, in an area that lies between 5,000 and 7,000 feet.

The Sebei appear to have migrated to Mount Elgon from the high plains to the east and north. They probably occupied the whole of the mountain until the late nineteenth century when pressures from Bantu peoples pushed them onto its sparsely populated northern face. Sebei occupation of the plains below this escarpment has apparently been sporadic; raids by the Karamojong, Pokot, Nandi, and Masai rendered the area largely untenable before the intervention of British police and military forces in 1914.

The economy of the Sebei rests on the cultivation of maize, millet, plantains, and other crops, including coffee which has become the principal cash crop. Cattle, sheep, and goats are grazed on the mountain, as well as on the plains below. The Sebei live in scattered households which are formed into neighborhoods. On the plains, stock is kept in thorn kraals; on the mountain, cattle are kraaled in small enclosures near the houses. Daily life centers upon the production and consumption of beer, an activity only slightly less vital to the Sebei than the care of their fields and stock—and a good deal more enjoyable than either.

In addition to their spatially defined neighborhoods, the Sebei also recognize larger units, or territories, as well as a number of sub-tribes with local territories, all amalgamated into the larger tribal entity. The dominant kin group is the patrilineal clan, which is divided into lineages. All men are inducted into age-sets by means of an elaborate ritual involving circumcision. Woman are also initiated, and undergo clitoral and labial excision as they are inducted into age-sets with names that are the counterparts of the male groups.

The Sebei previously recognized prophets who were often quite important. Now, they accord few special statuses, recognizing only elders or judges and some military leaders. Councils were held by neighborhoods, clans, and territories on various occasions, but these hearings were largely informal gatherings.

Sebei warfare in the past was largely defensive, although retaliatory raids were mounted then, as they are now. Present-day Sebei pastoralists are engaged in regular defensive actions, as well as some bloody retaliations against the Karamojong and the Pokot ("Karasuk").

The Sebei conduct a series of important purificatory rituals that extend across Sebei territory. Supernatural belief among the Sebei, as among all four tribes in this research, acknowledges a remote high god, but focuses upon evil spirits, divination, and witchcraft.

The Sebei of today are relatively heavily influenced by European dress, crops, material culture, and cash economy.[5]

The locations of the Sebei pastoral and farming study sites are shown in figure 5.

THE SEBEI FARMING SITE (SASUR)

The neighborhood of Sasur is located in the escarpment zone, toward the northwest portion of Sebei territory. Sasur is small, consisting of no more than 0.4 square mile, and it is crowded, containing 355 people, a density of 888 per square mile. Sasur is cool, green, and wet, with glossy *matoke* leaves, muddy paths, and coffee groves surrounding its maize fields. When the clouds and mists lift, the plains below the escarpment can be seen, shimmering in the heat and stretching far to the north beyond Lake Kyoga.

The large circular houses of the inhabitants of Sasur are sur-

5. For information concerning the Sebei, I am grateful to W. R. Goldschmidt. For additional description of the Sebei, see Goldschmidt (1967a), Huntingford (1953), Roscoe (1924), and Weatherby (1966).

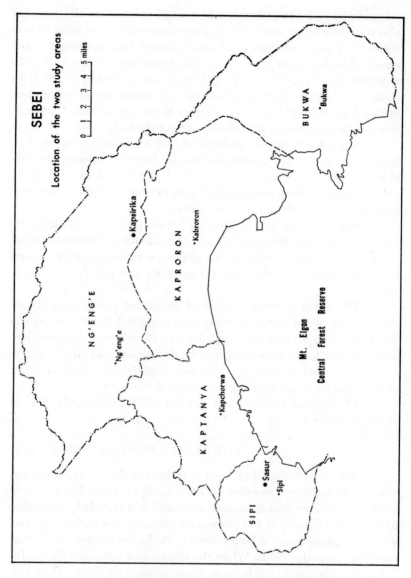

Figure 5. Locations
of the Sebei pastoral
and farming study
sites.

SEBEI

Location of the two study areas

0 1 2 3 4 5 miles

•Bukwa

BUKWA

•Kapsirika

•Kabroron

KAPRORON

NG'ENG'E

•Ng'eng'e

Mt. Elgon

Central Forest Reserve

•Kapchorwa

KAPTANYA

•Sasur

•Sipi

SIPI

rounded by soggy vegetation, and the insides of the houses are dark and cool. Men and women work, especially in the mornings, caring for their fields and their stock. By early afternoon the work is usually done and beer drinks are in progress, drawing eager men and women in droves.

So adequate is the precipitation in Sasur that two crop seasons are virtually without risk; therefore, although there is little cultivable land in Sasur (only 0.67 acre per capita are in crop), the average yield per acre is 2,350 pounds of edible food. This is 1,763 pounds of food per capita, by far the greatest agricultural yield of any of the sites studied.

But the Sebei of Sasur are poor in stock. A solitary cow is a great prize for most men; indeed, the average holding in livestock units is only 0.63 per capita, making Sasur the poorest of eight research sites in livestock ownership, and these few cattle are often kept in the kraals of men who live elsewhere. The Sebei of Sasur are farmers. More than any other people among those we studied, they depend upon the produce of their fields for sustenance.

Sasur is free of war or the threat of war. It is also relatively safe from animals, although leopards occasionally are encountered and poisonous snakes sometimes bite. It is relatively free of the diseases of tropical Africa, yet Sasur is sufficiently cold and damp that tuberculosis and pneumonia are threats to children and to the aged.

THE SEBEI PASTORAL SITE (KAPSIRIKA)

Kapsirika covers 47 square miles along the Sundet River on the savanna to the north and east of Sasur. Kapsirika is a flat grassland dotted by acacia woods, open except for the forest and brush along the river. Sebei homesteads in Kapsirika are scattered widely, surrounded by fields, pasture, and large thornbush kraals in which stock are held. Cultivation in Kapsirika employs the plow, not the hoe which is typical of Sasur.

The area is sparsely populated. There are only 287 Sebei in Kapsirika, six per square mile. These Sebei, like those of Sasur, cultivate, planting primarily maize and millet. Unlike well-watered Sasur, two crop seasons in Kapsirika are impossible, and even a single crop is likely to fail 25 percent of the time. The people of Kapsirika have cultivated only about one acre per person, leaving much land untouched; and their fields produce an average of no more than 510 pounds of edible food per acre. This low productivity is comparable to that of the Kamba pastoralists of Kilungu.

89

If the cultivation of the Kapsirika Sebei is far less intensive and productive than that of the Sebei of Sasur, their dependence upon livestock is far greater, and far more productive. There are approximately 4.18 livestock units per capita in Kapsirika, again comparable to the number of stock owned by the Kamba pastoralists of Kilungu. These animals, primarily cattle, are kept in kraals, are grazed, and are driven to salt and water within Kapsirika. These herds are sometimes endangered by predatory animals, especially the younger animals by hyenas, and they are often threatened by human predation. During the period of this research, the Karamojong made several large raids into the territory of the pastoral Sebei, and men of Kapsirika took the lives of several Karamojong while defending their herds. Thus, while the area is open to Western influence with roads here and there, and bicycles everywhere, the territory is every bit as endangered by warfare as is the far more remote area of the pastoral Pokot.

This chapter has introduced the tribes. It has also provided some initial comparisons between environmental and economic aspects of the eight study sites. Additional ethnographic material regarding these tribes is cited in the footnotes to this chapter, but for an adequate description of the tribes and the sites within them, a reading of the other monographs of the Culture and Ecology Project is essential.[6]

Chapter 3 extends this introduction to the eight populations in our study by providing some impressions of these people and the character of their daily life.

6. See the forthcoming volumes by members of the Culture and Ecology Project research team, including Conant's on the Pokot people, Goldschmidt's dealing with the culture and behavior of the Sebei, Oliver's on the Kamba of Kenya, Porter's study of the ecology and environment of East Africa, and Winans's description of the Hehe local neighborhoods.

An Observer's Impressions of Life Among Pastoralists and Farmers

3

In this chapter are presented my impressions of the people and the character of their lives in each of the eight research sites. I present these impressions for two reasons: first, to continue the introductory task begun in chapter 2 by adding something of a psychological dimension to the description of life in the pastoral and farming sites of each tribe; and second, to add an observational perspective to the interview findings that will shortly be considered. Thus, the vignettes offered here are both a part of the necessary background for an evaluation of interview findings, and a set of findings in themselves.

Most of my time in the field was devoted to the formal interviewing, and, consequently, large-scale systematic sampling and measurement of observed behavior was impossible. However, I was able to make certain kinds of observations of the behavior that made up everyday life in each of the eight sites in which we worked. As partial compensation for the limited time at my disposal, I was, unlike the ethnographers who were confined to one tribe, able to spend approximately equal time in each of the eight sites.

In order to take advantage of my opportunity for comparative analysis, I had to devise a program that would permit me to make roughly comparable observations in each site. I attempted to accomplish this, in the first instance, by making the same sorts of observations regarding the behavior of each respondent before, during, and after the interview. Since I had equal access to each respondent during this period, I was successful in making these observations in a comparable way. Of course, such a restricted set of observations was little more than a start. I also sought to make similar kinds of observations of everyday behavior in each site. Each day that I spent in the field had its breaks in the interviewing routine, and when I was not confined to the interviewing area waiting for respondents to make their appearance, I attempted to circulate through each site, at different times and in different places. In addition, I usually had time free from interviewing each morning and evening; and, in each site, I took a few days in which I devoted myself completely to observations. I sat and watched children at play, women at work, and men at their talk sessions. Sometimes, I played with the children, carried water for the women (to their amazement), and drank beer with the men. And I visited families during the day and evening. Of course, as any ethnographer would, I attended ceremonies, tended the sick, and came to know some people better than others.

What I was able to see was extremely limited. I had but about a month in each site, and most of that time was spent interviewing. What is more, I did not know the language, and when I observed behavior, I did not always have an interpreter with me. But I did have one advantage. I was sensitized to comparison, so that in each site I tried to make the same kinds of observations, and I sought the same kinds of insights. I was after the feeling tone of everyday life, and I believe that even within the limits of my opportunities it was possible to make similar inferences about the character of life in each place. I also wanted to know how people felt about each other and about themselves. This, of course, was more difficult to infer.

In making my observations, I had in mind our expected differences—of hostility, impulsivity, cooperation, and so forth. I looked for cues that people were or were not tense with each other, or that they did or did not have confidence in their worth as persons. But I do not believe that I biased my vision as a result, because I had no commitment to showing that pastoralists or farmers were either one kind of people or another. Neither was I enamored of one tribe over another, or one site more than any other. My bias lay in the fact that I searched for differences—and thus may have unknowingly exaggerated the differences that I saw—but I was not committed to finding any particular kinds of differences.

In addition to this observation and limited participation, I asked people about what I thought I had seen. If I felt that in witnessing a discussion between man and wife I was seeing an expression of male dominance and female resentment, I afterward asked the participants about their actions, their motives, their attitudes, and their goals—that is, about what they had done and why they had done it. I also asked bystanders for their views. Sometimes such questions led to an improved understanding, other times they did not.

In writing these sketches, I am aware that I saw far too little and asked far too clumsily about what I did see. But I have not attempted to say more than I saw. Nor have I knowingly contaminated my inferences from these observations with what I learned from the interview responses. Both in making these observations and in writing about them, I have attempted to set aside what I knew of these interview responses.

I have set down my impressions briefly, and I hope clearly, for I have tried not to employ technical terminology. If these short sketches add even a little to an understanding of the thoughts and feelings that accompany the action of men and women in these eight places, I have accomplished as much as I intended. As before, I have considered the tribes in alphabetical order, dealing first with the farmers, then the pastoralists. Within each tribe, I have made comparisons between the two sites.

HEHE FARMERS

The farming neighborhood of Ngelewala was quiet. It seemed even to lack the expected sounds of children and birds. It also appeared to be a serene place. There was nothing obviously ominous about its quiet. The pace of life was slow and even. The lack of bustle and noise came in part from the great dispersion of homesteads. No matter where one stood, the houses of these Hehe farmers remained hidden from view by their wide separation, their distance from the walking paths, and by the fringe of trees and crops that surrounded them. Much was hidden within these houses, too, for these massive, thick-walled enclosures seemed to stand as fortresses separating their occupants from the world outside. The people of Ngelewala were also hidden from view. The people were small in stature, graceful, and dignified, but they were not often in evidence. What was equally significant, when they did meet each other, they continued to hide, this time behind a mask of almost ritualized courtesy and etiquette. These rituals of deference were elaborate, formalized, and ever-present. They typified life in Ngelewala. Not only did these Hehe farmers greet their chiefs with exaggerated politeness, they greeted everyone with the same attention to decorum. At every encounter, formal salutations were expressed, hands were shaken, and polite utterances flowed for a goodly period of time. Then people parted, having done what was essential to maintain the apparent amiability of life in Ngelewala.

Even the most superficial observation of Hehe interaction was sufficient to call into question the sincerity of these polite, deferential encounters. The Hehe themselves readily admitted that they were insincere, and said that these expressions of concern and caution in their everyday relations with each other were essential to avoid serious affront or insult. The Hehe were astonishingly sensitive to insult; they lived in continual dread of affront, either given or received. It was for this reason, they said, that men feared each other and took such care not to give offense by the least breach of decorum.

When a breach occurred, the response was anything but amiable. In one such response to insult, which has been described in detail in an earlier paper,[1] an old woman who was hidden from view took grave offense that a young Hehe man did not see her and offer her the stylized greetings to which she was entitled. The young man accepted her vigorous rebuke seriously and went to great pains to rectify his inadvertent omission. I saw a similar readiness to take insult often, and sometimes the consequences were mercurial and serious; for when the Hehe became angry, they did so impulsively, without apparent control over the resulting verbal abuse or physical assaults. I have seen relatively elderly people, who were the most courteous and restrained of humans under ordinary circumstances, apparently lose control altogether under the provocation of what they took to be an insult; it often required the intervention of other persons to prevent their hot words from leading to physical combat. When such angry combats were not prevented, they could be dangerous; for when men fought, they did so with uncontrolled passion, swinging fists and nearby cudgels with abandon and also butting heads. While I was in Ngelewala, a man was killed by such a head butt.

With this uncontrolled fury went an intense suspiciousness. Sometimes, this suspiciousness went to such bounds that its institutionalized expression verged upon the ludicrous. For example, in Ngelewala, there were several wide paths that traversed the neighborhood. At certain times of the day, large numbers of people walked along these paths, passing each other and exchanging greetings. It was

1. Winans and Edgerton (1964).

94

notable that while men and women greeted each other formally, they rarely stopped to talk to one another. It was not the press of time or work to be done that caused this avoidance: it was a rule that said that a woman may not converse with any man who is not her husband. What was remarkable was that the application of this rule was extended to a public pathway on which any conversation would be observed and overheard by dozens of passersby. A wife's infidelity was constantly to be suspected. And so was the hostile intent of kinsmen and neighbors.

The strong press for deference and decorum in Ngelewala not only led to avoidances such as the one between men and women, but also placed each person behind a mask that was removed only by the occasional eruption of great anger. It is not difficult to sense that others are wearing masks: their control, evasion, stylized expression, and the like lead easily to this assumption. It is more difficult to demonstrate that this is so. In observing the Hehe farmers of Ngelewala, I was struck by the formal role-regulation of their public behavior, and I was equally struck that they could not easily remove their masks when they moved to less public places. No matter how many public versions of everyday life I saw, I saw a people who maintained a veil of secrecy and restraint which was never lifted. However, I assumed that within the sanctuary of their formidable houses, when they left the obviously constraining public encounters, they removed their role-masks, and, as it were, became themselves. I had thought, that is, that they would become more relaxed, less restrained, and less secretive.

I think that I was wrong in this assumption. For me, the truth of this matter and the essence of this Hehe farming world was expressed by an Ngelewala man who answered my question of how I could "get to know the Hehe better" by saying this: "You cannot. We Hehe are very good with secrets. We hide everything that we are thinking. How can you get to know us? We do not even know each other." For me, this was the last word on the Hehe of Ngelewala. The quiet of Ngelewala was the quiet of concealment, the more strongly maintained because of the explosive anger that everyone felt and feared.

HEHE PASTORALISTS

To leave the cool, green farmlands of Ngelewala for the dry, brown heat of Pawaga, in the basin of the Great Ruaha River, was to enter a strikingly different environment. Pawaga was oppresively hot, flat, dusty, and open. It was a different social world as well. Unlike Ngele-wala, one could see through the thornbush for great distances, and along the paths, both people and livestock seemed to exist in droves. Here, also unlike Ngelewala, the houses were packed together into nucleated settlements. But the houses were more open, with their thin walls, partial enclosure, and flimsy construction. Around these villages there were people, cattle, and much shouting and laughter.

The people were still small, but they lacked the farmers' grace and dignity of carriage. Instead they were ragged and dirty, without visible concern for niceties of dress or decoration. Here, people bustled about, and when their arms were not burdened with billhooks, babies, or dried fish, they tended to wave them about, gesticulating actively.

It was obvious that the veil of constraint and secrecy had been lifted. People were clearly more open, more spontaneous. They laughed and they quarreled openly. Everything they did was more animated. As women walked together or worked together, they chattered and giggled. At night, and even during the day, there was drumming, dancing, and singing. When men drank beer together, they talked and laughed loudly; and if they fought, as they frequently did, there were no signs of lingering acrimony.

In this respect, the men of Pawaga were dramatically different from the men of Ngelewala. In Ngelewala, men maintained great control over any expression of anger; yet aggression sometimes broke through the constraint, and when it did, it did so impulsively in an outburst of rage. In Pawaga, men displayed a constant readiness for combat. They lived in a dangerous world of large animals and human enemies. Lions, elephants, and hyenas were a continual threat to livestock, children, and adults. Hostile tribesmen, Gogo or Baraguyu, posed a violent threat as cattle thieves. In Pawaga, Hehe men displayed a constant readiness to fight—against animals, against men from other tribes, or against one another. But whereas fights among the Hehe farmers were few and terribly severe, in Pawaga, fights were frequent but inconsequential, usually being accompanied by neither serious injury nor lasting resentment. Here men fought casually, without hesitation, but with control. They fought fairly and sublethally, and the same man who one day fought with a friend might the next day submit without retaliation to a physical beating by his father. Physical combat in Pawaga was socially acceptable and socially controlled; and, perhaps because it was so readily accepted, it was readily maintained within socially controlled limits.

Among the pastoralists of Pawaga, the Hehe pattern of greeting and deference continued, but here it was briefer in its execution, and more perfunctory. Also, men and women were less rigid in their avoidance of one another in public places. They talked to each other in public; indeed, they sometimes talked at length without seeming to excite much suspicion. Men made public comments regarding their appreciation of a woman's beauty, and women flirted and flaunted their sexual attractiveness. Even when suspicion would have been well merited, the Hehe of Pawaga seemed to be more open about their conduct. For example, one could have walked through Ngelewala endlessly without blundering upon a man and a woman in an indiscreet act: avoidance and secrecy were far too intense. But in the plains of Pawaga, a chance stroll through the bush frequently would have brought you face-to-face with a man and woman in an adulterously compromising or even intimate circumstance.

Here one continued to see the face, the pride, the sensitivity to insult that so characterized the farmers, but the massive overlay of concealment and constraint was lacking. Here, pleasant or unpleasant, people's feelings were out in the open. The people of Pawaga were difficult for me to characterize. They were still Hehe. They differed from the farmers of Ngelewala only in degree, but the direction of that difference was clearly toward greater openness between people, and freer expression of emotions. There were still masks—as there will always be with any people—but here the mask was *not* everything.

KAMBA FARMERS

The farmers of Ngelani lived among a patchwork of terraced fields along the barren tops and eroded slopes of a line of hills. The hills were cool, sometimes even windswept and cold, and above all they were crowded, with people everywhere and seemingly no possibility of privacy, and no end to activity. Women were continually walking to some place, or were hard at work in the fields. Children played and wandered everywhere, across the fields, and along the paths. Here and there older men sat, talking and watching. There were few cattle or young men to be seen. The cattle were on the plains below, and the young men were in the nearby towns and cities.

Ngelani was a place of meetings. These Kamba farmers had their council of elders, and their clan councils, but they also had their *barazas,* general meetings in which almost everyone gathered to discuss the most recent issue. That people worked as well as talked was also

97

apparent, particularly among the women, who were always to be seen working at something. Usually they hoed in the fields; but whatever they did, their hands had to be busy, so that even when they walked or sat and talked, they were busy making string baskets.

The most eye-catching quality of Ngelani was the sense of calculation in the conduct of everyone. There was a remarkable lack of spontaneity in the action of these people. Every act, even the apparently trivial one, was apparently a matter for caution and forethought. Life here was deliberate, cautious, measured, and directed toward a common consideration. That consideration was property. When the Kamba farmers met to talk, when they worked, whenever they acted, it appeared that they did so with property in mind. If two men were seen talking along a path, the chances were that they were discussing property. It was the same when women sat together and talked; they gossiped and complained and joked, but the theme was usually property in one or another of its forms.

The Kamba continually said that the people "must be responsible." What a person had to be responsible about was property. If you watched the Kamba during an ordinary day, then stopped them to inquire about their thoughts at the time you were watching them, almost without exception (at least among those who could and would answer your question) they would say that they were thinking about their fields, or livestock, or money, or children. When asked why, they explained that they were "responsible," and that they "must care for the property." It seemed to me that virtually every act during the course of a day was a calculated one, and that the heart of the calculation was the relevance of the act in terms of property. This calculated approach to life had nothing of the ritual about it, as among the Hehe of Ngelewala. Instead, it had about it the commonsense wisdom of people who had learned that there was an advantage to cunning, to deceit, and to caution.

Every Kamba knows that property is difficult to come by, difficult to maintain, and more difficult still to increase. Yet each person knows that his acts will be accountable in terms of property: if a man violates a norm, he, or his clan, will be compelled to pay—in goats or in cattle, or in some other form of property. And everyone seemed to be measuring each act—his own and those of others—in terms of this calculus. For example, they seldom openly quarreled and still less often actually fought. To do so would be to risk the payment of heavy compensation to the wronged party. But when the Ngelani men drank, and they did so almost every day, they often fought. Even the elders sometimes fought, rolling ignominiously about on the ground feebly flailing at each other. It comes as no surprise that no one was held accountable for such drunken tussles, unless, that is, property damage or some personal injury occurred. Again, it is no surprise that these drunken fights rarely produced sufficient damage or injury to lead to any legal action (MacAndrew and Edgerton, 1969).

The following incident illustrates the way this property-oriented calculus operates. A Ngelani man was returning from a beer drinking session one day, and was feeling, I was told, a bit amorous. As he passed an unmarried woman working in a field, his amour became imperative and he "seduced" her. He did so in spite of the fact that both of her legs had been withered and deformed since birth. She charged rape, but he insisted that it was seduction. In proper Kamba fashion, she complained, and her family took action against the man, for it was believed by everyone that the woman was so deformed that she would surely die in childbirth. Should that have occurred, the responsible man would have been required to pay five cattle to the aggrieved relatives. This fine was quite standard. In this case, however, the now regretful man argued that he had been drunk, and moreover, that the girl was so badly crippled that she was worth little alive and no more than two cattle dead. Both of his pleas were rejected. The council ruled that, drunkenness and deformity notwithstanding, she was worth five cattle. Faced with this decision, the man decided to marry her because the required bridewealth was slightly less than the imposed fine of five cattle. This way, he reasoned, if she died he would owe nothing further, and if she lived, he would own a wife. If she produced a child, he would own still more. He could not lose. As the Kamba told the story, their delight in the man's shrewd judgment was obvious, because over the years since his calculated decision, the deformed woman has given this man three sons and a daughter, all of whom are fine strong children. I heard this story several times, and asked many Kamba farmers about it. No one ever included in his rendition of the story so much as a mention of any consideration not directly involved with property.

For me, this concern with property was the dominant factor shaping the Kamba farmers' behavior. By their own frank admission, they saw themselves and they saw others primarily in property terms. Men were wealthy or poor. Women were responsible or not, that is, good at maintaining or acquiring property, or not good. Of course, there are other themes that run through Kamba culture, but none explains so much of Kamba behavior as this one. These Kamba of

Ngelani are African Babbitts, pursuing property and security, and apparently unable to separate the two.

KAMBA PASTORALISTS

Among the Kamba, as with the Hehe, the physical world of the pastoralists contrasted sharply with that of the farmers. The pastoral area of Kilungu was a place of solitude and desolation. Much of the land was overgrown with dense, tall thornbush and thicket penetrated only by a few paths, and relieved only by baobab trees (the "upside-down" trees whose fat bottoms dwarf their small leafless branches) that rose above the tangle of brush. The people and their herds usually stayed to the few wide paths that crossed the area, for in some places it was possible to become lost in the brush, and it was also possible to come upon lions, rhinos, elephants, and buffalo. Other areas were flat and free of brush; hot and dusty, they were places for cattle.

The people of Kilungu have scratched some haphazard fields out of the bush, and they graze cattle in the less densely thicketed areas. Their homesteads were widely separated, and in most instances the nearest neighbor was many minutes away. There was no sense of crowding and little bustle of activity. Instead, there was a strong sense of solitude. The people themselves looked very different, too. In this hot land, the women were likely to be bare-breasted; and in this dangerous land, the men seldom strayed far from home without their bows and poisoned arrows. The people of Kilungu seemed to be alert —perhaps nervous—and they were easily startled.

Here, as in Ngelani, the concern with property continued, but it was no longer dominant. Perhaps that is inevitable where so many are poor and so few ever achieve any degree of wealth. Whatever the reason, here in Kilungu, other concerns seemed to be more important. One of the most obvious differences was the greater visibility of emotion. People in Kilungu displayed their emotions more openly: they laughed, yelled, shouted, even cried. They showed their emotions in public where anyone could see. If smiles, laughter, and affectionate gestures were counted, the people of Kilungu were usually less guarded with each other and more friendly than the people of Ngelani. But, at the same time, people in this pastoral area were tense and afraid. The people of Kilungu were fearful, not in hidden, subtle ways, but on the surface for anyone to see. A noise in the bush

54104

would startle a man and might send him to flight, trembling slightly with fear: the noise could have been a buffalo, or a snake. At the sudden approach of children, a group of women who had been gossiping would stop talking: children can tell tales, and who knows what they might say and to whom. Here, the death of a cow was more than a personal tragedy for its owner: it was an unquestionable sign of witchcraft. People were saying that the witch could have been anyone, and revenge, in the form of counterwitchcraft, was in everyone's mind. Such revenge sometimes goes astray, and innocent parties could be hurt. Who could say what might happen next?

Much of this fear and hostility was concentrated in the relations between husbands and wives. Such antagonism existed among the farmers, too, but among the pastoralists it was more obvious and more intense. Men often beat their wives and abused them. Sometimes they did so where I could witness them. They also refused to show affection for their wives, saying it would be demeaning to do so. In turn, women expressed their own anger in covert ways, including adultery, witchcraft, and poisoning. Yet at the same time, here in Kilungu, both men and women were markedly more expressive of sexuality and affection. But sex and affection had to be found outside marriage, not with one's spouse. And so, men and women sought each other out for moments of illicit sex, and for the kind words that sometimes went with such lovemaking. There was a kind of desperation, and a futility, about these searches for sex or love; and these people appeared to be sad more often than they appeared to be happy. They said that they were not happy, and they often behaved in a way that confirmed this assertion.

Their world was a place of danger, where the wives were bitter, the animals were lethal, the husbands were brutal, warfare was a threat, starvation was never far away, and witches were everywhere. It was a place of fear, not anxiety of a diffuse sort, but fear that was openly expressed, and clearly caused by the tangible dangers in their world. Here, as among the farmers, security was the first issue, but here the accumulation of property was less pressing than the daily concern with survival.

POKOT FARMERS

Tamkal Valley was a lush green enclosure, surrounded by massive, cloud-covered peaks that were streaked with glistening waterfalls. The Pokot farmers had opened some of this land to cultivation and had dotted it with their conical huts, but much of the valley was still covered by green shrubs and trees. It was a cool place, without many insects, or large animals, and relatively free of disease. It was so beautiful, that it was all one could do to believe that the people who lived in this place were unhappy. But to look at these people was to remove all doubt.

Both men and women worked in Tamkal, sometimes hard, grubbing in the fields, cutting back brush, getting hot and dirty. The women sometimes sang when they worked, and chatted, but they often grumbled too. And the men were very often drunk and in bad temper. This set the tenor of Tamkal; the people were moody and dour. They quarreled, and they were violent. Their expressions were very often set in a scowl, and not even the children seemed to laugh very much. Not that Tamkal was quiet. It was noisy, but the shouts were joyless or angry. Two women seemed unable to meet at the river to fetch water without quarreling about something, and men not only quarreled, they fought, and even bit each other. They were an argumentative lot, and their arguments sometimes led to violence. Men often beat their wives, and wives fought back, sometimes with surprising success. Old people quarreled too. When there had been drinking, the quarrels were more frequent and more serious.

When I asked about the cause of these quarrels and of the sullen, sour faces I saw, I got few answers beyond what I already knew—that the people were often moody, unhappy, or quarrelsome. Women did say that they had too little of what counted in life, food and sex, and that their husbands were woefully inadequate in every way. And men lamented their poverty, pointing to the scarcity of cattle in Tamkal. Others said simply that they fought because, living together as they did, no one could reasonably avoid doing so.

Going beyond the words and actions of these people, I felt that I was seeing people who were living in a society where cattle above all were valued, but were scarce, and where beautiful women were next highly esteemed, yet men could not command the bridewealth to acquire such women as wives. They were the poor relations, not only compared to the pastoral Pokot, but also compared to the farming Pokot in other parts of Pokot territory.

The people of Tamkal complained that life was better in other parts of Pokotland, and they bemoaned their own condition, but they said they could see no way out. They said that there was nothing they could do. So, they seemed to lash out at their frustration with anger and then retreat into their moods of self-recrimination and self-pity.

The pastoral Pokot of Masol referred to these farmers as *kapartab,* "little boys." For me, this label led to an understanding. I began to ask men whom I met why the pastoralists called them this. The responses were interesting: for every answer that struck back at the pastoralists by calling them stupid, brutal, vainglorious boasters, or something else pejorative, there were a dozen that took "little boys" to heart and said that men in Tamkal Valley were indeed poor in cattle and afraid of warfare, and that while this was sad, it was true. And Pokot farming women reacted to this same question about "little boys" with a torrent of scorn: it was true, they said, that their men lacked cattle, and spears, and courage and feathers—the important and beautiful things they ought to have. As one woman said: "What good is a farm when I have no milk? What good is a man who has no cattle? What good is such a life?"

I am certain that this reaction was overdrawn, that both men and women had sources of self-esteem that I did not see in their conduct, nor hear in their talk, but nevertheless, these people, above all others whom I saw in the eight sites, appeared to doubt their self-worth, and to wish to be something they were not. Perhaps this lack of self-esteem was related to the kind of social malaise I felt; perhaps it even produced the sullen and quarrelsome people I saw. Perhaps it did not. But I felt that these Pokot farmers were poor relations—and they knew it.

POKOT PASTORALISTS

The plains of Masol were hot and dry and sparsely studded by brush. They were open plains, not thickly covered like the flatlands of Kilungu. Large herds of cattle sometimes were to be seen, and vast numbers of flies were always there to be seen, and felt. There was no great sense of crowding in Tamkal, but here, the dispersion was extreme. Homesteads were widely spaced, and the land seemed to be vast and vacant. Even the usual large animals seemed to be few.

In watching the Pokot pastoralists who lived in this land, one seemed to be witnessing the Pokot dream come true—a land where cattle and women were bountiful, yet where disease was not too virulent, where dangerous animals were not too numerous, and where enemies were no longer able to raid, at least not often, nor openly. It was a land where there was time for beauty and sexuality, and for a kind of military posture that was exciting but not too serious. It was the life the people of Tamkal longed for, but could not attain.

103

The Pokot who lived in this seemingly idyllic world sometimes found reason to complain, but these people who were so envied by their farming brethren seemed to be quite pleased with themselves. The women in Masol complained far less, and even complimented their men from time to time for their wealth and for their sexual prowess. These Pokot women were formidable, with calloused hands, strident voices, and demanding ways; but more often than not, they admitted that their men were as acceptable to them as men were ever likely to be.

That the Pokot pastoral men should merit this respect was, at first appearances, most unlikely. These men were every bit as foppish as those Victorian cavalry officers who lisped their way from drawing room to parade ground, strutting for the ladies, yet now and then won, or at least survived, battles. The Pokot farmers were stolid, muscular, unadorned fellows. The pastoralists were weakly muscled dandies who spent hours over their hairpieces, and they did, in fact, lisp. They also sang in falsetto, carried spears flamboyantly, and adorned themselves with every bangle and feather they could lay hands on. Indeed, they did not scruple to pull the feathers out of a lowly chicken destined for our stew pot. Yet it would be wrong to think of them merely as poseurs. They exuded bravado, but they managed their swagger with a confidence not wholly feigned. They could throw their spears if need be, and they were able to control their women, beating them severely when necessary. They also managed their herds well. Older men displayed real battle scars, and real wealth in their large herds. Younger men did, now and then, go on cattle-stealing raids, even against the feared Turkana, and, now and then, they were successful.

Here, preeminently, was a people who were living a life they valued, and everything about them suggested that they esteemed themselves while doing so. Of course, they had their fears. For one thing, the truculent Turkana were nearby. And, they had their quarrels, but seemingly few in comparison to the farmers. But they had a fundamental confidence, too, a sense that they could cope with whatever would be. One woman who was raised in a farming area but had moved to the plains to marry a pastoral man put it into words: "It is hot here, and water is far away but I am happy. There are many cattle here and many handsome men. I would never want to go back to my farm."

SEBEI FARMERS

The neighborhood of Sasur was cool and green, high enough that mist and clouds sometimes shrouded the large leaves of the banana trees and obscured the panorama of the plains far below. The soggy dampness of Sasur muffled its noise and bustle, even though the people were active, often appearing to be working even when they were not.

No one could enter this Sebei world without an immediate awareness of one central feeling tone, felt and seen everywhere. For want of a better word, call it hostility. In some ways, this hostility was visible, as in the constant gossip, criticism, and corrosive humor of both men and women. These Sebei could also phrase their hostility in an abrasive form of bluster, threat, and posture that was certain to annoy everyone, but was not so extreme that it would lead to open conflict. The Sebei of Sasur avoided open conflict. They were a devious people. Just as hostility was central to their character, so was deviousness.

With the farming Sebei, examples of hidden hostility are so numerous that it is difficult to know where to start, but the preferred form of seduction is one useful illustration. Seduction was accomplished through trickery and, if necessary, by threat. A man did not ensnare his heart's delight through romantic niceties, nor by acts of derring-do, not even by his family's wealth or his own physical prowess. He did it by filching the beads she wore around her waist. Since a girl could not return home bereft of these beads without calling her chastity into doubt, she would stay with her boyfriend and try to recapture her beads. Yet, the man had an advantage for he would threaten to tell everyone the worst unless she submitted to his advances. Men said that they were proud of their ability to trick and coerce women in this way. Women recalled such experiences with anger, speaking of men as "dogs" who would stop at nothing where sex was concerned.

Quarrels regularly took the same oblique course. Men would quarrel, but avoid a showdown in favor of some indirect retaliation. A favorite was witchcraft, done with much innuendo and sly threatening. Another was arson. An angered Sasur farmer might well choose to burn the house of his enemy, but he would do so at night, when there was no danger of discovery. Even the children I saw avoided the direct fight, and ran away where they pouted and plotted the demise of their enemy. Sasur children did not even fight in play very much;

of all the children I saw at the eight interview sites, Sasur children were least given to the widespread East African sport of wrestling.

In Sebei perspective, such caution, and such devious means of expressing hostility were essential, for the Sebei said that they saw every man—and especially every woman—as a potential enemy, a person with the power and the probable intent to destroy crops, to sicken children or cattle, to cause a woman to miscarry, to bring death to an entire family. They lived with fear and tension, and their mistrust of each other was so basic that I sometimes wondered how the tasks of everyday life got done. In fact, the tasks of everyday life were done because mistrust and fear and hatred were kept below the surface, where everyone *could* see them, but no one *had* to see them.

Two illustrations may provide some sense of this aspect of Sebei character. The first comes from what I saw every afternoon as I sat, partially obscured, on a large rock that overlooked what took place on a small plateau below me. Scarcely a day passed that I did not see a Sebei man or woman hide behind a bush or tree to watch the activities of some other Sebei. And, sometimes, I saw still another Sebei watching the watcher. This was *very* Sebei, people furtive and alert, watching other people, and in turn being watched by still others. This watching was not casual: it was prompted by fear. In characterizing the Sebei of Sasur, I remember a man's typical reaction to my question about whether people were ever so worried that they did not sleep well. He said this: "Who can sleep well? Who does not have worries? Who does not know that someone wants to kill them? No one! Not even a child!"

SEBEI PASTORALISTS

From Kapsirika, the plains stretched out in an open savanna from the base of Mount Elgon far into the north, where the Karamojong and other warlike tribes posed a continual threat to the Sebei pastoralists. But the threat did not seem oppressive. The people, their homesteads, and their herds spread over a large area that undoubtedly included as many large, wild animals as it did people, but when several pastoral Sebei were together, I was struck instantly that they did not appear to be living under the cloud of mistrust and fear that covered the farming Sebei. Here, people were not as guarded, not as wary, and not as tense. Here anger did find open expression as children fought, husbands cuffed their wives, drunken men brawled with each other, and occasionally there was armed combat with the

Karamojong or the Karasuk. Military pride was evident, and men were concerned with strength and courage. Emotion of all sorts was more freely expressed. Anger as well as laughter, despair as well as elation, could be seen on many public occasions. But the pervasive hostility of Sasur was far less obvious.

The pastoral Sebei also looked different, for while they will never rival the Pokot pastoralists for sartorial elegance, the men did sport the occasional feather, and women did wear more beads and bracelets than their farming counterparts. Furthermore, each sex seemed to be more aware of the dress of the other. Men and women ogled each other, and nervously shifted their attire when someone of the opposite sex happened by. These pastoralist women were much more lusty and provocative than their farming counterparts. They were also more loving, warm, and responsive to their children.

Not that all was warmth or gaiety by any means. There was also gloom and sadness, freely expressed, but here they did not result so much from the fear of one's neighbors or relatives as from bad luck, God's will, disease, old age, or the threat of enemy raiders. Even witchcraft, which still occurred, changed its character. Here it was more open, and when it struck, it was more often cattle than humans who were the victims.

There was no distinctive feature, or set of features, that epitomized the Sebei pastoralists for me. Rather, there was a continuity with the farming Sebei. There can be no doubt that these people were still Sebei, were still sometimes hostile, reserved, and devious. But they were far less so. I saw no hidden figures watching furtively, and no one told me that even children lived in fear of other Sebei.

CONCLUSION

I know that the sketches offered in this chapter have been partial and selective. In presenting these depictions of life, I have proceeded as if these eight places were without variability, complexity, or contradiction. I have done so in order to seek a simplified portrait of central themes, focal points, or characterizing features. Obviously, I have made no attempt to present a complete or balanced portrait of any site. I am aware that my characterizations are subjective; they could hardly be otherwise. Indeed, in a sense, they cannot be verified, for no one else can ever see the same people under the same circumstances that I did. Still, some assessment of the accuracy of these sketches is possible, because the interview findings presented later focus upon many of the issues I have raised here. What is more, each ethnographer outlines his own understanding of the pastoral and farming people in each tribe. These ethnographies, detailed and independent views of each tribe, are, of course, important sources of of confirmation and clarification for all the findings reported in this monograph.

I shall not try to review or to summarize the sketches presented in this chapter, for they have reflected many diverse observations and inferences, but I hope that these sketches have at least had the virtue of adding another perspective to the interview data. I hope, too, that this perspective will improve our understanding of the differences between life in the farming and pastoral sites. In conclusion, I shall offer only this comparative judgment derived from the sketches presented here. I believe that, despite many differences among pastoralists and farmers in different tribes, there exist these similarities: (1) in three tribes (the Kamba are the exception), the farmers are more anxious and more hostile than the pastoralists of that tribe; (2) in all four tribes, the pastoralists are more direct in their actions, and more open with their feelings, than their farming counterparts.

As subsequent chapters will demonstrate, these findings concur with those derived from the interview, and I believe that they represent important basic differentials between farmers and pastoralists.

Before continuing with an analysis of the differences between farmers and pastoralists, there are questions to be asked. Chapter 4 is an analysis of the success of the interview in characterizing not pastoral or farming subgroups, but tribes themselves.

Cultural Distinctiveness: The Unique and Characteristic Responses of Each Tribe

4

In this chapter I shall begin the consideration of the interview responses by reporting what was unique and characteristic about each tribe's pattern of responses. I begin this consideration with what I have referred to as cultural distinctiveness because all of our assumptions about the nature and direction of environmental adaptation rest upon an understanding of the cultures undergoing ecological change. We could not concentrate our attention upon differences in attitudes and values as the end products of an adaptive process without also considering the relative importance and stability of these attitudes and values within each cultural and social system. What I undertake in this chapter, therefore, is the description of that commonality of culture in each tribe which is shared by pastoralists and farmers alike.

There are many reasons for this concern with a distinctive core of attitudes, values, and personality characteristics shared by both the pastoral and farming populations within a tribe. For one thing, it permits us to specify the nature of a cultural core from which adaptation to changing ecological circumstances must take place. It also permits us to consider responses with greater regard for their *relative* emphasis within a tribe, and thus, we may be able to determine that a small difference between pastoralists and farmers in some kinds of attitudes may be more significant than a large difference in others.

Second, description of these cultural emphases in response may contribute to an improved understanding of these, or related, East African societies. There is still relatively little material available which is relevant to the attitudes or the psychological orientation of African people, particularly material that is amenable to cross-cultural comparison.[1] Finally, the elucidation of distinctive and characteristic tribal response patterns may serve to increase our confidence in the adequacy of the interviewing procedures. We should surely have had little confidence in an interview that failed to discriminate among four independent tribal populations. Of course, if the distinctive response patterns elicited by the interview appear to be consistent with what is already known about these tribes, then our confidence should be increased still more.

THE FINDINGS

Before presenting the distinctive response patterns of each tribe, I should clarify what is meant by "distinctive." First, it means that the responses so designated are uniquely emphasized by that tribe: they differ from the responses of the other tribes to a statistically significant degree. Consequently, unless otherwise stated, every response pattern mentioned here as being culturally distinct is statistically significant at the 0.01 level. Although the findings presented in this chapter are based on the nominal scale and content analysis categories described in chapter 1, I have sometimes combined these categories into more general ones in referring to the tribal emphases.

These distinctive responses are also characteristic. They do not merely differ from the responses of the other tribes in the study; they characterize the responses of the tribe that made them. They are frequently, emphatically, and variously made, and therefore they are said to characterize or to pervade the overall response pattern of the tribe.

Each feature presented here as being tribally distinctive and characteristic is shared by both farmers and pastoralists. Unless both pastoral and farming respondents made the response in question with similar frequency and emphasis, and in similar contexts, the response was not included in this chapter. For each tribe, these features are presented in approximate order of their importance.

1. For a review, see LeVine (1961). Since LeVine wrote there has been some improvement in the situation, but LeVine's conclusions still hold. For example, see Crijns (1966).

THE HEHE

The interview responses point to six distinctive emphases among the Hehe: (1) impulsive aggressiveness, (2) "face"—extraordinary sensitivity to insults, (3) self-control, (4) relative sexual constraint, (5) concern with formal authority, and (6) secrecy.

References to impulsive aggression pervade the Hehe responses to the interview. Not only did the Hehe—both men and women—repeatedly say that the least grievance was likely to erupt in physical combat, they insisted that a fight, once started, would be almost impossible to stop ". . . because we Hehe have very hot tempers and when we are fighting we cannot know what we are doing. We can even kill someone who tries to stop us." Another typical comment is: "When we lose our tempers, we must fight. Words alone could never

TABLE 3

RESPONSES TO VALUES PICTURE 5: WHAT WILL THIS PERSON (THE THIRD PERSON) DO?

Answer	Hehe	Kamba	Pokot	Sebei
He will stop the fight	19	121	73	72
He will try to stop it but will fail	71	0	12	17
He will do nothing	5	0	13	18
*He will help one man against the other	0	0	1	1
No answer or don't know	28	5	29	20
Total	123	126	128	128

NOTE: $\chi^2 = 236.40$, P $\ll$ .001, df = 9
*Omitted in computation.

stop the Hehe." Both the belief that physical combat is the likely outcome of any annoyance, and the belief that fighting, once started, is virtually impossible to stop, were expressed much more often among the Hehe than among members of any of the other tribes (P < .001). A good example is provided in values picture 5[2] (two men in a posture that could be seen as threatening, being watched by a third man): in response to this picture, all but one of the 123 Hehe men and women who were interviewed said that the two men were fighting. Again, when asked what the third man who was watching "the fight" would do, the Hehe had a distinctive response (see table 3). The results of

2. The values pictures appear as Appendix I of this volume.

table 3 make the point clearly: although almost all of the Hehe respondents believed the onlooker would attempt to stop the fight, most Hehe said he would fail.

Related to Hehe impulsivity is an intense sensitivity to insult; a mild slight may give grave offense and precipitate great anger, an anger that may easily burst into physical onslaught. Hehe concern with insults is far greater than that of any other tribe (P < .001). Unless full apology is quickly and sincerely offered, the Hehe believe that insult will inevitably provoke physical attack, or, when women are involved, the use of witchcraft. For example, the following response by a Hehe woman was made to values picture 4 (a sick person and a diviner): "This woman is angry and this man is apologizing to her for the insult. I can see by his raised hands that he is apologizing. If her heart cools, all will be well. If not, she will fight with witchcraft." Also, the Hehe are unique in the degree to which they attribute the cause of suicide to improperly avenged insult. They are also unique in their expression of the belief that suicide is often the result of losing one's temper. Thus they say, "He lost his temper and became so angry with himself that he committed suicide."

Hehe concern with self-control is a related emphasis, and it is equally distinctive (P < .001). In five separate questions and in the content analysis, the Hehe reiterated their concern lest they lose control: women feared that they would kill one another; men worried that, in their anger, they would kill their own children; all feared that, once they were angered, they would lose control and kill indiscriminately. It is not only anger that must be controlled, so must sexual desire: the Hehe are also fearful their sexual impulses will prove to be beyond their control.

The next Hehe cultural characteristic is their relatively strong sexual constraint. Not that they are to be confused with the Puritans; but, compared to the other tribes in this study, they are notable in their emphasis upon the control of sexual desire, and upon sexual sin and concealment. Both sexes repeatedly said that men and women must learn to control their desires for sexual intercourse, yet both sexes admitted to having strong desires. For example, 89 Hehe said that girls should not have sexual relations before marriage; only 59 persons in the other three tribes combined gave the same answer. Another 45 Hehe said that it was morally wrong for young men to have sexual relations before marriage; only 25 persons in the other three tribes combined agreed. Both young men and women who have premarital sexual relations are referred to as "harlots." And in the content analysis, the Hehe had the lowest expressed concern with physical beauty and sexuality although they were fairly high on the nonsexually defined concerns of love and affection. Hehe men and women criticized persons who thought too much of sex, and several respondents said that a man who too often engages in sexual intercourse was certain to "ruin his character"; other tribes often noted that such men were likely to tire themselves and thus be poor warriors, but the notion that sexual excess was sinful was confined to the Hehe. The Hehe also say that anything that produces sexual excitement should be carefully controlled, and thus women's breasts which "make men excited" must be covered. Proper Hehe conceal their sexual enjoyment; it is not something to be reveled in, as members of other tribes often do.

The Hehe also express great respect for chiefly authority. For example, when asked the open-ended question, "Whom can a person trust?" forty-four Hehe said "Chief." In all three of the other tribes combined, the chief was mentioned only five times. And the Hehe protocols are filled with respectful (and, less often, fearful) remarks about the various "chiefs" in the modern Hehe political system. Since the Hehe are a formerly highly successful kingdom based upon a panoply of local and regional chiefs, this respect is not surprising, especially so because, among the Hehe, it is the chiefs who control the use, distribution, and ownership of land.

Finally, the Hehe response pattern is also characterized by secrecy. Secrecy involves more than mistrust. For one thing, mistrust alone is hardly distinctive: all four tribes are markedly mistrusting. But the Hehe brand of mistrust is singularly involved with secrecy. The Hehe said they trusted "no one," and men often remarked upon the delight women take in telling secrets to their daughters, while women complained that men have their own secrets. The Hehe mentioned secrecy—of all sorts—far more often than any other tribe. And they mentioned lying—by virtually everyone, from one's father to one's children—with a similarly unique high frequency.

With regard to possible ethnographic support for these response patterns, I can say only that, in my experience with the Hehe, each of these emphases was clearly expressed and frequently acted upon in everyday life.

THE KAMBA

The Kamba responses were distinguished by seven characteristic emphases: (1) a fear of poverty, (2) extreme male dominance, (3) male-female antagonism, (4) the importance of the clan, (5) concealment of emotion, (6) a need for affection, and (7) the value of the land.

The Kamba are dominated by a dread of poverty which for them implies not merely loss of prestige, but hunger, ridicule, and death. Typical Kamba responses to the question, "How do the Kamba feel about a poor man?" took this form: "He should go away and die like a dog!" "Kill him, he is not a man!" "Leave him alone, let him suffer." "Let him die! He was careless, so let him die." "Why not bury him alive? Why should I have to see such a man?" For the Kamba, the worst thing that can happen in life is poverty, and the best is wealth. They are almost univocal in this orientation. For example, 93 of the 126 respondents said "poverty" in response to the question, "What is the worst thing that can happen to a man?" They gave this answer significantly more often than did members of any other tribe (P < .001). Kamba women want to marry rich men: for them there is no other alternative (120 of 126 Kamba said this was the kind of a man a woman wants to marry). For 95 of 126 Kamba, "wealth" was the reason for happiness; for 116 of 126, the most respected man was a rich man; and so on, throughout their entire response protocol. It is difficult to imagine a more emphatic or pervasive emphasis.

Extreme male dominance and antagonism between men and women are also characteristic of Kamba culture. For example, when asked, "What is the most important thing for parents to teach a toddler?" 105 of 126 Kamba said, "To say the word 'father.'" In none of the other tribes was a similar response given. In Kamba culture, a child learns to say "father" (dada) before it learns to say "mother" (mwaitu). But there are many other examples of male dominance: men dominate women in every area of life, and they profess to have no sympathy for their wives' problems. Unlike men in the other tribes, Kamba men say they do not attempt to give their wives any satisfaction in sexual relations; indeed, they say that should a man admit that he has done so, he would become the object of ridicule. In marked contrast to the other tribes, the Kamba say that men choose wives principally on the basis of how "polite," "obedient," or "responsible" they are (P < .001). And men emphasize their "ownership" of women, saying that, "We buy them, we sell them—they are just like cattle." Not surprisingly, the antagonism between the sexes is great:

men say that women "are like children" with "small" and "smooth" brains which are "incapable of thinking," while women speak of men as "drunkards" and "animals." The Kamba protocols overflow with such reciprocal recriminations, although women do tend to be somewhat less open in the expression of their antagonism.

The Kamba response pattern is also marked by a strong valuation of the clan, markedly higher than that found among members of any other tribe (P < .001). For example, when presented with a choice between fellow clansmen and friends, 113 of 126 Kamba chose the clan, and all but one Kamba chose their clan over their age-group in a similar forced situation. No other tribe had a comparable emphasis. The Kamba typically say, with feeling: "The clan is the most important of all." "My clan must help me whether they like me or not." "Clan members are better than anything." "My clan will never desert me." "The clan cannot be compared to anything else." "The clan is above any other thing." They also say that a man who was refused help by his clan (something that does occasionally happen to some incorrigible rule-breaker or psychotic) would have no choice but to commit suicide.

Kamba personality is reflected in two strikingly distinct features. The first is a need for affection that expresses itself in a strong desire for soft-cuddling, but nonsexual, physical contact, and an interest in "soft," "furry," and "warm" things. This emphasis is clearly shown in the Rorschach responses. At the same time, the Kamba do *not* openly express affection, being much the lowest of the four tribes in the mention of nonsexual affection (P < .001). Both sexes lament the lack of affection in their lives (e.g., "No one cares about us—who is there to love us? No one. Not our children, not our fathers, no one!"), but they do not attempt to express any affection that they may feel for others. This is consistent with the second Kamba tendency, that of restraining emotion. In 1913, Charles Dundas wrote: "I have heard Akamba say that they dislike all foreigners, but hate each other." And, "The Mkamba is much too mistrustful and suspicious to make it possible for him to ever work to any extent in combination with others." [3] The Kamba themselves often made similar comments in 1962: "I must hide my feelings and my plans from everyone; otherwise, I can do nothing, because other Kamba will always try to thwart me if they can." Or, "Never tell anyone what you plan to do. If you do, they will try to stop you; someone may even try to kill you." This

3. Dundas (1913), pp. 485–487.

sort of mistrust and concealment of motives is *not* unique to the Kamba. It exists in all four of these tribes. What is distinctive is the extent to which the Kamba conceal their feelings, and the frequency with which they say that it is proper to do so.

Finally, the Kamba value land more than any other tribe. Where mere mentions of land are concerned, the content analysis shows that the Kamba mention land more often than any other tribe. They also value it more often (P < .001) and speak of land in rapturous terms. It is not unusual for the Kamba to say that the first thing a young man must learn before he marries is "where his father's fields are, and to think always about caring for them and inheriting them." Respondents in other tribes often spoke highly of land versus cattle, saying that while cattle die, "land lives forever," but the Kamba said such things more often and with greater fervor. One Kamba pastoralist who obviously loved his cattle summed up this Kamba feeling when he said: "Cattle are beautiful, but land is life."

My observations of the Kamba strongly confirm the presence of five of these seven emphases. For two, concealment of emotion and need for affection, I had insufficient ethnographic grounds for making a judgment.

THE POKOT

The Pokot response pattern is overwhelmingly devoted to three concerns: (1) cattle, (2) physical beauty, and (3) sexual gratification. Although there are additional distinctive concerns, for example, independence, respect for the prophet, military bravery, and depression, these are secondary in relative emphasis.

The Pokot are a cattle-oriented people. All tribes were asked this question: "If a man could have anything he wanted, what should he choose?" Out of the large number of culturally possible answers, "cattle" was the one given by 101 of 128 Pokot. Members of other tribes also answered "cattle," but much less (P < .01) frequently (40 Sebei, 32 Kamba, and 19 Hehe). What is more, the Pokot had much the highest frequency of mentioning and valuing cattle throughout their entire protocols—more than twice as many valuations of cattle as the next most cattle-oriented tribe. But the most compelling evidence of their cattle orientation is seen in their response to this forced choice question: "Would you rather own good farming land but no cattle or good cattle but no farming land?" Of the Sebei, 114 chose land and only 14 chose cattle; 112 Hehe chose land and only 11 chose cattle; 109 Kamba chose land and only 17 chose cattle; but only 24

Pokot chose land while 104 Pokot (51 farmers and 53 pastoralists) said, and emphatically, "cattle."

The following Pokot comments to the slides showing cattle are typical of the Pokot, but they would be most unusual coming from members of the other tribes: "This is what I live for—I love them!" "Beautiful! Cattle are even more beautiful than women!" "This is what I want! I'll give you my daughter for them." "If I had these cattle, I would look at them all the time, and I would sing songs to them to make them happy." "What a beautiful ox—with him in my kraal, I am a man!" "Cattle! They are the best of all. Having only a farm is not living at all." All of these comments, and many others like them, were made as often by Pokot farmers as they were by Pokot pastoralists, and with the same emphasis. It is not only the pastoralists among the Pokot who cherish cattle, it is *all* Pokot.

Second only to cattle in the interest of the Pokot is physical beauty. In terms of the frequency with which physical beauty is mentioned throughout the protocols, the Pokot lead the next tribe by more than three to one. But the clearest understanding of the Pokot concern with beauty is seen in their responses to questions about what kind of a person a man or woman wants to marry. When the question, "What kind of woman does a man want to marry?" was asked, the answer, "a beautiful one," was given by 22 Sebei, 22 Hehe, 14 Kamba, and 95 Pokot. Still more remarkable are the answers to, "What kind of man does a woman want to marry?" The tribes gave a variety of answers, but "a handsome man" was answered by only 13 Sebei, 3 Hehe, and no Kamba; however, 87 Pokot (43 men and 44 women) said that a Pokot woman wanted to marry a handsome man. When they were shown the color slides of men and women, the Pokot respondents typically erupted in a long and appreciative comment on the relative beauty of the persons pictured. For example, a woman said: "Oh, oh! What a handsome man. He is more than I can look at. He makes me feel weak. I should have married this man. I would like to have such a man in my bed." Men were equally ecstatic about the beauty of women they saw, enthusing at length about their most beautiful features, the number of cattle they were worth, and about their probable skill in sexual matters.

The third major focus is upon sexual gratification. Like cattle and physical beauty, sexuality pervades the Pokot responses. For example, the Pokot were the only tribe of the four to insist that young men should learn how to have sexual intercourse before marriage (P < .001); they also were the only tribe to answer regularly that the

117

most important thing for young women to learn before marriage was how to please men sexually (P < .01). Thus it is no surprise that 98 Pokot said that it was perfectly acceptable for unmarried girls to have sexual relations with several men. No other tribe gave this answer as often (P < .01). Neither is any other tribe as given to delight, freely and joyously stated, in sexuality. Men happily said that when they were making love to a woman, "not even a lion could bother me, I am too busy enjoying myself." No Pokot woman responded routinely to a question about a woman's enjoyment of sex. This answer is typical: "I love it. As soon as he finishes I give him food and let him sleep and then I wake him up and we do it again; we can do this all night. He works very hard to make me happy. I must have it ten times —or more." Indeed, a woman who is not satisfied by her husband's sexual performance may subject him to public humiliation and torture.[4] And in response to the values pictures showing men and women together, both men and women saw sexuality, pleasurably engaged in; they did not, as did members of the other tribes, often see either violence or nonsexuality. Instead, they made enormously detailed and imaginative comments about the presumed sexual anatomy and technique of the persons involved. The more graphic, the more ribald, the more the Pokot exulted in the discussion of sex.

The Pokot have four additional response emphases, each of which is distinctive of them (P < .01). First, the Pokot mentioned independence of action ("I am a man, no one commands me.") more often than any other tribe. Their mention of depression, particularly on the part of older men, similarly was greater than that of any other tribe. The Pokot also expressed a unique respect for their prophet (laibon), saying: "When he speaks, all the Pokot must obey." Finally, they stand out from the other tribes in their valuation of bravery in warfare. They spoke of spears and battle scars, and when they mentioned warfare, they, more than any other tribe, saw victory as the outcome. They particularly value courage when it is involved in cattle raiding. Women and men both said that men should have the courage to steal cattle by raiding and to defend cattle against enemy raids. For example, an elderly Pokot respondent said: "A man must go and steal cattle from the Turkana. I have stolen many and I have killed eight Turkana. That is why the people respect me."

Although all four of these response emphases are distinctively

4. For additional information about the actions of women who are sexually deprived, see Edgerton (1965) and Edgerton and Conant (1964).

Pokot, they lack the emphasis and frequency of mention accorded the three major foci: cattle, physical beauty, and sexuality. My own ethnographic experiences tend strongly to confirm the importance of these major Pokot concerns in everyday life. The four minor emphases also appear ethnographically in everyday life, but they do not seem to be central concerns.

THE SEBEI

The Sebei are difficult to characterize as a tribe, not because they lack distinctive responses, but because these response patterns, although they are pervasive, lack the dramatic, positive emphasis found among the other tribes. Still, it is possible to identify six distinguishing response patterns: (1) fear of death, (2) diffuse anxiety, (3) fear of the malignant power of women, (4) profound jealousy and hostility, (5) desire for population increase, and (6) respect for seniority.

The Sebei have a virtual obsession with death. Thirty-four Sebei said that death was the worst thing that could happen to a man; only ten persons in the three other tribes combined gave this response. When asked the totally open-ended question about the worst thing that could happen to a woman, sixteen Sebei gave "death" as the answer, compared to only three such answers from the other three tribes combined. In the content analysis, the Sebei were conspicuous by their frequent concern over death ($P < .01$); they spoke somberly of burial, putrescent bodies, the agonies of serious illness. But the flavor of this concern is even more striking than the frequency of its expression. It is not a perfunctory concern: it is a fearful dread. For example, when Sebei become drunk, their most typical worry is about death. It is quite common for a man in his cups—a quite robust man at that—to begin weeping and say: "Nothing is worse than death; I want life, I don't want to die!" It is not the means of death that the Sebei fear: disease, violence, and witchcraft are equally to be feared. It is death itself that terrifies them: "A man should not die; what could be worse than that?"

This fear of death is associated with a general fearfulness of so diffuse a nature that it can properly be called anxiety. The Sebei are fearful, not merely of specific dangers, but of everything: "We are afraid of everything," or, "We Sebei are cowards, we are afraid even to fight. We are all afraid." Among the four tribes, only the Sebei regularly commented that the two men who face each other in threatening posture in values picture 5 are afraid to fight: "They are afraid

119

—they will not fight"; or again, "They are bluffing, they are trying to win without fighting." Similarly, there is great concern with protection against vague dangers—with dogs to warn of sounds in the night, with friends to protect one against one's clan, with clansmen to protect one against one's friends, with luck to protect one against everything. Even where adultery is concerned, the Sebei are anxious. For example, members of all four tribes expressed some fear lest they be caught in the act of adultery, but only the Sebei responded to the picture of the man and woman in values picture 8 as follows: "He is saying, 'Let us do it quickly before someone comes and finds us.' " In the Rorschach and throughout the response protocol, the Sebei made more anxious remarks than did members of any other tribe.

Sebei jealousy and hostility is likewise a related emphasis. Of all the tribes, the Sebei rank lowest on cooperation (P < .01). Their profound jealousy is not confined to wealthy men: "We are jealous of everyone!" And, "Everyone hates me—my clan, everyone." Or, this: "Perhaps my friends may plot to kill me. Who will protect me?" Or this, in response to values picture 9: "We Sebei always backbite; we talk against everyone. That is why I like these people who are drinking their beer happily without quarreling." The Sebei often express their jealousy in theft. For example, only the Sebei saw values picture 4 (a sick person seated next to a diviner) in this, typically Sebei, manner: "An old man here . . . he is sick, covered with a cloth. A pot behind him. Another man kneels here in front of him. *What will happen?* I think that this one kneeling is going to steal something, thinking that no one is home." Referring to a wealthy man, this respondent's comment is characteristic: "If people who hate him are able to kill him, perhaps I'll be able to steal some of his possessions." And, in answer to the question of how a poor man can become wealthy, we heard: "Steal! It is the fastest way." [5]

The Sebei also focus upon the malignant power of women. It is not simply that the Sebei are hostile toward women, for although they *are* hostile toward them, they are not as hostile as the Kamba. The Sebei *fear* their women. They fear their supernatural power as witches, and their secular power as shrews. For example, it is typical for the Sebei to see, as in values picture 6, that a man is hiding from a woman, not in order to rape her or attack her, as is the common response of other tribes, but because he "fears" her. Fathers caution their sons not to fall under the malignant spell of their mothers, and

5. For an additional note on this Sebei concern with theft, see Gold-schmidt (1967a), pp. 180 ff.

women admit that men fear them, with good reason: "A man must treat me well; if he does not . . . well, he will regret it." A most characteristic Sebei response involves suicide. The typical Sebei suicide is said to be one in which a man is caught in an attempted theft; when he returns home, his wife berates him, heaping invective upon him. He says nothing, but meekly goes to bed. During the night, he murders his wife while she sleeps, then kills himself. Women, say the Sebei, "are worse than anything . . . except death."

The Sebei, in one of their unusual positive emphases, do respect seniority: 87 Sebei said that it is never correct for a younger brother to tell an older brother that he is wrong; only five persons in the other three tribes combined gave this answer. The Sebei also expressed significantly greater respect for their fathers and for old men than did members of any other tribe (P < .001). As one young man put it, "The father is my god; any older person is better than I am. I must respect them. They are good because they give good advice."

Finally, the Sebei have a unique interest in repopulation. They do not voice this interest simply as a desire for more children as wealth, or as security. They specifically speak of the need to "produce more children" in order to "increase the population." In response to a question asking why they desired children, 73 Sebei answered that it was to increase the Sebei population ("I must produce more children to add to the Sebei people."); not one single person in the other three tribes gave this answer. This emphasis becomes less mysterious when it is understood that the Sebei have a history of being outnumbered, and encroached upon, by their enemies. Several respondents made replies similar to that of a man who said: "If war comes, we need more sons to defend us."

My ethnographic observations agree with this interview portrait of general fearfulness—of death, of women, and of many unspecifiable dangers. The pervasive jealousy and hostility of the Sebei is also obvious. I also heard a desire for population increase expressed in everyday life, but less often. According to Walter Goldschmidt, the Sebei are fully socialized to accept dominance based on age. It is permissible for any initiated man to chastise and punish any uncircumcised boy or girl. The precircumcised are aware that they may be made to cry by magical means at circumcision by any adult whom they have angered, a notion that gives sanction to the authority that derives from seniority; and there are many other customary reinforcements of this attitude.

Despite the fact that it has been possible to adumbrate some distinctive features of the Sebei response pattern, the Sebei as a people remain shadowy. That the reality of the Sebei responses should prove to be so illusory may in part result from the extreme variability of their responses: of all the tribes, their responses are most varied (Appendix VI). More striking is their lack of positive expression in their beliefs, attitudes, and values. It is very much as though they had no commitment to them, no favorable sentiment about their world. What stands out about the Sebei is the negative, hostile, and fearful quality of their interaction and, also, of their interview responses. Anything positive in their response pattern is contrapuntal to this negative background.

COMPARING THE BANTU AND KALENJIN TRIBES

The preceding effort to locate distinctive and characteristic response patterns for each of the four tribes was not at all difficult, for each tribe produced a set of remarkably distinctive responses. There were commonalities, of course, for all these tribes share some common social and cultural features that are reflected in similar patterns of interview response. However, many of the questions in the interview were open-ended and thus permitted a wide range of response. To this kind of question, as well as to the values pictures, the tribes produced quite divergent emphases in their answers. In spite of this divergence in response from one tribe to the next, when the two Bantu-speaking tribes (Hehe and Kamba) were compared with the two Kalenjin-speaking tribes (Pokot and Sebei), there were some consistent response differentials between the two pairs of tribes.

The Pokot and Sebei are quite close to one another, both geographically (some of the pastoral Sebei are in contact, which is sometimes warlike, with some of the pastoral Pokot) and linguistically. Both speak Nandi or Kalenjin languages that belong to the Eastern Sudanic branch of the Chari-Nile grouping within the Nilo-Saharan language family.[6] In historical perspective, the two tribes are also close. For example, Murdock places both tribes—he calls them the "Suk" and "Sabei"—together in the "Nandi cluster" of what he refers to as "Cushitized Nilotes." [7] Huntingford, a Nandi specialist, agrees that the Sebei and Pokot belong within the Nandi group of tribes.[8]

6. Greenberg (1963).
7. Murdock (1959).
8. Huntingford (1953).

Following local East African usage, I shall refer to this pair of tribes as the Kalenjin peoples.[9]

The two Bantu-speaking tribes are separated by many hundreds of miles, and they are far more distantly related linguistically and culturally. For example, Murdock assigns the Kamba to the "Kenya Highland Bantu," a congeries of seven tribes of relatively homogeneous culture.[10] He regards the Hehe as members of the "Tanganyika Bantu," placing them in the "Rufiji Cluster" with such tribes as the Bena and Sangu.[11] As Oliver points out in his Culture and Ecology Project monograph, however, the Kamba themselves believe that they migrated north from Tanzania, and they claim close kinship with the Nyamwezi, a Tanzanian tribe located relatively close to the Hehe. Even should the Kamba and Hehe be more closely related than Murdock and others believe, it remains true that today they are widely separated, speak mutually unintelligible versions of Bantu, and live under quite different cultural and social conditions; therefore, it comes as no surprise that the Kamba and Hehe response patterns are markedly different, bearing little apparent similarity to one another on most points. It is surprising, however, that the response patterns of the Pokot and the Sebei differ to the same marked degree. With the Kalenjin tribes, as with the Bantu tribes, the differences between tribes are *far* greater than the similarities.

Despite this finding that the linguistically related pairs of tribes are strikingly different in their interview responses, it is, as I noted before, possible to locate some similarities in response that appear to reflect meaningful differences between the two sets of tribes. Comparable similarities between nonrelated pairs (e.g., Sebei-Kamba) were not found.

To warrant consideration as such a difference between the Bantu and Kalenjin tribes, a response pattern must be contributed to equally by both tribes in a pair. For example, we cannot claim that the Kalenjin tribes exceed the Bantu tribes in their expressed interest in cattle, because while one Kalenjin tribe (the Pokot) is very high in its frequency of mention of cattle, the other Kalenjin tribe (the Sebei) is not. Only if both Kalenjin tribes expressed a similar interest in cattle and this interest were substantially greater than that expressed by the two Bantu tribes would this constitute a difference between the two sets of tribes.

9. Weatherby (1963).
10. Murdock (1959), p. 342.
11. Murdock (1959), p. 359.

Following this procedure, it was possible to find some twelve statistically significant response differences between the Bantu and the Kalenjin tribes. Some of these differences were rather inconsequential, but may be interesting enough to merit brief mention. For example, the two sets of linguistically related tribes differed in their views of which diseases were "the worst a person can have." The Kalenjin specified smallpox as such a disease 41 times, compared to only 7 such mentions by the Bantu; in addition, the Kalenjin mentioned dysentery twice as often as the Bantu did. The Bantu, on the other hand, specified leprosy as the worst disease 37 times, while only 5 Kalenjin respondents mentioned leprosy. Thirty-six Bantu mentioned epilepsy, compared to one such mention by the Kalenjin. The high incidence of smallpox and dysentery in the areas occupied by the Pokot and Sebei is amply documented. I do not know what the relative incidence of leprosy and epilepsy is among the four tribes.

Another difference concerns preferences in feminine beauty. When all men in the four tribes were asked to view color slides of young women from different tribes (Nyoro, Masai, Giriama, and Gusii) and to indicate the woman they most favored, 101 Bantu said the Nyoro girl, but only 32 Kalenjin chose her. Asked to specify the girl they thought to be most unattractive, 109 Bantu said, often emphatically, the Masai; only 14 Kalenjin selected the Masai. On the contrary, 101 Kalenjin thought the Gusii woman to be least attractive, a decision shared by only 7 Bantu. Such consensus in choice regarding four sets of rather fetching young ladies is notable, especially so as it seems closely to follow Bantu, non-Bantu, lines.

The third difference has somewhat greater import; it involves expectations of military prowess. When asked to indicate the probable outcome of the conflict shown in values picture 3, in which armed raiders are engaged in cattle theft, the Bantu and Kalenjin respondents differed. Fifty-eight Kalenjin, farmers and pastoralists alike, compared to only 19 Bantu, said that the enemy in the picture would be defeated or driven off. This is a substantial difference, but its meaning is difficult to determine. While it may well point to fundamental differences in the military experience and attitudes of the two sets of tribes, it may also reflect quite recent changes in military orientation brought about by European police presence, which is probably more effective in preventing raiding in the Bantu areas than in the Kalenjin territories. The possible significance of this military differential as a pastoral response is developed in later chapters.

124

Another difference that is difficult to interpret concerns shame. The Bantu say that they feel no shame when one of their relatives commits suicide; the Kalenjin have considerable shame over such an event. For example, only 10 Bantu said that shame would follow a relative's suicide; 143 Kalenjin said that suicide would cause shame among relatives. My ethnographic investigations suggest that this difference does exist, but I am unable to explain it.

Another difference relates to an apparently lesser respect for certain kinds of authority among the Bantu. For example, asked when a younger brother might properly correct an older brother, 145 of the Bantu said an older brother could properly be corrected whenever he was wrong; only 20 Kalenjin were similarly willing to give the younger brother the right to correct the older whenever he was wrong. With regard to a young man's right to correct an elder, the same pattern resulted: 153 Bantu said that an elder could be corrected whenever he was wrong, an answer given by only 18 Kalenjin. The same degree of difference occurred in response to values picture 1, which was identified to respondents as a son being disobedient and disrespectful to his father. Forty-one Kalenjin respondents said that the proper course of action was one in which the father treated the son's disobedience mildly, seeking to reach an understanding with him; however, 125 Bantu respondents said that such an accommodation was the proper course of action for the father. Conversely, 183 Kalenjin, and only 116 Bantu, said that it was proper for the father to take serious measures against the disobedient son, measures that included beating, disinheriting, banishing, cursing, or bewitching the son. Therefore, with regard to at least these three authority relationships, the Kalenjin maintain greater respect for persons in authority and react more harshly to instances of disrespect. This difference may reflect the greater importance of age-sets among the Kalenjin peoples.

In expressing their preference concerning the sex of their children, the Bantu chose boys but the Kalenjin wanted both boys and girls. Table 4 indicates the magnitude of the difference. This difference may relate to the relative wealth of the Kalenjin peoples in cattle, a wealth that makes daughters more valuable as a source of bride-price. Additionally, among peoples whose primary orientation is to land, sons who can help with the land, and inherit it, may be favored over daughters whose direct economic usefulness ends with their marriage.

Other differences also seem to be related to a differential involvement with land. The Bantu both mentioned and valued land more than the Kalenjin did; members of both Bantu tribes did so

almost twice as frequently as the Kalenjin. They also valued industriousness more often, mentioning hard work seven times as often as
the Kalenjin did. Whereas the Bantu tend to select spouses on the
basis of their ability to work hard, the Kalenjin respondents are far
more concerned with physical beauty. For the Sebei as well as for the
Pokot (for whom it is a central focus), beauty is an important criterion

TABLE 4

WOULD THE (TRIBE) PREFER TO HAVE SONS OR DAUGHTERS?

Answer	Bantu	Kalenjin
Sons	198	54
*Daughters	3	5
Both	48	197
Total	249	256

NOTE: $\chi^2 = 172.87$, $P \ll .001$, df $= 1$
*Omitted in computation.

in the selection of a wife or a husband. Throughout the interview, the
Kalenjin mentioned physical beauty almost seven times as often as
the Bantu respondents did.

Another set of differences appears to point to problems in the
control of hostility. For example, the Bantu as a pair of tribes are
more concerned with self-control. This concern was expressed most
often by the Hehe, as I have already noted, but it was shared by the
Kamba, so that together the Bantu tribes mentioned and valued
self-control almost twice as often as did the Kalenjin tribes. In what
may be a related differential, the Bantu tribes mentioned hatred—
without aggression—almost twice as many times as the Kalenjin tribes.

Finally, and most pervasively, the Bantu and Kalenjin differ
in their concern with witchcraft. The Bantu are very much given to
sorcery and witchcraft, the Kalenjin much less so. For example, in
discussing causes of suicide, twice as many Bantu (101) as Kalenjin
(54) mentioned witchcraft. Or, concerning the etiology of psychosis,
120 Bantu implicated witchcraft, whereas only 19 Kalenjin offered
this cause. Finally, the content analysis showed that throughout the
entire response protocol, the Bantu respondents mentioned witchcraft
or sorcery over three times as often as did the Kalenjin. This differen-

tial is so consistent that it suggests a fundamental difference between the Bantu and Kalenjin peoples. Indeed, LeVine (1966*a*, p. 114) has indicated that this same difference is reported between other East African Bantu and Kalenjin, or Nilotic, tribes.

CONCLUSION

A previously published brief account of some of these data (Edgerton, 1965) has already been utilized in another comparative study in East Africa,[12] suggesting that these findings may indeed prove to be of use to those whose research centers upon East Africa. Of course, conclusions regarding the degree to which these interview-based characterizations of the tribes and the sets of linguistically related tribes agree with what is known of these peoples from other sources must be made by independent investigators. I have already expressed my belief that they fit the ethnographic accounts quite well.

These findings should not be pushed beyond their limitations, however, for they are not meant to be comprehensive accounts of the cultural and psychological conditions of any tribe or its people. Neither are they meant to serve more global purposes. For example, because the Kalenjin tribes are also Nilotic, or more specifically, Nilo-Hamitic, it may be tempting to generalize from these findings about two tribes to more generic differences about the Nilotes as compared with the Bantu, differences that have already been speculated about in the literature with ample enthusiasm, if few data.[13] The data presented in this chapter are not meant to serve such a purpose, but only to establish the existence of certain response differentials between tribes, and between two Bantu-speaking and two Kalenjin-speaking tribes. This presentation was undertaken because if there were such differences, it might well be that they indicated long-standing orientations in culture. Such long-standing orientations might prove to be highly resistant to change, even though substantial ecological change might occur. This question of the differential sensitivity to change of the basic response patterns is central to our concern with ecology, and it is examined in later chapters. Do distinctive and characteristic re-

12. LeVine (1966*a*).

13. For description of the Nilotes, as well as bibliography, see: Murdock (1959); see also Fleming (1969). For speculation, see Burke (1966). For rare examples of specific comparisons of Bantu and Nilotic peoples, see LeVine (1960, 1962, 1966*a*, *b*).

sponse emphases persist despite ecological change, or do they vary as readily as do the less focal responses that typify neither tribes nor language groupings?

Before this question can be considered directly, it is necessary to observe the effects that the sex, age, and acculturation of the respondents had upon the response patterns.

The Relationship of the Respondents' Age and Sex to the Response Pattern

5

The nature of the relationship between the age and sex of the respondents and their interview response patterns is explored in this chapter in order that the way may be cleared for a discussion of other variables, particularly those related to ecological variation. The relationship between the age and sex of these African respondents and their attitudes, values, and personality characteristics is particularly relevant and interesting because these societies are divided into age classes, and they are characterized by social distinctions and psychological tensions between the sexes.

THE INFLUENCE OF AGE

These four societies, like so many in East Africa, have accorded an unusual importance to age distinctions. Therefore, much that a person is, and much that he does and thinks and feels, is directly influenced by his age, and by the age of others. Two of these four societies (Pokot and Sebei) have complex age-grade systems, one (Kamba) recognizes three formal age classes, and one (Hehe) recognizes less formal age classes but nonetheless makes important age distinctions. For example, all four societies tend toward gerontocracy, with wealth, supernatural power, and political influence largely in the hands of the old. In such societies, the potential for intergenerational conflict is great, and the need for institutional control of such conflict is imperative. What is more, the decline of warfare, which has deprived the young men of their traditional role as warriors, may have contributed to the tensions ordinarily present between the generations.[1]

With such distinctions and intergenerational tensions being so common in East Africa, we felt that it was essential for us to explore the extent to which age differences in the societies we studied were accompanied by differences in values, attitudes, or personality characteristics. We did not anticipate that any of the four societies would be beset by the massive cleavage between the young (warriors) and the old (elders) that is so central a problem for some East African societies, as for example, the Samburu of Kenya as described by Spencer (1965); but we did expect that some of responses elicited by the interview would be influenced by the age of the respondent.

As was noted in the discussion of sampling in chapter 1, we chose to interview only married adults. This decision was in keeping with our concern for locating broadly shared differentials among eight populations. The values and attitudes of children and adolescents would have made an interesting counterpoint to this adult focus, but within the design and resources of this project we were unable to extend the investigation beyond adults. In fact, however, we did include very young men and women in the sample because in all four tribes both sexes now marry when they are quite young.

We decided to focus upon married persons because it is marriage that inducts a person fully into adult status in these societies, removing "boys" or "girls" from the low prestige and limited participation of the not-yet-married. A newly married person does not yet have the prestige or power or knowledge that can be expected in later years, but being married is seen by the young and old alike as the essential and desirable entree into adulthood.

Although sampling within each of the eight interviewing sites was designed to provide a representative age distribution of married persons, it was occasionally necessary to exclude a very elderly person from the sample because of blindness, deafness, or infirmity. Fortunately, only a very few extremely elderly persons were so excluded, and the sample did include a substantial number of quite elderly respondents.

The age of each person to be interviewed was estimated by such considerations as age-grade membership, year of circumcision, and approximate age at the time of known historical events, and by matching age with other persons born in the same year for whom a better date was available, by inferences based upon the person's physi-

1. LeVine (1966b).

cal appearance, and finally, by the "informed" guess of the interpreter. Out of this set of facts and estimates, an age was determined which was later compared with the age independently estimated for the same person by the resident ethnographer. Where discrepancies existed, the mean of the two estimates was taken. The ages finally assigned to the respondents are obviously no better than approximate, but the degree of accuracy is probably within a year or two for young adults, increasing to a probable error of five or more years for the most elderly persons in the sample. Table 5 presents the age distribution of the persons interviewed in each of the eight interviewing sites.

The Hehe, Pokot, and Sebei samples are very similar in age, but the Kamba samples, especially the farmers, are notably older. The greater age of the Kamba is due to local economic conditions which have caused large numbers of young men (with and without their wives) to move to nearby cities and European farms in search of employment. Thus, the age distribution of the Kamba samples accurately represents the ages of married persons living in the two areas chosen for study (widows and widowers were not included). In seven of the eight sites, the sampling universe of married women was younger than the universe of married men. This difference is a reflection of the realities of polygynous marriages (with older men acquiring younger wives) in these areas.

What effect does age have upon the responses? To answer this question, all respondents were placed in one of three age categories: 20 to 35 years (N = 196), 36 to 55 (N = 198), and 56 and over (N = 110).[2] These categories seemed best suited to reflect culturally meaningful age distinctions in the four tribes. The categories cannot be claimed to match exactly any existing age-class distinctions such as "warrior," "married man," or "elder," but they do provide an approximation of recognized distinctions between the young adult, the man of middle years, and the elder. For analytic comparison, many other age categories such as deciles and quartiles were also examined, but the results of these various breakdowns did not differ in any significant fashion from the three-category comparison. Consequently, the three-category system was retained, and is used here.

Examination of all responses to the interview in relation to the ages of the respondents indicated that age exercised very little influence upon the response patterns. When age influence is examined within each tribe, minor differences can sometimes be noted. For

2. One case in age category 56+ was unintentionally omitted.

TABLE 5
AGE DISTRIBUTION OF RESPONDENTS IN ALL INTERVIEWING SITES

Tribal group	Number	Mean age	Standard deviation	Range
Hehe farmers				
Men	31	42	14	23–74
Women	30	36	15	20–74
Both sexes	61	39	15	20–74
Hehe pastoralists ·				
Men	31	39	14	19–77
Women	31	34	11	20–56
Both sexes	62	36	13	19–77
Kamba farmers				
Men	31	51	14	28–89
Women	31	52	17	25–90
Both sexes	62	51	16	25–90
Kamba pastoralists				
Men	32	52	15	25–99
Women	32	41	13	23–68
Both sexes	64	47	14	23–99
Pokot farmers				
Men	33	40	14	23–85
Women	32	35	14	20–60
Both sexes	65	38	14	20–85
Pokot pastoralists				
Men	31	44	17	25–85
Women	32	38	15	20–77
Both sexes	63	42	16	20–85
Sebei farmers				
Men	34	44	17	22–79
Women	31	34	17	21–78
Both sexes	65	40	17	21–79
Sebei pastoralists				
Men	31	41	12	19–78
Women	32	33	11	23–67
Both sexes	63	37	12	19–78

example, older Kamba (56+) are likely to be more enthusiastic about the pleasures of old age than are younger Kamba, and younger persons among the Hehe (20–35) are more likely than older ones (36+) to say that they do not know the answer to a question. But, to an overwhelming degree, such differences are few in number, relatively small in terms of statistical significance, and trivial in importance. In 96 percent of the possible age comparisons within each of the tribes, there are no statistically significant or theoretically intriguing differences between the age categories. Indeed, the *agreement* between age categories is frequently very impressive. For example, table 6 illustrates the degree of agreement often found in response to an interview question.

TABLE 6

Age-Categorized Answers of All Four Tribes to the Question:
How Can a Poor Man Become Wealthy?
(In percentages)

Answer	Age category		
	20–35 (*N* = 196)	36–55 (*N* = 198)	56+ (*N* = 110)
By working hard	21.0	24.2	16.4
By farming well	49.5	48.0	56.4
By working for a rich man	10.2	7.6	6.4
By working for wages	3.1	4.5	0.9
By trading	4.6	5.6	5.5
By "selling" his daughters for the bride-price	2.6	3.0	0.9
He cannot become rich	2.0	2.0	5.5
By luck or act of "God"	1.0	1.0	1.8
Other (own beehives, steal, or poach ivory)	6.1	3.5	6.4
No answer, or don't know	0.0	0.5	0.0

Strong agreement across age categories of the kind shown in table 6 was characteristic throughout, even extending to Rorschach responses. For example, there is marked agreement in the frequency of "texture" responses (cF and Fc) in the Rorschach; a "texture" response emphasizes the tactual softness, hairiness, smoothness, and so on, of the ink blot. Such responses are traditionally interpreted as being indicators of an awareness of affective needs, sometimes involving tactual contact. Table 7 gives the percentages of age-categorized "texture" responses to all ten blots of the Rorschach. Again, persons of similar age are combined, irrespective of their tribal affiliation.

The agreement across age categories shown in table 7 is only slightly greater than was characteristic. Moreover, even where one might well anticipate age differentials, few appear. For example, table 8 gives the age-differentiated responses of all respondents (this time separated by tribe) to the question: "Under what circumstances can a young adult man tell a *mzee* ["old man"] that he is wrong?" Al-

133

though this question is obviously one that might discriminate between age categories, simple inspection of these answers is sufficient to indicate that the answers given in each tribe were largely unrelated to the age of the respondent.

Perhaps one additional example will provide adequate illustration of the minimal influence of age-differentials upon responses

TABLE 7

PERCENTAGE OF "TEXTURE" (FC) RESPONSES GIVEN
TO ALL TEN RORSCHACH BLOTS
(In percentages)

	Age category		
Number of "Texture" *(Fc) Responses*	*20–35* *(N = 196)*	*36–55* *(N = 198)*	*56+* *(N = 110)*
None	32.1	32.8	33.6
One	46.4	47.0	46.4
Two	14.3	15.1	15.5
Three	5.1	4.0	4.5
Four	2.0	1.0	0.0

that we might have expected to be age-related. In all four tribes, rich men tend to be older men, and rich men tend to be envied, and often hated. Table 9 lists the answers members of all four tribes gave to the question: "How do people feel about a rich man?" Here again, the influence of age upon the responses is inconsequential. Although small differences between age categories do occur—as they do in regard to most sets of answers—they are so small (with the possible exception of the Hehe) that it is unreasonable to conclude that age has exerted any important influence upon the response patterns.

When all four tribes are compared, again we find remarkably few age-related responses. Indeed, of over 200 comparisons made, only eight showed age to be statistically significant at the 0.01 level in all four tribes.

The eight age-influenced responses that occurred in all four tribes were:

1) Young people (ages 20-35) said that women want to marry handsome men; the middle-aged (36-55) and older (56+) people said that women want to marry rich men.

134

TABLE 8

UNDER WHAT CIRCUMSTANCES CAN A YOUNG ADULT MAN TELL A *mzee* ("OLD MAN") THAT HE IS WRONG?
(In percentages)

Answer	Hehe age category			Kamba age category			Pokot age category			Sebei age category		
	20-35 (N = 53)	36-55 (N = 45)	56+ (N = 25)	20-35 (N = 21)	36-55 (N = 63)	56+ (N = 42)	20-35 (N = 58)	36-55 (N = 49)	56+ (N = 20)	20-35 (N = 62)	36-55 (N = 43)	56+ (N = 22)
Never	2	7	—	—	—	2	2	—	—	85	70	73
If he wastes property	—	—	—	5	3	10	53	55	50	3	9	9
If he refuses to pay the bridewealth	—	—	—	—	—	—	—	—	—	3	7	9
If he beats his wife, or wives, too much	—	—	—	10	2	5	15	12	10	—	—	—
If he is too abusive or quarrelsome	—	—	—	19	27	29	21	27	25	—	—	—
If he too often commits adultery	8	7	8	—	2	2	3	—	5	—	—	—
If he lies	28	26	24	—	—	—	—	4	—	—	—	—
Whenever he is wrong	58	60	68	66	66	52	3	2	10	9	14	9
Other	—	—	—	—	—	—	3	—	—	—	—	—
No answer	4	—	—	—	—	—	—	—	—	—	—	—

2) The young most respected a chief or headman; the middle-aged and older most respected a rich man.

3) The young said that men worry that they cannot please their wives sexually; the middle-aged and the old said that men do not so worry.

4) The young tended to say that it is correct for a son to argue with his father "if he is wrong"; the middle-aged and older persons said that the father "should be obeyed," simply "because it is right."

5) Younger respondents tended to value their age-group more than middle-aged and older persons did (this excludes the Hehe who have no age-grades).

6) Middle-aged and older people were much better able to correctly identify a picture showing a traditional native doctor at work (values picture 4); the young less often recognized the traditional costume or paraphernalia.

7) In response to the Rorschach, the younger persons tended to focus their responses more often upon tiny portions of the blot (d); the middle-aged and older respondents more often used the entire blot (W). This could reflect nothing more than a loss of close vision among the old.

8) There was a tendency for middle-aged and older persons to give more form-determined (F) responses to the Rorschach; the responses of the young were somewhat more diversely determined.

These examples emphasize the finding that, for the most part, the age of the respondent had little relationship to the responses given. Only in a few instances were age-significant responses noted, and these differences failed to cohere into any dominant pattern. There was, for example, no sign of the expected tension or conflict between the young and the old. The most that can be said is that with greater age comes an increase in the appreciation of wealth, a depreciation of the sexual and romantic, a loss of interest in one's age-mates (who, at this age, are more likely to be deceased), and a somewhat more constricted set of Rorschach perceptions. None of these patterns should come as a surprise; indeed, they have about them such a familiar ring that they could apply to the aging in our own society, and many others.[3] This finding is important because it permits us to

3. For reviews of social and psychological dimensions of aging, see; Anderson and Clark (1967), Arth (1965), Birren (1968), Brehm (1968), Clark (1967), Havighurst (1968), Shanas (1963), Shanas and Strieb (1965), Shelton (1965), Simmons (1945), Simmons (1960), Talland (1968), and Talmon (1968).

TABLE 9

How Do People Feel about a Rich Man?
(In percentages)

Answer	Hehe age category			Kamba age category			Pokot age category			Sebei age category		
	20-35 (N = 55)	36-55 (N = 45)	56+ (N = 25)	20-35 (N = 21)	36-55 (N = 63)	56+ (N = 42)	20-35 (N = 58)	36-55 (N = 49)	56+ (N = 21)	20-35 (N = 62)	36-55 (N = 43)	56+ (N = 22)
They like and respect him	9	4	16	5	11	—	59	70	62	16	30	18
They like him if he is generous	9	17	20	19	27	26	17	12	23	23	23	27
They think he is lucky	4	13	8	—	—	2	—	—	—	—	—	—
They have no feelings	4	9	16	—	—	—	—	—	—	2	—	—
He is criticized	20	2	—	—	—	5	5	2	5	—	—	—
They are jealous; they hate him	20	31	28	71	60	62	12	16	10	56	37	41
They employ witchcraft against him	28	22	12	5	2	5	7	—	—	3	10	14
Other	4	—	—	—	—	—	—	—	—	—	—	—
No answer	2	2	—	—	—	—	—	—	—	—	—	—

follow the analyses into different areas, confident that where age becomes significant, it does so in these aforementioned familiar ways.

THE INFLUENCE OF SEX

We had every reason to expect that the sex of the respondents would have a substantial effect upon the response patterns. Our question was not whether sex would be relevant, but rather how much of an effect it would have and where this effect would be most pronounced. A diverse literature has shown that men and women in many societies express differing attitudes, values, and personality-linked preferences, and that these differences can readily be detected by interviewing techniques.[4] The extensive literature on Africa has repeatedly noted that men and women live in clearly differentiated social worlds and that male and female perspectives upon life and upon each other correspondingly vary. Although research in Africa has been peculiarly lacking in psychological focus, it has not been—as has been true in some parts of the world—excessively male-oriented. The separation of women from men in the house-property complex, women's relative inequality vis-à-vis men, and their antagonism toward men have been described in several parts of Africa. African women have been the subject of large, if not fully proportionate, share of research interest. This may in part be the result of the activity of so many female fieldworkers; among well-known contributors, one must include Richards, Hunter, Thomas, La Fontaine, Wilson, Kuper, Albert, Smith, Leith-Ross, Krige, Tew, and Paulme, to name but a few. In addition, many male researchers have also written extensively about African women.[5] Nonetheless, little systematic quantitative research comparing the attitudes or values of men and women has been reported.

The present study assumed that there might be important differences between men and women, although neither the nature nor the extent of these differences could be fully specified in advance. Because of our anticipation of sex-specific response patterns, we decided to avoid a male-centered study by assuring that women were fully represented, even though implementation of this desired female

4. For discussions of male-female differences, see: La Fontaine (1967), LeVine (1966b), Rocheblave-Spenlé (1964), Spindler (1962), and Whittaker (1967).

5. An extensive bibliography of work to 1960 is available in Paulme (1963).

representation might prove difficult. And, in fact, it *was* more difficult to interview women than men. In most instances, women were busier than men, and their essential activities often made them unavailable for the interview. They said, no doubt truthfully, that their husbands were not eager to see economic duties suspended, even for a few hours. Furthermore, once they were in the interview situation, women were often more timid than men. Motivating women to appear for the interview and to complete it was disproportionately difficult. Nonetheless, equal numbers of women and men were interviewed. Immediately after each interview, I made judgments concerning the relative interest and effort invested in the interview by male and female respondents in all tribes, taking into account the respondents' interest, efforts to respond fully and thoughtfully, complaints, positive remarks, reluctance to complete the entire interview, and so forth. With the exception of the Kamba pastoralists, where there was no male-female difference, and the Pokot pastoralists, where women were slightly more interested than men, women were somewhat less interested in the interview and devoted less effort to it than men did. While this lesser degree of interest and effort by women should be borne in mind, it should also be noted that overall interest (by women as well as men) was quite high. I should add that analysis of the responses showed that the only discriminable effect of low interest or effort was a tendency for such persons to reject more cards on the Rorschach and to give slightly shorter answers to some questions. In no other way do the answers of the more poorly motivated respondents differ from those of the better motivated ones.

When male and female responses are compared within each of the eight interviewing sites, differences sometimes do emerge. For example, as table 10 illustrates, the Hehe pastoralists disagreed on

TABLE 10

ANSWERS OF HEHE PASTORALISTS TO THE QUESTION:
WOULD THE HEHE PREFER TO HAVE SONS OR DAUGHTERS?

Answer	Men	Women
Son	23	9
*Daughter	0	2
Both	8	19

NOTE: $\chi^2 = 10.48$, P $< .005$, df $= 1$
*Omitted in computation.

their preference for sons or daughters. Another example comes from the Kamba pastoralists, where men and women made quite different replies when asked, "whom can a person trust?": men said that they trusted their fathers while women said that they trusted their "in-laws" (particularly their husbands' fathers). Also, Sebei farming women mentioned witchcraft significantly more often than Sebei men did (P < .01). And Pokot pastoral men mentioned cattle more often than women did (P < .01).

Often, however, when male-female differences existed in the responses to one question or picture, they were counterbalanced by the responses to a related stimulus. The Pokot pastoralists provide one such example. When presented with a 35mm color slide of several ochrous and beaded Samburu warriors brandishing spears, men and women among the Pokot pastoralists responded differently: 29 men sniffed a neutral "so what" or "they aren't so much," and two men said nothing; but 25 of the 32 women were nearly ecstatic in their response. These 25 Pokot women squealed with pleasure and unfailingly commented upon the beauty and virility of the men in the color slide. Seventeen of the women went on to say how delighted they would be to receive the amorous attention of such men. Said one Pokot woman with characteristic enthusiasm: "I would do anything to sleep with such a man. How beautiful! How wonderful! How can I get such a man to sleep with me? Can you help me meet such a man?" And when the same Pokot pastoralists were presented with a color slide of a Pygmy man who was totally without decoration, and was standing alone displaying a large, protruding stomach, the response was different. Pokot men either dismissed the Pygmy as a small and fat man, or said nothing at all; but 30 of 32 women literally screamed with horror at the sight of the unfortunate Pygmy. Their comments frequently made it clear that they would "rather die than sleep with such a man": "If such a man tried to sleep with me, I would kill him; if I couldn't kill him, I would kill myself. Only an animal would sleep with such creature." Yet when the slides shown were those of women, it was the Pokot men who waxed lyrical and the women who said little. Consequently, when the entire response protocol is considered, Pokot pastoral women and men spoke of beauty and sexuality with equal frequency and intensity.

Additional male-female response differentials could be mentioned in all eight sites; however, such differences are small and few in number. In all four tribes the responses of men and women are overwhelmingly in agreement. Of all possible comparisons in re-

140

sponses between men and women in the pastoral and farming sites of all four tribes, fewer than 5 percent showed statistically significant differences. On most attitudes, most values, even on most personality characteristics, the responses of these African men and women did *not* differ. In fact, the agreement between the sexes is very often remarkable. Many examples of this impressive agreement could be given; the example presented in table 11 was selected at random from many

TABLE 11

MALE VERSUS FEMALE RESPONSES TO THE QUESTION:
WHAT MAKES A MAN A GOOD FRIEND?

Tribal group	(1) Being generous	(2) Providing beer	(3) Being polite	(4) Being trustworthy	(5) No answer OR Don't know
Hehe farmers					
Men	7	12	3	9	0
Women	9	13	3	4	1
Hehe pastoralists					
Men	11	15	1	2	2
Women	6	21	3	0	1
Kamba farmers					
Men	0	25	2	4	0
Women	0	28	0	2	1
Kamba pastoralists					
Men	0	27	0	5	0
Women	0	25	0	7	0
Pokot farmers					
Men	0	18	0	15	0
Women	0	17	0	15	0
Pokot pastoralists					
Men	1	12	0	18	0
Women	0	17	0	15	0
Sebei farmers					
Men	1	29	3	0	0
Women	1	23	2	2	3
Sebei pastoralists					
Men	2	26	2	0	1
Women	0	29	4	0	0

others that share this same, typical, degree of agreement between men and women.

But even though less than 5 percent of the response varies between men and women, almost all of this variance clusters in one

TABLE 12

MALE VERSUS FEMALE RESPONSES TO VALUE PICTURE 7: WOMAN WATCHED BY MAN

Response	Hehe				Kamba				Pokot				Sebei			
	Farmers		Pastoralists		Farmers		Pastoralists		Farmers		Pastoralists		Farmers		Pastoralists	
	Male	Female	Male	Female	Male	Female	Male	Female	Male	Female	Male	Female	Male	Female	Male	Female
She is just working	1	7	1	0	0	0	0	0	7	6	3	0	18	18	12	10
They are quarreling	10	17	8	4	3	10	0	0	4	5	4	8	3	6	4	3
It is a sexual tryst	9	3	4	6	1	0	27	25	13	12	8	10	7	5	9	14
It is a rape	8	3	17	14	21	18	3	5	2	3	16	13	5	2	5	2
A jealous husband is watching his wife	2	0	0	5	0	0	0	0	0	0	0	0	0	0	0	0
Other, or don't know	1	0	1	2	6	3	2	2	7	6	0	1	0	0	1	4

area: relations between men and women. In fact, questions that dealt directly with relations of men to women typically elicited substantial male-female response differentials. In some instances where relations between men and women are involved, the differences were small, as in the responses to the values picture 7 (showing a woman carrying water along an isolated path while a man, who crouches behind a bush, watches her) shown in table 12.

Most stimuli in the interview dealing directly with relations between men and women showed greater differentials than those presented in table 12. And one question is the ultimate in differentiating men from women, that is, whether wives obey their husbands. Table 13 shows the responses to this most discriminating question. This

TABLE 13

MALE VERSUS FEMALE ANSWERS TO THE QUESTIONS: DO WIVES OBEY THEIR HUSBANDS? AND IS IT RIGHT FOR THEM TO DO SO?

Tribe	Wives obey and they should		Wives disobey but should not		Wives disobey and should when the husband is wrong	
	Male	Female	Male	Female	Male	Female
Hehe						
Farmers	0	0	25	7	6	23
Pastoralists	0	13	28	18	3	0
Kamba						
Farmers	1	1	30	20	0	10
Pastoralists	20	24	10	5	2	3
Pokot						
Farmers	13	12	20	7	0	13
Pastoralists	19	30	12	2	0	0
Sebei						
Farmers	12	15	20	14	1	2
Pastoralists	1	13	29	19	0	1

question alone among all those in the interview provoked differences in all eight communities. Inspection of table 13 reveals two obvious points. First, not a single person of the 505 interviewed failed to answer: this is a topic about which every adult apparently had an opinion. Second, the answers do not merely differ between men and women, they do so in a consistent direction: men said wives disobey their husbands and should not; wives said either that they did obey, or that they disobeyed but were within their rights in doing so!

The striking similarity of most male and female responses is accentuated when the responses of all women in all tribes are compared with those of all men in all tribes. By combining responses in this manner, rather large comparison groups are formed (253 men and 252 women), and differences between these large groups stand out clearly. By now, it should come as no surprise to learn that there were very few such differences. In addition to the aforementioned difference concerning whether or not wives obey husbands, when all men are compared with all women, only five statistically significant areas of male-female difference were found:

1) Men tended to prefer sons to daughters; women tended to evaluate sons and daughters equally (P < .001).

2) Men explained their preference for sons in terms of a desire to perpetuate their name within the clan or lineage; when women did say that sons were preferred, they rarely mentioned perpetuation of a name as the reason for their preference (P < .001).

3) Men tended to use the entire blot (W) in their Rorschach responses, whereas women more often confined their responses to a part of the blot (P < .01). The use of the entire blot is often interpreted as a sign of an organizational bent, and the use of parts (D) is taken to indicate a more matter-of-fact, particularistic approach to life. This same response tendency has sometimes been recorded among European populations.[6]

4) Women sometimes trusted their husbands, but men *never* trusted their wives. Thus, 67 women said (in answer to the question, "Whom can a person trust?") that they trusted their husbands, but not a single man in any tribe said that he trusted his wife.

5) In answer to the question, "What is the worst illness a person can have?" more than twice as many women as men answered "venereal disease," citing as their reason the fear of becoming infertile. Men more often than women mentioned smallpox and epilepsy as the worst afflictions (P < .001).

These five differences notwithstanding, the similarity in response between all men and all women is massive. A few examples might help to emphasize this point. In the content analysis, the mean number of mentions of land for men was 47.9; for women, it was 47.5. Again in the content analysis, men gave an average of 51 scorable mentions of hatred; women gave 50.7 similar mentions. And in men-

6. See Ames et al. (1959).

tions of physical beauty, the male mean score was 15.62; the female mean score was 15.61. Such agreement was evident throughout the protocol. For example, in the values picture 4 (showing a native doctor in traditional garb), 93 men and 94 women identified the doctor, while 160 men and 158 women did not. Faced with a choice between land and cattle, 179 men and 179 women chose land, while 73 men and 73 women selected cattle (one man could not decide). This extraordinary agreement was also maintained in the open-ended questions to which many differing responses were given, as these randomly selected examples will demonstrate. The question, "What is the first useful task a young girl is given?" would seem to offer men and women considerable opportunity for disagreement; but the male and female replies listed in table 14 show striking agreement. That this question

TABLE 14

MALE VERSUS FEMALE ANSWERS TO THE QUESTION:
WHAT IS THE FIRST USEFUL TASK A YOUNG GIRL IS GIVEN?

Answer	All males	All females
To farm	71	70
To milk cattle or herd goats	7	11 ·
To grind grain	41	48
To do housework	41	47
To learn obedience to adults	9	8
To cook	25	22
To fetch water	41	29
To learn proper morality	10	6
Other	3	1
Don't know	5	9
Total	253	251

NOTE: $\chi^2 = 5.38$, P $< .75$, df $= 8$

does not evoke greater response differences may be surprising, but the same lack of difference is consistent throughout the interview.

Table 15 is another randomly selected example of answers to a question that might well have been expected to elicit male-female differences in responses: "If a man could have anything he wanted, what should he choose?" Once again, we find phenomenal agreement.

A scene showing the disagreement between a son and his father might also be expected to produce response differences, with men and women disagreeing regarding the severity of punishment a father

TABLE 15

MALE VERSUS FEMALE ANSWERS TO THE QUESTION:
IF A MAN COULD HAVE ANYTHING HE WANTED, WHAT SHOULD HE CHOOSE?

Answer	All males	All females
Wealth	64	58
Cattle	94	98
Land	29	22
Money	9	8
A wife	39	44
Children	10	6
*Feathers	0	1
*Spears	1	1
*Other	6	1
*Don't know	1	13
Total	253	252

NOTE: $\chi^2 = 5.36$, $P < .50$, df = 6
*Omitted in computation.

TABLE 16

MALE VERSUS FEMALE RESPONSES TO VALUES PICTURE 2:
ONE OF THREE SONS DISOBEYS HIS FATHER

Response	All males	All females
*The son is right	0	2
*Father should "peacefully" correct son	10	3
Father should give one last warning	22	24
Father should take matter to the elders	56	50
Father should beat son	31	39
Father should disinherit son (refuse to pay bride-price)	39	38
Father should banish son from home	57	59
**Father should curse son (a destructive magical oath)	15	18
**Father should bewitch son (a fatal act)	2	2
Don't know	21	17
Total	253	252

NOTE: $\chi^2 = 3.71$, $P < .90$, df = 7
*Combined for computation.
**Combined for computation.

ought to direct upon such a son. Table 16 reports the responses to just such a scene, as portrayed in values picture 2. Once more, men and women agreed upon the action that should be taken.

This sameness of response is not merely found in the answers that reflect what we may assume to be widely shared understandings, values, or attitudes; it also obtains in the responses to the Rorschach. As was so in the intratribal analysis, when all men are compared to all women, their Rorschach responses are very much alike. For example, table 17 indicates the frequency of color responses (CF, FC, C) given to the ten Rorschach blots, and this Rorschach example is but one of

TABLE 17

FREQUENCY OF COLOR RESPONSES BY MALES VERSUS FEMALES
TO ALL TEN RORSCHACH CARDS

Number of responses	*All males*	*All females*
None	126	125
One	68	65
Two	31	37
*Three	13	9
*Four	3	4
*Five	2	2
Total	243	242

NOTE: $\chi^2 = .87$, $P < .90$, df = 3
*Combined for computation.

many showing a similar degree of agreement. The only Rorschach differences of any consequence are these:

1) Women tended to reject the blot without responding ($P < .05$).
2) As mentioned earlier, women tended to respond to a part of the blot rather than to all of it ($P < .01$).
3) Women were somewhat more willing to accept the percepts that were suggested in card 1 ($P < .01$).
4) Women saw the "popular" winged creature (usually a bird or a bat) in card 5 somewhat less frequently than did men ($P < .01$).

With the possible exception of the last-mentioned difference, these female response tendencies appear to be linked to a lesser effort on the part of women. On all other major quantitative dimensions of the Rorschach performance, men and women are alike. Possible differences of a more subtle qualitative kind are discussed in chapter 8, which deals specifically with Rorschach performance.

CONCLUSION

In general, we may conclude that the responses of men and women differed little. They differed consistently only when the concern was directly that of relations between men and women. To an overwhelming extent, men and women, like persons of different ages, expressed similar values, attitudes, and emotions. Why such agreement should occur is theoretically intriguing. It may represent some artifact of the interview's construction or of its administration, or it may reflect something basic to these particular societies. There is reason to suspect that all these factors are involved. But whatever the source, this similarity well serves our comparative purposes. I have already noted that the interview was designed to elicit shared attitudes, beliefs, and perceptions, rather than idiosyncratic ones. It was directed toward a homogeneity of response by many factors, probably the most important of which was the use of an impersonal ("What do the Hehe think . . . ?") rather than a personal ("What do you think . . . ?") format. (The Rorschach, which may be an exception to this format, is considered later.) But I would also conclude, as I think we must, that there is substantial sharing—cognitive, affective, and valuative—between men and women, between young and old, in these societies. In fact, I suspect that attitudinal consensus is more widespread than the literature on East Africa has heretofore suggested. Indeed, I suspect that conflict between men and women is far more common than is fundamental disagreement on values, attitudes, and feelings.

In conclusion, it is sufficient to record here that in this study, the influence of the respondents' age upon the response pattern was slight and predictable, while the influence of their sex was minimal and confined to one area, relations between men and women. With this differential response fully noted, it is possible to examine subsequent findings without a continual harkening back to possible age or sex-specific response differences. Henceforth, analyses usually combine the responses of men and of women of all ages. Of course, where sex or age is relevant to the findings at issue, these variables are considered in appropriate detail.

148

The Problem of European Acculturation 6

An understanding of the possible impact of European acculturative influences was essential to the research design of this study, for it was obvious that should there be major differences in the degree of European acculturation among the respondents of the various tribes, then the interpretation of the interview data could be massively confounded. Without some measure of the relative acculturation of the respondents it could, in fact, be impossible to evaluate these data at all, for it might well be that all the variance in interview response could be accounted for by differences in the acquisition of European values and the degree of European involvement. Hence, we were greatly concerned that the sites selected for study be as little acculturated as possible and that the European acculturative influences that might prevail be measured in some comparable fashion. This chapter reports our efforts to minimize acculturative differences between sites. It also presents our "index of acculturation" by means of which we attempted to measure the degree of acculturation in each site. Finally, it analyzes the interview responses to determine the extent to which these responses were related to differential European acculturation.

East Africa at the time of this research was a kaleidoscopic scene of competing acculturative influences. Principal among these influences was the increasing acceptance of European values, economic practices, and material culture, but there was also a welter of changing and commingling African cultures, not to mention the influences of Arab and Somali traders and large numbers of Indian merchants. We tried to take into account all these forms of acculturation, but most particularly the European kinds, since these were the most widespread and influential.

The degree of acculturative influence of one African tribe upon another varies throughout the area from the widespread, almost "pan-pastoralist," influence of the Masai to more locally confined influence, such as that of the Kikuyu upon the Kamba or the Turkana upon the Pokot. These various influences are so complex, so reciprocal, and of such long duration that any effort we might have made to assess them —particularly in a comparable way from tribe to tribe and from site to site—could not have been more than a gloss of the complexities of a process of change. In this research, we assumed that all tribes in East Africa have been affected by their African neighbors and that these influences continue; but we also assumed, and we believe justifiably, that these influences were relatively incommensurable, being as varied as they were from tribe to tribe. Conversely, although European influence was itself complex and somewhat variable from place to place, it nonetheless had sufficiently common, recurrent features that we believed we could derive a fair estimate of its relative presence in one tribe or another.

Our concern with the differential spread of European influence among the tribes in our study was made urgent by the obvious fact that European acculturative influence in these areas was more prominent in the highlands, where all four of our farming sites were located, than it was in the lowlands, where all of our pastoral sites were situated. Consequently, we faced the possibility that, in each of the tribes we studied, we would encounter differential exposure to European influence, with the farmers in the tribe being more acculturated than the pastoralists. Thus, the measurement of European acculturation was imperative.

Our first efforts to reduce the possible influence of European acculturation consisted of avoidance procedures. We sought first to avoid selecting sites for study which were greatly influenced by European acculturation. This meant avoiding areas close to European towns, cities, or experimental agricultural stations, and areas greatly involved in cash cropping or wage work, and so on. Obviously it was impossible to avoid all such influences and still locate appropriate and accessible study areas, yet all reasonable care was taken. For example, the Hehe farming community of Ngelewala was chosen despite its proximity to Iringa, a European town and administrative center. Ngelewala was quite close to Iringa: the trip from one to the other took 20 minutes by car, 45 minutes by bicycle, or a little more than an hour by foot. However, from our inspection of Ngelewala and many more distant neighborhoods, and from our comparison of travel and wage work records, it became apparent that the neighborhood of Ngelewala was no more acculturated than were other areas that were as much as 15 miles farther away from Iringa. Many of these more distant areas, in addition to being far less accessible to research activities (especially during the rainy season), were heavily populated by immigrant Bena, Kinga, and Sangu. Hence Ngelewala was selected.[1]

We also attempted to avoid areas of intensive African acculturation. As with the aforementioned Hehe, some areas were heavily peopled by immigrants from other tribes, and other areas were dominated by the culture of a neighboring tribe. The latter problem was particularly evident in areas close to the tribal boundaries in the lowland pastoral areas. For example, some Hehe pastoralists were culturally influenced by, and were in hostile contact with, the Baraguyu, as were some Kamba with the Masai, some Pokot with the Turkana, and some Sebei with the Pokot and the Karamojong. Such border areas were avoided whenever possible.

Furthermore, once a site was selected for study, certain "atypically acculturated" persons were avoided. This practice required that the resident ethnographer identify those persons who were to be excluded on the grounds of atypical acculturation. Thus a few persons, although resident within the sampling universe, were excluded from the sample. In all, there were three exclusions because of atypically high European acculturation (one Sebei farmer who was involved in national politics, one Kamba farmer with an extensive government employment record, and one Pokot farming chief with some knowledge of English). In addition, a few persons in several sites were excluded because they were, by their own admission and in the opinion of the residents of that site, entirely, or in large measure, a member of another tribal society. In all, approximately twenty persons were excluded for this reason.

Despite these avoidance and exclusion procedures, some obvious differences in the degree of European acculturation existed, not only among the sites but also within them. Thus, even though the interview was composed of items that were thought to be minimally sensitive to the effects of European acculturation, it was impossible

1. A more complete discussion of these considerations is available in Winans's forthcoming Culture and Ecology Project monograph on Hehe local neighborhoods.

to reject the possibility that European acculturation might yet have played a decisive role in the responses that were given.

In view of these evident differentials in acculturation, it was imperative that I obtain a measure of the relative European acculturation for each individual who was to be interviewed. Although the search for measures of acculturation is a common one in anthropology, few explicit models for a formal index of acculturation were available.[2] Of these models, we were most influenced by the work of the Spindlers among the Menomini.[3] The literature concerning East Africa contained numerous useful fragments of information, but we were aware of neither a systematically organized nor an up-to-date guide for the development of an index of European acculturation.[4] Consequently, we attempted to develop our own index.

As a first step toward the development of this index, I asked each ethnographer to attempt to identify for his own tribe those criteria that would best indicate a person's degree of European acculturation. This each ethnographer did during his field research. Then, as I visited each site during the field research period, I recorded my observations concerning possible measures of acculturation, and Porter did likewise in the course of his travels from tribe to tribe. Goldschmidt also made brief visits to each site and he, too, systematically noted relevant differences in acculturation. Toward the close of the field research period, the combined research staff met to attempt the construction of an index of acculturation. Since we hoped to develop an index of items that would permit us to compare the relative acculturation of all eight sites, we could consider only those items that were equally applicable in all communities. After we eliminated those items that were not relevant for all communities, we drew up a general list of possible acculturation items, and the ethnographers returned to the field to collect any necessary data not already available. Because there were limitations of time and access to information, and because in all sites men were, without exception, more influenced by European culture than were their wives, it was also decided to collect systematic acculturation data for men only.

After examination of the data collected in the field, I selected ten items for inclusion in the index: (1) education of self, (2) sons'

2. For examples of varied approaches to the problem of conceptualizing and measuring acculturation, see, Eisenstadt (1954), Graves (1967), Humphrey (1944), Peterson and Scheff (1965), and Roy (1962).

3. G. Spindler (1955) and L. Spindler (1962).

4. See Ainsworth (1959), Ainsworth and Ainsworth (1962a–d).

education, (3) daughters' education, (4) religion, (5) footwear, (6) cleanliness of clothes, (7) travel, (8) roofing type, (9) participation in cash economy, and (10) wage work. The relevance of most of these items is obvious. For example, the amount of European education a man has received (education of self), or the amount of time spent in European towns (travel), is an obvious indicator of his exposure to European culture. But others require some explanation. The extent to which a man's sons receive European primary education is generally a function not so much of the sons' ability or motivation as it is of their father's willingness to pay for and encourage this education; and hence the father's own views on the value of education are directly at issue. The same holds true for the education of daughters, only more so, since only a relatively few men will encourage and pay for the education of their daughters. Both of these items concerning education of sons and daughters are essential additions to the index; "education of self" is inadequate as a single item, because older men had little opportunity for European education when they were young, whereas their children had much easier access to schooling within the expanding educational opportunities of East Africa. Religion was included because it was assumed that there was a meaningful difference in acculturation between men who professed only to a tribal religion and men who were self-professed Christians. The extent to which a man had become involved in the European cash economy was also thought to be important; thus the amount of wage work done and the degree of participation in the cash economy were included. Three less obviously relevant items were also included. The type of roof that a man had on his house (grass or other native materials versus sheet metal) was a mark of European acculturation in all eight sites, even though there were no metal roofs in some of the sites. So too was a man's footwear. European sandals and shoes were generally coveted and worn as items that signified actual or aspired-to European acculturation. The cleanliness of a man's clothing was similarly significant of "Europeanization." The British standards of cleanliness had made themselves widely known over East Africa, and clean clothing had consequently become prestige-relevant for any African who aspired to move upward through the complexly ordered strata of European acculturation.

Each of these ten items was ordinally ranked from least significant as an acculturation item to most significant. For example, "wage work" was ranked "none," "intermittent," or regular by each ethnographer. However, the problem remained of assigning numerical weights to the various ranks in order that we might give each individual man a numerical score that would represent his acculturation. The assignment of such numerical weights was difficult because, although each of the ten acculturation items was applicable in all eight sites, there was some variation in their importance from tribe to tribe. In order to represent these variations in the final weights, each of the four ethnographers was asked to add his judgment of the appropriate weightings to mine.

The method of weighting employed was as follows: Each one of the 38 categories for each of the ten items was placed on a separate card. For example, one of the 38 categories was "Wage Work—none," another was "Wage Work—intermittent," and still another was "Wage Work—regular" (for all 38 categories, see table 18). These 38 cards were then shuffled, and an identically ordered copy was mailed to each of the four ethnographers. In order to establish an upper and lower baseline, I arbitrarily assigned weights to two of the 38 items. As a zero point I took "Education of Respondent—none," and as an upper limit I gave 10 points to "Education of Respondent—9 or more years." I then asked each ethnographer to assign relative weights to the remaining 36 items in terms of their relevance for his own tribe. My instructions were as follows:

> Please assign a score of from zero to ten to each of 36 items. Zero has been assigned to Item No. 1 (Education of Respondent—none); please assign a score of zero to any other item which like No. 1 represents *no* European acculturation. The criterion for the maximal score of ten points is Item No. 5 (Education of Respondent—9 or more years). Assign ten points to any other item which in your judgment is *equivalent* in acculturative importance to Item No. 5. For example, consider Item No. 21 (Footwear—good European shoes and good socks). If you believe that knowing that a man in your tribe wears good shoes and socks is, in general, as good an indicator of his acculturation as knowing that he has 9 or more years of schooling, then score this item ten points. If you think it less important, then give it correspondingly fewer points.
>
> Please pay especial attention to Items No. 6–No. 10 (Sons' Education) and No. 11–No. 15 (Daughters' Education). As you may recall, the education of each son and daughter (of school age) was compared with the child's age so that a year of schooling for each school-eligible-year is given a perfect score of 1.00. Less than perfect school attendance has been divided into five categories in order to approximate the categories used for "Education of Respondent." To recapitulate:

TABLE 18
Weights Assigned to 38 Items in Index of European Acculturation

Item number	Item	Conant (Pokot)	Goldschmidt (Sebei)	Winans (Hehe)	Oliver (Kamba)	Edgerton	Mean score
	Education of respondent						
1	None (arbitrarily assigned weight zero)	0	0	0	0	0	0
2	1–4 years	7	3	7	3	2	4.4
3	5–6 years	9	5	9	7	4	6.8
4	7–8 years	10	10	9	9	7	9.0
5	9 or more years (arbitrarily assigned a weight of ten)	10	10	10	10	10	10.0
	Average of sons' education						
6	Zero	0	0	0	0	0	0
7	.01–.25 years	3	3	5	4	2	3.40
8	.26–.50 years	7	5	7	6	4	5.80
9	.51–.75 years	8	9	8	8	7	8.00
10	.76–1.0 years	9	10	9	9	10	9.40
	Average of daughters' education						
11	Zero	0	0	0	2	0	0.4
12	.01–.25 years	7	3	9	5	4	5.6
13	.26–.50 years	8	6	9	7	6	7.2
14	.51–.75 years	9	10	10	9	10	9.6
15	.76–1.0 years	10	10	10	10	10	10.0
	Religion						
16	Native only	0	0	0	0	0	0
17	Nominal world religion	6	3	8	3	2	4.4
18	Practising world religion	10	8	10	7	7	8.4
	*Footwear						
19	Native	0	0	0	0	0	0
20	European sandals or worn European shoes	5	2	5	2	2	3.2
21	Good European shoes and good socks	10	6	7	4	5	6.4
	*Cleanliness of Clothes						
22	Very dirty	1	0	2	1	0	.75
23	Dirty	1	1	3	2	1	1.60
24	Clean	8	2	4	3	2	3.80
25	Very clean	10	4	6	4	4	5.6
	Travel						
26	Tribal area only	0	0	0	0	0	0
27	Local European town only	6	1	3	1	2	2.6
28	Distant European towns	8	6	6	5	5	6.0
29	Frequent and/or prolonged visits to distant European towns	10	9	10	7	8	8.9
	**Roofing Types						
30	Native	0	0	0	0	0	0
31	Metal	9	6	8	4	3	6.0
	Participation in cash economy						
32	None	0	0	0	0	0	0
33	Minimal	2	1	4	3	1	2.2
34	Considerable	7	6	8	7	4	6.4
35	Intense	9	9	10	9	8	9.0
	Wage work						
36	None	0	0	0	0	0	0
37	Intermittent	3	1	5	5	3	3.4
38	Regular	7	8	10	7	7	7.8

*I collected these data in the field.
**The data on roofing were collected by Porter.

if a man sent all his sons to school each year that they were of school age until they were 18, the score would be 1.00. The same is true, of course, for daughters.

Please attempt to rank-order the 38 items—using Items No. 1 and No. 5 as your zero and ten baselines—before you assign weights to any of these items. All scores given will be averaged, and the final weight for each of the 36 items will be the mean score of all five judgments (those of each of the four ethnographers and my own).

The results of this weighting procedure are shown in table 18.

Using the mean scores shown in table 18, a score was computed for each of the 253 men who were interviewed. By adding these scores, it was possible to assign a single summative score to each of the eight sites as its collective acculturation score. The mean scores for each of the ten items in the index, as well as the sums of these items for each site, are shown in table 19.

A glance at the standard deviations shown in table 19 will suffice to make it clear that there is substantial individual variation within each of the eight sites. The nature of these individual differences and their possible significance is discussed in detail in chapter 9. The point at issue here is the possible significance of the differences in acculturation between population aggregates, that is, among the eight sites. It is immediately apparent that while there is a strong relationship between each of the ten items, the relationship is by no means perfect, and in some instances there are obvious anomalies. For example, the Hehe pastoralists scored disproportionately high on religion (IV); The Hehe farmers scored very high on footwear (V); and the Pokot pastoralists scored surprisingly high on travel (VII). Furthermore, two items, footwear (V) and roof type (VIII), contributed very little to the overall index. Finally, it might be argued that the index is too heavily skewed toward education, with three of the ten items devoted to that one interest.

All of these criticisms have some merit, but none, it seems to me, is particularly damaging. We would hardly expect so gross an index to have all ten items perfectly correlated; if it did, there would be no need for more than one item. Although some items contribute little to the sum of acculturation in any community, they all contribute something; and none obviously contradicts the other (only two of the scales have a correlation with the overall scale that is below .70, and none is below .60). As for an education bias in the index, I would only say that, given the nature of European influence in East Africa,

TABLE 19

Mean Acculturation Scores for All Eight Sites

Site	(I) Education of respondent	(II) Sons' Education	(III) Daughters' Education	(IV) Religion	(V) Footwear	(VI) Cleanliness	(VII) Travel	(VIII) Roof type	(IX) Cash economy	(X) Wage work	(XI) Total	(XII) Standard deviation
Kamba farmers	3.93	4.83	5.06	3.36	0.86	2.20	5.50	0.72	5.56	2.06	34.06	14.08
Hehe farmers	2.24	3.86	2.03	4.58	2.46	2.55	5.48	0.72	4.86	4.65	32.27	15.43
Sebei farmers	2.58	4.06	2.61	2.78	0.00	1.75	6.81	0.42	3.96	2.75	27.72	13.32
Kamba pastoralists	1.28	3.28	1.06	0.93	0.37	1.43	5.90	0.87	5.28	1.84	22.24	10.97
Sebei pastoralists	1.90	3.03	1.63	2.16	0.00	2.26	6.33	0.00	2.93	1.93	22.17	12.93
Hehe pastoralists	1.36	2.72	1.48	3.21	0.54	2.12	5.54	0.00	2.54	1.84	21.35	10.59
Pokot farmers	1.27	0.78	0.48	0.93	0.00	1.33	2.81	0.00	2.12	1.81	11.53	5.88
Pokot pastoralists	0.46	0.36	0.46	0.00	0.00	0.13	4.80	0.00	2.43	1.56	10.20	5.61
*Correlation coefficient	.866	.970	.835	.856	.632	.793	.605	.717	.811	.615		

*Correlation coefficient between each scale and the total scale

TABLE 20

Subjective Ratings of the European Acculturation of the Eight Sites

Date	Acculturation rating scale							
	Less acculturation	0	5	10	15	20	25	30	More acculturation

Sept. 29, 1962 — Less acculturation · 0 · 5 (PP) · 10 · 15 (PF, SP/KP/HP) · 20 · 22 (SF/KF/HF) · 25 · 30 · More acculturation

Jan. 20, 1963 — Less acculturation · 0 · 5 (PP) · 10 · 12 (PF) · 15 (SP/KP/HP) · 20 · 22 (SF/KF/HF) · 25 · 30 · More acculturation

May 16, 1963 — Less acculturation · 0 · 5 (PP) · 10 · 12 (PF) · 15 (SP/KP/HP) · 20 · 23 (SF/KF/HF) · 25 · 30 · More acculturation

Sept. 19, 1963 — Less acculturation · 0 · 5 (PP) · 10 · 18 (PF SP HP KP) · 20 · 24 (SF/KF/HF) · 25 · 30 · More acculturation

Index of acculturation totals from table 19

PP	PF	HP	SP	KP	SF	HF	KF
(10.20)	(11.53)	(21.35)	(22.17)	(22.22)	(27.72)	(32.27)	(34.06)

Key:
PP = Pokot Pastoralists   SP = Sebei Pastoralists   KP = Kamba Pastoralists
HP = Hehe Pastoralists   PF = Pokot Farmers   SF = Sebei Farmers
KF = Kamba Farmers   HF = Hehe Farmers

if we erred in the proportional weight given to education in the index, it was by giving it too little importance, not too much.

How accurate is this index? Is the sum of these individual ratings a proper reflection of the acculturation of a community? As I have emphasized before, the concern of this chapter is the relative acculturation of each site as an aggregate of its individual members. For this kind of comparison, I believe that the index is sufficiently precise and accurate. Surely it does show differences between the sites, and the magnitude of these differences is considerable. The most acculturated community, the Kamba farmers, is over three times as acculturated as the Pokot pastoralist community at the antipodal end of the scale. Unfortunately there is no objective, independent criterion with which we can compare and hence "validate" this index; however, there is a subjective criterion available in the form of impressionistic ratings of the differential acculturation of the eight sites, made before the results of the quantitative index were known. On the basis of my impressions and field notes, I attempted to rate the eight sites along a continuum from most to least European acculturation. I made the first such rating only a few days after leaving the last of the eight sites. I made three subsequent ratings, each three months apart, in order to determine how well my "independent" ratings would agree over the passage of time and with the blurring of my impressions. Each time I made the ratings, I reexamined my notes and reordered my recollections, but I did not look at my previous ratings. Table 20 presents the results of these ratings.

It is apparent that while my ratings vary somewhat over time, the *order* does not vary in any significant way. Comparing my subjective ratings with the quantitative ordering given in Scale XI, table 19, two major differences appear. In the first place, I allowed less overall spread (from the bottom to the top of the scale) than the quantitative index showed. In this instance I would judge that the quantitative ranking is more nearly correct. On the other hand, my subjective rating shows greater distance between the Pokot pastoralists and the Pokot farmers than the quantitative index does. Here, I feel that the quantitative index is misleading because its score for the Pokot pastoralists is inflated by a large amount of "travel," which was probably less significant as a vehicle for cultural contact than this index indicates.

Except for these two points, my subjective ratings and the quantitative index agree quite well. Certainly my subjective ratings are no more than that—subjective. But they do represent my best ef-

159

forts to compare the eight sites, and I have confidence in the results. My confidence was increased when Philip Porter, the project's geographer who, like I, visited all eight sites, independently ranked the sites and placed them in the same order that I, subjectively, and the index, "objectively," had.

Thus, despite some minor inaccuracies, the quantitative index is, I believe, a very good approximation of the relative degree of European acculturation present in the samples taken from each site.

THE RELATIONSHIP OF EUROPEAN ACCULTURATION TO THE RESPONSE PATTERN

Our concern with European acculturation was prompted by our suspicion that the farming sites in each tribe would be more influenced by European culture than the pastoral sites. As we have now seen, this suspicion was well founded; in each tribe, the farmers in our samples were more acculturated as a group than their pastoral counterparts.[5] This difference in acculturation is the central issue of this chapter. If every pastoral site was less acculturated than the farming site within the same tribe, how can we be certain that differences in interview responses between pastoralists and farmers were not the product of differences in acculturation rather than differences in economic mode of life? To answer this question we must examine the relationship between relative acculturation and interview response patterns.

One means of examining the relationship of relative European acculturation to the response patterns would have been to rank-order all the male respondents, irrespective of tribe or site, by their total acculturation score; this rank-order could then have been divided into convenient (e.g., quartiles) categories for comparative purposes. Such rank-ordering was not feasible, however, because the Pokot respondents so clustered at the bottom of the order that any such comparison was certainly to be culturally biased. A more efficient, less culturally contaminated, means of examining the response patterns

5. The differing acculturation of farmers and pastoralists has already led to discussion between McLoughlin (1966) and Goldschmidt (1967b). McGloughlin (1966, p. 1008) contended that, compared to pastoralists, farmers are *less* drawn into modern life, and are *less* receptive to European acculturative influence. Goldschmidt (1967b, p. 223) has effectively rebutted McGloughlin on the basis of the four tribes studied in the Culture and Ecology Project.

for the possible influence of acculturation was to deal with each site internally, by comparing the responses of, for example, the more acculturated Sebei farmers with those of the less acculturated Sebei farmers. Such comparisons were made in each site between various percentile groupings (e.g., deciles and quartiles), but considering the small numbers that were involved, the smaller percentile groupings were impractical. However, it was possible to rank-order all men in each site from most to least acculturated, and then to divide the rank-ordering of these men into quartiles, thirds, and halves. Because there were no statistically significant differences seen in results between quartiles, thirds, and halves, I will speak here of only one such analysis, by means of which the men in each interviewing site were rank-ordered from least to most acculturated and then divided into halves, all those above the median versus all those below the median.

When this comparison was made for each of the items in the interview, including the various content analysis variables, it was abundantly clear that the effect of a man's acculturation upon his responses was minimal. Although a few differences between the less and more acculturated respondents did occur in each site, these differences were typically minor and inconsistent. That is, responses that appeared to be linked to acculturation in one question would consistently be contradicted by the responses to a related question. What is more, almost without exception, differences that appeared to be related to acculturation were entirely specific to one site. In only one instance was there an acculturation-linked response difference that was shared by more than two of the eight sites.

Thus, among the Sebei, of all the responses given to the interview, only three statistically significant differences could be found. In the content analysis, the more acculturated Sebei farmers were four times as aggressive as the less acculturated Sebei farmers, and the more acculturated pastoralists were twice as fearful as their less acculturated counterparts. The more acculturated Sebei, both farmers and pastoralists, chose friends over age-mates, while the less acculturated valued age-mates over friends. There were only two such differences among the Pokot: more acculturated Pokot farmers tended (P < .10) to seek the intervention of the chief when conflict occurred, whereas the less acculturated Pokot farmers tended to say that they would act individually without consideration of the chief's authority. And, among the Pokot pastoralists, there was significantly more talk concerning warfare and bravery among the more acculturated men than among the less acculturated (P < .05). This difference is difficult

161

to interpret because there is such a slight difference in acculturation between the more and less acculturated Pokot pastoralists.

The sole acculturation-linked response differential among the Hehe was one concerning desirable conduct in wives (P < .01): the less acculturated men (both farmers and pastoralists) stressed the need for a wife to perform housework well, but the more acculturated men often spoke of the need to find a wife who could brew beer well (beer thus brewed could profitably be sold for cash). Among the Kamba, both farmers and pastoralists, there were no statistically significant response differentials between the more and the less acculturated.

By far the most striking finding to emerge from these comparisons was the agreement in response between the two acculturation classes. (I should repeat that this agreement was found to an equal degree when the rank-ordering was divided into quartiles and thirds.) Only one response difference between the more and less acculturated was found to hold up in more than one of the tribes; that was a response to the Rorschach that was found to be characteristic of the more acculturated persons in all sites. The more acculturated men projected more Western objects (e.g., airplanes, machines of various kinds, tools, maps, Christian crosses, and the like) into the content of their responses, whereas the less acculturated persons tended to mention animals or parts of animals. However, this difference did not extend to any of the interview questions: here more acculturated men did *not* speak of items of European material culture more often than less acculturated men did. Neither did they more often value money or European education. Thus, not only were there few response differentials of any kind between the more and less acculturated, even where we might expect to find European values or preferences expressed—as in answer to questions of the best or worst things in people or in life—there were no response differences that could be linked to differences in acculturation.

Perhaps the lack of differentiation between acculturation categories is best exemplified by a presentation of the data from one of the content analyses. Instead of dealing with mean scores here, I use sums in order to *increase* the apparent magnitude of any differences that occur. In table 21 are the sums of all mentions of 15 content analysis categories listed by acculturation category (respondent's placement below or above the median of a rank-ordering of all men). For greater simplicity of illustration, only two sites, chosen at random, are presented.

It should be apparent that the differences between persons above and below the median on a rank-order of acculturation are extremely slight. The same degree of agreement prevails for the other six sites, with the partial exception of the Sebei farmers, who (as previously mentioned) do show a statistically significant difference concerning "direct aggression."

A final examination of the influence of acculturation upon the response differentials was to correlate the acculturation scores of each

TABLE 21

COMPARISON OF CONTENT ANALYSIS DATA BY ACCULTURATION CATEGORY

Content analysis category*	Total number of mentions by acculturation category			
	Hehe pastoralists		Pokot farmers	
	Above median	Below median	Above median	Below median
Adultery	20	19	12	12
Affection	39	34	92	97
Bravery	0	1	19	19
Cattle	118	118	347	345
Clan	27	20	18	23
Cooperation	101	123	121	139
Direct aggression	187	192	221	208
Fear	58	69	91	90
Hatred	71	83	50	71
Industriousness	20	26	12	12
Insults	61	67	45	72
Land	90	92	78	75
Physical beauty	8	5	41	48
Valuation of cattle	86	94	209	190
Witchcraft	14	20	9	14

*These 15 categories were chosen at random from the full list of 31 content analysis categories shown in tables 2 and 22.

of the eight sites with all 31 content analysis categories. Because, like the acculturation scale, these content analysis data constitute an interval scale, they can be employed in such a statistical test. To determine the degree to which any of these 31 categories was related to acculturation, each of these response categories was correlated with the rank-order of sites by total acculturation score. Table 22 represents the results of this comparison.

Because the correlation coefficient (r) tends to exaggerate the degree of similarity between these scales, I have included the actual mean scores in table 22. Before the high correlation coefficients are

TABLE 22
Acculturation Index Compared with Content Analysis Scores

Content analysis category	Correlation(r) between CAS* and acculturation index	Content analysis scores of tribal sites							
		Kamba farmers	Hehe farmers	Sebei farmers	Kamba pastoralists	Sebei pastoralists	Hehe pastoralists	Pokot farmers	Pokot pastoralists
1. Adultery	−.055	.46	1.83	1.54	2.08	1.76	4.11	.90	1.34
2. Affection	−.891	.80	2.36	1.90	1.85	2.78	5.14	6.60	9.20
3. Cattle	−.865	18.39	14.51	14.90	18.33	16.90	19.92	25.71	25.69
4. Clan	.648	5.78	2.77	3.20	3.47	3.20	3.08	1.87	2.88
5. Concern with death	−.258	8.58	12.86	19.97	13.74	22.88	15.55	14.18	15.40
6. Concern with wrongdoing	.080	18.59	24.04	10.55	23.82	16.83	28.74	21.94	12.94
7. Conflict avoidance	.288	2.87	2.85	1.98	3.08	1.51	2.44	2.98	1.60
8. Cooperation	−.561	8.41	9.86	7.85	9.70	8.06	17.60	17.34	11.20
9. Depression	−.853	1.35	.99	.98	1.83	1.54	1.44	2.01	2.87
10. Desire for friends	−.349	2.19	1.26	2.35	2.79	4.23	.90	7.14	.76
11. Direct aggression	−.536	21.64	23.64	17.50	26.95	19.46	32.13	24.21	28.56
12. Disrespect for authority	.389	3.17	4.12	3.32	.29	1.03	.42	4.20	.16
13. Divination	−.270	1.04	.00	.06	1.69	1.82	.49	.22	1.59
14. Fatalism	−.084	.17	1.68	1.65	.09	2.13	2.65	1.34	.90
15. Fear	−.758	6.32	5.62	6.20	5.70	8.55	7.20	8.96	8.06
16. Fear of poverty	.049	4.00	1.87	.98	4.05	3.07	4.75	3.48	1.24
17. Guilt-shame	−.388	1.62	.21	.77	.80	1.58	.41	1.81	1.32
18. Hatred	.538	10.03	12.47	9.59	13.01	6.25	11.05	9.26	5.06
19. Hostility to opposite sex	.255	2.11	1.50	.92	3.28	.88	2.72	1.14	.81
20. Independence	−.822	1.23	1.80	1.55	3.00	2.36	2.71	2.58	3.05
21. Industriousness	.318	1.39	1.96	.90	1.93	.80	3.21	.89	.51
22. Insults	.330	6.67	20.19	6.60	7.77	4.15	17.71	8.18	4.86
23. Jealousy of wealth	.239	.82	1.92	.97	2.74	2.28	1.34	1.32	.10
24. Land	.406	12.76	6.19	8.60	10.24	8.13	14.52	8.77	2.18
25. Litigiousness	−.257	1.22	5.98	2.74	2.22	3.30	10.97	8.40	2.25
26. Physical beauty	−.695	.39	.65	4.85	1.46	1.67	.75	7.49	4.74
27. Respect for authority	−.412	4.25	3.47	4.63	5.74	7.03	5.94	4.86	5.12
28. Self-control	.293	9.06	15.91	5.91	11.33	6.17	16.47	6.66	8.42
29. Valuation of Cattle	−.754	7.65	3.93	2.37	6.36	4.41	6.19	12.15	12.93
30. Valuation of Independence	−.639	.46	.43	.81	2.78	1.94	2.40	1.02	2.99
31. Witchcraft	.228	.50	5.87	1.88	7.16	1.01	2.57	1.62	.95
Acculturation scores		34.06	32.27	27.72	22.24	22.17	21.35	11.53	10.20

taken too much to heart, I suggest that the reader examine the actual scores for each category.

A glance at this table is sufficient to indicate that most of the scores for the 31 content analysis categories do not correlate well with the acculturation index scale. Only six of these categories are strongly correlated (.70 or greater) with the acculturation scale. These six are: affection (no. 2), −.891; cattle (no. 3), −.865; depression (no. 9), −.853; fear (no. 15), −.758; independence (no. 20), −.822; and valuation of cattle (no. 29), −.754. In examining these six high correlations to see to what extent they appear to reflect differences in acculturation, we find that the content analysis score for the first of these, affection, does correlate in a high negative fashion with the acculturation score. It is not apparent why such a relationship should exist; indeed, theoretical support for this relationship is difficult to provide. And upon closer examination of the relationship, the high correlation is less impressive, being anchored at one pole by the low affection of the Kamba (a culturally stable trait) and at the other pole by the high affection of the Pokot (also a cultural trait). Thus it may be that the relationship is more apparent than real, being an artifact of a scale that opposes the Kamba and the Pokot. The two categories involving cattle (nos. 3 and 29) are also anchored, and heavily influenced, by the cattle-oriented Pokot. Here, too, the correlation appears to tell us more about cultural emphasis than acculturation. The other relationships, independence, fear, and depression, like the first three, show a high negative relationship to the acculturation scale.

What we appear to find, then, is that, as men in these four tribes become more acculturated, they become less affectionate, less concerned with cattle, less independent, less fearful, and less depressed. It seems to me unlikely that this complex of traits accords with any theory of the effects of acculturation in East Africa. It does, however, fit well with the nature of pastoralism in this area. Indeed, as we see in chapter 9, where these variables are again examined in relation to acculturation, each of these variables is better explained by recourse to ecology than by reference to acculturation. Recall, too, that when more and less acculturated men within each site were compared, none of these six variables was found to vary with degree of acculturation.

How then are we to resolve the central question raised by the fact that all farming sites are more influenced than their pastoral counterparts by European culture? I believe that the answer is clear. When men who are more acculturated are compared to men who are less acculturated, we find that their responses to the interview seldom differ. Conversely, when we relate these same responses to economic and environmental differences, as subsequent chapters do, a great many consistent differences occur. Thus, although the final assessment of the role of acculturation in determining interview response cannot be offered until the last chapter is reached, at this point in the analysis I believe it is correct to conclude that differential European acculturation appears to have had no significant influence upon the interview response patterns; therefore, we have no reason to believe that the systematic response differentials between pastoralists and farmers examined in chapters 7 are a product of differences in acculturation.

Initial
Pastoral-Farming
Comparisons

7

We turn now to a preliminary comparison of the interview responses of pastoralists and farmers. The way has been cleared for this comparison by the prior analyses of the possible influences of age, sex, and acculturation upon the responses. Some other variables could have been examined—and some are examined in later chapters—but sex, age, and acculturation were considered to be the major relevant variables, and their relationship to the response pattern has been found to be very slight.

This chapter presents a general review of the fundamental response differences between farmers and pastoralists. This comparison follows the original "four farming sites versus four pastoral sites" design of the research. To recapitulate for a moment, the design of the Culture and Ecology Project called for the controlled comparison of four societies, each of which contained the "same" internal differentiation into farming and pastoral sectors. Ideally, the four farming sectors would be highly similar as would the four pastoral sectors. It must be reiterated that the original design was not based upon the assumption that all four pastoral sites would be identical, nor that the four farming sites would be indistinguishable one from the other in their essential features, but it did anticipate a greater degree of similarity among related sites than was in fact found. As I have already mentioned, and as I discuss further in subsequent chapters, ethnographic realities were difficult to mold to the requirements of our original comparative design. For example, while the four farming sites were relatively similar in their essential economic and physical environmental features, the four pastoral sites were relatively dissimilar, with only the Pokot pastoralists providing a satisfactorily close approximation to our hypothesized pastoral economic model.

Thus, even if the pastoral and farming models should prove to be entirely correct, it would be unreasonable on our part to expect completely consistent response differentials between the farmers and pastoralists in all four tribes. Furthermore, it would be naïve to *confine* the analysis of the responses to this comparison of pastoral sites versus farming sites. These cautions notwithstanding, it is important to *begin* the analysis by looking for just such response differences, for it is basic to our inquiry to determine whether or not there are responses that do vary consistently between the farmers and pastoralists in all four societies. Of course, the inquiry should not stop at this point. Other inquiries must follow, and subsequent analyses of the same data will offer more varied and sophisticated perspectives upon the possible relationship between pastoralism or farming and evoked values, attitudes, and personality characteristics.

THE FINDINGS

The responses presented in this chapter include all instances in which a response pattern differed between farmers and pastoralists in all four tribes. In addition, some findings that differed in three out of the four tribes are reported when they are of particular significance. As before, I avoid complicated statistical procedures. The findings are presented in as direct and straightforward a manner as possible, for here, without question, if meaningful differences exist, it should be a simple matter to locate and describe them. And no complex tests of statistical significance should be required to establish the importance of these differences. The findings are grouped into general categories. Each set of findings is discussed, but, in this context, extended reference is not made to the original hypotheses. These hypotheses are examined in detail in the final chapter where all the relevant findings can be brought together.

CATTLE VERSUS FARMING LAND

One of the most fundamental, and seemingly most obvious, questions in the interview concerned preferences for cattle as opposed to farming land. It was anticipated that, given a meaningful choice between the two, pastoralists would more often choose cattle and farmers would more often choose land. In theory, nothing could have been more simple. In fact, however, while responses did differ in the direction expected in all four tribes, the responses constituted a surprise, both in magnitude and in kind. Table 23 presents the responses to the question that most directly posed the choice between cattle and farming land.

TABLE 23

RESPONSES OF PASTORALISTS AND FARMERS TO THE QUESTION: WOULD YOU RATHER OWN GOOD FARMING LAND BUT NO CATTLE, OR GOOD CATTLE BUT NO FARMING LAND?

	Response	
Tribe	Land	Cattle
Hehe		
Farmers	59	5
Pastoralists	55	9
Kamba		
Farmers	56	5
Pastoralists	56	6
Pokot		
Farmers	14	51
Pastoralists	10	53
Sebei		
Farmers	59	2
Pastoralists	49	15

In every one of the four societies, pastoralists said "cattle" more often than farmers did, but, obviously, the margin of difference is minute. For example, the Pokot pastoralists responded as expected with an overwhelming preference for cattle. Surprisingly, however, the Pokot farmers expressed a preference for cattle that was almost equally strong. Conversely, in the other three tribes the choices were dominated by an emphasis upon land, even among pastoralists. Perhaps, however, the choice offered by this question was not a meaningful one, being too elementary in its all-or-nothing phrasing. What we appear to find are culturally relative emphases, with only the Pokot, as noted in chapter 3, according cattle a primacy over land.

Other evidence, however, shows that pastoralists *did* more often express a valuation of cattle. Thus, when mean scores from the manifest content analysis category—all mentions of the desirability of cattle—were totaled, we found the distribution shown in tables 24 and 25.

Only among the Kamba did farmers mention the desirability of cattle more often than did pastoralists. The repeated references by Kamba farmers to cattle may reflect frustrated or wishful desire, or they may indicate economic valuation, for cattle are a principal means of storing wealth acquired by farming, and the Kamba farmers have far more wealth to store than do the pastoralists (see chapter 10). In-

TABLE 24

MEAN NUMBER OF MENTIONS PER PERSON OF THE VALUATION OF CATTLE

	Farmers		Pastoralists	
Tribe	Mean number of mentions	Sample variance	Mean number of mentions	Sample variance
Hehe	3.93	1.59	6.19	4.45
Kamba	7.65	9.61	6.36	7.45
Pokot	12.15	37.33	12.93	27.46
Sebei	2.37	1.04	4.41	1.61

deed, the situation is admirably stated by this aforementioned, wistful comment of an elderly Kamba farmer who thought about the relative merits of cattle and land and then said, sadly but realistically: "Cattle are beautiful, but land is life." For the pastoralists in all tribes, cattle are no less beautiful, but they can also be life.

TABLE 25

ANALYSIS OF VARIANCE OF EFFECTS OF TRIBAL AFFILIATION AND ECONOMIC MODE UPON VALUATION OF CATTLE RESPONSES

Source	df	MS	F
Tribal affiliation (A)	3	2,041.36	178.58 **
Economic mode (farmer/pastoralist) (B)	1	113.12	09.90 *
A × B	3	233.72	20.45 **
Error	496	11.43	

*$P < .001$
**$P < .0005$

When mentions of land are tabulated, as in tables 26 and 27, we find that, with the exception of the Hehe, farmers more often than pastoralists refer to land. The significance of these differentials is explored in greater detail in chapter 10, but for now I should say that the frequency of mention of land by pastoralists was no surprise; pastoralists may prefer cattle, but they also (except for the Pokot) value farming land, especially among the Hehe where cultivable land is in exceedingly short supply.

SOME RESPONSES THAT REFLECT THE PHYSICAL HABITAT

Although the influence of the physical environment upon the responses is often discernible, especially in the hot, dry, barren, and dangerous pastoral areas, it is seldom as directly related to the re-

TABLE 26

MEAN NUMBER OF MENTIONS PER PERSON OF FARMING LAND

Tribe	Farmers		Pastoralists	
	Mean number of mentions	Sample variance	Mean number of mentions	Sample variance
Hehe	6.19	9.18	14.52	62.25
Kamba	12.76	10.37	10.24	36.48
Pokot	8.77	16.81	2.18	13.84
Sebei	8.60	76.04	8.13	89.49

sponse differentials as it is in the few responses described in the paragraphs that follow.

For example, answers to the question, "What is the first useful task that a young girl is given?" corresponded very neatly to differ-

TABLE 27

ANALYSIS OF VARIANCE OF EFFECTS OF TRIBAL AFFILIATION AND ECONOMIC MODE UPON MENTIONS OF FARMING LAND

Source	df	MS	F
Tribal affiliation (A)	3	877.44	187.56**
Economic mode (farmer/pastoralist) (B)	1	12.30	2.63*
A × B	3	1,257.86	268.88**
Error	496	4.68	

*$P < .05$
**$P < .0005$

ences in the physical environment. Among the Kamba, Pokot, and Sebei, the farmers said that a young girl should be taught to farm; the pastoralists said that a young girl should be taught to fetch water. The differences here are quite marked, as shown in table 28.

Hehe responses to the same question did not follow this pattern. Their answers mentioned "grinding grain," "doing housework," "learning to obey adults," and "cooking," not farming or fetching water. Although it is not clear why the Hehe farmers should not have mentioned farming, it is obvious why the Hehe pastoralists did not

TABLE 28

Combined Kamba, Pokot, and Sebei Responses to the Question: What Is the First Useful Task That a Young Girl Is Given?

| | Response | |
Interview group	Farm	Fetch water
Farmers	109	12
Pastoralists	20	55

Note: $\chi^2 = 82.76$, $P \ll .001$, df $= 1$

mention fetching water: they lived along the banks of a river, and water was readily at hand.

Another difference occurred when the question was: "What is the first useful task a boy is given?" In all four tribes the predominant response was "herd small animals [goats or calves]"; however, in all tribes the pastoralists replied, "herd small animals," more often than the farmers did (229 pastoralists to 188 farmers). The difference is not great, but it is present in each of the four tribes.

The final example reflects the relatively greater safety of living in the mountainous farming areas. Historically and to this day, life has been safer in the mountains of East Africa than it has been on the open plains below. In pre-British days, intertribal warfare made life on the plains perilous, and sometimes altogether impossible. And even in the 1960s, the pastoral areas of these four tribes were subject to occasional cattle raids in the course of which human life was sometimes lost. Life on the plains was also in jeopardy from snakes and large animals such as lions, hyenas, and buffalo (the latter animal took several lives among the populations with which we worked during the course of this research). In addition, malaria was common on the plains, as were tse-tse flies and several endemic diseases such as smallpox and viral meningitis, both of which reached epidemic proportions during the period of our research. In short, from disease, from animals, and from man, the threats to life are greater on the pastoral plains than they are in the highland farming areas. This is not to suggest that the farming areas are completely tranquil sanctuaries. Far from it. Farmers have their problems from disease,

TABLE 29

MEAN NUMBER OF MENTIONS PER PERSON OF A CONCERN WITH DEATH

Tribe	Farmers		Pastoralists	
	Mean number of mentions	Sample variance	Mean number of mentions	Sample variance
Hehe	12.86	28.52	15.55	62.25
Kamba	8.58	10.37	13.74	36.48
Pokot	14.18	16.81	15.40	13.84
Sebei	19.97	76.04	22.88	89.49

drought, and witchcraft; but, relatively speaking, in terms of objective threats to life and limb, living is more hazardous in the lowland plains.

When a content analysis of a concern for, or fear of, death is made, this relative emphasis is borne out. As seen in tables 29 and 30,

TABLE 30

ANALYSIS OF VARIANCE OF EFFECTS OF TRIBAL AFFILIATION AND ECONOMIC MODE UPON MENTIONS OF CONCERN WITH DEATH

Source		df	MS	F
Tribal affiliation	(A)	3	2,418.18	57.60*
Economic mode (farmer/pastoralist)	(B)	1	1,130.22	27.00*
A × B		3	1,591.01	38.01*
Error		496	41.85	

*$P < .0005$

pastoralists in all four tribes mentioned a fear of death more often than their farming counterparts did. This relatively greater concern over death among pastoralists accords well with the realities of life in these environments.

KINSHIP PREFERENCES

Another set of responses that differed between farmers and pastoralists concerns preferences for various categories of kinsmen. In the course of the interview, several questions were asked that posed explicit choices between various classes of kinsmen and nonkinsmen. Responses to several of the questions failed to discriminate between farmers and pastoralists. Other questions, however, did elicit con-

TABLE 31

RESPONSES OF PASTORALISTS AND FARMERS TO THE QUESTION: IS IT BETTER TO HAVE MANY FRIENDS OR MANY KINSMEN (WHO ARE NOT CLANSMEN)?

Tribe	Response			Statistical difference
	Friends	Kinsmen	No answer*	
Hehe				
Farmers	17	44	0	$\chi^2 = 3.72$
Pastoralists	8	51	3	$P < .10$
				df = 1
Kamba				
Farmers	19	43	0	$\chi^2 = 1.77$
Pastoralists	13	51	0	$P < .20$
				df = 1
Pokot				
Farmers	42	23	0	$\chi^2 = 12.53$
Pastoralists	21	42	0	$P < .001$
				df = 1
Sebei				
Farmers	33	30	1	$\chi^2 = 1.76$
Pastoralists	26	38	0	$P < .20$
				df = 1

*Omitted in computation.

trasting response patterns. Thus, as is shown by table 31, when faced with a choice between friends and kinsmen (who were not clansmen), pastoralists in all four tribes tended to choose kinsmen, whereas farmers tended to choose friends.

Although the differences in each of these tribes do not always reach statistical significance, they are always in the same direction. That friends should have received greater preference in the farming areas was something of a surprise, although a partial explanation of this preference may be available, as we shall see in the course of subsequent discussions of this and other questions concerning the meaning of various kinship preferences.

A second, related difference involves a pastoralist emphasis upon the clan. Manifest content analysis of the number of times the clan was mentioned in a positive context (as distinguished from a neutral or derogatory one) indicates that, among the Hehe, Pokot, and Sebei, pastoralists mentioned the clan 25 percent more often than farmers did. Among the Kamba, the number of mentions of the clan among farmers and pastoralists was approximately equal. This same pattern was found in the answers to the following question: "Is it better to have many friends or many clansmen?" Again, the pastoralists more often chose clansmen, particularly among the Pokot. There appears to be a plausible explanation for this pastoral emphasis upon the clan; namely, that when clansmen are fewer in number because they are more widely dispersed, their importance in economic exchanges, particularly in bridewealth cattle exchanges, increases. This explanation was suggested by ethnographic and follow-up interviews in several sites. It should be recalled that both dispersion of clansmen and the importance of bridewealth cattle exchange is greater in pastoral areas. We might also suggest that among farmers everyday interaction focuses upon one's neighbors, those nonkinsmen who live nearby. Among pastoralists, it tends to focus upon kinsmen in extended families. In addition, among pastoralists the clan appears to possess important juridical functions, whereas these powers are often lost to some form of community-wide legal action among farmers.

Contrary to our expectations, preferences concerning age-mates did *not* differ between pastoralists and farmers. Neither when the choice was between friends and age-mates, nor when it was between clansmen and age-mates, was there any consistent pattern of response that distinguished farmers from pastoralists. The prevailing evaluation of age-mates (in all sites where they existed) was ambivalent. Mention of age-mates was as much negative as it was positive, and many respondents expressed both negative and positive feelings at the same time. This finding did not support our expectation that age-mates would be more important among pastoralists, but it may accurately reflect the diminishing importance of age-grades in present-day East Africa.

RESPECT FOR AUTHORITY

Farmers and pastoralists differed prominently in their expressed attitudes toward authority. Pastoralists were more given to express respect for authority, and not simply in the quantitative sense of mentioning respect for authority somewhat more often than did the farmers. A qualitative difference was also involved. Pastoralists

TABLE 32

MEAN NUMBER OF MENTIONS PER PERSON OF RESPECT FOR AUTHORITY

	Farmers		Pastoralists	
Tribe	Mean number of mentions	Sample variance	Mean number of mentions	Sample variance
Hehe	3.47	1.71	5.94	4.58
Kamba	4.25	2.79	5.74	3.92
Pokot	4.86	4.84	5.12	4.54
Sebei	4.63	5.81	7.03	12.82

expressed a sincere and deferential respect for the authority of various persons; in contrast, farmers expressed contempt, ridicule, or disrespect for the same categories of persons. An overall indicator of this difference can be seen in the content analysis category "respect for

TABLE 33

ANALYSIS OF VARIANCE OF EFFECTS OF TRIBAL AFFILIATION AND ECONOMIC MODE UPON MENTIONS OF RESPECT FOR AUTHORITY

Source	df	MS	F
Tribal affiliation (A)	3	64.51	12.51*
Economic mode (farmer/pastoralist) (B)	1	732.19	141.94*
A × B	3	492.78	95.53*
Error	496	5.16	

*$P < .0005$

authority." When all instances in which respect for, or obedience to, a person in a position of authority (e.g., father, chief, elder) were counted, the results were as shown in tables 32 and 33.

Obviously, in all four tribes the pastoralists expressed respect for authority more often than did the farmers, and in three of the four tribes (Hehe, Kamba, and Sebei), the magnitude of difference is substantial. When only traditional authority is considered (fathers, elders, prophets, etc.) and chiefs are excluded, this differential becomes still larger, increasing the number of respectful mentions by

TABLE 34

MEAN NUMBER OF MENTIONS PER PERSON OF DISRESPECT FOR AUTHORITY

	Farmers		Pastoralists	
Tribe	Mean number of mentions	Sample variance	Mean number of mentions	Sample variance
Hehe	4.12	4.33	0.42	0.029
Kamba	3.17	2.62	0.29	0.012
Pokot	4.20	1.25	0.16	0.006
Sebei	3.32	1.19	1.03	0.176

pastoralists over farmers to more than two to one. Conversely, the farmers in all four tribes expressed at least three times as many disrespectful or contemptuous mentions of authority as did the pastoralists. These responses are shown in tables 34 and 35. As before, when

TABLE 35

ANALYSIS OF VARIANCE OF EFFECTS OF TRIBAL AFFILIATION AND ECONOMIC MODE UPON MENTIONS OF DISRESPECT FOR AUTHORITY

Source	df	MS	F
Tribal affiliation (A)	3	75.22	63.49*
Economic mode (farmer/pastoralist) (B)	1	1,312.51	1,107.81*
A × B	3	1,771.67	958.80*
Error	496	1.18	

*$P < .0005$

the pastoralists were disrespectful, it was usually toward nontraditional authority, principally their chiefs. The farmers were equally disrespectful toward everyone in authority.

Three questions elicited clear pastoral-farming differences in attitudes toward authority: (1) "Under what circumstances can a younger brother tell an older brother that he is wrong?" (2) "Under

177

what circumstances can a young adult tell a *mzee* ['elderly man'] that he is wrong?" (3) "Should a man always obey his father without argument?" In each instance, pastoralists expressed much greater respect for the senior person than the farmers did. For example, table 36 lists the responses to the first of these three questions.

TABLE 36

RESPONSES TO THE QUESTION: UNDER WHAT CIRCUMSTANCES CAN A
YOUNGER BROTHER TELL AN OLDER BROTHER THAT HE IS WRONG?

	Response			
Tribe	*Never (or only if he is very wrong)*	*Whenever he is wrong*	*No answer**	*Statistical difference*
Hehe				
Farmers	16	45	0	$\chi^2 = 8.24$
Pastoralists	31	29	2	P < .01
				df = 1
Kamba				
Farmers	4	58	0	$\chi^2 = 45.53$
Pastoralists	41	23	0	P ≪ .001
				df = 1
Pokot				
Farmers	31	34	0	$\chi^2 = 24.94$
Pastoralists	56	7	0	P < .001
				df = 1
Sebei				
Farmers	30	33	1	$\chi^2 = 25.27$
Pastoralists	57	7	0	P < .001
				df = 1

*Omitted in computation.

The differences between farmers and pastoralists are substantial, with the pastoralists expressing respect for the older brother more often than the farmers. And I should repeat the earlier finding from chapter 6 that neither this difference, nor the differences in response to questions about the *mzee* or the father, is merely a product of greater acculturative disorganization in the lives of the farmers. On the contrary, it appears to represent a basic and perhaps long-standing difference between pastoralists and farmers in these four tribes. To clarify this difference, I should add that respect on the part of the pastoralists is backed by realities of economic existence in the protection, management, and accumulation of herds that may make the competence of older brothers and the wisdom of older men more important. And, of course, where cattle inheritance is so essential, respect for one's father is vital, for he holds these cattle as security against any sign of disrespect.

It may well be that these findings reflect the pastoralists' commitment to gerontocracy, not their respect for authority per se. In any event, it is clear that the findings do not relate directly to our hypothesis that formalized office would more often be found among farmers, whereas the pastoralists would more often give respect to achieved status. The findings discussed here are much more related to seniority than to these matters. Although ethnographic findings tend to support our anticipations about formal office and achieved status, the interview unfortunately did not elicit responses that bore directly upon these questions.

AGGRESSION

Several of the findings relate to aggression, and they all point to the same distinction between farmers and pastoralists: when the pastoralists spoke of aggressive action, they more often spoke of direct aggression; the farmers, on the contrary, were more likely to mention

TABLE 37

MEAN NUMBER OF MENTIONS PER PERSON OF DIRECT AGGRESSION

Tribe	Farmers		Pastoralists	
	Mean number of mentions	Sample variance	Mean number of mentions	Sample variance
Hehe	23.64	31.92	32.13	77.26
Kamba	21.64	23.23	26.95	21.25
Pokot	24.21	61.31	28.56	45.56
Sebei	17.50	38.56	19.46	26.11

an indirect method of aggression. An indication of this difference is seen in the content analysis category "direct aggression." When all mentions of direct verbal or physical aggression were totaled, the results were as shown in tables 37 and 38.

Although the differences between farmers and pastoralists were not great, pastoralists did express more direct aggression in every one of the four tribes. Consistent with this difference, pastoralists more often gave expression to a need for self-control. By self-control is meant an internal, psychological restraint rather than a social-

TABLE 38

ANALYSIS OF VARIANCE OF EFFECT OF TRIBAL AFFILIATION AND ECONOMIC MODE
UPON MENTIONS OF DIRECT AGGRESSION

Source		df	MS	F
Tribal affiliation	(A)	3	2,250.34	55.35*
Economic mode (farmer/pastoralist)	(B)	1	3,184.75	78.33*
A × B		3	4,435.27	109.54*
Error		496	40.66	

*P < .0005

TABLE 39

MEAN NUMBER OF MENTIONS PER PERSON OF THE NEED
FOR PERSONAL SELF-CONTROL

Tribe	Farmers		Pastoralists	
	Mean number of mentions	Sample variance	Mean number of mentions	Sample variance
Hehe	15.91	44.76	16.47	38.94
Kamba	9.06	16.56	11.33	29.16
Pokot	6.66	8.12	8.42	11.29
Sebei	5.91	5.43	6.17	10.11

TABLE 40

ANALYSIS OF VARIANCE OF EFFECT OF TRIBAL AFFILIATION AND ECONOMIC MODE
UPON MENTIONS OF NEED FOR PERSONAL SELF-CONTROL

Source		df	MS	F
Tribal affiliation	(A)	3	2,523.65	123.85**
Economic mode (farmer/pastoralist)	(B)	1	185.25	9.09*
A × B		3	281.19	13.80**
Error		496	20.38	

*P < .001
**P < .0005

institutional form of external constraint. When all mentions of a need for personal self-control were tabulated, the results were as shown in tables 39 and 40. The differences between farmers and pastoralists that are presented in these tables correspond well to those concerning direct aggression: the greater the expression of direct ag-

TABLE 41

MEAN NUMBER OF MENTIONS PER PERSON OF THE DESIRE TO AVOID CONFLICT

Tribe	Farmers		Pastoralists	
	Mean number of mentions	Sample variance	Mean number of mentions	Sample variance
Hehe	2.85	0.76	2.44	0.38
Kamba	2.87	0.59	3.08	1.17
Pokot	2.98	0.85	1.60	0.21
Sebei	1.98	0.36	1.51	0.14

gression, the greater the expressed concern with self-control.

On the other hand, the control mechanisms most often mentioned by farmers were social. When all mentions of the need for various persons to cooperate together, and to conform to custom in order to prevent the outbreak of conflict, were tabulated (tables 41 and 42), the farmers took the lead. The one exception to the pattern

TABLE 42

ANALYSIS OF VARIANCE OF EFFECTS OF TRIBAL AFFILIATION AND ECONOMIC MODE UPON MENTIONS OF THE DESIRE TO AVOID CONFLICT

Source	df	MS	F
Tribal affiliation (A)	3	45.67	81.72*
Economic mode (farmer/pastoralist) (B)	1	33.09	59.21*
A × B	3	58.19	104.13*
Error	496	0.56	

*$P < .0005$

of greater farming concern with social rather than personal control was the Kamba. As we shall now see, the Kamba continued to provide the exception to the rule that farmers more often expressed indirect aggression.

181

The following three instances illustrate differing aspects of the farming preference for indirect, rather than direct, means of aggression. First, farmers more often said that an insult had occurred, but they did *not* refer to direct confrontations in which one person openly insulted another. Instead, they made reference to oblique insults, saying that an act of omission gave insult, that a remark that was overheard was offensive, or that one person "intended" to insult

TABLE 43

MEAN NUMBER OF MENTIONS PER PERSON OF INSULTS

	Farmers		Pastoralists	
Tribe	Mean number of mentions	Sample variance	Mean number of mentions	Sample variance
Hehe	20.19	62.25	17.71	51.70
Kamba	6.67	4.45	7.77	9.86
Pokot	8.18	13.32	4.86	2.96
Sebei	6.60	4.28	4.15	6.25

another. When pastoralists mentioned insults, they typically referred to a direct verbal affront of one person by another in a face-to-face situation. Table 43 totals all mentions of insults of *both* kinds. The analysis of variance of the effect of tribal affiliations and economic mode upon these mentions is presented in table 44.

TABLE 44

ANALYSIS OF VARIANCE OF EFFECT OF TRIBAL AFFILIATION AND ECONOMIC MODE UPON MENTIONS OF INSULTS

Source		df	MS	F
Tribal affiliation	(A)	3	5,056.62	265.07*
Economic mode (farmer/pastoralist)	(B)	1	402.60	21.10*
A × B		3	661.48	34.67*
Error		496	19.08	

*P < .0005

Thus we see that not only were the insults different in kind (the farmers' insults were indirect, the pastoralists' were direct), but the farmers (except for the Kamba) mentioned insults more often.

The same pattern held for expressions of hatred. In tabulating mentions of hatred, every instance was counted in which it was said that one person hated, or wished serious harm or misfortune to, another, without mention of actual verbal or physical aggression. The results are shown in tables 45 and 46.

The farmers not only mentioned hatred more often than the pastoralists did, they also mentioned witchcraft more often. In much of Africa, witchcraft is perhaps the most common, and is certainly the most feared, form of indirect aggression. When all mentions of witch-

TABLE 45

MEAN NUMBER OF MENTIONS PER PERSON OF HATRED

| | Farmers | | Pastoralists | |
Tribe	Mean number of mentions	Sample variance	Mean number of mentions	Sample variance
Hehe	12.47	29.27	11.05	15.68
Kamba	10.03	11.49	13.01	29.38
Pokot	9.26	17.47	5.06	4.24
Sebei	9.59	13.47	6.25	20.98

craft (for these purposes it was not distinguished from sorcery) were counted, the results were as seen in tables 47 and 48.

Except for the consistently divergent Kamba, the farmers gave considerably greater evidence of a concern with witchcraft. All of these points about direct and indirect aggression are discussed in more detail in subsequent chapters. It is sufficient here to note that in three of the four tribes differences in aggression between farmers and pastoralists are impressively consistent, and these differences are in the direction that we had expected. The anomaly of the Kamba is considered further in subsequent chapters.

SEXUALITY

Another set of findings suggests that there was a heightening of sexuality among pastoralists. The first example comes from the responses to values picture 7, depicting an attractive woman carrying water as she walks along a secluded path. In this picture, a man is crouching behind a bush and watching the woman as she approaches him. Although the picture could have been interpreted as a sexual liaison, or as impending rape, it could as easily have been given a

TABLE 46

ANALYSIS OF VARIANCE OF EFFECT OF TRIBAL AFFILIATION AND ECONOMIC MODE
UPON MENTIONS OF HATRED

Source		df	MS	F
Tribal affiliation	(A)	3	687.96	38.78 **
Economic mode (farmer/pastoralist)	(B)	1	140.82	7.94 *
A × B		3	707.45	39.88 **
Error		496	17.74	

*P < .001
**P < .0005

TABLE 47

MEAN NUMBER OF MENTIONS PER PERSON OF WITCHCRAFT

Tribe	Farmers		Pastoralists	
	Mean number of mentions	Sample variance	Mean number of mentions	Sample variance
Hehe	5.87	4.88	2.57	0.828
Kamba	0.50	0.008	7.16	1.66
Pokot	1.62	0.16	0.95	0.036
Sebei	1.88	0.31	1.01	0.063

TABLE 48

ANALYSIS OF VARIANCE OF EFFECT OF TRIBAL AFFILIATION AND ECONOMIC MODE
UPON MENTIONS OF WITCHCRAFT

Source		df	MS	F
Tribal affiliation	(A)	3	310.46	318.13 *
Economic mode (farmer/pastoralist)	(B)	1	26.11	26.75 *
A × B		3	619.19	634.48 *
Error		496	0.976	

*P < .0005

TABLE 49

FARMER VERSUS PASTORALIST RESPONSES TO VALUES PICTURE 7:
WOMAN WATCHED BY MAN

	Response			
Tribe	No sex mentioned	Sex mentioned	No answer*	Statistical difference
Hehe				
Farmers	35	25	1	$\chi^2 = 16.29$
Pastoralists	13	46	3	P < .001
				df = 1
Kamba				
Farmers	15	40	7	$\chi^2 = 18.82$
Pastoralists	0	60	4	P < .001
				df = 1
Pokot				
Farmers	22	30	13	$\chi^2 = 4.00$
Pastoralists	15	46	2	P < .05
				df = 1
Sebei				
Farmers	45	19	0	$\chi^2 = 5.74$
Pastoralists	29ᶜ	30	5	P < .02
				df = 1

*Omitted in computation.

nonsexual interpretation. The responses are listed in table 49. There is nothing in the picture itself to account for this marked difference in response between farmers and pastoralists. Neither was there anything in the next values picture to account for the differential response pattern that it elicited. Values picture 8 depicted the inside of a house in which a man and woman were together in what could easily have been interpreted as a sexual embrace. The responses elicited by this scene are shown in table 50.

Both of these values pictures evoked marked quantitative differences in response between farmers and pastoralists: the pastoralists mentioned sex and adultery far more often than the farmers did.[1] In

1. The Pokot version of values picture 8 was, as mentioned earlier, drawn in error so that the man was identified by his mudpack as being unmarried. This fact may have influenced the Pokot pastoralists to see the scene as adultery, for the actors could *not* be seen as a married couple. However, the Pokot farmers, who are also familiar with the symbolism of the mudpack, did *not* see the scene as adultery, so the insignia of the mudpack may not have influenced response to any great degree.

addition, the content analysis confirmed the relatively greater pastoral emphasis upon adultery. Tables 51 and 52 give the results of the content analysis of all mentions of adultery. It is not merely that the pastoralists in all four tribes more often mentioned adultery, for such a differential might mean only that the pastoralists, who own more cattle and value them more, were more fearful that, in being apprehended in adultery, they would lose their cattle through legal fines. More than mere frequency of mention is involved. The pastoralists

TABLE 50

FARMER VERSUS PASTORALIST RESPONSES TO VALUES PICTURE 8:
MAN AND WOMAN TOGETHER INSIDE A HOUSE

	Response			
Tribe	No adultery mentioned	Adultery mentioned	No answer*	Statistical difference
Hehe				
Farmers	20	39	2	$\chi^2 = 15.93$
Pastoralists	3	57	2	$P < .001$
				$df = 1$
Kamba				
Farmers	52	10	0	$\chi^2 = 83.86$
Pastoralists	1	59	4	$P \ll .001$
				$df = 1$
Pokot				
Farmers	35	21	9	$\chi^2 = 42.14$
Pastoralists	3	55	5	$P \ll .001$
Sebei				$x^2 = 16.86$
Farmers	55	9	0	$P < .001$
Pastoralists	30	28	6	$df = 1$

*Omitted in computation.

emphasized their mentions of adultery and they enjoyed describing adulterous activities.

And so it was with all mention of sexual conduct. When sex was mentioned, there was a profound qualitative difference between the farming and pastoral responses. The pastoralists more often delighted in seeing sex; they reveled in it, exclaimed about it, grinned and chortled at the very thought of it, and, in short, thoroughly enjoyed themselves. When the pastoralists saw adultery, they did so with a vigorous "Aha!" quality: they were emotionally involved and often acted out their excitement with vivid gestures and facial expressions. In contrast, even when the farmers mentioned sex or adultery, they rarely (except for the Pokot!) invested their responses about either one with any visible emotion. Indeed, they were quite matter-of-fact.

Mention must also be made of two additional differential responses to sexuality. When asked about the proper sexual conduct for

TABLE 51

MEAN NUMBER OF MENTIONS PER PERSON OF ADULTERY

	Farmers		Pastoralists	
Tribe	Mean number of mentions	Sample variance	Mean number of mentions	Sample variance
Hehe	1.83	0.240	4.11	2.624
Kamba	0.46	0.012	2.08	0.533
Pokot	0.90	0.058	1.34	0.162
Sebei	1.54	0.36	1.76	0.281

unmarried males and females, farmers and pastoralists responded differently. Farmers tended to be very permissive for both males and females, saying that it was permissible for both sexes to have sexual relations before marriage. Pastoralists, on the other hand, tended to encourage male sexuality by saying that boys "needed" to have sexual

TABLE 52

ANALYSIS OF VARIANCE OF EFFECTS OF TRIBAL AFFILIATION AND ECONOMIC MODE
UPON MENTIONS OF ADULTERY

Source		df	MS	F
Tribal affiliation	(A)	3	89.28	159.60*
Economic mode (farmer/pastoralist)	(B)	1	163.75	292.72*
A × B		3	246.23	440.17*
Error		496	0.559	

*$P < .0005$

experience, but at the same time they more often said that female premarital sexual relations were decidedly improper. It was admitted that girls engaged in sexual relations before marriage, but such actions were deplored. Men and women agreed upon this view. Thus,

187

while it was clear that sexuality was accorded high value among the pastoralists, it was also indicated that this should be a male-oriented sexuality before marriage, becoming equally shared by males and females only after marriage.

7. PSYCHOSIS

When the respondents were asked to describe the behavior of a psychotic person, an interesting and entirely unanticipated difference between farmers and pastoralists emerged. The farmers were

TABLE 53

FARMER VERSUS PASTORALIST RESPONSES TO THE QUESTION:
HOW DOES A PSYCHOTIC PERSON BEHAVE?

| Tribe | Response | | | Statistical difference |
	Socially disturbing	Socially benign	No answer*	
Hehe				
Farmers	22	39	0	$\chi^2 = 12.44$
Pastoralists	5	52	5	$P < .001$
				df = 1
Kamba				
Farmers	32	20	0	$\chi^2 = 1.53$
Pastoralists	26	38	0	$P < .30$
				df = 1
Pokot				
Farmers	47	9	9	$\chi^2 = 22.82$
Pastoralists	19	30	14	$P < .001$
				df = 1
Sebei				
Farmers	21	42	1	$\chi^2 = 1.94$
Pastoralists	13	46	5	$P < .20$
				df = 1

*Omitted in computation.

more inclined than the pastoralists to describe psychotics in terms of socially disruptive conduct. The results are shown in table 53.

Although the differences were large in only two of the four tribes (the Hehe and the Pokot), the differences are in the same direction in all four tribes. Because the details of the methods by which this question and others concerning psychosis were asked and analyzed are described in another publication (Edgerton, 1966), considerations of methodology will not be gone into here. The essential point that needs to be repeated is this: all respondents were referring to the same term for a psychotic (the Swahili term, *wazimu*), a term that was used and understood in all tribes.

The findings presented in table 53 indicate that farmers tended to think of psychotic behavior as socially disturbing, while the pastoralists thought of it as relatively benign. It should be noted that these differentials were only seen in response to this, the first, question about psychosis. Two additional questions were asked: "How else do psychotics behave?" and, "Can you tell me about a specific psychotic person whom you have seen?" When the answers to these questions were examined, the pastoral-farming response difference disappeared. That is, when pastoralists and farmers gave their initial, their tip-of-the-tongue, impressions, they differed in the degree to which they described psychotics as dangerous, disturbing people; but when they were asked a second and third time to describe psychotic behavior, their answers no longer differed. I would conclude that there is no reason to believe that the psychotic behavior itself actually differed between pastoral and farming areas, but only that farmers and pastoralists were selective in their memory or feelings about such behavior. This interpretation is supported by other data concerning conceptions of psychosis in these four tribes (Edgerton, 1966).

This response differential is difficult to interpret. I would have expected just the opposite of what was found, with pastoralists having the lower tolerance for psychotic deviance. Apparently, however, it is the farmers who have less tolerance, perhaps because of the vulnerability of their crops to theft by psychotics, perhaps because of their fear of physical assault. Both are common reasons given for fear of psychotics.

The six remaining categories are relatively minor in emphasis, representing but one or two response differentials, rather than a set of related responses. As before, each of these categories is described and discussed separately.

MILITARY PROWESS

Values picture 3 presented a scene in which a number of spear-waving warriors were rushing toward some cattle being protected by nothing more than a few small boys. As shown in table 54, the responses to this scene indicated that there was a somewhat greater confidence in the outcome among pastoralists. Even though the dif-

189

ferences are small, they are consistently in the direction of a greater sense of military prowess among pastoralists. And, here, as before, simple inspection of the table is a better guide than any test of statistical significance. Throughout the protocols, farmers in their mountain sanctuaries spoke grandiosely about their courage and skill in military affairs, but whenever the rhetoric was cast aside, as I believe it was in the responses shown in table 54, pastoralists more often displayed quiet confidence in their military skills.

SUICIDE

Beliefs concerning suicide also differed between pastoralists and farmers. Pastoralists tended to say that women were more likely

TABLE 54

FARMER VERSUS PASTORALIST RESPONSES TO VALUES PICTURE 3:
ENEMY WARRIORS STEALING CATTLE

Tribe	Response			
	Enemy will steal cattle and escape	Enemy will be repulsed or pursued and killed	No answer or Don't know	Statistical difference
Hehe				
Farmers	53	4	4	$\chi^2 = 6.57$
Pastoralists	52	10	0	P < .05
				df = 2
Kamba				
Farmers	61	0	1	$\chi^2 = 17.36$
Pastoralists	46	5	13	P < .001
				df = 2
Pokot				
Farmers	19	13	33	$\chi^2 = 2.20$
Pastoralists	19	19	25	P < .50
				df = 2
Sebei				
Farmers	40	10	14	$\chi^2 = 5.31$
Pastoralists	27	16	21	P < .10
				df = 2

than men to kill themselves. This difference in response obtained in all four tribes, although it was large only among the Kamba and the Pokot.

When asked why men and women killed themselves, respondents in all four tribes agreed that men killed themselves because of poverty or quarrels with their wives or children, or because they were bewitched by a wife, a son, or an enemy. Women were said to kill themselves because of grief over the death of a child, because they were forced to marry a man whom they detested, or because their husband's protective magic had punished them for an act of adultery. Thus we see that the reasons for male suicide were problems that were common among farmers, while the reasons for female suicide were problems that were more characteristic of the pastoralists. Con-

TABLE 55

MEAN NUMBER OF MENTIONS PER PERSON OF DIVINATION

	Farmers		Pastoralists	
Tribe	Mean number of mentions	Sample variance	Mean number of mentions	Sample variance
Hehe	0.00	0.00	0.49	0.026
Kamba	1.04	0.073	1.69	1.08
Pokot	0.22	0.002	1.59	1.25
Sebei	0.06	0.0001	1.82	1.06

sequently, the reasons men and women were said to kill themselves fit well with the problems of everyday life in farming and pastoral areas, with men more subject to suicide risk in farming areas, and women more subject to this risk in pastoral areas. Unfortunately, I have no data that indicate the actual incidence of suicide in any of the tribal areas.

DIVINATION

As is evident from the content analysis data shown in tables 55 and 56, there was a greater mention of divinatory practice among pastoralists than there was among farmers. We originally hypothesized that this difference would exist because of the greater individuation and uncertainty of postoral life. Not only are there, in our view, more situations in which a pastoralist (we are speaking here principally of men) must make an explicit choice between alternatives, but there are also more in which he must do so without the guidance of routine, or tradition, or the counsel of his fellows. When these choices involve the imponderables of weather, enemy raiders, and wild animals among other things, recourse to divination seems a reasonable means by which an individual can reduce uncertainty. The data presented in tables 55 and 56 suggest that pastoralists are indeed

191

more involved with divination than are farmers. The ethnographic and follow-up data suggest that the data shown in the tables are probably an underestimate of the degree to which pastoralists are involved with divination. In fact, the interview was not well constructed for the elicitation of divination, and the mention of divination (even more so than most variables) can be taken only as a relative, not an absolute, indication of the importance of divination in the lives of these eight populations.

AFFECTION

Not only was there a heightening of sexuality among the pastoralists, there was a greater expression of nonsexual affection as well. As used here, affection is defined as nonsexual. It includes expressions

TABLE 56

ANALYSIS OF VARIANCE OF EFFECTS OF TRIBAL AFFILIATION AND ECONOMIC MODE
UPON MENTIONS OF DIVINATION

Source		df	MS	F
Tribal affiliation	(A)	3	49.37	112.14*
Economic mode (farmer/pastoralist)	(B)	1	143.58	323.91*
A × B		3	102.10	231.93*
Error		496	0.440	

*$P < .0005$

of love, tenderness toward a child, a strong positive emotional attachment to another person, and the like. All mentions of such expressions are tabulated in tables 57 and 58.

Although the pastoralists have a "reputation" for brutality in many parts of East Africa and this reputation appears to be deserved, they also gave a freer expression to affection. Indeed, it may well be that they are more willing, and perhaps more able, than farmers to express affect of all kinds, positive as well as negative. This point is elaborated in chapter 8, which deals more explicitly with personality.

DEPRESSION

If pastoralists were more given to the expression of positive affect, so were they more likely to express depression. In all four tribes, pastoralists more often expressed gloom, despair, pessimism, and a strongly depressive feeling tone. In tabulating mentions of de-

TABLE 57

MEAN NUMBER OF MENTIONS PER PERSON OF AFFECTION

Tribe	Farmers		Pastoralists	
	Mean number of mentions	Sample variance	Mean number of mentions	Sample variance
Hehe	2.36	0.672	5.14	1.99
Kamba	0.80	0.677	1.85	0.436
Pokot	6.60	7.34	9.20	16.00
Sebei	1.90	0.884	2.78	1.90

TABLE 58

ANALYSIS OF VARIANCE OF EFFECT OF TRIBAL AFFILIATION AND ECONOMIC MODE UPON MENTIONS OF AFFECTION

Source	df	MS	F
Tribal affiliation (A)	3	1,052.79	285.79*
Economic mode (farmer/pastoralist) (B)	1	420.81	114.23*
A × B	3	591.83	160.66*
Error	496	3.68	

*$P < .0005$

TABLE 59

MEAN NUMBER OF MENTIONS PER PERSON OF DEPRESSION

Tribe	Farmers		Pastoralists	
	Mean number of mentions	Sample variance	Mean number of mentions	Sample variance
Hehe	0.99	0.084	1.44	0.25
Kamba	1.35	0.221	1.83	0.462
Pokot	2.01	1.23	2.87	1.61
Sebei	0.98	0.185	1.54	0.578

pression, expressions of fear of death were not counted, for, as has already been indicated, the pastoralists were also more involved than the farmers with such fears. Tables 59 and 60 are a tabulation and analysis of these depressive responses.

The nature of this depression among pastoralists was varied and included grief over the loss of a loved one, sadness over advancing age, a sense of despair over bad fortune, and, quite often, a concern with impotence. Frequently, however, it was a generalized sadness or

TABLE 60

ANALYSIS OF VARIANCE OF EFFECTS OF TRIBAL AFFILIATION AND ECONOMIC MODE
UPON MENTIONS OF DEPRESSION

Source		df	MS	F
Tribal affiliation	(A)	3	40.60	69.65*
Economic mode (farmer/pastoralist)	(B)	1	43.49	74.60*
A × B		3	59.39	101.88*
Error		496	0.583	

*P < .0005

hopelessness, one without a specific referrent or antecedent. This matter, too, is examined in detail in chapter 8. Here, I should note only that this differential was entirely unexpected. We had not anticipated that depression would differentiate farmers and pastoralists at all, much less that it would characterize pastoralists.

INDEPENDENCE

This final difference between pastoralists and farmers is one of the most important, for, perhaps more than any other, it serves to characterize pastoral values and personality. This difference concerns independent action. When the number of mentions of an individual's explicitly taking independent action was tabulated, the distribution shown in tables 61 and 62 resulted.

We had predicted that independence of action would typify pastoralism, and tables 61 and 62 make it obvious that there was a greater number of such mentions among pastoralists in all tribes. What is more, when all mentions of instances in which independent action is valued—that is, when it was highly praised or said to be desirable—were tabulated (tables 63 and 64), the differences were still more impressive.

194

Thus, when the valuation of independent action was considered, the pastoral response remained high, but the farming response decreased markedly. It would appear that independence of action is a pastoral trait, par excellence, and so it should be in an environment

TABLE 61

MEAN NUMBER OF MENTIONS PER PERSON OF INDEPENDENT ACTION

Tribe	Farmers		Pastoralists	
	Mean number of mentions	Sample variance	Mean number of mentions	Sample variance
Hehe	1.80	0.774	2.71	2.02
Kamba	1.23	0.423	3.00	1.35
Pokot	2.58	1.416	3.05	1.72
Sebei	1.55	0.548	2.36	1.12

where individuals must make many decisions regarding themselves and their herds, usually without recourse to tradition, or group consultation, and, what is more, without delay. In a world where man and his animals are vulnerable to so many threats, life without independent decisions, rapidly made and carried out, would be fragile indeed.

CONCLUSION

Each one of the categories that was described so briefly here could have been the subject of an extended analysis. Indeed, each

TABLE 62

ANALYSIS OF VARIANCE OF EFFECT OF TRIBAL AFFILIATION AND ECONOMIC MODE UPON MENTIONS OF INDEPENDENT ACTION

Source	df	MS	F
Tribal affiliation (A)	3	38.41	32.79*
Economic mode (farmer/pastoralist) (B)	1	123.48	105.39*
A × B	3	174.28	148.76*
Error	496	1.17	

*P < .0005

one would have been, were a final understanding of the issues at hand to be attempted in this chapter. Such an understanding was not intended, however, for this chapter is no more than an introduction to the basic differences in response among all four pastoral sites and all four farming sites.

In conclusion to this introductory appraisal we must ask how successful the original comparative design was. How many basic differences could have been expected, and how many were, in fact, found? Such an appraisal is more difficult than it sounds, because not every question in the interview was expected to produce pastoral-farming differences; nevertheless, some evaluations are possible. For example, the 85 questions that were asked in the interview were reduced to 66 coded sets of answers. Of these 66, about 20 percent showed differences between pastoralists and farmers in all four tribes. When it is considered that some of the 66 questions were general-pur-

TABLE 63

MEAN NUMBER OF MENTIONS PER PERSON OF THE
VALUATION OF INDEPENDENT ACTION

| | Farmers | | Pastoralists | |
Tribe	Mean number of mentions	Sample variance	Mean number of mentions	Sample variance
Hehe	0.43	0.005	2.40	1.96
Kamba	0.46	0.014	2.78	2.46
Pokot	1.02	0.078	2.99	1.88
Sebei	0.81	0.026	1.94	1.08

pose probes rather than specific questions to which we had anticipated differential response, the findings become increasingly positive. Thus, if we eliminate the 20 or so questions that were intended to be general probes, then some 40 questions remain for which we had anticipated response differences. Of these, over 30 percent showed differences between pastoralists and farmers in all four tribes.

In addition to these questions, there were nine values pictures. Each one of these was directly intended to evoke differences between pastoralists and farmers. Of the nine pictures, three (or 33 percent) showed differences between pastoralists and farmers in all four of the tribes. Finally, there were 31 content analysis categories, all but a few of which were expected to reflect pastoral-farming differences. Ten of these (over 30 percent) showed differences between pastoralists and farmers in all four tribes (another five showed differences in three of the four tribes).

What can we conclude concerning the probabilities that these pastoral-farming differentia were no more than the product of chance? First, it seems highly unlikely that chance would have directed so many of these response differentials to conform to our expectations based upon the pastoral and farming models. Most of these differentials *were* anticipated. What is more, although I am reluctant to invoke strict probabilistic formulas, in this instance, it may be useful to do so. If we convert the farming-pastoral differences into a binary (yes-no) set, such as that in a coin flip, then the probability that the pastoral sites will differ from the farming sites in all four tribes on any given question is one in sixteen. By this criterion, all the findings—from the 66 questions, from the 31 content analyses, and

TABLE 64

ANALYSIS OF VARIANCE OF EFFECTS OF TRIBAL AFFILIATION AND ECONOMIC MODE
UPON MENTIONS OF VALUATION OF INDEPENDENT ACTION

Source		df	MS	F
Tribal affiliation	(A)	3	10.49	11.16*
Economic mode (farmer/pastoralist)	(B)	1	430.07	457.54*
A × B		3	581.76	618.92*
Error		496	0.94	

*$P < .0005$

from the nine values pictures—could be expected to have occurred by chance less than one time in one thousand.

I think we must conclude that there are differences between the responses of farmers and pastoralists which could merit further investigation.

197

The
Rorschach 8
Findings

To imagine an anthropologist happy with the Rorschach as a key to
personality is every bit as difficult as Camus's task of imagining Sis-
yphus happy. Yet, with Sisyphus-like dedication, anthropologists continue to toil over Rorschach's ink stains. My own decision to confront
unsuspecting Africans with the task of finding meaning in these blobs
of ink was a calculated risk that was informed by several considerations. As I indicated in chapter 1, the Rorschach was utilized because
I wanted to present respondents with some sort of ambiguous stimulus material. The pretest had shown, as had much cross-cultural research by others, that nonliterate persons are able to project meaning
into the Rorschach blots. The existence of this body of comparative
research was an additional inducement for the use of the Rorschach
in this study.[1] Furthermore, the research design of the Culture and
Ecology Project offered opportunities for comparison that most Rorschach studies have lacked.

Yet, like so many anthropologists and psychologists before me,
I was uneasy about the technique as a research device, for, as a massive
literature has made clear, Rorschach technology has continued to
suffer from the basic antimony between qualitative sensitivity and
methodological precision. As critics have justly pointed out, the technique has built-in configurational biases (e.g., bilateral symmetry),
procedural tactics that make rigorous comparison difficult (e.g., the
"inquiry"), and criteria for interpretation that must still be treated

1. For a review of the use of the Rorschach in cross-cultural research,
see Hallowell (1956) and Lindzey (1961). For Africa, see especially
Pfeiffer (1959), Pfeiffer et al. (1963), and Thomas (1959, 1963).

as being largely conjectural. As a result, validation studies often render negative conclusions.[2]

In an effort to minimize these objections and still retain the fundamentals of the technique, I made a number of modifications in procedure (principally, the use of the first card as an instruction card, confining scoring to the first response per card, and the omission of the inquiry). As a result, it is only fair to say that my use of the Rorschach may distress many clinicians. By proceeding as I did, I have also reduced the comparability between my findings and those from other Rorschach research that have followed clinical protocol more or less exactly. It must also be admitted that I have reduced the richness and individuality of response that has stood as the hallmark of the technique.

My reasons for so abbreviating and altering the standard Rorschach procedure were partly statistical (as I mentioned in chapter 1), but they were also dictated by the practical realities of Rorschach research in tribal Africa. The inquiry had already been rejected by African respondents in Doob's[3] research, and in my own pretest. Moreover, the responses given during the pretest were almost without exception quite brief, even terse. Rarely was more than one response given to each blot, and that response was seldom long or detailed. Thus, had I expected these eight populations to produce several long and revealing responses to each card, I would have guaranteed the incommensurability of my findings. Instead, I chose to use the Rorschach technique so that it was acceptable to the least perceptive and articulate of the 500 respondents. I wanted everyone to respond, not the articulate few; and I wanted to be able to compare what was said by inarticulate pastoralists in the Masol plains with what was said by the relatively expressive farmers in the Sebei highlands. I concluded that the most I could expect from every respondent in the sample was one brief response. I did not exclude the possibility of more voluble response, but neither did I depend upon it. My intent, of course, was to maximize comparison within the four tribes and eight sites of this study. Possible comparison with populations studied by others, should that prove useful, had to remain a secondary consideration.

Except for the departures already mentioned, administration of the Rorschach followed procedures detailed in Klopfer et al. (1954), and so did the scoring of the response protocols. Although Rorschach

2. For example, see Lindzey (1961) and Zubin (1954).
3. Doob (1960).

administrative procedures are relatively uniform, there are several scoring (and related interpretive) systems for the Rorschach, among the best known of which are those of Beck and Klopfer. In scoring, if not always in interpretation, I have followed Klopfer's system. In this system, there are both quantitative and qualitative scoring procedures. The qualitative system, which analyzes both the content and the sequence of responses, follows a complex series of cues to be located in the sequence of responses given to each card. The system is complex and subjective. The quantitative scoring system is only slightly less complex, but it is a good deal less subjective. It consists of a large number of criteria by which each response is classified with regard to its "location" (all or some part of the blot), its "determinants" (e.g., form, color, movement, shading, or several of these), its "content" (animal, human, abstract, etc.), and its "form level" (the degree to which the analyst believes that the percept the respondent gives corresponds to the actual configuration of the blot). In the scoring of all of these quantitative features except form level, I have followed the Klopfer system to the letter. All the response protocols were scored by me and by a graduate student in clinical psychology who had been trained in the Klopfer technique. Differences between our scoring were resolved by the mediation of a third person, a psychologist experienced in the use of the Klopfer scoring system. There were few occasions where mediation was necessary, however, as the overall interjudge agreement between the two sets of scores was .91. The relevant quantitative findings will be presented first; the qualitative analysis will follow.

SOME FINDINGS COMMON TO ALL TRIBES

In some significant ways, most of the tribal Africans who responded to these Rorschach cards were alike. Most striking was their low ambiguity tolerance, an inability or unwillingness to accept the blots as ambiguous stimuli. For most of the respondents, each card was *a* picture of *a* particular thing. It was this fixed idea that led me to employ the first card as an instruction card designed to point out the possibility that many "things" could be carved out of a single blot; however, this instruction card notwithstanding, there remained a marked tendency to reject ambiguity. In all tribes, responses tended to be highly form-specific, but what is more, respondents typically made it clear that they were engaged in finding the one and only thing hidden in the blot. I saw no evidence to suggest, however, that most respondents felt that they were involved in a test on the basis of which they would somehow be evaluated. Rather, it seemed that they simply could not easily accept the suggestion that the blots were basically ambiguous.

Strict reality orientation of this sort is not uncommon among nonliterate peoples,[4] but these four African populations appeared to be extreme in their lack of tolerance for ambiguity. Those who wish to speculate might note that these four societies also tend to be quite specific and concrete in their approach to life (I am tempted to say in their cognitive style), and they are uniformly lacking in plastic art. Neither do they possess any sort of elaborated oral literature. Even the Kamba, who have recently taken up wood carving for a commercial market, exhibit not the least sign of improvisation in their "art." These carvings are as stereotyped as if they were produced by machine, and new designs, when they occur, seem to be the inventions of non-Kamba who control the industry.[5]

Although it is quite common for nonliterate populations to produce heavily form-determined Rorschach responses (responses that appear to be determined by form alone, not by color, shading, or movement), the African records from these four societies were unusually lacking in the perception of humans in motion, yet animals in motion and inanimate objects in motion were seen relatively frequently. If one were to follow traditional Rorschach interpretation of these ratios, the conclusion might be that these Africans are relatively anxious and impulsive, yet lacking in strong inner controls and imaginal ability. This high anxiety and poor imaginal ability would fit well with the ethnographic picture; the high impulsivity and poor self-control are less easy to assess. I believe that these Africans worry considerably about controlling their impulses but that they achieve control under most circumstances. The adequacy of this summary depiction will be clarified when more of the evidence has been presented.[6]

These Africans also displayed far greater difficulty in responding to the so-called "soft" colors (pastels) of the last three cards than they did to the "hard," bright reds of the second and third blots. For example, the reaction time (the latency period between picking up

4. Hallowell (1956); see also Kaplan and Lawless (1965).

5. Elkan (1958).

6. For a review of inferences regarding personality in Africa, see Crijns (1966).

the blot and responding) was longer for the soft-color blots; these blots were more frequently rejected (not responded to); and the responses that were given to these pastel blots were lower in form level than were the responses to the blots containing bright colors. A traditional interpretation of this finding might have it that these people were not shocked or troubled by what is harsh or challenging or brutal about their world, but that the more soft or tender experiences were difficult for them. This interpretation, too, is consistent with my ethnographic observations concerning these people: they are more at home with harsh emotions than tender ones.

On the basis of the frequency with which certain concepts are seen in certain cards by European populations, some responses have been designated as "populars" (very frequently seen percepts). For example, the Klopfer system recognizes ten such popular responses (card 1, winged creatures; card 2, animal in black portion of card; card 3, two humans in a bending position; card 3, the center red area seen as a bow tie or butterfly; card 5, any winged creature; card 6, the skin of any animal; card 8, a four-legged animal in motion; card 10, to the blue area, a many-legged animal such as a crab; to the center green area, an elongated animal such as a caterpillar or snake). As Hallowell has noted, to the surprise of no one, populars based upon Western Rorschach records are not necessarily seen with similar frequency in non-Western populations.[7] However, based upon his analysis of six American Indian populations, Hallowell did find four "universal" populars, percepts that were seen in all tribes. In order of their universality in these six Indian tribes, they were: "animals" in card 8, "animals" in card 2, "rabbits" in card 10, and "winged creature" in card 5.

The findings from the four African populations provide an interesting comparison. The "animal" in card 8 was seen by at least 80 percent of the respondents, men and women, in all four tribes. Typically, the animal was seen in motion. The "animal" in card 2, however, was seen by only a handful of respondents among the Hehe, Pokot, and Sebei, but 97 out of 126 Kamba saw this "popular." Rabbits in card 10 were never seen, not even once in any of the tribes. Approximately 40 percent of the respondents among the Hehe, Pokot, and Sebei, but only 6 percent of the Kamba, saw the "winged creature," a bird or a bat, in card 5. The remaining 94 percent of the Kamba respondents saw a rabbit in this card.

All of the American Indian "universal" populars are animals,

7. Hallowell (1956).

a point which Hallowell noted. However, one of the most theory-laden populars in the Klopfer system is human: two human figures in a bending position, seen in action, in card 3. This popular was seen 35 times by the Hehe, 21 times by the Kamba, 7 times by the Pokot, and 39 times by the Sebei. When this popular was seen, it was seldom seen in motion. Rather, it was given as a static, emotion-free response. Contrariwise, another Klopfer popular, the red butterfly in card 3, was seen by only four respondents all told (all four of these were Sebei). The blue, many-legged animal Klopfer popular in card 10 was likewise rarely seen.

In conclusion, it seems reasonable to suggest that while the frequency with which certain allegedly "popular" concepts are seen will vary from population to population, that even populations from quite dissimilar environments may be able to see some of the same populars seen by American respondents. The animals in card 8 are a case in point. They are a popular in the Klopfer system, they are the leading universal among Hallowell's six American Indian samples, and they were seen by over 80 percent of the respondents in these four East African tribes.

Turning to form level, I must first say that efforts to evaluate the degree to which an African respondent's percept "fits" the objective configuration of an inkblot are difficult at best, and without benefit of a prolonged inquiry of the kind that I avoided, such evaluations must remain highly tentative. Nonetheless, I attempted to judge the form level of the responses and found that, with the exception of a very few responses (usually global and vague responses to the entire blot), the responses were both specific and accurate. I was able to locate each response on a standard location sheet with no more difficulty than I would have with most American records I have seen. The vast majority of responses in all study sites were accurate ones; they fitted the blots well.[8]

One of the most striking findings emerges from the content of these African responses. Throughout the Rorschach protocols in all tribes there was a remarkable lack of hostile responses, and there were still fewer overtly aggressive ones. Even such characteristic non-Western "aggression" responses as "two animals fighting over something" were quite uncommon, while actual conflict between humans was mentioned *only twice* out of the several thousands of responses that were given. Furthermore, witchcraft was not mentioned *even*

8. I used a simplified scoring system which included a basic estimate of accuracy as well as two decrements for inaccuracy and two increments for exceptional accuracy.

once in any Rorschach response. Overtly sexual responses were only slightly more frequent: all four tribes combined produced only 17 responses that mentioned sex in any way, and 14 of these were Hehe responses concerned with menstruation.

This absence of aggression and sexuality in the responses is notable. Throughout the rest of the interview, respondents freely referred to all manner of aggression, including witchcraft, and sexual matters were a common subject of discourse by men and women alike. Yet neither subject was common in the Rorschach which instead typically elicited percepts involving animals, or features of the physical environment. Even here, however, there were anomalies. For example, such a ubiquitous aspect of African life as cattle was never once mentioned in a Rorschach response in any tribe!

All this, I think, points to the low ambiguity tolerance of these Africans. They saw what was for them *most* realistic—certain animals, birds, insects, fields, trees, landscapes, clouds, rocks, and material objects. They neither carried over the content of their previous interview response by mentioning sex, aggression, poverty, cattle, or the like, nor projected into the Rorschach blots any manifest content of a sort *not* mentioned in the remainder of the interview. That is, they did not often reveal hidden wishes, secret desires, or unconscious fantasy material.

Their approach to the Rorschach cards was typically matter-of-fact, literal, and parsimonious. Of course, it may be that this kind of approach was dictated by some subtle feature of the interviewing situation, but if so, it did not affect all respondents. In each of the eight sites, a few individuals did invest themselves in the Rorschach with the same loquacious delight typical of graduate students in the United States. In seven of the sites, only two or three persons (women as often as men) produced such remarkable responses; among the Sebei farmers, however, there were seven or eight persons who gave such Rorschach performances. These unusual individuals produced richly complex, sometimes even fantastic, responses, and they reveled in the ambiguity of the blots. Such individuals produced 40 or 50 complex responses with ease, and I could no more have quenched their pleasure in dealing with the ambiguity of the Rorschach than I could have produced similar delight in the majority of the respondents.[9] Since these unusual individuals were responding to the same instructions and situation that produced the relatively sparse re-

9. An analysis of these unusual individuals is in preparation.

sponses of the majority, I conclude that it is not to the situation but to the people themselves that we must look for an explanation of the findings. (I should note, however, that even these inventive respondents saw little sex or aggression, and no cattle.) Although I have emphasized the commonality of response among these African tribesmen, it is proper that I conclude by calling attention to the variability that was also seen. There can be no doubt that there are substantial individual differences in all of these tribes, yet it is the commonality, not the individuality, of these Rorschach performances that is so impressive.[10]

A QUANTITATIVE COMPARISON OF PASTORALISTS AND FARMERS

Quantitative analysis of the Rorschach responses pointed to some statistically significant differences between farmers and pastoralists. Some of these differences involved the general approach to the task. For one thing, pastoralists less often than farmers accepted any of the suggested percepts in card 1 (P < .001); that is, pastoralists invented their own responses, while farmers were satisfied to use one of those I had already suggested. But pastoralists also rejected more of the blots without responding than farmers did (P < .01). Finally, when pastoralists did respond, they did so after a longer delay, with delays of 30 seconds before responding being common (P < .01). In all of these instances, the differences between pastoralists and farmers were present in all four tribes. I believe this suggests that the farmers' perceptual and verbal skills were more facile, more attuned to the task of responding to the Rorschach blots, and that the farmers were also more eager to please, less prideful, and less arrogant than the pastoralists, who retained their independence even in the Rorschach performance.

There was another difference involving the location of the percepts that were seen. Farmers tended to utilize the entire blot in their responses, whereas pastoralists more often used relatively small portions of the blots for the location of their responses (P < .01). These whole-blot responses of the farmers were neither intricate nor well organized; instead they tended to be rather vague and global perceptions of the cards. Conversely, the pastoralists' use of smaller parts of the blots was marked by a greater precision and specificity.

10. For further discussion of variability, see chapter 9.

There was one reversal of this trend; the farmers more often (P < .01) than the pastoralists tended to use tiny portions of the blots (dd). Klopfer et al. (1954) hypothesized that such an emphasis on tiny (dd) details of the blot represents obsessional, meticulous, or pedantic trends. Thus, combined with the earlier mentioned tendency to respond with rather vague whole-blot responses, we find an approach by the farmers that was, alternatively, imprecise and global, and immensely meticulous. Conversely, the pastoralists were neither overly vague nor overly precise. They regularly carved their responses out of moderately sized portions of the blots.

With regard to the determinants of the responses, there was a striking difference: in all tribes, the farmers' responses were more diversely determined than were the pastoralists'. The pastoralists gave form-determined (F) responses; the farmers used movement, shading, texture, color, and achromatic color—all to a greater degree than did the pastoralists (P < .01). This difference was particularly marked for inanimate movement (m) and human movement (M). Traditional interpretations of these two differentia suggests that the first, inanimate movement, reflects anxiety, especially of a sort produced by an awareness of threatening forces beyond personal control. The second, human movement, involves perhaps the most complicated of Rorschach interpretations. There is no simple nor widely accepted interpretation available, but the use of human movement is generally taken to be a positive sign, variously said to indicate high intelligence, good imaginal ability, positive self-concept, empathy, inner stability, inner controls, and the like. In these African protocols, examination of the ratio of human movement responses to other determinants unfortunately does nothing to clarify the possible significance of this use of human movement. We are left with a pattern that apparently balances anxiety with sources of strength, stability, and control.

The comparison of content and form level was unavailing, for in neither instance were there statistically significant differences between farmers and pastoralists. Except for the aforementioned tendency of the farmers to employ more Western material objects in their responses, the farmers and pastoralists saw the same things in the blots, and they saw them with similar accuracy.

On the basis of these quantitative scores and ratios, comparatively little can be concluded with confidence, even if we were to accept the traditional Rorschach hypotheses available in the literature. The most I feel comfortable in saying is this: farmers' Rorschach responses reflect a greater volubility, a more complex imaginal ability, and a greater readiness to generalize; the pastoralists, on the contrary, were more particularistic, tied closely to the form properties of reality, and more limited, or less flexible, in their perceptual style. These conclusions are tentative and meager, I am aware. They are also more relevant to a discussion of what is usually meant by perceptual style than what is generally meant by personality. Unfortunately, quantitative analysis of the previous kind can tell us little more than this, unless one is willing to indulge in cross-cultural psychodynamic speculation of a sort that these data can do nothing to support.

Because, as any Rorschach analyst would insist, quantitative findings tell only part of the story, we must also consider some qualitative aspects of these Rorschach performances.

QUALITATIVE ANALYSIS

It has become almost *de rigueur* for anthropologists who bring Rorschach records back from the field to submit them to a Rorschach "expert" for "blind" analysis. Such sightless collaboration usually pleases no one, neither the Rorschacher nor the anthropologist, both of whom usually feel that their hands have been tied, and especially not the critics, who often find reason to suspect that the analysis was not truly "blind." [11]

I chose not to invite a "blind" reading of these African protocols. Instead, I worked in collaboration with an experienced Rorschach analyst, Florence Brawer. Dr. Brawer was for several years an assistant to Bruno Klopfer, and she had previously analyzed non-Western Rorschachs.[12] We read each protocol together, and as she offered interpretations, I provided answers to her questions about the idiomatic expressions being employed by respondents, about material culture, and so forth. As a result, Dr. Brawer knew she was seeing protocols from Africans, from pastoralists, or from farmers, and she knew something of the culture of each tribe involved. However, she was never told anything about the kinds of differences that were anticipated between pastoralists and farmers; indeed, she was not look-

11. This practice began with DuBois and Oberholzer and has since involved some of the most illustrious names in the field of culture and personality research.

12. Boyer et al. (1964).

ing for differences at all, but was merely trying to characterize each population.

Obviously, then, the analytic procedure was an interchange of information, not an independent, much less a "blind," analysis. The interpretations to be offered here are a product of that interchange. The insights are frequently hers, but the portraits drawn here are entirely mine. She is in no way responsible for the use I have made of her inferences, especially so because I have freely altered some of her own emphases, omitted some of her inferences, and added others of my own in order to satisfy my own understanding of these Rorschach patterns.[13]

In what follows, I shall deal briefly with each individual tribal site, examining first the farmers, then moving to the pastoralists of that same tribe. In this way I hope to be able better to draw out subtle differences that may have ecological significance. Finally, I shall summarize the differences that I believe may exist between the pastoralists and the farmers. As before, I begin with the Hehe for alphabetical reasons.

HEHE FARMERS

Although the Hehe farmers were relatively diverse in their approach to the Rorschach, there were no appreciable differences between men and women or the young and the old. The most prominent feature of these protocols was the clearly expressed sense of unease that ran through them. One way of talking about this quality of response would be to refer to it as anxiety of a particularly diffuse sort. Thus, while the Hehe farmers approached the Rorschach without visible discomfort, and while they responded in a relatively wordy way, their response regularly reflected dysphoria. For example, they, almost alone among the tribal populations, gave some evidence of hostility in their responses. A continual theme in these tense responses was blood, seen in many contexts. Several respondents, both men and women, saw menstrual blood, and others saw illness or death in the Rorschach blots. A few respondents saw animals or humans with their legs, arms, or even heads cut off, and blood was sometimes seen as an indication that someone had just been killed. For example, the bright red in card 3 evoked this response: "It looks like two people looking at some blood; it is the blood of someone they have killed." Or this: "Looks like a human being with legs and head cut off and the blood running out." Following such bloody responses, the Hehe

13. I am most grateful to Dr. Brawer for her assistance.

farmers often "retreated" from their sanguinary view of the blots, by offering "safe" topics such as clouds or hills or crops. The force of this description derives from the response sequence: first, a response of blood and gore to a red card ("blood—someone has been killed; dying people"), then clearly expressed unease, as in facial expression and shifting about, and sometimes taking the form of rejection of the next card, then a change of subject toward something innocuous such as clouds ("something like a cloud; clouds over the hills; nice clouds"). In general, the Hehe did not respond to soft color. Indeed, they often were unable to respond at all to the pastel colors of the last three cards. Nor did they employ texture in their responses. Their sensitivity was to the bright red, which appeared to trouble them, and they found refuge in the gray world of natural objects.

This portrait of the Hehe farmers as people who are uneasy about the potential violence of their world fits well with the ethnographic observations and the interview data. These *are* hostile people. The Rorschach responses do not, however, specifically suggest the concern with impulsivity and self-control that was so clearly expressed by Hehe farmers in other parts of the interview.

HEHE PASTORALISTS

It was immediately apparent that, compared to those of the farmers, the protocols of the pastoralists were shorter, less complex, and less differentiated. The pastoralists rejected many cards, but without apparent pattern. Again, there were no differences between men and women or among the age categories. The pastoralists' approach was basically simple: they saw animals and aspects of their physical world in large parts of the cards (D's). They displayed a pronounced tendency to linger over the gray portions of the blots, often responding to them as clouds that were dark, rainy, or gathering. Such an emphasis could be interpreted as anxiety. Or, in an environmental context, as a concern with rainfall in a dry land. I was more struck by another inference. From the Hehe farmers to the pastoralists, there was a notable shift in sensitivity from the bright reds that so intrigued the farmers, to the dark gray and black portions of the blots. At the same time, the pastoralists were less expressive of hostility and aggression, concentrating instead upon food and hunger, a theme that ran through their responses. When the pastoralists did give hostile responses, the hostility concerned food, as, for example, in this response: "Some people waiting for something to eat, animals eating blood—

209

hungry—birds and animals fighting over food." That the pastoralists concentrated upon the achromatic portions of the blots could be interpreted as a depressive sign. There is support for such an inference in the Rorschach literature.[14] Support also comes from the gravity of sadness and despair that often accompanied these responses. In any event, the shift in responsivity from red among the farmers to black among the pastoralists was so marked that it constituted the fundamental difference between the two sets of protocols.

As the ethnographic observations suggested, the pastoralists were more open and direct in the responses. Unlike the farmers, whose suppressed aggression comes through in the Rorschach, the open aggression of the pastoralists was not reflected in the Rorschach responses. The depressive quality of the responses was, at least to a degree, suggested by the content analysis, but the dominant depressive emphasis was unanticipated.

KAMBA FARMERS

The search for a modal pattern among the Kamba farmers was simple because, of all the tribal sites, here there was the least variability. This consistency of response among all ages and both sexes carried over to the mode of approach which was, almost without exception, open, direct, and uncomplicated. There were very few rejections; and these respondents, more so than those of any other site, enjoyed looking at the Rorschach blots. In spite of this enjoyment, the Kamba farmers were neither complex nor inventive in their response pattern. They often gave whole-blot responses, frequently of a quite simple sort (e.g., tree, cloud, flower). Indeed, these farmers strongly emphasized their environment and the weather, especially rivers, clouds, and soil erosion. This emphasis was not surprising among a people who suffer recurrent drought and flood.

There was no general indication of anxiety, hostility, or aggression among these people; however, there was a dominant focus evident in their responses: the frequent use of texture. The Kamba farmers saw many animal skins which they sometimes touched, rubbed or referred to as being soft, fluffy, smooth, hairy, and the like. This sort of response, which Klopfer calls Fc (or cF), is interpreted by him as follows: "Fc responses indicate an awareness of and acceptance of affectional needs experienced in terms of desire for approval, belongingness, and response from others, retaining a passive recipient flavor but refined beyond a craving for actual physical con-

14. Klopfer et al. (1954).

tact."[15] To transfer so experimental an hypothesis from the Western world to East Africa may be incautious, but this depiction seems to me to apply to the Kamba quite well, for these are people whose protocols, including their response to soft color, are suffused by a concern for softness. Perhaps this focus is not too surprising among a people who express so little affection in everyday life.

KAMBA PASTORALISTS

Like the Kamba farmers, the Kamba pastoralists were open and direct, but they did not express any enjoyment over the blots. They did not follow the previously noted pattern of a less complex response pattern among pastoralists. In fact, their responses were longer, more complex, and more variable than those of the Kamba farmers. They continued the use of whole responses, but they added a large number of responses that used smaller parts of the blots. When these responses focused upon fields, flowers, and grazing areas, that is, upon matters of sustenance, the responses were unusually long and complex.

Like the farmers they were not very responsive to color; neither did they show any sign of depression. The focal interest of the farmers in texture did carry over to the pastoralists, but in a somewhat reduced intensity and frequency. Instead, these pastoral responses were marked by anxiety, clearly expressed as fear, worry, or as concern over the outcome of events. What is more, there was a pattern of responses that could easily be called, to borrow an appropriate psychoanalytic term, oral aggressivity. This, the pastoralists' most striking pattern, combined animals in movement with food concepts: baboons who wanted a single ear of maize, two dogs with one bone, etc. Bright color, in particular, seemed to evoke food responses, often with some implied competition. This latter pattern fits well with the greater impoverishment of this area as compared with the much richer upland farming area, and the greater danger of life in this area.

The anxiety expressed in this pastoral site is consistent with the differences noted in chapter 7, where it was reported that the Kamba were unique among the four tribes in that their pastoralists exceeded their farmers in such related matters as hatred, insults, witchcraft, and other anxiety-related variables. However, among a people so given to antagonism between the sexes, it was surprising that there was so little difference between men and women in Rorschach performance.

15. Klopfer et al. (1954), p. 273.

POKOT FARMERS

The Pokot farmers provided terse responses to the Rorschach, a pattern that was somewhat more noticeable among the old than among the young, but was shared by men and women. The approach was one of indifference, not as a product of poor motivation, but as a more basic psychological set that led to a distinct readiness to reject cards and to give quite brief responses.

There were several particularly distinctive response features. The first was but another version of the anxiety seen among respondents in other sites. The Pokot version of unease was marked by perseveration (carrying a response from one blot, where it may be appropriate, to subsequent blots, where it is not) and rejection after some "disturbing" blot was encountered. Color, particularly bright color, often seemed to touch off this avoidance. Indeed, so unpredictable and impulsive was the response to bright color that, in Rorschach parlance, the pattern is suggestive of hysteria. In a pattern marked by anxiety, bright color seemed to "shock" the Pokot farmers: their color concepts were loosely formulated, and were followed by overt content disruption, perseveration, and rejection.

The Pokot farmers also tended to concentrate upon what are considered to be the phallic features of the blots. Their percepts centered upon almost every elongated projection in all of the cards. In this concentration, the women, if anything, exceeded the men. Finally, the Pokot farmers had a distinctive emphasis upon the sun in their responses. When they responded to a bright color, they often saw it as the sun. This response is intriguing because the sun is quite important in Pokot cosmogony, so much so, in fact, that it is not a great exaggeration to speak of them as sun worshippers.[16]

The Rorschach did not appear to indicate any of the low self-esteem that I had earlier suggested was a central problem among these farming Pokot. It does, however, strongly suggest that relations among these people are, indeed, difficult and joyless.

POKOT PASTORALISTS

The Pokot pastoralists approached the blots with an even greater disdain, lack of involvement, and readiness to reject a card than did the Pokot farmers. The emphasis upon the sun continued, as did the concentration upon elongated, "phallic" projections; but,

16. See Conant (1966) and Schneider (1956) on the place of the sun in Pokot religion.

in contradistinction to the farmers, signs of anxiety decreased markedly, and color seemed to be less of a problem for the pastoralists. They did not perseverate, nor did they show as much impulsivity in their responses as did the Pokot farmers.

The content of these pastoralist responses was highly specific, consisting principally of animals and features of the physical habitat. A unique response was the *manyatta* (a kraal in which cattle are kept), but cattle themselves were not mentioned. And, despite the remote location of these pastoralists, far from European contact, they did mention airplanes quite often. Even in remotest East Africa, airplanes fly overhead, and it was these pastoralists who mentioned them most frequently. Throughout, the pastoralists' approach was rigid and form-determined, lacking any sign of flexibility or innovation.

In their overall performance, these pastoralists were impassive. They seemed to be in perfect command of the situation. Nothing flustered them, nothing intrigued them. For a people who made such copious use of color in their everyday clothing and ornamentation, they displayed almost no interest in color in the blots. There was a clear depressive flavor to the responses of older people, both male and female, but the dominant aspect of these performances was the distance, the composure, of all respondents. They came to look at the blots and they did so. As far as I could ascertain, they were little affected by the experience. This, too, is consistent with what we already know about these haughty pastoralists.

SEBEI FARMERS

Nowhere were Rorschach responses as diverse as they were among the Sebei farmers, although even here there were only minimal differences between men and women, young and old. These responses were remarkably complex and, in many instances, quite inventive. Some individuals produced protocols that were frankly amazing in their creative richness. Yet, in the main, the records were marked by a pattern of inconsistency—a careful, complex response followed by a vague, indifferent concept. Throughout, the Sebei farmers evinced a pronounced ebb and flow of interest in the Rorschach, but they were always able to avoid full involvement of themselves in the perceptual tasks before them. They held the task at a distance by using such innocuous percepts as rocks and clouds, and by qualifying the reality of what they saw: "It is an animal that does not live in this country," or, "It might be a rock," or, "It looks like something I have seen, but it is not quite right—it must be something else, I don't know what," or, "It is a shadow of a person, not a real person." Such imprecise concepts were regularly followed by intricate and accurate responses.

But the most compelling aspect of these protocols was their troubled quality. Not that they contained open signs of aggression, only a hidden hostility that sometimes broke through ("Here is someone, trapped, testicles bleeding, leg broken—but, of course, I don't know who it is!"). They have a feeling tone of coldness to people, of distaste for positive emotions, and of fearfulness, both open and diffuse ("It is a man. There is something bad here. Maybe he is dying. I think something is dying, maybe a man"; "Here is an arm reaching for something. I don't know what he wants."). Out of a welter of long and complex responses, there was no sign of anything that touched upon empathy or compassion. Such a lack came as no surprise in the brief, terse responses of the other tribes. But in the rich Sebei responses, one is not only impressed by the lack of such feelings but by the presence of avoidance or evasiveness so marked that we can refer to it as deviousness. Sometimes this deviousness is even expressed directly ("It is a man hiding himself in a skin. He is going to do something secret.").

These Sebei did not seem to be responding directly to color, or shading, or texture or movement. Instead, they seemed to be driven by an internal directive to avoid contact, to escape involvement, and to prevent the feelings of others from touching them. Typical of this characteristic, even if it be merely symbolic of it and not directly related, was the Sebei concentration upon so-called vista responses, responses in which a three-dimensional depth perspective is combined with form to give the impression of a vista or space perception in a landscape ("There is someone standing on a cliff looking down below. You can see lakes on the plains below. Rivers, too. This man is all alone. Maybe he wants to jump off."). This response was extremely rare in other tribes (although others, particularly the Kamba farmers, also had vast panoramic views), but it was frequent among the Sebei farmers. This tendency to see their environment at a distance may simply derive from life upon a mountain escarpment from which one can see great distances down to the plains below, but it also serves, however metaphorically, to characterize Sebei perception. For the Sebei, not only the landscape but the people in it were seen at a distance.

SEBEI PASTORALISTS

The Sebei pastoralists were entirely different. They were far more open and direct in their approach, and their responses were much fewer in number, less complex in their subject and organization, and far less varied. The pastoralists were definite, simple, and concrete in their perceptions. They saw animals, often in movement, and their view of these animals was entirely uncomplicated. This concentration upon animals in a plains world filled with animals was as direct a reflection of the environment as was the farmers' use of the vista, and so was it an insight into their perceptual approach to the Rorschach. The pastoralists were confined to a simple, matter-of-fact view of the blots ("This is fat from the stomach of an antelope."). There was much less evidence of concealment, or anxiety, or coldness toward people. Neither was there the ebb and flow of involvement that characterized the farmers. This is not to say that there was evidence of great warmth, but only that instead of a negative affectivity, we find a more neutral, bland tone ("Two women—making a fire."). There was a suggestion of depression in their strong reactivity to the dark portions of the blots and a content that tends to be gloomy ("This is an old house, around which the grass is dying. The roof is rotten and is falling down. There is death here."), but there was nothing in the pastoralists' responses comparable to the farmers' fearfulness and avoidance of each other.

CONCLUSION

Any reader who has followed these impressionistic depictions is as well aware as I am that there are few outstanding response tendencies that serve to characterize all farmers, or all pastoralists. Perhaps this was to be expected of such subjective accounts of Rorschach performances. Nevertheless, there are some response tendencies that appear to qualify as pastoral-farming differentia. The first is anxiety, which we had anticipated would be more common among farmers than pastoralists. Indeed it was, except for the Kamba, whose pattern was not merely discrepant but was a consistent reversal of what was found among the other three tribes. Still, among the Hehe, Pokot, and Sebei, the farmers did give both quantitative and qualitative evidence of being more anxious. The second difference was consistent, intriguing, and unanticipated. It involved sensitivity to the gray and black (achromatic) parts of the blots. In all four tribes, the pastoralists were more responsive to achromatic stimuli than were the farmers.

Conversely, while color responsiveness was never high,[17] in all four tribes (although the tendency was weak among the Sebei) the farmers were more responsive to bright red than were the pastoralists. This difference lends itself to a traditional Rorschach interpretation which would say that the pastoralists tended to depression and the farmers were troubled by interpersonal challenges.[18] Although this interpretation is based upon Western Rorschach testing, and sometimes appears to be a naïve kind of argument by analogy, there is additional evidence in these African Rorschach performances and in the remainder of the interview to suggest that the farmers were indeed troubled by interpersonal relations and that pastoralists were in fact somewhat inclined to depression.

Another major difference involves cognitive rigidity. As we had expected, compared to the farmers, the pastoralists gave more stereotyped responses; their responses were largely determined by form and consisted of a more limited array of content and a less varied set of locations. Pastoral rigidity often took the form of perseveration in which a single concept, location, or determinant was repeated over and over without regard to the changing configurations of the blots. Conversely, the farmers responded to the ambiguous stimuli of inkblots more freely and creatively, restructuring them and assigning them meaning more flexibly. Similarly, the farmers seemed to enjoy fantasy more than the pastoralists did; surely, they were more often able to produce responses that integrated fantasy with the properties of the blots. A few individuals in each tribe were extremely skilled in organizing complex perceptions of the blots within their highly imaginative responses but, in general, the farmers far exceeded the pastoralists in this ability.

These are the principal, easily recognized differences between pastoralists and farmers. I shall not continue this analysis of Rorschach performance in a search for less obvious sorts of differences, for I believe that it is possible to labor too long over these inkblot responses in our pursuit of that will-o'-the-wisp called personality. Whatever personality is, it is not fully or solely knowable from Rorschach testing. In subsequent chapters, when these findings can better be seen in context, I shall return to many of the issues raised in this chapter.

17. Doob (1960).
18. Klopfer et al. (1956), pp. 297–298.

Many of the analyses in earlier chapters were confined to generalized or modal contrasts involving the comparison of various estimates or measures of central tendency. The impressionistic contrasts were phrased in terms of modal differences, and the interview responses were sometimes presented as mean scores. In these analyses, individual behaviors or responses were "averaged," with a resulting loss of a sense of the variability within the populations being contrasted. It is sometimes simpler to use such an approach than it is to report the full variability of response of behavior at every step along the path of an analysis. In this research, however, more than convenience is involved. To risk belaboring a point, the basic purpose of this research was the comparison of eight populations. We were expressly concerned with locating differences among these populations which were widely shared, because we hoped to learn whether the ecological variation among our populations would be accompanied by corresponding variation in their interview response patterns. Hence, the search for modal comparisons was fundamental to our research design.

It was the conclusion of chapters 7 and 8 that statistically significant differences in response did exist among the various sets of pastoral and farming populations; and, for what it is worth, some of these differentials were supported by more impressionistic observations. Yet, throughout the course of these analyses, I was mindful of the conclusion of Wallace, Lindzey, and others on modal personality,[1] that personality variables are unlikely to be shared by a substantial majority of any population, nor could I easily ignore Bert

1. An introduction to this question is available in Wallace (1961).

Kaplan's comments on the use of projective techniques to "discover" modal tendencies.[2] Kaplan pointed out that no matter what the responses to these tests might be, they can always be "averaged" to provide measures of central tendency, measures that may well be misleading. As Kaplan said: "When such averages are unaccompanied by measures of variability, they are worse than worthless since they have left the worker satisfied and pleased with his errors." [3]

The question, then, is this: How much error has resulted from my use of averages?

THE VARIABILITY OF THE RESPONSES

In some of the findings reported earlier, actual frequency counts were given in which the variability of the various responses in each site was apparent at a glance. In other instances, however, particularly with regard to the content analysis, mean scores and sums were reported, sometimes without mention of the standard deviation. Of course, there were differences between sites in the variability of interview responses, just as there were differences within sites in response variability from one question to the next. I did not feel that such differences were of critical importance in understanding these earlier findings. I was concerned only with demonstrating that there *were* differences among the mean scores of various sites. Matters cannot be left at that, however. The present task calls for an examination of response variability to determine its extent and its possible relevance to our understanding of pastoral and farming response differences. This examination is presented here in a single section rather than piecemeal in earlier portions of the book so that the importance of this variability may be better evaluated.

For each site, the variability of every response—to a question, the Rorschach plates, slides, or values pictures—was recorded. Because the means of these eight sets of responses were often quite different, it would be misleading to report only the absolute magnitudes of the standard deviations. As Blalock has pointed out,[4] one would expect that a very large mean would carry with it a large standard deviation. Thus a more informative comparative measure of variability would be one that indicates the size of the standard

2. See Kaplan (1961).
3. Ibid., p. 236.
4. See Blalock (1960a), pp. 73–74.

deviation relative to the size of the mean. The coefficient of variability (V) does this by dividing the standard deviation by the mean. Thus, the larger the coefficient of variability, the greater is the variability of response.

Since the content analysis scores were routinely presented as mean scores in the foregoing analysis, and since these scores take a central place in subsequent analyses, it is upon the dispersion around these mean scores that we must now concentrate. The variability of the interview responses that were coded in nominal categories and presented as frequencies in earlier chapters is considered in Appendix VII. When the eight study sites are compared with regard to the variability of their content analysis scores, some differences do appear. For example, table 65 presents the average coefficient of variability for the combined content analysis categories in each of the eight sites. A glance at this table is sufficient to confirm that while differ-

TABLE 65

AVERAGE COEFFICIENT OF VARIABILITY SCORES*

Study site	Mean coefficient of variability
Hehe farmers	.327
Hehe pastoralists	.358
Kamba farmers	.334
Kamba pastoralists	.335
Pokot farmers	.360
Pokot pastoralists	.327
Sebei farmers	.377
Sebei pastoralists	.433

*All 31 content analysis categories used.

ences between the sites in the variability of their responses do not appear to be greatly discrepant, there are some differences.

Unfortunately, there does not appear to be any criterion by which it is possible to decide when response variability is homogeneous enough to warrant satisfaction or, conversely, when it is so great that the use of measures of central tendency is inadvisable.[5] In this particular instance, I can reach no confident conclusion. I do not feel that the variability was so extreme that the use of mean scores, or modal patterns, made a mockery of reality. On the other hand, I

5. Of course, statistical tests of the significance of differences between means do take variability into account.

take it as given that any such measure of central tendency always distorts understanding of the actual distribution of responses and of the relationships among them. For this reason, it is necessary to examine the actual responses of individual persons, without further assumptions about the adequacy of mean scores or modal patterns.

MULTIVARIATE ANALYSES

Previous chapters have reported differences between pastoralists and farmers as seen in mean or modal comparisons. The task at hand is to determine what happens when those variables that best reflected pastoral-farming differences in these earlier analyses are reexamined by taking the responses of individual persons into account without reference to the tribe or the site of that person. Do any of the same patterns that were seen in earlier chapters persist? Does such a procedure produce patterns of response that are similar, or ones that are entirely different? To answer these questions, it is first necessary to define the individual as the unit of analysis, and therefore to examine his particular response, not the mean or modal response of all persons in the site in which he lives, or the economic mode to which he belongs. One way of achieving this examination is to employ a multivariate statistical technique that permits an analysis of the relationships among responses of many individual persons.

In spite of increased computer capabilities and the impressive ingenuity of programmers, it remains true that there are limits to the numbers of variables that even multivariate techniques can employ. And, of course, if too many variables are utilized, the analyst also runs the risk of becoming fuddled. At the time of this analysis (1966), the upper limit of variables for the available programs was 50. Consequently, I attempted to reduce the hundreds of potential variables representing each individual to a more limited number that would still be an efficient sample of those responses that had appeared to represent pastoral-farming differentia.

To begin, I selected 29 of the 31 content analysis categories. Two others, "valuation of cattle" (with "cattle") and "valuation of independence" (with "independence"), were largely redundant and were consequently highly correlated; therefore, the first variable of each pair was omitted. These content analysis categories were included because they are relatively abstract, because they range across a wide area of interest, and because many of them had shown pastoral-farming differences. And, of course, it is these content analysis variables that were previously treated as averages, without apparent regard to their dispersion.

In addition, fourteen other variables were selected. Three of these, labeled "fantasy," "impulsivity," and "other-direction," were derived from the Rorschach. "Fantasy" refers to the ability of the person to see complex and unusual percepts in the Rorschach; "fantasy," as defined here, refers to unique responses, matched by no one else's in the sample, that are at the same time highly inventive, complicated perceptions. "Impulsivity" derives from two ratios of traditional Rorschach scores: the ratio of animal movement (FM) to human movement (M), and the ratio of color combined with form (FC) to color without form (CF). "Other-direction" refers to the content of the Rorschach responses, specifically the frequency with which the individual saw other human beings in the Rorschach. The greater the frequency of such human percepts, the more that person was considered to be "other-directed." Needless to say, all three of these variables merely reflect Rorschach hypotheses, and while they derive some support from Western Rorschach research, they lack demonstrable predictive validity for non-Western societies.

Two other variables were developed from my own evaluation of the entire interview response protocol. These were labeled "brutality" and "anxiety." In reviewing each protocol, I scored "brutality" whenever there was mention of the infliction of a substantial amount of physical pain or emotional suffering upon a person or animal; this was scored without regard to the respondents' efforts to justify the pain or suffering. "Anxiety" was scored for every indication of fearfulness without a clear and specific referent. Thus, "This man is afraid of that snake" would *not* be scored as anxiety, but "This man looks worried" would be scored as anxiety.

Two variables came from the demographic interview forms collected in the field by each ethnographer. The first variable was relative "social prestige" (low, average, or high); the second was "relative wealth" (poor, average, or wealthy). Both variables are relative to the site to which they refer. Thus, a man with high social prestige among the Kamba farmers might not be so regarded among the Kamba pastoralists. Similarly, wealth among the Sebei farmers might consist of land, livestock, and money, whereas wealth among Pokot pastoralists would consist almost entirely of livestock. Consequently, while neither social prestige nor wealth as here estimated can be translated from one site to the next, these two variables do permit us

221

to estimate the relative prestige and wealth of a man as judged by his neighbors.

Six variables represented differential acculturation. Four of these were taken from the "acculturation index" (chapter 6): "education of respondent," "travel," "participation in cash economy," and "wage work." Two other variables represented the individual's place in a rank-ordering of respondents by acculturation score. The first of these, "intratribal acculturation," indicates the individual's place in a rank-ordering of all male respondents in his tribe; the second, "overall acculturation," represents his rank-order relative to all male respondents, irrespective of their tribe.

Finally, the age of each person was also included. In all, there were 43 variables. Although other data could have been included, this array seemed to me to provide a range of important variables—ones that had already been implicated in one or another pastoral-farming differential, as well as some new variables that might be related to these differentials and help to explain them. Furthermore, the array was not so large as to preclude analysis by available multivariate statistical techniques.

Because the necessary data for many of these 14 new variables were not available for the female respondents, the 43 variables represent male respondents only. Although this is regrettable, it should be recalled that there were no statistically significant differences between men and women on the 31 content analysis variables for which female data did exist, nor were there any substantial differences between males and females in the variability of these responses.

SMALLEST SPACE ANALYSIS

Among the many techniques available for the analysis of a complex system—multiple regression, multiple analysis of variance, iterative least squares, and so on—the two techniques that most appealed to me were factor analysis and smallest space analysis. Factor analysis is one of the most widely employed techniques developed for the handling of problems involving large numbers of variables. Used appropriately, the technique can reduce a large number of operational indices to a much smaller number of conceptual variables. It may be used to confirm relationships that theory has already pointed to, but it may also be used to discover previously unnoticed relationships between variables.[6] Despite its utility in social science, however, the technique has received more than its share of criticism. Factor analysis is regularly accused of being more art than science, and a few critics have even suggested that magic is involved, perhaps black magic at that. Much of my own concern about the technique involves the interpretation of the factors that are extracted. First, there is the analyst's problem of interpretation, but there is also the problem of communicating these interpretations to readers who may not be familiar with the technique. The unsophisticated reader is often at a loss to evaluate the factors that the analyst presents to him.

Smallest space analysis, recently developed by Guttman and Lingoes,[7] overcomes some of these ambiguities of interpretation by presenting its results in a diagrammatic form that permits simple, visual interpretation of the data. Whereas factor analysis relies upon a distance function for analysis and interpretation of data (that is, it is based upon conventional metric assumptions), smallest space analysis is a nonmetric technique that is concerned with relative distances within a set of points. With nonmetric techniques, neither linear nor distributional assumptions need be made; therefore, it is possible to use such techniques in analyzing such measures as probabilities, likelihoods, frequencies, correlations, or virtually any kinds of coefficients.[8] Like factor analysis, smallest space analysis begins with a data matrix, in this instance, with coefficients of correlation (Pearson's r). The technique makes few assumptions about the data (here again, those for Pearson's r would apply, but this is not a limitation of smallest space analysis), the only important one being monotonicity, the assumption being that the physical distance between any two points in the space diagram is inversely related to the size of the correlation coefficient computed on the joint distribution of those two traits.[9]

Smallest space analysis seeks to find the minimal number of dimensions in which data (consisting of any measure of distance be-

6. The literature on factor analysis is large, but for an introduction see Thurstone (1947) or Cattell (1952).

7. See Bloombaum (1968), Laumann and Guttman (1966), and Lingoes (1965).

8. See Coombs (1964) and Lingoes (1966).

9. "A function $(Y = f(X)$) is said to be *monotone-increasing* if an increase in the value of X in the domain of the function always is accompanied by an increase in the corresponding value of Y. A *monotone-decreasing* function has the opposite property: an increase

TABLE 66

CORRELATION MATRIX (PEARSON'S r) FOR THE 43 VARIABLES

Row	Variable	1	2	3	4	5	6	7	8	9	10	11	12	13	14	15	16	17	18
1	(1) Impulsivity	.00	.02	.10	−.16	.15	.13	.06	.13	.03	.19	−.05	−.05	.02	.04	.05	.03	.01	.04
2	(2) Insults	.02	.00	.34	−.43	−.04	−.17	.13	.02	−.22	−.22	.24	−.20	−.13	.36	−.09	−.27	.10	−.09
3	(3) Fear	.10	.34	.00	−.24	−.06	−.06	.12	−.01	−.15	−.08	.02	.03	−.13	.27	−.10	−.04	.01	−.05
4	(4) Cattle	−.16	−.43	−.24	.00	−.20	.08	−.11	−.10	.24	−.09	−.25	.07	.07	−.35	.07	.22	−.07	−.00
5	(5) Land	.15	−.04	−.06	−.20	.00	−.16	−.10	.11	−.03	.24	.08	.10	−.01	−.07	.21	−.03	.09	.16
6	(6) Independence	.13	−.17	−.06	.08	−.16	.00	.07	.04	.07	.04	.09	.07	.14	−.24	−.12	.30	.00	−.01
7	(7) Fatalism	.06	.13	.12	−.11	−.10	.07	.00	−.16	.07	−.04	−.23	−.13	−.19	.11	−.20	.09	−.32	−.13
8	(8) Avoidance of conflict	.13	.02	−.01	−.10	.11	.04	−.16	.00	−.02	.26	.10	−.07	.21	−.11	.03	−.01	.22	.40
9	(9) Depression	.03	−.22	−.15	.24	−.03	.07	.07	−.02	.00	.05	−.15	.11	.04	−.19	−.08	.32	−.04	.06
10	(0) Respect for authority	.19	−.22	−.08	−.09	.24	.04	−.04	.26	.05	.00	.11	.19	.13	−.23	.11	.08	.02	.09
11	(A) Jealousy of wealth	.05	.24	.02	−.25	.08	.09	−.23	.10	−.05	.11	.00	.07	.11	−.00	.20	.00	.27	.06
12	(B) Desire for friends	−.05	−.20	.03	.07	.10	.07	−.13	−.07	.11	.19	.07	.00	−.07	−.01	.08	.11	.10	.05
13	(C) Hostility to opposite sex	.02	−.13	−.13	.07	−.01	.14	−.19	.21	.04	.13	.11	−.07	.00	.25	.15	.08	.16	.07
14	(D) Litigiousness	.04	.36	.27	−.35	−.07	−.24	.11	−.11	−.19	−.23	−.00	−.01	−.25	.00	−.06	−.16	.04	−.10
15	(E) Hatred	.05	−.09	−.10	.07	.21	−.12	−.20	.03	−.08	.11	.20	.08	.15	−.06	.00	−.12	.34	−.01
16	(F) Direct aggression	.03	−.27	−.04	.22	−.03	.30	.09	−.01	.33	.08	.00	.11	.08	−.16	−.12	.00	−.05	−.01
17	(G) Fantasy	.01	.10	.01	−.07	.09	.00	−.32	.22	−.04	.02	.27	.10	.16	.04	.34	.05	−.13	.01
18	(H) Witchcraft	.04	−.09	−.05	−.00	.16	−.01	−.13	.40	.06	.09	.06	.05	.07	−.10	.11	−.01	.22	.00
19	(I) Brutality	−.05	−.11	−.16	.00	.06	.02	−.01	−.02	.08	.03	.15	.03	.18	−.12	.22	.00	.13	.01
20	(J) Anxiety	.13	.09	.00	−.13	.09	−.03	−.11	.19	.01	.17	.09	.12	.15	.08	.03	−.06	.14	.18
21	(K) Interest in physical beauty	−.08	−.15	−.12	−.03	.12	−.04	−.16	.09	.02	.14	.05	.10	.06	−.13	.06	−.04	−.06	.12
22	(L) Self-control	.02	−.14	−.15	.18	−.01	.09	−.13	−.02	.16	.04	.05	.07	.13	−.25	.12	.08	.15	.03
23	(M) Disrespect for authority	−.08	.06	.09	.05	−.22	.03	.23	−.20	−.06	−.20	−.15	−.10	−.13	.09	−.05	.04	−.05	−.17
24	(N) Adultery	−.00	−.16	−.10	−.11	.15	−.00	−.11	.10	.01	.16	.07	.11	.06	−.12	.05	−.04	−.06	.09
25	(O) Concern with death	.03	−.20	−.11	.13	.26	−.04	−.17	.09	.13	.25	.11	.13	.15	−.16	.11	.07	.08	.16
26	(P) Fear of poverty	−.06	−.07	.04	−.04	−.12	.07	.08	−.06	.02	−.02	−.01	.14	−.07	.02	.02	.09	−.17	−.07
27	(Q) Clan	.05	.12	.12	−.09	−.05	−.08	.14	−.05	−.08	−.07	−.01	.14	−.17	.21	−.00	−.03	−.01	−.11
28	(R) Cooperation	.05	.12	.13	−.15	.05	.09	−.03	.04	.06	.04	.01	.12	.07	−.05	−.12	.07	−.12	−.05
29	(S) Affection	.00	−.03	−.09	.03	.05	−.03	−.09	.09	−.11	.09	−.09	.01	.00	−.14	−.04	−.02	.09	.08
30	(T) Guilt-shame	.09	−.11	−.02	−.02	.22	.07	−.00	.14	.15	.19	.02	−.17	.20	−.24	−.12	.19	−.18	.14
31	(U) Concern with wrongdoing	.08	.13	−.03	−.24	.14	−.03	.11	.15	−.02	−.04	.09	−.06	.08	.09	.14	−.13	.20	.16
32	(V) Divination	−.03	−.15	.02	.10	−.11	−.10	.07	.14	.13	−.09	−.17	−.05	.04	.08	−.07	.19	−.07	.09
33	(W) Other-direction	−.09	.09	.08	−.16	−.17	.17	−.07	.05	−.03	−.05	.07	−.04	.10	.09	.07	.06	.26	.00
34	(X) Youth	−.08	.14	−.01	−.03	−.28	.05	−.27	.05	−.05	−.05	.32	−.01	.14	.10	.10	.09	.34	.03
35	(Y) Industriousness	.03	−.10	−.02	.00	.18	.16	−.10	.35	.17	.14	.12	.11	.27	−.18	.11	.19	.32	.19
36	(Z) Education	.00	−.12	−.11	.03	.14	−.04	−.18	.08	.10	.06	.11	.06	.03	−.08	.10	.07	.03	.11
37	($) Travel	.11	.04	.21	−.14	.15	−.00	−.03	−.01	−.00	.05	.19	.13	.04	−.07	.05	−.01	.04	.06
38	(.) Participation in cash economy	−.04	−.02	−.08	.08	.04	.04	−.27	.14	.03	.06	.20	.05	.15	−.22	.03	.01	.14	.14
39	(,) Wage work	−.07	.19	.07	−.06	−.03	−.08	−.05	.07	.04	−.03	.15	.03	−.10	.08	−.09	.08	.03	.09
40	(=) Intratribal acculturation	.02	.03	.04	−.00	−.03	−.03	−.12	.00	.01	−.04	.13	.10	−.01	.07	−.00	.05	.10	.11
41	(') Overall acculturation	.09	.26	.07	−.21	.22	−.15	−.22	.16	−.16	.09	.31	.03	.06	.02	.12	−.11	.20	.19
42	(() Social prestige	−.03	−.01	−.07	.12	−.01	.16	.09	−.09	.10	−.07	−.08	.06	.01	−.08	−.02	.02	−.05	−.08
43	()) General wealth	−.13	.02	−.03	.10	.05	.06	−.01	.06	.08	−.06	.12	.09	.01	−.12	−.04	.07	.01	−.01

tween two variables) can be adequately represented. The technique establishes distances among variables by considering their complete multibivariate distribution, that is, the set of bivariate distributions of all possible pairs of variables. The task of the numerical calculations performed by the computer is to express the distances between variables in an actual Euclidean space.[10] The computer plots the space of lowest dimensionality which maintains the rank-order of the sizes of the input coefficients, whatever they may be. Each variable is represented by a point in an m-dimensional space. If several points are clustered together in one region of space, it means that the traits represented by these points are relatively closely associated. The distance between points or sets of points indicates the amount of correlation between these points. Thus by simple visual inspection of the resulting space diagrams it is possible to comprehend the empirical

---

in the value of X in the domain is accompanied by a decrease in the value of Y. Linear functions are always monotone, but so are many other functions that are definitely not linear (Y = X3, Y = log X, and so on)" (Hays [1963], p. 642).

10. See Laumann and Guttman (1966).

TABLE 66 (*continued*)

CORRELATION MATRIX (PEARSON'S r) FOR THE 43 VARIABLES

Row	20	21	22	23	24	25	26	27	28	29	30	31	32	33	34	35	36	37	38	39	40	41	42	43
1	.13	-.08	-.02	-.08	-.00	.03	-.06	.05	.05	.00	.09	.08	-.03	-.09	-.08	.03	.00	.11	-.04	-.07	.02	.09	-.03	-.13
2	.09	-.15	-.14	.06	-.16	-.20	-.07	.12	.12	-.03	-.11	.13	-.15	.09	.14	-.10	-.12	.04	-.02	.19	.03	.26	-.01	.02
3	.00	-.12	-.15	.09	-.10	-.11	.04	.12	.13	-.09	-.02	-.03	.02	.08	-.01	-.02	-.11	.21	-.08	.07	.04	.07	-.07	-.03
4	-.13	-.03	.18	.05	-.11	.13	-.04	-.09	-.15	.03	-.02	-.24	.10	-.16	-.03	.00	.03	-.14	.08	-.06	-.00	-.21	.12	.10
5	.09	.12	-.01	-.22	.15	.26	-.12	-.05	.05	.05	.22	.14	-.11	-.17	-.28	.18	.14	.15	.04	-.03	-.03	.22	-.01	.05
6	-.03	-.04	.09	.03	-.00	-.04	.07	-.08	.09	-.03	.07	-.03	-.10	.17	.05	.16	-.04	-.00	.04	-.08	-.03	-.15	.16	.06
7	-.11	-.16	-.13	.23	-.11	-.17	.08	.14	-.03	-.09	-.00	-.11	.07	-.07	-.27	-.10	-.18	-.0	-.27	-.05	-.12	-.22	.09	-.01
8	.19	.09	-.02	-.20	.10	.09	-.06	-.05	.04	.09	.14	.15	.14	.05	.05	.35	.08	-.01	.14	.07	.00	.16	-.09	.06
9	.01	.02	.16	-.06	.01	.13	.02	-.08	.06	-.11	.15	-.02	.13	-.03	-.05	.17	.10	-.0	.03	.04	.01	-.16	.10	.08
0	.17	.14	.04	-.20	.16	.25	-.02	-.07	.04	.09	.19	-.04	-.09	-.05	-.05	.14	.06	.05	.06	-.03	-.04	.09	-.07	-.06
1	.09	.05	.05	-.15	.07	.11	-.01	-.01	.01	-.09	.02	.09	-.17	.07	.32	.12	.11	.19	.20	.15	.13	.31	-.08	.12
2	.12	.10	.07	-.10	.11	.13	.14	.14	.12	.01	-.17	-.06	-.05	-.04	-.01	.11	.06	.13	.05	.03	.10	.03	.06	.09
3	.15	.06	.13	-.13	.06	.15	-.07	-.17	.07	.00	.20	.08	.04	.10	.14	.27	.03	.04	.15	-.10	-.01	.06	.01	.01
4	.08	-.13	-.25	.09	-.12	-.16	.02	.21	-.05	-.14	.24	.09	.08	.09	.10	-.18	-.08	-.0	-.22	.08	.07	.02	-.08	-.12
5	.03	.06	.12	-.05	.05	.11	.02	-.00	-.12	-.04	-.12	.14	-.07	.07	.10	.11	.10	.05	.03	-.09	-.00	.12	-.02	-.04
6	-.06	-.04	.08	.04	-.04	.07	.09	-.03	.07	-.02	.19	-.13	.19	.06	.09	.19	.07	-.01	.01	.08	.05	-.11	.02	.07
7	.14	-.06	.15	-.05	-.06	.08	-.17	-.01	-.12	.09	-.18	.20	-.07	.26	.34	.32	.03	.04	.14	.03	.10	.20	-.05	.01
8	.18	.12	.03	-.17	.09	.16	-.07	-.11	-.05	.08	.14	.16	.09	.00	.03	.19	.11	.06	.14	.09	.11	.19	-.08	-.01
9	.06	.01	.13	-.10	.00	.13	.01	-.06	-.00	.00	.14	.07	-.11	.11	.12	.25	.00	.08	-.01	-.30	-.24	-.03	.21	.20
0	.00	.13	-.04	-.35	.10	.10	-.16	-.02	.19	-.05	.07	.18	-.05	.05	.15	.23	.09	.08	.11	.06	.06	.20	.00	.01
1	.13	.00	.07	-.40	.93	.28	.01	.07	-.01	.02	.06	.09	-.10	.01	.00	.09	.15	.01	.12	.07	-.03	.08	.03	.05
2	-.04	.07	.00	-.07	.06	.15	.08	.09	-.12	-.04	-.08	.06	-.03	.08	.07	.09	.04	.02	.06	-.08	.03	-.01	.09	-.05
3	-.35	-.40	-.07	.00	-.44	-.41	-.02	-.02	-.15	.01	-.21	-.10	.12	-.02	-.07	-.19	-.06	-.07	-.26	-.06	-.03	-.22	-.01	-.09
4	.10	.93	.06	-.44	.00	.30	.04	.10	.00	.02	.07	.08	-.10	.01	-.02	.09	.13	.06	.13	-.07	-.02	.08	.03	.06
5	.10	.28	.15	-.41	.30	.00	-.04	-.06	-.06	.00	.17	.09	-.11	.09	.05	.21	.09	.08	.25	.09	.06	.14	.00	.08
6	-.16	.01	.08	-.02	.04	-.04	.00	.20	.15	-.01	-.03	-.00	-.07	-.01	.00	.02	.05	.03	.02	.09	.09	.03	.04	.02
7	-.02	.07	.09	-.02	.10	-.06	.20	.00	-.10	-.02	-.04	-.00	.02	-.02	-.02	.04	.01	.07	-.00	.13	.12	.08	.07	.10
8	.19	-.01	-.12	-.15	.00	-.06	.15	-.10	.00	.00	.15	.04	-.05	.09	.02	.21	.02	.08	-.02	.01	-.03	.07	.00	.03
9	-.05	.02	-.04	.01	.02	.00	-.01	-.02	.00	.00	-.01	.01	-.03	.02	.00	.00	-.02	-.11	-.05	-.08	-.11	.00	-.04	.04
0	.07	.06	-.08	-.21	.07	.17	-.03	-.04	.15	-.01	.00	.05	.09	-.08	-.10	.23	.12	.12	.18	-.03	-.03	.14	.06	.13
	.18	.09	.06	-.10	.08	.09	-.00	-.00	.04	.01	.05	.00	.13	.08	.15	.15	.14	-.04	.07	.05	.04	.20	.06	-.01
	-.05	-.10	-.03	.12	-.10	-.11	-.01	.02	-.05	-.03	.09	-.13	.00	-.01	-.07	.01	.05	-.0	-.02	-.04	.08	-.10	-.02	-.10
	.05	.01	.08	-.02	.01	.09	-.07	-.02	.09	.02	-.08	.08	-.01	.00	.21	.18	-.04	-.01	.04	-.02	.07	-.02	.05	.06
	.15	-.00	-.07	-.07	-.02	.05	-.01	-.02	.02	.00	-.10	.15	-.07	.21	.00	.11	-.06	.01	.08	.09	.03	.07	-.08	-.02
	.23	.09	.09	-.19	.09	.21	.00	.04	.21	.00	.23	.15	.01	.18	.11	.00	.13	.13	.21	-.09	.07	.19	.08	.24
	.09	.15	.04	-.06	.13	.09	.02	.01	.02	-.02	.12	.14	.05	-.04	-.06	.13	.00	.17	.17	.11	.28	.00	.10	
	.08	.01	.02	-.07	.06	.08	.05	.07	.08	-.11	.12	-.04	-.09	-.01	.01	.13	.17	.00	.06	.06	.30	.40	.03	.07
	.11	.12	.06	-.26	.13	.25	.03	-.00	-.02	-.05	.18	.07	-.02	.04	.08	.18	.21	.17	.06	.00	.37	.45	.21	.45
	.06	-.07	-.08	-.06	-.07	.09	.02	.13	.01	-.08	-.03	.05	-.04	-.02	.09	-.03	.11	.06	.37	.00	.45	.46	-.07	.04
	-.03	-.03	-.03	-.02	.06	.09	.12	-.03	-.11	-.03	.04	.08	.07	.03	.07	.28	.30	.45	.45	.00	.64	.11	.18	
2	.20	.08	-.01	-.22	.08	.14	.03	.08	.07	.00	.14	.20	-.10	-.02	.07	.19	.28	.40	.51	.46	.64	.00	.03	.17
	.00	.03	.09	-.01	.03	.00	.04	.07	.00	-.04	.06	.06	-.02	.05	-.08	.08	.00	.03	.21	-.07	.11	.03	.00	.49
	.01	.05	-.05	-.09	.06	.08	.02	.10	.03	.04	.13	-.01	-.10	.06	-.02	.24	.10	.07	.45	.04	.18	.17	.49	.00

structure of the relationships among all the variables included in the analysis.

Table 66 presents the correlation coefficients among all 43 variables in the analysis. It is immediately apparent that most of the correlations are quite low. In fact, approximately 90 percent of the correlation coefficients are between ± .20, suggesting that most of the variables are unrelated. The absolute magnitude of these coefficients does not pose a problem for the smallest space analysis because all the linear distances in the space diagram which this analysis produces are relative under the constraint of the assumption of monotonicity.

The smallest space analysis (SSA-I) was performed at the University of Hawaii.[11] Three solutions were provided: one with two

11. Milton Bloombaum, associate professor of sociology, performed the analysis using Smallest Space Analysis-I; this routine is appropriate here because the matrix of intercorrelations is symmetrical. The computations were done on the IBM-7040 at the University of Hawaii's Statistical and Computing Center. The computing routine was provided through the courtesy of Louis Guttman, scientific director at the Israel Institute of Applied Social Research and professor of social and psychological measurement at the Hebrew University, Jerusalem.

dimensions, a second with three dimensions, and a third with four dimensions. The goodness of fit of any m-space (dimension = m) to a data matrix does not depend upon an arbitrary choice of coordinate axes for this space. The computer routine employed converges to a set of coordinates for a best fit in a given m-space.[12] The adequacy of each solution is represented by the coefficient of alienation, the computation of which is described elsewhere.[13] It is necessary here only to note that the smaller the coefficient, the better the fit. The coefficient of alienation for each of the three solutions was as follows: $m = 2$, .318; $= 3$, .232; $m = 4$, .165. It is apparent from the decreasing coefficients that each additional dimension improves the fit, with the four-dimensional solution being the best one.

Unfortunately, the visual representation of a three or four-dimensional space diagram is anything but simple,[14] and this analytic technique was chosen in large part because of the simplicity of its visual presentation. Therefore, I have chosen to confine visual presentation to the much less complex two-dimensional solution. For purposes of comparison, the coordinates for the four-dimensional solution, as well as the coordinates for the three-dimensional solution, are given in Appendix VIII.

The space diagram shown in figure 6 presents the actual linear distances between each of the 43 variables as seen in two dimensions. It is obvious that some variables cluster together, while others are more dispersed. Nonetheless, it must be emphasized that the way in which the analyst defines and labels any set of variables is somewhat arbitrary; the structure of the variables is invariable, so that the decision to define some set of variables as a "cluster" is dictated by the theoretical perspective of the analyst. From my theoretical perspective, I first chose to define two separable macroclusters—I call them domains—in this structure of variables. I think that my distinction between Domain I and Domain II is an obvious one. Not only are the two clusters of variables separable, but the 15 variables in Domain I are ones that were previously identified as being "pastoral" (that is, as occurring more frequently in the responses of pastoralists). Most of the remaining 28 variables were previously identified as being "farming" variables, as occurring more often in the responses of

12. See Laumann and Guttman (1966), p. 177.

13. Ibid., p. 172.

14. See Guttman (1968) and Guttman, Guttman, and Rosenzweig (1967).

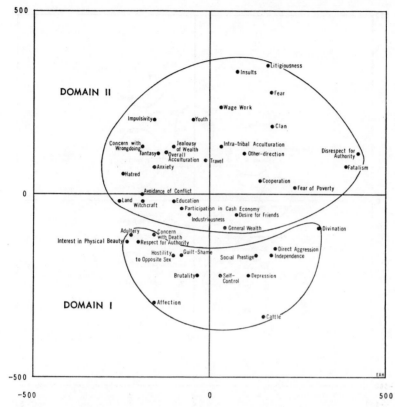

Figure 6. Two-dimensional space diagram: farming and pastoral domains.

farmers, or being mixed as regards pastoral or farming orientations.

I find this solution extremely interesting, for it suggests that when the responses of individuals are considered quite independently of their tribe or of any identification as pastoralists or farmers, some variables which were associated in prior analyses continue to cluster together. The variables that I have included in Domain I are: (1) cattle, (2) divination, (3) direct aggression, (4) independence, (5) social prestige, (6) depression, (7) self-control, (8) brutality, (9) affection, (10) guilt and shame, (11) hostility to the opposite sex, (12) concern with death, (13) respect for authority, (14) concern with adultery, and (15) interest in physical beauty. This cluster of variables includes almost every variable that earlier analyses had tentatively identified as being associated with pastoralism. Of the 28 variables that constitute Domain II, two (fear and clan) were previously identified as being associated with pastoralism, and two others (litigiousness and concern

227

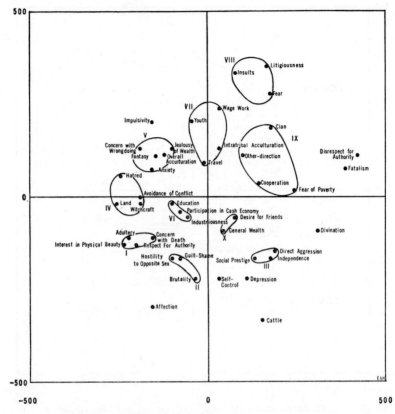

Figure 7. Two-dimensional space diagram: ten subclusters.

with wrongdoing) tended to be pastoral. In addition to the variables earlier identified as being associated with farming, Domain II includes all of the acculturation variables, once again suggesting that acculturation is more likely to be associated with farming variables than with pastoral ones.

Within these two basic domains, there are several significant clusters. I have defined ten such clusters which are shown in figure 7; each cluster is defined primarily by the close association of the variables in it, and secondarily by my ability to provide a plausible account for this association.

Turning first to clusters within the pastoral domain (Domain I), I would like to call attention to three particularly close associations of variables. Cluster I includes four variables: interest in physical beauty, concern with adultery, respect for authority, and concern

228

with death. The association of the first two of these variables, physical beauty and adultery, is hardly surprising, suggesting as it does only that those men who talk about beautiful women also talk about adultery. It should be noted that, in table 66, the correlation (r) between these two variables is .93, by far the highest correlation between any two variables in the correlation matrix. But this cluster also suggests that such men respect authority. At first glance, this association appears to be anomalous, but in fact it is not. In these four societies, and particularly in the pastoral sectors of these societies, the acceptance of a man's interest in beauty and in pursuing it, even with other men's wives, is an obvious fact of everyday life. It is also accepted that men caught in such acts bear the responsibility to pay compensation. Thus, it is not at all surprising that a respect for authority should be related to so well-established a practice as adultery. I have also made the nearby variable, concern with death, a part of this cluster. I have done so because, while in fact men do not kill each other over adultery (at least they very rarely do so), they do *talk* about killing each other. That the talk is largely rhetorical is clear. Whether it lends excitement to the chase or harkens back to earlier, more violent days varies from tribe to tribe. Nevertheless, talk about violent death continues to be associated with the amatory subjects of beauty and adultery.

The second cluster consists of the extremely close relationship of two variables, hostility to the opposite sex and guilt and shame, and the more distant association of a third variable, brutality. This cluster is close to the center of the pastoral domain, and it is among the pastoralists that male dominance and, thus, hostility to the opposite sex, is most extreme. I had not previously found much reason to believe that men felt guilt or shame over their openly expressed hostility to women, or women's expressed hostility to them, but this cluster suggests that just such a relationship may exist. It also suggests that brutality may be related to these two variables as well. Thus, rather than confirming a previously established association, this cluster points to an intriguing hypothesis, one, by the way, that could not have been inferred from an examination of the r matrix (table 66) alone. However, when a 20 percent sample of the response protocols was reexamined following the suggestion of this cluster, it was found that over 50 percent of all indications of guilt, shame, or brutality by men were associated with antagonism between the sexes.

Cluster III is a tight one, consisting of social prestige, direct aggression, and independence. That direct aggression and independence should be so closely associated makes obvious sense, although the correlation between the two is not high ($r = .30$) It is especially noteworthy that social prestige is closest to these two variables, suggesting that both independence and direct aggression are highly rewarded by pastoralists. That the variable depression should be so close is not consistent with our expectations. We saw earlier that depression is more frequent among pastoralists, but I had assumed that depression was related to fear, age, failure, and the like, not that it was a correlate of prestige. Indeed, I would have anticipated that the closest variable to social prestige would have been cattle, which is, although relatively nearby, somewhat more distant than depression.[15]

Within the pastoral domain as a whole, the centrally located variable might be self-control, yet it stands as an isolate. Its closest association is with depression, an interesting concatenation. Two other variables that are central to the pastoral world, affection and cattle, are also isolates, as is divination. Although these variables were previously seen as essential designata of the pastoral response pattern, and while they continue to be pastoral, they are not closely linked with any other variables. In all three instances, this degree of isolation is surprising.

Domain II is more dispersed, more heterogeneous, and more complex than the pastoral domain. This, too, may be theoretically significant, for the models from which this research derived always assumed that pastoral values and attitudes would be more "tightly" related than would be any corresponding attributes of farming life.[16] Despite the complexity of the domain, there are some theoretically meaningful clusters within it. The first of these, Cluster IV, is particularly important. It includes four variables: witchcraft, avoidance of conflict, land, and hatred. This clustering is a striking parallel to our original formulation about a central farming social dilemma. This formulation can be synopsized as follows: a shortage of land pro-

15. As a clinical phenomenon, depression is highly diverse. Explanations of its origins are not only diverse, they are often contradictory, ranging from ungratified sexuality and aggression to loss of self-esteem. This latter and more obvious connection best relates to the pastoral response pattern. For a review of depression, see Beck (1967). I might mention the apparent congruence of these findings with Cohen's (1961) social cohesion thesis, or with the psychoanalytic "doing defense" thesis (Mandell, 1970). Without further investigation, however, these data can support neither position.

16. See Walter Goldschmidt's introduction to this book.

duces hatred, but because farmers must live together, they must avoid overt conflict; hence direct aggression must be avoided but indirect aggression will be more frequently expressed in the form of witchcraft. The extremely close association of witchcraft with avoidance of conflict in this cluster is particularly interesting. Of all the clusters in what I have called the farming domain, none is more paradigmatic, or clearly defined, than this one.

Cluster V is complex, but it might best be seen as a blend of acculturation with previously mixed farming-pastoral attitudes. It includes the most fundamental acculturation variable—high rank in an overall acculturation scale—but it also contains these three variables: anxiety, jealousy of wealth, and concern with wrongdoing. Anxiety clearly identifies farmers, but the other two variables are not clearly defined as pastoral or farming. Still, that these variables should be related is no surprise; the logic of explanation might be similar to that used in Cluster IV, namely that jealousy of wealth, whatever its relationship to direct conflict, can be expected to relate to a concern with wrongdoing and general anxiety. The final variable, fantasy, has an uncertain background, although chapter 8 did suggest that it was *not* associated with pastoralism. It has been associated with both farming life and acculturation, and perhaps it serves to characterize this cluster which is related both to the farming dilemma seen in Cluster IV and to acculturation. Indeed, perhaps the entire cluster should be seen as an acculturation-influenced relative of Cluster IV.

Cluster VI is far less difficult to interpret. Its three variables, education, involvement in the cash economy, and industriousness, mark it as a clear-cut acculturation cluster, one that has significance above the ordinary in its linkage of education with industriousness. This combination has been commented upon by several observers of East African farming populations. The present analysis offers support for that speculation, but adds participation in the cash economy as a variable that intervenes between education and industriousness.

Cluster VII is yet another acculturation subcategory. It associates youth with three indices of acculturation: participation in wage work, high intratribal rank, and travel. This association is perfectly reasonable, if not very significant. The major surprise is the separation of this cluster from Cluster VI, when we might have expected to find a closer relation of youth to education. As an added point, although impulsivity is not included in this cluster, it does seem to be more closely related to youth than any other variable. This sort of association, too, appeals to our Western common sense.

Cluster VIII, fear, insults, and litigiousness, is an isolated but

231

interesting one which may well point to a separable aspect of life. I interpret the association of these three variables as follows: an insult leads to litigation, which in turn leads to a fear of the consequences of court action. In all tribes, not only among the Hehe who were so obsessed with face, an insult can lead to litigation. Again, all tribes had one or another version of the saying, "Courts make enemies," thus reaffirming the belief that litigation is not without danger. But there is an anomaly here. Litigiousness and fear have previously been seen as primarily pastoral variables, while insults is primarily a farming one. This cluster seems to indicate that all three are closer to other farming responses than to pastoral ones. Note, for example, the distance that separates this cluster from Cluster III (direct aggression, independence, and so on), an opposition that serves well to differentiate the farming world from that of pastoralists in terms of conflict and its resolution.

Cluster IX is frankly speculative. All of these variables are mixed in pastoral-farming affiliation, but they have previously tended to be more pastoral than farming in orientation. An interpretation of any association between these four variables may be forced, but clan concern, other-direction, cooperation, and fear of poverty do share a relationship. For example, clan responsibility requires cooperation; about this there can be no question. Clan members share corporate responsibility for the actions of other clan members. And one concern that clan members, with their corporate responsibility, must have is poverty; they soon weary of the need to aid indigent clansmen. Other-direction has a more tenuous connection; it may be involved in cooperation, or it may not. It is, by linear distance, actually closer to the variable intratribal acculturation than any other and perhaps it more properly belongs in Cluster VII. Similarly, it could be argued that the variable clan belongs with fear in the litigation cluster (VIII). In short, this cluster is weak and tenuous, yet the association of clan, fear of poverty, and cooperation is plausible.

The so-called farming domain (Domain II) also contains some interesting "isolated" variables. The first is a curious pairing of fatalism with disrespect for authority. Unless this relationship signals a kind of African estrangement, a loss of faith in authority combined with an acceptance of life as it is, I do not understand this pairing. The two variables could be seen with equal ease as either contradictions or a unity. I must leave them as a puzzle. The second puzzle is impulsivity. This variable stands off by itself, on the edge of the farming cluster. It could be linked to youth, and thus to several measures of acculturation, or it could be related to concern with wrongdoing. But it seems to me to stand alone. As the final cluster, Cluster X, we find wealth and desire for friends linked. These variables are located almost in the center of the space diagram, approximately midway between the farming and the pastoral domains. Yet neither variable is very closely related to any other variable. One could make a case for associations with industriousness or with social prestige, but both are actually fairly distant variables. It seems to be more correct for wealth to stand alone, related only to a desire for friends. This cluster suggests, as does some ethnographic evidence, that rich men are lonely, and that, perhaps as a consequence, they seek friends. This wistful note can serve to mark an end to the interpretation of the space diagram.

A FACTOR ANALYSIS

The Guttman-Lingoes smallest space analysis has examined a matrix of correlation coefficients and has shown the ways in which these many variables cluster together in Euclidean space. After this analysis, the same data matrix was reexamined by means of factor analysis in an effort to discover any latent dimensions that might serve to complement the understandings produced by the smallest space analysis.

Before presenting the findings of this factor analysis, I should clarify my decision to employ factor analysis in this role. Earlier, I mentioned the ambiguity that was sometimes involved in the interpretation of the factors extracted by factor analysis. The interpretative process of these factors can indeed be complex, but this is only one of the criticisms frequently leveled against the technique. Roiling debate over the properties of factor analytic procedure has involved virtually every step of the analysis: the number of factors that should be extracted, the methods of extraction, the criteria for estimating communalities, the means of rotating factors, and so on. While many of these criticisms have merit, others seem to reflect sectarian zeal more than an effort to understand and improve the procedure. I believe that the technique has demonstrated that it can be of value for many problems that require the simultaneous handling of a large number of variables.[17] When factor analysis is used as I have used it here, as an additional means of examining a large matrix of correlation coefficients, I believe that its value far outweighs its possible disadvantages. Other studies have shown that while the results of small-

17. For example, see Driver and Schuessler (1957), Gouldner and Peterson (1962), and Minturn and Lambert (1964).

TABLE 67

ROTATED CENTROID FACTORS

Variable	1	2	3	4	5	6	7
1. Impulsivity	.10988	.01044	-.01097	.27176	-.08793	-.06093	.08132
2. Insults	-.06620	-.49146	-.17486	.40309	.26514	.13888	-.05368
3. Fear	-.10503	-.16842	-.12089	-.36922	.08772	.20734	-.08680
4. Cattle	.06581	.37901	-.08370	-.57800	-.16189	.00069	-.14338
5. Land	.25091	-.17647	.17292	.16040	-.35581	-.14188	.39927
6. Independence	-.00459	.42187	-.03390	.07417	.15539	.03175	.02956
7. Fatalism	-.37413	.08507	-.14166	.29535	-.24488	.01500	-.12972
8. Avoidance of conflict	.57671	-.00454	.05198	.15134	.06329	-.11349	-.05861
9. Depression	.03918	.48598	.04995	-.04312	-.04196	-.05711	-.03099
10. Respect for authority	.25538	.11370	.19789	.10290	-.18040	-.11373	.22635
11. Jealousy of wealth	.13310	-.08503	.06577	.10684	.35105	.07453	.37228
12. Desire for friends	-.02900	.15330	.16536	-.08923	.00086	.26506	.18995
13. Hostility to opposite sex	.31697	.22692	.03980	-.03263	.20467	-.17929	.12652
14. Litigiousness	-.26338	-.41897	-.07741	.25363	.21639	.09762	-.19420
15. Hatred	.10988	-.18667	.05491	-.26815	.12126	-.14105	.39693
16. Direct aggression	.00413	.58167	-.02892	.04420	.03106	.03975	-.03998
17. Fantasy	.33765	-.17302	-.09792	-.17546	.46950	-.02333	.27222
18. Witchcraft	.49122	-.02553	.06738	-.02006	-.00328	-.05890	.01658
19. Brutality	-.00898	.16234	-.00368	-.05205	.12308	-.06519	.52520
20. Anxiety	.31423	-.04166	.18440	.24337	.19569	-.05608	.02108
21. Interest in physical beauty	.07871	-.04160	.91634	-.08987	-.00245	.04711	-.04105
22. Self-control	.06031	.17068	.06784	-.29129	.10885	.10543	.15556
23. Disrespect for authority	-.33294	-.04284	-.49927	-.11381	-.05833	-.04113	-.13031
24. Adultery	.05686	-.03552	.93050	-.01005	-.02790	.07713	.00642
25. Concern with death	.24019	.14352	.36862	-.08873	-.00697	-.07749	.25112
26. Fear of poverty	-.13429	.12087	.02731	.01549	-.05871	.38913	.04134
27. Clan	-.13029	-.10562	.07714	.05250	-.01798	.41017	-.02264
28. Cooperation	.06130	.17328	.02504	.39805	.03501	.08256	.04138
29. Affection	.14478	-.08895	-.03875	-.10650	-.12621	.00336	.05588
30. Guilt-shame	.31406	.28105	.07402	.31031	.24311	-.00097	.09416
31. Concern with wrongdoing	.20193	-.18727	.08770	.11093	.18757	-.07103	.15234
32. Divination	.10040	.16265	-.13672	-.02218	-.08970	-.01862	-.29572
33. Other-direction	.00954	.06369	.00188	.06630	.45210	-.00867	.06873
34. Youth	.08102	.00582	-.00849	-.07759	.62218	.03268	.04952
35. Industriousness	.43556	.30545	.06350	.15763	.18022	.05721	.25280
36. Education	.20578	.07037	.14035	-.03594	-.07213	.06564	.08063
37. Travel	.18350	.01396	-.02679	.05437	.02029	.17440	.54870
38. Participation in cash economy	.26696	-.14752	-.09541	.03655	-.19936	.26888	.30451
39. Wage work	.14060	-.13514	-.05412	-.01056	.11545	.50041	-.00483
40. Intratribal acculturation	.30581	-.25076	-.11825	.00755	.23877	.37658	-.05770
41. Overall acculturation	.21525	-.43857	.00760	.15554	-.01034	.25630	.16102
42. Social prestige	.04593	.03526	.04667	.20440	-.01847	.22501	.28663
43. General wealth	.43360	.06794	.10570	-.09880	.07727	.24330	.07840

est space analysis and factor analysis differ, the two techniques can be made to complement each other.[18]

A principal components analysis of the same 43 × 43 correlation matrix was carried out. Unities were inserted in the diagonals, and all factors with latent roots greater than 1.00 were accepted.[19] The seven resulting factors were rotated to simple structure (Varimax) by the method of simple plane. These factors were orthogonal; that is, each factor was independent of every other factor. The loadings of all 43 variables on seven factors are shown in table 67.

In interpreting these seven factors, the following points should be kept in mind. The loadings on each factor vary in size. The larger

TABLE 68

FACTOR 1: CONFLICT AVOIDANCE

Number	Loading	Variable
8	.58	Conflict avoidance
18	.49	Witchcraft
35	.44	Industriousness
43	.43	General wealth

NOTE: All loadings on all factors are shown in Table 67. In tables 68-74, variables with loadings below .40 are only rarely shown.

a variable's loading the greater its correlation with the "factor," or "dimension," that is presumed to underlie the array of variables included in the factor. Thus, a variable with a loading in the high .90s would have a very strong relationship to the putative underlying factor. Variables with lesser loadings would be weaker measures of this underlying dimension. Factors may contain negative as well as positive loadings. The positive and negative poles of these "bipolar" factors are opposites.

Loadings for the variables in factor 1 are shown in table 68. I have named this factor conflict avoidance after its most prominent variable. Naming factors, of course, is arbitrary, and can be misleading. Ideally, names should suggest the factor's common, underlying dimension, but actually they more often reflect the analyst's willingness to speculate about this dimension. Since my aptitude for such

18. Comparisons of smallest space analysis and factor analysis are available in Nutch and Bloombaum (1968) and Schubert (1967).

19. See Kaiser (1960).

factorial archaeology is limited, I shall use the name of each factor as its label, not necessarily as its explanation.

Factor 1 is clearly concerned with the relationship of witchcraft to the avoidance of conflict, a relationship that also showed up clearly in the smallest space diagram (figure 7). It also links industriousness with general wealth, a relationship that was not as evident in the space diagram, although the two variables were quite close to each other. Nonetheless, the relationship is one that would seem to "make sense." Furthermore, there is substantial ethnographic evidence to indicate that, while industry does often lead to wealth, wealth

TABLE 69

FACTOR 2: AGGRESSION

Number	Loading	Variable
16	.58	Direct aggression
9	.49	Depression
5	.42	Independence
4	.38	Cattle
14	−.42	Litigiousness
41	−.44	Overall acculturation
2	−.49	Insults

makes a man especially vulnerable to witchcraft. This knowledge might make a wealthy man eager to avoid any conflict that could cause an aggrieved party to employ witchcraft against him. At least, such an explanation is plausible. More important for the theoretical position of this research is the close association of witchcraft with avoidance of conflict. We presumed that such a relationship would obtain, and would tend to characterize farmers. We continue to find evidence to support this view.

Factor 2 (table 69) seems to be polarized around the question of aggression. It indicates that direct aggression goes with depression, independence, and cattle—a cluster that also appeared in the space diagram—but is opposite to litigation. The negative pole of this factor seems to suggest that, among acculturated men, when insult is given, it leads to court, not to combat. This interpretation is not inconsistent with the space diagram, nor is it at odds with ethnographic reality. We anticipated just such a distinction, with direct aggression being a pastoral trait, opposed to litigation. This factor tells us little that was not apparent from the smallest space diagram except that it tends to link litigiousness more clearly to acculturation than that diagram did.

Factor 3 (table 70) is a replica of Cluster I within the pastoral domain of the space diagram. Once again it shows the extremely close relationship of adultery and physical beauty and the lesser relationship of concern with death and respect for authority. Here, however,

TABLE 70

FACTOR 3: ADULTERY

Number	Loading	Variable
24	.93	Adultery
21	.92	Concern with physical beauty
10	.37	Concern with Death
23	−.50	Disrespect for authority

TABLE 71

FACTOR 4: CATTLE

Number	Loading	Variable
2	.40	Insults
28	.40	Cooperation
4	−.57	Cattle

the factor analysis differs from the space diagram by not including respect for authority; instead, it has moved completely across the space diagram to include, as a polar negative, disrespect for authority.[20] The result has the same meaning as did the smallest space analysis.

Factor 4 (table 71), for which I have found no fully appropriate label, is extremely difficult to interpret. It moves from cattle (its

20. As Appendix IV indicates, "respect for authority" and "disrespect for authority" are not merely two sides of the same coin. The former refers to *any* authority, such as that of a man or woman, or the old over the young, and so on. The latter variable refers only to authority vested in a formal status or office (for example, chief or elder). Thus, there is no necessary relationship, either positive or negative, between the two variables. Indeed, as table 66 shows, the correlation between them is − .20.

heaviest loading) at the bottom of the space diagram, through co-operation in the middle of the diagram, to insults at the diagram's upper edge. The three variables are thus "lined up" in a curious fashion, but other than this specious lineality, their association is obscure. Insults and cattle certainly do belong to opposite domains: the first is a farming trait, the second is clearly a pastoral one; and this the factor clearly indicates. The linkage to cooperation does not seem to fit either the space diagram, or any theoretical interpretation I can provide.

TABLE 72

FACTOR 5: YOUTHFUL SENSITIVITY

Number	Loading	Variable
34	.62	Youth
17	.47	Fantasy
33	.45	Other-direction

Factor 5 (table 72) makes an interesting cluster of three variables that had not previously been suspected to relate closely to one another. The association between youth, fantasy, and other-direction can be interpreted as a sensitivity dimension. Indeed, I am tempted to think of it as the Janus-faces of African youth; one face alertly looking to people in the outside world, the other face dreamily sensitive to an inner world of fantasy. Whatever the relevance of this speculation, this factor suggests a radically different interpretation of these three variables than the one offered in the space diagram. In that diagram, I placed each of these three variables in separate clusters within the farming domain. The factor analysis suggests that another, more intriguing, unity may tie them together.

TABLE 73

FACTOR 6: POVERTY

Number	Loading	Variable
39	.50	Wage work
27	.41	Clan
26	.39	Fear of poverty

Loadings for variables in factor 6 are shown in table 73. This small unipolar factor seems to me to make a kind of practical sense. Although these three variables (wage work, clan, and fear of poverty) have a tenuous relationship in the space diagram, I saw no reason to cluster all three together. The association between a fear of poverty and a concern with the clan, as the social agency most responsible for and worried about indigency, has already been discussed, and these two variables were placed together in Cluster IX (figure 7). The factor analysis adds wage work, suggesting, possibly, that men who fear poverty may view wage work as a source of wealth, and thus as a solution to their problem, either as poor men themselves, or as clansmen weary of supporting poor men. An alternative explanation might be that men who engage in wage work have acquired some wealth, and have spoken of the clan and of poverty as an expression of their fear of losing their wealth.

TABLE 74

FACTOR 7: BRUTALITY

Number	Loading	Variable
37	.55	Travel
19	.53	Brutality
5	.40	Land
15	.40	Hatred

Factor 7 (table 74) is a surprising one. It combines the closely associated variables land and hatred with travel, which is some distance away on the space diagram. What is more, it includes brutality, which in the smallest space analysis is situated in the center of the pastoral domain, far from these other variables. Thus, this factor points to a dimension that runs through the farming domain into the pastoral one—a plausible enough possibility—to link such strange bedfellows as travel and brutality. An interpretation could take this form: farmers (men who mention land) are given to hatred by the many frustrations of farming life, so they travel and give evidence of little kindness to their fellowmen. But, of course, this is no more than a guess, and a wild one at that. If this factor is to be taken seriously, then we can only assume that travel and brutality are both products of something more basic—perhaps the underlying relationship of hatred and land (or land shortage) that we have already noted.

239

These seven factors do not exhaust the significant relationships among the 43 variables. For example, all seven factors together account for only 32 percent of the total variance in the original correlation matrix. However, these seven factors represent 70 percent of the total variance accounted for by all possible factors.[21] I believe that these seven factors did succeed in adding some new dimensions to our previous understanding of this mass of variables.

ACCULTURATION REVIEWED

Finally, we must return to the perplexing problem of European acculturation, the subject of chapter 6. As reported there, acculturation became a problem for us because, as we had anticipated, all four farming populations were more acculturated than their pastoral counterparts, and consequently "farmingness" and acculturation were confounded. Chapter 6 attempted to disentangle the two by an internal analysis of the responses of persons in each of the four societies. When the responses of the more acculturated farmers were compared to those of the less acculturated farmers in that same society, it was discovered that there were very few differences. So few were these differences that it was possible to conclude, with a few specified exceptions, that the systematic response differentials between farmers and pastoralists could not be explained by differences in acculturation.

Turning first to the smallest space analysis, it is clear that when individual interview responses and various other variables (including six measures of individual acculturation) are intercorrelated, the acculturation variables all fall within what I have referred to as the farming domain (figure 6). This association confirms the earlier findings about the relatively greater acculturation of farmers. As figure 7 shows, however, most of the acculturation variables included in the smallest space analysis cluster together, rather than being closely associated with what we have come to regard as the centrally important farming variables. Thus, we find that all six acculturation

21. All positive eigenvalues accounted for 46 percent of the total variance in the original correlation matrix. The seven factors that were rotated account for the following percentages of the total variance: factor 1, 9 percent; factor 2, 6 percent; factor 3, 5 percent; factor 4, 3 percent; factor 5, 3 percent; factor 6, 3 percent; and factor 7, 3 percent.

variables are located in only three clusters. Indeed, five of these variables occur together in two clusters (figure 7; see Clusters VI and VII). It is obvious, therefore, that these variables have relatively weak association with farming variables. The sixth acculturation variable, overall acculturation, falls into Cluster V, a cluster that does contain some possible farming variables, namely concern with wrongdoing, fantasy, jealousy of wealth, and anxiety. However, three other farming clusters, including Cluster IV which is the most central cluster in terms of our model, are not associated with *any* acculturation variable. Thus, we find that while there is some association between acculturation and farming variables in the smallest space analysis, this association is relatively tangential.

When the factor analysis of these same variables is considered, this association again appears to be weak. Of the seven factors presented in chapter 9, three include acculturation variables. In factor 2 (aggression), the variable overall acculturation is related to litigiousness and insults, all three of which are negatively related to the pastoral variable, direct aggression. In factor 6 (poverty), wage work is related to clan and fear of poverty. There is nothing central to "farmingness" in either of these two factors. Factor 7 (brutality) associates the farming variables land and hatred with the pastoral variable brutality and the acculturation variable travel. This factor does include some important farming variables. There were, however, no acculturation variables in factor 1 (conflict avoidance); and in terms of our theory, this was the most important "farming" factor. The factor analysis, then, does associate acculturation variables with some farming variables; and while this association is difficult to interpret, we cannot deny that there is *some* relationship of acculturation variables to farming variables. Therefore, we must examine an additional source of information, the correlation matrix upon which both the smallest space analysis and the factor analysis were based.

This matrix (see table 66) presents the intercorrelations among all 43 variables, and consequently it provides us with an opportunity to make some simple comparisons. You will recall that most of the intercorrelations in this matrix are quite low, with 90 percent falling between ± .20. Using this figure as a criterion, we can examine the strength of the correlations among the 6 acculturation variables and the remaining 37 variables in this matrix. There are 222 correlations among the 6 acculturation variables and the 37 nonacculturation variables; of these 222 correlations, only 15, or less than 7 percent, are greater than $\pm$ .20. On the other hand, of all possible correlations among the 6 acculturation variables themselves, over 66 percent are greater than $\pm$ .20. What is more, the magnitude of these correlations also differs. The average correlation between acculturation variables is .41; the average correlation between acculturation variables and nonacculturation variables is .26. It is certainly not surprising that the acculturation variables should correlate more highly with themselves than they do with nonacculturation variables, but it is significant that acculturation variables correlate so very weakly with nonaccultura- tion variables, there being only 15 of 222 correlations over the $\pm$ .20 criterion. What is still more significant, of these 15 correlations greater than $\pm$ .20, only two are with variables previously found definitely to be associated with farming, and four others are with variables that *may* have farming associations.

Thus we see that although acculturation variables are more highly related to farming variables than to pastoral variables, this re- lationship is far less impressive than it originally appeared. We must conclude that while the farming response patterns are influenced by acculturation, it is by no means true that these farming patterns can be accounted for as well by the respondents' acculturation as by their identification as farmers.

CONCLUSION

The smallest space analysis indicated that the 43 individual inter- view responses and attributes were roughly separable into two do- mains, one clearly pastoral, and the other largely farming. Within these theoretical domains of variables there were a number of clusters of more closely related variables. The factor analysis served to con- firm several of these clusters, but it also pointed to some previously unexpected combinations of variables. Several of these variable clus- ters, both those seen in the space diagram and those derived from the factor analysis, could be made the focus of future investigations. Others have immediate relevance for many of the pastoral-farming differentials that we had sought to locate in this research. Still others clarify the role of European acculturation.

Perhaps the most significant of these findings, however, is the fact that most of those variables previously associated with farming continue to be clearly distinguished from those previously linked with pastoralism. This chapter sought to determine whether or not pastoral-farming differences that were built up out of averaged interview responses and modal sketches would hold up when the responses of individuals were examined without regard to tribe or site. I believe that this chapter has shown that pastoral-farming differences that appeared in the earlier, more generalized, analyses also appear when individual responses and attributes are examined in multivariate perspective.

The Environment:
A Search for
Some Sources
of Ecological
Differentiation 10

This research was directed toward a search for covariation in the attitudes and values of ecologically different populations, and therefore the discovery and documentation of response differentials between farmers and pastoralists was our primary goal. In addition, however, we were interested in the *sources* of covariation. We sought, that is, to explain how and why it was that farmers and pastoralists became different. Thus, we predicted that the attitudes, values, and personality features of farmers and pastoralists would vary *because* of certain variations in their environments (including their economies and technologies). In this chapter I attempt to locate some of the sources of pastoral-farming response covariation by turning to a consideration of the physical, social, and economic environments with which these populations have come to terms.

This chapter explores relationships between environmental and attitudinal variables in a search for causal linkages. Before discussing these explorations, we should reiterate the conceptual and theoretical underpinnings of our concern with the environment. The central theoretical position has been stated by Goldschmidt in *Man's Way,* and in a series of working papers prepared for the *Culture and Ecology Project.*[1] The position is summarized in the introduction to this volume. As a theory of cultural evolution, it is related to several past and present theoretical systems, from the "cultural materialism" of the nineteenth century to the "evolutionism" of such anthropologists as Julian Steward and the psychologically focused schemata of Abram Kardiner and John Whiting. Although these formulations dif-

1. See Goldschmidt (1959) and (1965).

fer in their conceptualizations of "environment," they are alike in the nature of their causal assumptions. Thus, the physical habitat is seen as setting limits upon the economic uses peoples may make of it. A second limitation is what might be called the "stock of technological knowledge at hand" by which a people may establish their economy. This set of technological and economic knowledge and practices in turn determines limits to and makes demands upon the kinds of social arrangements and interpersonal relationships that may be established. And, finally, these institutionalized social patterns influence the thoughts and feelings of men, and the practices to which these thoughts and feelings are related. These formulations, and ours, agree that livelihood comes first, that social institutions are given shape by economic factors, and that ideology and personality are formed by social institutions.

Some of these formulations employ a language that is unabashedly causal, or deterministic. Others, perhaps the majority, veil causal assumptions in an elliptical idiom. It is not simply that these elliptical versions see laws as being probabilistic, they so ensnare themselves in contingencies, interactions, and "on the other hand" equivocations that causality and explanation are emasculated or lost altogether. So it is that some modern versions of ecology, although retaining the idea that populations "adapt" to their "environments," seem to speak as if human populations develop their behaviors, maintain them, and change them by some internal servomechanism which makes any discussion of "efficient cause" unnecessary, an anachronism of a pre-systems theory era.

I return to questions of causal inference in our research in the final chapter. Here, it is necessary only to reaffirm that our theory *is* causal, and that we sought the "ultimate" causes of attitudes, values, and feelings in men's technological and economic relationships to their environments. Of course, we invoke such disclaimers as "in the long run," or "for the most part," or "on the average," for the influence of the environment is neither immediate nor is it uniform. About this, too, I say more in the last chapter.

We must also note that our perspective was not merely a *simpliste* version of habitat, economy, and society; it was a version of ecology. Therefore, we were influenced by those related perspectives known as functionalism, equilibrium, or general systems theory. Thus, we were concerned with populations as sociocultural systems, as organized wholes of which the parts are in complex and dynamic relationships with each other. In ecological theory, because of the

245

complexity of processes by which animals relate themselves to their environments, these ecological processes have increasingly come to be seen in systems theory terms. What is more, in anthropology in general, functional theory and equilibrium theory have been modified by encounters with systems theory. Systems theory, consisting of various borrowings from thermodynamics, information theory, cybernetics, and systems engineering, has, as Watt has pointed out, directed the study of ecology to a greater attention to social systems as input-output informational structures and processes, characterized by steady states and feedback.[2] Our own theory of ecology was modified by some of these understandings, although the modification was through the eclectic borrowing of concepts and ideas, rather than through adoption of any formal systems analytic position.

Our systems-influenced ecological position led to the construction of a research design in which we were concerned not to do unnecessary violence to "natural" sociocultural systems; therefore, we selected tribes and communities, rather than sampling population aggregates as if they were randomly occurring individuals. Within these sociocultural systems each ethnographer made every effort to understand the networks of interrelationship that organized them, as well as the articulations between social and economic systems. However, a precisely measured analysis of a complex sociocultural system is a formidable undertaking. To have attempted such a comparative analysis of eight systems, as was required by our research design, was far beyond our resources. The size of the systems, the numbers and types of variables involved, the different levels of organization, the interlocking cause-effect pathways produced so complex a problem for comparative analysis that neither our measurement techniques nor our manpower could possibly have permitted a formal quantitative analysis of each system as a *system*.

Instead, we followed what conventional wisdom in ecology—animal as well as human ecology—has put forth as an essential operating principle: extremely complex systems can most easily be understood when they are dissected into a large number of very simple unit components, rather than a small number of relatively complex systems.[3] Consequently, in my efforts to correlate interview responses with features of the environment, I have chosen to examine several relatively simple unit relationships rather than a few highly complex ones.

2. Watt (1966), Miller (1965).

3. Watt (1966), p. 3.

THE RESEARCH

In one sense, the controlled comparison that constituted the basis of the Culture and Ecology research design was intended to "hold the environment constant"; however, it was always assumed that this environmental constancy would be approximate, not perfect. Consequently, each of the eight environments in which research was located became the subject of intensive study by the project's geographer, Philip Porter.

Porter's task was to examine all eight study sites in order to document the prevailing patterns of environmental use. In addition, he was asked to assess the potential of each environment both with regard to its present use and with regard to other, technologically feasible uses. Finally, he was asked to explain how the observed economic and technological systems were organized and how they were related to their environments.

Porter's mandate took him to each study site, where he gathered a vast array of data on such matters as soils and land forms, vegetation, land and water use, settlement patterns, arrangement of domiciles, layout of fields, grazing routes, marketing and the flow of commodities. In addition, he made daily measurements of maximal and minimal temperature, rainfall, evaporation, solar radiation, wind, and soil moisture. He also collected a host of ethnogeographic conceptions concerning time, distance, location, climate, soil, vegetation, disease, and the like. In pursuit of these and many other diverse indices of economic and technological use of environment in East Africa, his itinerary took him to and from the eight study sites, in the course of which he, as I, was plagued by the exigencies of drought and deluge. A full account of his procedures, concepts, and findings is available in his monograph in the Culture and Ecology series.

SELECTION AND MEASUREMENT OF VARIABLES

Although a series of project conferences that dealt with general ecological theory and with our own formulation of this theory helped to give us a common perspective for viewing relevant features of the environment, when it came to the actual selection of environmental variables, and systems of variables, for study, the crucial problem continued to be measurement. Theory directed us to measure a great many aspects of the environment; on that account we had no shortage of potential variables. Our problem was one of measurement.

Neither our theory nor any other modern version of sociocultural evolution or ecology postulated any immediate and inevitable (or necessary and sufficient) causal link from features of the physical habitat to social organization to ideology. Without consideration of the critical intervening features of economy and technology, study of the physical habitat in relationship to ideology becomes virtually meaningless. Hence, most of the environmental variables that were easily measured—amount of rainfall, elevation, evaporation, temperature, and the like—were not what we had conceived of as independent variables. Instead, we had to find means of measuring relationships that combined technological, economic, or demographic variables with features of the physical environment.

Furthermore, we were faced with a need for relatively precise measurement. One dimension of this problem is familiar to geographers, namely, the problem of scale. It would have been foolish for me to collect interview data with great care and to quantify them precisely, only to correlate precise data with gross estimates of, for instance, economic potential. Similarly, many of Porter's precise measures, such as those pertaining to solar radiation derived from the Gunn-Bellani, were far more precise than any of my data. Thus I sought some degree of equivalence between Porter's many environmental data and my interview data, hoping all the while to avoid measurement by fiat or by statistical sleight of hand.[4]

Perhaps an example of the difficulties we faced would provide a useful illustration of this problem. Our theory, like most social theories, would look to high mortality as a stress that would predictably cause widespread social system strain taking the form of, for example, fear, a proliferation of witchcraft, a desire for more offspring, and so on. Mortality, I need hardly explain, is scarcely less difficult to measure in East Africa than the Holy Grail is to find—anywhere. Infant mortality is almost inaccessible to recovery; questions about it elicit avoidance routines or embarrassingly faulty memories. Adult mortality is also tricky to determine. One can derive a fair estimate of adult mortality for a recent period—say a year—but it is almost impossible to be precise about mortality in the more distant

4. For useful discussions of reason in statistics, see Cicourel (1964) and Kaplan (1964).

past. And we have good reason to suppose that current attitudes and ideologies are largely a product of past catastrophes. We know, that is, that people of today remember and fear past epidemics, wars, droughts, crop failures, and the like. Those cataclysmic disasters shape their attitudes and their willingness to risk economic innovations. Yet, how does one measure, comparatively, memories of wars, army worm infestations, smallpox, and a host of equally horrendous events for which nothing more precise than temporally nonspecific human memory is available? I should also say, however, that a great many deceptively simple matters were equally nonsusceptible to measurement. For example, we sought to determine the relative presence of disease and warfare in each of our eight sites. The variables were theoretically relevant, to be sure, but even at the minimal level of a rank-order scale, we could not agree. Or if we did agree, it was for different reasons. Thus it was that a great many theoretically important variables proved to be incommensurable from one site to the next.

Fortunately, it was never my intention to attempt to correlate all theoretically relevant indices of the environment with all of the interview variables. At best, I sought only a limited number of environmental variables which would provide a theoretically important sample of a potentially much larger array of environmental features. By correlating this set of environmental variables with some of the interview response variables, I hoped to identify dimensions of environment-attitude covariance that would at least suggest causal linkages and might provide directions for further investigation. Consequently, I have taken ten environmental variables from Porter's research which I believe provide a useful sample of the relevant dimensions of the "environment." These variables are diverse, representing as they do aspects of the physical, human, and animal environment. Most of them reflect an interaction between physical environmental features and economy or technology. Of the ten environmental variables selected, three could be measured at no better than an ordinal level. The remaining seven were formed into interval scales. All ten variables and their correlations with 31 content analysis categories are presented in table 75.

SCALE 1: LAND SHORTAGE

Scale 1 attempts to rank the eight sites according to the degree of pressure upon the land present in each. For us, land shortage was a theoretically significant variable, one that we believed would be

TABLE 75

RANK-ORDER CORRELATION COEFFICIENTS BETWEEN 31 INTERVIEW RESPONSE VARIABLES AND 10 ENVIRONMENTAL VARIABLES

Content analysis category	(1) Land shortage*	(2) Crowding within residence*	(3) Population density	(4) Homestead clusters	(5) Water management*	(6) Food production*	(7) Farming feasibility	(8) Livestock ownership	(9) Index of cattle concern	(10) Pastoral farming index
1. Adultery	−.190	.667	−.420	−.146	.214	−.077	−.157	.577	.866	−.558
2. Affection	−.310	.143	−.559	.437	.786	−.561	−.367	.404	−.093	−.705
3. Cattle	.024	−.381	−.516	.327	.738	−.612	−.566	.368	−.398	−.538
4. Clan	.190	−.190	.311	−.232	−.500	.075	−.161	.081	−.085	.521
5. Concern with death, disease	−.357	.048	−.133	.492	.143	.004	.145	.117	.127	−.127
6. Concern with wrong doing	.190	.500	−.416	−.377	.286	−.084	−.310	.246	.557	−.407
7. Cooperation	.119	.238	−.439	−.233	.810	−.154	−.297	.275	.288	−.539
8. Depression	−.595	−.143	−.633	.654	.833	−.847	−.652	.528	−.454	−.656
9. Desire for friends	−.405	−.548	−.028	.093	−.286	.050	−.055	−.347	−.535	.148
10. Desire to avoid conflict	.190	−.357	.197	−.666	−.048	.255	.056	−.343	−.056	.182
11. Direct aggression	−.024	.310	−.687	.146	.881	−.650	−.589	.715	.300	−.845
12. Disrespect for authority	.310	−.310	.705	−.550	−.524	.759	.697	−.926	−.204	.693
13. Divination	−.595	.048	−.596	.771	.333	−.821	−.759	.662	−.304	−.379
14. Fatalism	.095	.548	−.180	−.020	.048	.237	.200	.119	.722	−.242
15. Fear	−.262	−.310	−.527	.552	.500	−.443	−.444	.287	−.242	−.389
16. Fear of poverty	.167	.119	−.412	−.254	.310	−.226	−.618	.435	.239	−.210
17. Guilt-shame	−.190	−.667	−.132	.416	.095	−.333	−.420	.016	−.744	.147
18. Hatred	.286	.262	.299	−.744	−.262	.452	.294	−.301	.329	.197
19. Hostility to opposite sex	.357	.095	−.190	−.412	−.071	−.125	−.356	.361	.311	−.183
20. Independence	−.548	.190	−.831	.542	.905	−.782	−.624	.665	.001	−.921
21. Industriousness	.524	.405	−.184	−.553	−.167	.122	−.109	.315	.807	−.264
22. Insults	.429	.262	−.012	−.548	.071	.331	.270	−.093	.784	−.190
23. Jealousy of wealth	.500	.381	−.207	.048	−.048	−.004	−.064	−.032	.168	−.090
24. Land	.524	−.214	.096	−.634	−.048	.297	−.152	.152	.389	.234
25. Litigiousness	.048	.310	−.309	−.355	.333	.130	−.026	.125	.616	−.417
26. Physical beauty	−.429	−.571	.105	.151	.238	.022	.185	−.299	−.575	−.024
27. Respect for authority	−.548	.190	−.653	.581	.548	−.541	−.612	.697	.112	−.474
28. Self-control	.310	.619	−.234	−.401	.333	.017	−.050	.242	.782	−.378
29. Valuation of cattle	−.119	−.310	−.459	.322	.667	−.625	−.562	.291	−.486	−.459
30. Valuation of independence	−.524	.048	−.770	.597	.786	−.820	−.684	.858	.070	−.825
31. Witchcraft	−.143	.310	−.041	−.204	.012	.044	.155	−.118	.216	−.199

*Correlation coefficients in these columns are Spearman rank correlation coefficients; all others are Pearson product moment correlations.

related to a host of social arrangements. We believed that, for farmers in particular, a shortage of land should be reflected in many social institutions (see Goldschmidt's introduction). Hence we were eager to locate the eight sites along a continuum of most to least population pressure upon the land. The resulting scale reflects such differential pressures, not only as they affect the farming populations, but also as they influence the life activities of the pastoralists. The ordering of this scale, like the next two scales, is only ordinal; such a complex phenomenon as this, involving both availability of land and its effective utilization, could achieve no greater precision. Thus, while Porter and I were able to agree upon this rank-order of the eight sites, it was not possible to specify the intervals between the sites on this scale.

SCALE 1

LAND SHORTAGE

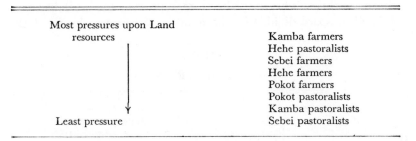

Most pressures upon Land resources	Kamba farmers
	Hehe pastoralists
	Sebei farmers
	Hehe farmers
	Pokot farmers
	Pokot pastoralists
	Kamba pastoralists
Least pressure	Sebei pastoralists

The ordering of this scale differs considerably from most of the other scales, and the correlations with response categories, although rather low, are interesting. Thus, we see that where pressure upon the land is greatest, these three responses are emphasized: industriousness (.524), land (.524), and jealousy of wealth (.500). These responses are consistent with what we would expect from a population that is pressing upon its land resources. Conversely, the following responses are negatively correlated with land shortage: depression (−.595), divination (−.595), independence (−.548), respect for authority (−.548), and valuation of independence (−.542). All, quite clearly, are pastoral emphases.

Even though a pastoral population (the Hehe, see chapter 2) is ranked near the top of this scale, along with the four farming populations, the results indicate an unequivocal polarity between a core of "farming" and "pastoral" responses. More significantly, we find a suggested linkage between land shortage and three central farming responses: industriousness, land, and jealousy of wealth (in this instance, the wealth would consist primarily of land).

SCALE 2: CROWDING WITHIN RESIDENCES

Scale 2 indicates the degree of physical crowding within individual dwelling structures in each site. Physical distances between family members within family dwelling units differ from site to site, particularly so where sleeping quarters are concerned. The following scale is an estimation of the average physical proximity of sleeping quarters within all dwelling structures located in the sampling universe of each site. We attempted this measurement because physical crowding was a central variable in our understanding of pastoral-farming differences (we anticipated that crowding, in general, would be more extreme among farmers). One index of crowding we were able to agree upon was that of physical distance between persons within dwellings. This scale, therefore, represents the available unit of dwelling space divided by the number of persons who regularly

SCALE 2

CROWDING WITHIN RESIDENCE

Greatest	Hehe farmers
	Hehe pastoralists
	Sebei pastoralists
	Pokot pastoralists
	Kamba pastoralists
	Kamba farmers
	Sebei farmers
Least	Pokot farmers

spend the night in that unit of space. Because dwellings in these societies were occupied primarily at night, this index best reflects talking and sleeping proximity. It need not reflect sexual relationships, many of which occur out-of-doors. Thus, the scale suggests some of the same concerns voiced by John Whiting and his colleagues in their studies of the spatial arrangements of sleeping quarters.[5]

As before, the scale is ordinal; and while measurement of proximity was difficult, especially in polygynous families where each wife

5. See, for example, Whiting (1961).

has a separate dwelling, Porter and I were able to agree upon this scale. Again the scale is mixed as to its farming-pastoral polarity, but the greatest crowding within dwellings usually occurs among the pastoralists. The positive correlates of physical crowding within dwellings appears to be these: adultery (.667), concern with wrongdoing (.500), fatalism (.548), and self-control (.619). Three response categories were negatively correlated: desire for friends ($-.548$), guilt-shame ($-.667$), and physical beauty ($-.571$). It is interesting to note that all of these correlates have a pronounced "moral" or "sexual" tone. If this finding is more than an artifact (and we should note that the correlations are not impressively high), perhaps its significance may be clarified by subsequent investigations. Although this scale did not measure physical crowding in the manner we had originally intended (the number of persons per unit of space in continuous, direct interaction), it did provide one measure of proximity. The high and low correlations to this scale do not conform to any of our original expectations; however, since they are so intriguingly "moral," they are presented here in the hope that they may be clarified by future investigators.

SCALE 3: POPULATION DENSITY

A related crowding variable of substantial theoretical interest in any consideration of the differences between the eight sites is population density. Because of the difficulties involved in finding a unit of measurement which was appropriate for each site, the measurement of the density of population in each of the eight areas is inexact. The unit of measurement finally employed was a square mile surrounding the site in question. Thus the unit of analysis was less arbitrary for some sites (those that did cover a square mile) than for others that occupied a larger or smaller area. Furthermore, enumeration within a square mile was never perfect. Thus the counts given in this scale should be understood to be estimates of population within a standard but somewhat arbitrary area. Nevertheless, I am confident that the error in enumeration for any site was never as great as 5 percent of the total. Furthermore, for many of the sites, the magnitude of the differences in population density are so great that any errors in measurement seem to be of relatively minor significance. Consider, for example, the difference between the population density of the Sebei farmers (888 per square mile) and that of the Sebei pastoralists (7 per square mile). Consider, too, that the densities of the farming

253

sites are not only high by East African standards, they are high by world standards as well.[6]

This scale arrays farmers against pastoralists in a consistent manner. As we shall see, the scale is quite similar to four other scales soon to be presented: food production, livestock ownership, farming feasibility, and the pastoral/farming index (see Appendix IX). Re-

SCALE 3

POPULATION DENSITY

Site	Number of persons per square mile
Sebei farmers	888
Kamba farmers	556
Hehe farmers	430
Pokot farmers	244
Kamba pastoralists	142
Sebei pastoralists	7
Hehe pastoralists	6
Pokot pastoralists	4

sponse correlation, too, is consistent and will soon become familiar. Strongly correlated with the farming end of the scale is only one variable: disrespect for authority (.705). The following high negative correlations have all been previously identified as "pastoral" responses: depression (−.623), divination (−.596), direct aggression (−.687), independence (−.831), respect for authority (−.653), and valuation of independence (−.770).

Thus, we see a pattern that will be repeated often: high correlations with several response categories that we have earlier recognized to be pastoral in nature, but low correlations with most farming response patterns. For example, we note the low values for hatred (.299), desire to avoid conflict (.197), land (.096), and witchcraft (−.041). Although these correlations are, as we could expect, related to the farming end of the scale, they are extremely low.

I think that it is fair to conclude that while population density is negatively correlated with certain pastoral responses, these correlations are not particularly strong. Still more disappointing is the failure of the scale to correlate positively with more than one of the "farming" responses. While it is widely recognized that population

6. For example, see Brass et al. (1968) and Porter (1966).

density per se has been a far less reliable predictor of human be-havior and attitudes than ethological research would have led us to believe, it is nonetheless surprising that the correlations to this scale are as weak as they are relative to those that we shall see in subse-quent scales. In this regard, the research of Gulliver comparing the Arusha and Nyakyusa of Tanzania is relevant in showing that neither land shortage nor population pressure is sufficient to explain the oc-currence of witchcraft or social conflict.[7]

SCALE 4: DISPERSION OF HOMESTEAD CLUSTERS

For the last index of crowding, we turn to a consideration of the dispersion of homesteads. This scale measures the mean distance between homestead clusters, between, that is, each dwelling or cluster of dwellings that is formed as the "natural" residential unit by a mar-ried man, his wife or wives, his wives' children, and by whatever additional persons may occupy them. By computing the mean dis-tance between such clusters of dwellings (or single dwellings), we find that there are considerable differences among sites in the disper-sion of homesteads. These differences are of theoretical importance for they provide us with another indicator of the crowding in each site. Several of our basic assumptions about the nature of farming life as opposed to pastoral life are founded on the condition that farmers' families be clustered together in nucleated or compacted settlements and that pastoralists' families be far more distantly sep-arated one from the other.

Averaging the linear distances between homesteads, Porter ranked the eight sites as shown in scale 4.

It is immediately apparent that our expectations were not as well founded as we would have wished. The most "nucleated" site was the Hehe pastoralists, *not* the farmers, and even here the mean distance between homesteads was 58 yards—hardly cheek by jowl! What is more, in one farming site (the Pokot), the average distance between homesteads was 200 yards! Nevertheless, in general it was true that the farmers were more closely clustered together than were the pastoralists. Two "pastoral" response categories show a moder-ately high positive correlation with this scale: depression (.654) and divination (.771). More interesting is the finding that suggests as

7. Gulliver (1961) argues for the crucial role of social factors con-cerning inheritance and social control in explaining the occurrence of witchcraft; LeVine's work (1962) on co-wife proximity and popula-tion density in relation to witchcraft is also relevant.

SCALE 4

DISPERSION OF HOMESTEADS

Site	Mean distance between homesteads (In yards)
Sebei pastoralists	670
Pokot pastoralists	633
Kamba pastoralists	300
Pokot farmers	200
Hehe farmers	133
Sebei farmers	67
Kamba farmers	65
Hehe pastoralists	58

homesteads are clustered closer together, one finds greater expression of (1) conflict avoidance (−.666), (2) hatred (−.744), and (3) interest in land (−.634). This set of "farming" responses is quite significant, for it confirms our expectations that crowding on the land is related to hostility and, because direct aggression is impractical, to a desire to avoid conflict.

SCALE 5: WATER MANAGEMENT

We turn now to the first of several critical considerations of the relationships between the physical environment and certain economic and technological conditions. Scale 5 indicates the extent to which people in each site must engage in the sharing and management of water resources. A predictable, manageable water supply is essential both for crop production and the maintenance of livestock. Therefore, both farming and pastoral economies are involved. Unfortunately, no simple formula can express the moisture availability needs in these diverse African environments and economic systems. For example, one must consider far more than the amount of rainfall; its regular occurrence throughout the annual cycle is crucial, as are such matters as predictability within any given season, from season to season, and from year to year. There are also questions of the intensity of rainfall and thus of relative runoff, of erosion, and of flooding. One must likewise consider the availability of permanent or seasonal water supplies from rivers, lakes, springs, wells, and the like. The moisture needs of various crops in various soils are also diverse and complicated. In short, as Porter points out in his Culture and Ecology series monograph, the question is complex.

This scale reflects the relative need for people to organize themselves in order that the available water may be made adequate for them, their crops, and their livestock. This scale therefore represents such diverse organizational needs as devising planting schedules, carrying out irrigation, digging step wells, carrying water from distant streams, arranging watering schedules for livestock, and the like. Although there can be no precise measurement of so complex a phenomenon, Porter has attempted to estimate the totality of the need within each site to organize the management of water resources.

SCALE 5

WATER MANAGEMENT

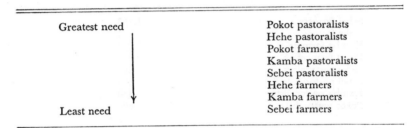

This scale is somewhat mixed as regards a pastoral-farming continuum (recall that the Pokot farmers practice irrigation). Despite this, the resulting high positive correlations are primarily "pastoral": affection (.786), cattle (.738), cooperation (.810), depression (.833), direct aggression (.881), independence (.905), valuation of cattle (.667), and valuation of independence (.786). The highest negative correlations are clan ($-.500$) and disrespect for authority ($-.524$). The positive correlations are quite high, and the pattern is intriguing.

It appears that the need to manage water correlates with much that is central to the pastoral response pattern; however, as before, "farming" responses are few and only weakly correlated: desire to avoid conflict ($-.048$), fear of poverty (.310), land ($-.048$), witchcraft (.012), and so on. Thus, while this scale appears to be an excellent predictor of pastoral response, it is far less successful as a key to farming response patterns.

SCALE 6: FOOD PRODUCTION

A second variable relating technological and economic factors to the environment is the relative ability of persons in each site to produce vegetable food. There should be no need to justify food productivity as a potentially important determinant of attitudes and values. When the production of all food from agricultural sources is tabulated (food from livestock sources is not included), scale 6 results.

From the 1,763 pounds of food per capita of the Sebei farmers to the total absence of horticultural produce among the Pokot pastoralists, we have an impressive difference. Indeed, the scale grades nicely from the Sebei farmers, through the other farming sites to the

SCALE 6

VEGETABLE FOOD PRODUCTION

Site	Pounds of edible food per capita per annum *
Sebei farmers	1,763
Hehe farmers	1,284
Kamba farmers	1,009
Pokot farmers	907
Hehe pastoralists	802
Sebei pastoralists	510
Kamba pastoralists	430
Pokot pastoralists	000

*Details of this estimation are included in Porter's forthcoming Culture and Ecology Project monograph on the ecology and environment of East Africa.

least farming-oriented pastoral site. The association between this scale and the various categories of interview response is once again familiar. The correlations again show a number of high negative "pastoral" responses: cattle $(-.612)$, depression $(-.847)$, direct aggression $(-.650)$, divination $(-.821)$, independence $(-.782)$, valuation of cattle $(-.625)$, and valuation of independence $(-.820)$. The only high positive ("farming") correlation is a familiar one: disrespect for authority $(.759)$. Thus, we see essentially the same pattern we have seen before, the strong correlation of several "pastoral" responses, and the weak association of "farming" responses.

SCALE 7: FARMING FEASIBILITY

When we turn away from actual production of food to a consideration of the extent to which farming is feasible in each site within the prevailing stock of technological knowledge and skills, we derive a somewhat different ordering of the eight sites. The calculation of such an index is a complex undertaking, one that Porter describes in suitable detail in his monograph. For present purposes, it is suf-

SCALE 7

FARMING FEASIBILITY

Site	Index of feasibility
Sebei farmers	1.90
Kamba farmers	1.88
Hehe farmers	.97
Pokot farmers	.81
Sebei pastoralists	.75
Kamba pastoralists	.51
Hehe pastoralists	.10
Pokot pastoralists	.00

ficient to note in shorthand fashion that the scale was derived by taking the number of usable seasons in each site and adding their probabilities. The higher the sum obtained, the greater the feasibility of farming within the existing technology of each site.

The interview response correlations do not differ notably from those found for scale 6, Food Production; the two scales are highly intercorrelated (.885). They include these high positive correlations, disrespect for authority (.697) and fear of poverty (.618); and these negative correlations, depression ($-.652$), divination ($-.759$), independence ($-.624$), respect for authority ($-.612$), and valuation of independence ($-.684$). In general, however, the correlations are weaker than those previously seen, except that where concern with cattle and direct aggression weakens greatly, expressed fear of poverty increases.

SCALE 8: PER CAPITA LIVESTOCK OWNERSHIP

When the focus is shifted from agricultural food production to per capita livestock ownership, the scale is reversed and altered. It was not possible to obtain faultless counts of livestock holdings; men lie about their herds, and the animals themselves are often herded miles away so that it is not possible for an investigator to count them. However, by questioning a number of persons about a man's livestock holdings, it was usually possible to reach what was probably a fairly good approximation. Our best possible enumeration of the number of livestock per capita in each site produced scale 8.

The response category correlations are largely unchanged from those seen in the preceding food production scale. Again, there are high correlations (this time positive) with direct aggression, div-

259

SCALE 8

Per Capita Livestock Ownership

Site	Livestock units per capita*
Hehe pastoralists	5.99
Pokot pastoralists	5.16
Sebei pastoralists	4.18
Kamba pastoralists	4.04
Kamba farmers	2.59
Pokot farmers	1.35
Hehe farmers	.69
Sebei farmers	.63

*For details of this compilation, see Porter's forthcoming Culture and Ecology Project volume. In brief, a "livestock unit" is 1 head of cattle, or 5 goats, sheep, or calves.

ination, independence, respect for authority, and valuation of independence. There is also an exceptionally high negative correlation with disrespect for authority ($-.926$). Despite the potential significance of livestock ownership as an environmental variable linked to interview response, this scale tells us nothing that earlier scales have not already shown. For a differing perspective upon this same phenomenon, we turn to the next scale.

SCALE 9: INDEX OF CATTLE CONCENTRATION

Because cattle are both highly prized and a principal measure of wealth in all eight sites, if per capita livestock ownership does not greatly discriminate between the various sites' modal response pattern, then we might at least reasonably expect that men who own many cattle would express attitudes and values that differ from those expressed by men who own few cattle, or none at all. Indeed, we might well anticipate that the modal response patterns of sites would differ as a function of the degree to which all cattle in those sites were owned by a few wealthy men, rather than being held in approximately equal numbers by all adult males. An indication of the extent to which cattle are concentrated in the hands of a few men, rather than being randomly distributed among all men, is given in scale 9.

Thus we see that, in the sample taken by Porter, there are substantial differences among the eight sites in the degree to which the actual distribution of cattle (I_e) departs from a random allocation of equal numbers of cattle to all heads of household (I_c). Among

SCALE 9

INDEX OF CONCENTRATION OF CATTLE IN EIGHT SITES

Site	Number of men*	Number of cattle	I_e (obs.)**	I_c (expected)***	Difference
Hehe pastoralists	47	1041	0.96	0.116	.884
Hehe farmers	52	187	0.92	0.290	.630
Sebei pastoralists	42	866	0.60	0.124	.476
Sebei farmers	40	125	0.73	0.299	.431
Kamba pastoralists	52	1025	0.49	0.126	.364
Kamba farmers	50	935	0.48	0.126	.354
Pokot pastoralists	29	744	0.46	0.115	.345
Pokot farmers	20	131	0.48	0.215	.265

NOTE: Information for this index was obtained from Porter's Culture and Ecology Project monograph.

*Heads of household.

**I_e (obs.) = the actual (observed) distribution of cattle.

***I_c (expected) = a random allocation of equal numbers of cattle to all heads of household.

the Hehe pastoralists, we find that most cattle are concentrated in the herds of a very few men, whereas among the Pokot, in contrast, cattle are much more evenly shared among the heads of household. The scale is highly culture-specific, moving as it does from the Hehe down through the Sebei to the Kamba and finally to the Pokot. Yet in each tribe we note that cattle are somewhat more equally shared among farmers than among pastoralists.

When we examine the association between this scale and the various response categories, we find several strong positive correlations: adultery (.866), fatalism (.722), industriousness (.807), insults (.784), litigiousness (.616), self-control (.782). There is only one strong negative correlation, guilt-shame ($-.744$). Thus, we see that this scale is the best thus far for yielding correlations with "farming" variables. We might infer that it is not merely land shortage, but cattle shortage as well, that evokes such attitudes as industriousness, insults, and litigiousness. Yet the admixture is curious for it places with these variables adultery and fatalism, and opposes to all of them guilt-shame. Although livestock ownership does not correlate with response patterns in any simple "farming" versus "pastoralism" manner, it does provide a key to farming response patterns.

SCALE 10: A PASTORAL/FARMING INDEX

All of the foregoing scales have been relatively specific and none has served, or attempted to serve, as a definitive index of pastoral versus farming economic-environmental orientation. The final scale to be discussed is a very general one that combines a number of variables within a single index. It *does* attempt to stand as a pastoral/farming index. To derive such an index, Porter calculated the tonnage of edible food produced per annum in each site and has contrasted this figure with the number of livestock units owned in that site.

This index provides a ready measure of the ratio of available agricultural food to livestock resources in each site. The higher the score, the more agricultural the site. Whether one chooses to believe that people produce what they *want* to produce, or what they *can* produce, this scale indicates that the Sebei farmers are most involved in, and dependent upon, their crops. As we might expect, there is a

SCALE·10

A PASTORAL/FARMING INDEX (I_{pf})*

Site	$\dfrac{T^{**}}{LSU}$	I_{pf}	Standard score
Sebei farmers	$\dfrac{279.6}{222}$	1.259	100
Hehe farmers	$\dfrac{177.1}{190}$	0.932	74
Pokot farmers	$\dfrac{71.7}{213}$	0.337	27
Kamba farmers	$\dfrac{222.1}{1,139}$	0.195	15
Hehe pastoralists	$\dfrac{87.4}{1,305}$	0.067	5
Sebei pastoralists	$\dfrac{73.2}{1,200}$	0.061	5
Kamba pastoralists	$\dfrac{74.8}{1,406}$	0.053	4
Pokot pastoralists	0.0	0.000	0

*For details, see Porter's Culture and Ecology Project monograph.
**T = tonnage of agricultural food; LSU = Livestock units.

positive correlation with the ubiquitous "farming" variable disrespect for authority (.693), but there are also these strong "pastoral" negative correlations: affection (−.705), depression (−.656), direct aggression (−.845), independence (−.921), and valuation of independence (−.825). But, once again, there is no corresponding set of strong correlations with the farming end of the scale.

That this scale is completely satisfactory as a definitive index seems to be questionable. For example, this scale places the Pokot farmers ahead of the Kamba farmers in degree of "farmingness." I suspect, and strongly so, that the only reason the Kamba farmers have more cattle than the Pokot farmers lies in the greater *wealth* of the Kamba, not in their lesser involvement with *farming*. In fact, it seems obvious that farmers in all four sites acquire as many cattle as they can afford. Thus, it may well be that the simpler measure of agricultural productivity (scale 6) may be a better indicator of farming orientation than is this index.

Rather than attempting to evaluate the relevance of each scale at this point, however, let us instead examine the 31 interview response variables in turn, in an effort to determine how each is associated with any or all of the 10 environmental scales that have been presented here.

REVIEWING THE INTERVIEW VARIABLES

1. Adultery.—This response category was previously found to be associated with pastoralism. Its highest correlation is with scale 9, Index of Cattle Concentration (.866). There is also a high correlation with scale 2, Crowding within Residences (.667). No other correlation is over .600. While a correlation of .558 with scale 10, the Pastoral/Farming Index, suggests that this variable tends toward pastoralism, its status is not greatly clarified by these scalar analyses, especially so since it is so often opposed to, rather than related to, physical beauty and other variables with which it had previously been associated.

2. Affection.—Affection continues to present a pastoral picture. It is correlated (.786) with scale 5, Water Management, and it is negative (−.705) on scale 10, Pastoral/Farming Index. Although it is related to the pastoral poles of only two scales, these relationships are relatively strong.

3. Cattle.—Cattle has only two reasonably high correlations, .738 with scale 5, Water Management, and −.612 with scale 6, Food Production. Thus, although cattle is surely a "pastoral" variable, it is not a particularly strong nor interesting one, largely so, I suspect, because farmers as well as pastoralists value cattle.

4. Clan.—Clan is another weak variable, with only two correlations as high as .500. One is —.500 with scale 5, Water Management; the other is .521 with scale 10, the Pastoral/Farming Index. Thus, these environmental scales have done little to increase our understanding of this "social organizational" variable.

5. Concern with death.—This variable has no high correlations; its strongest correlation is .492 with scale 4, Homestead Clusters.

6. Concern with wrongdoing.—Most correlations between this variable and the ten environmental variables are low. The highest are .500 with scale 2, Crowding within Residences, and .557 with scale 9, Index of Cattle Concentration. Thus, the significance of this variable—one we had previously seen to have mixed pastoral-farming associations—is difficult to assess. The correlations are too weak to permit any confident inferences.

7. Cooperation.—This variable has only one strong correlation, .810 with scale 5, Water Management. It is reassuring that a scale which necessarily measures cooperation succeeds in "discovering" this relationship; yet, further discoveries are lacking.

8. Depression.—This variable is clearly associated with the pastoral end of many of the environmental scales. Its highest correlation is —.847 with scale 6, Food Production. One might conclude, probably too glibly, that the more food that is produced, the less will people be depressed. Unfortunately, it is also strongly correlated (.833) with scale 5, Water Management, putting an end to such easy speculation.

9. Desire for friends.—This variable has only two moderately high correlations, —.548 with scale 2, Crowding within Residences, and —.535 with scale 9, Index of Cattle Concentration. We must infer that we know no more about this anomalous variable than we did before these analyses were performed.

10. Conflict avoidance.—This variable has only one relatively strong correlation, —.666 with scale 4, Homestead Clusters. This variable, earlier found to be a farming response category, is aligned with the "farming" end of the scale to which we would most have expected it to be related. It is surprising, however, that its correlations with all other scales are so low (see table 75).

11. Direct aggression.—This variable is often highly correlated with environmental variables, and the direction of this correlation is always with the pastoral end of the scale. The values are high, as, for example, are these: .881 with scale 5, Water Management, —.845 with scale 10, Pastoral/Farming Index, —.689 with scale 3, Population Density, and .715 with scale 8, Livestock Ownership. We see, then, that this variable is identified as being strongly "pastoral."

12. *Disrespect for authority.*—Disrespect for authority is, it would seem, the quintessential farming diagnostic. It repeatedly stands as being strongly correlated with the farming poles of these environmental scales. Its strongest correlation is —.926 with scale 8, Livestock Ownership. Thus, we see that where livestock are plentiful in a site—that is, the more pastoral the site is—the less is disrespect for authority expressed.

13. *Divination.*—This variable has high correlations with the pastoral end of several scales: for example, —.821 with scale 6, Food Production; —.759 with scale 7, Farming Feasibility; and .771 with scale 4, Homestead Clusters. From the strength of these associations, divination is clearly a pastoral variable. Yet, it is not possible to locate any specific "environmental" linkage for this variable.

14. *Fatalism.*—This variable is highly correlated with only one scale: —.722 with scale 9, Index of Cattle Concentration. This would seem to suggest that fatalism is a product of a situation in which a few men own many cattle, while most men own very few cattle and some, none at all. This inference is intriguing, and if it is correct, opens the way for an understanding of fatalism that has heretofore been lacking. I should caution against taking this inference too far, however, especially since the correlation upon which it is built is only moderately high.

15. *Fear.*—Fear is not highly correlated with any scale. It is —.527 with scale 3, Population Density, and .522 with scale 4, Homestead Clusters. It is, therefore, tending toward pastoralism, but it has a rather weak association.

16. *Fear of Poverty.*—This variable has only one noteworthy correlation, —.618 with scale 7, Farming Feasibility. Fear of poverty may, therefore, be said to tend toward the pastoral, but the association is weak.

17. *Guilt-shame.*—This variable has two reasonably strong correlations, both of which are pastoral in direction: —.667 with scale 2, Crowding within Residences, and —.744 with scale 9, Index of Cattle Concentration. Although we must conclude that this previously noted "pastoral" variable has not been clarified by its correlations with the environmental scales, we can nonetheless point to

the guilt-shame engendering potential of close sleeping quarters and an unequal distribution of cattle.

18. Hatred.—This presumed "farming" variable has but one significant correlation, —.744 with scale 4, Homestead Clusters. This indicates that the closer homesteads are clustered together the greater is the expression of hatred, and this confirms one of our most basic hypotheses about farming life. It is surprising, however, that this variable is so weakly correlated with other "farming" scales, such as Land Shortage, Food Production, and the like.

19. Hostility to the opposite sex.—All correlations between this variable and the environmental scales are low. None is over .500, with the highest being —.412 with scale 4, Homestead Clusters.

20. Independence.—This variable is often highly correlated with the pastoral poles of the environmental scales. Many values are quite high, but the highest is —.921 with the scale 10, the Pastoral/Farming Index. This variable, therefore, stands as an excellent "pastoral" diagnostic, one that consistently relates to pastoral social imperatives. For example, it correlates (.905) with scale 5, Water Management, and is negatively correlated (—.831) with scale 3, Population Density. Note also, however, that its relationships to Food Production and Farming Feasibility are weaker, (—.782) and (—.624), respectively, and that it has near zero correlation with scale 9, Index of Cattle Concentration. Not only have these scales confirmed the "pastoral" nature of independence, they have pointed to several aspects of the environment as principal sources of the expression of independence.

21. Industriousness.—The principal correlation of industriousness to the environmental scales is .807 with scale 9, Index of Cattle Concentration. A secondary relationship is .542 with scale 1, Land Shortage. This combination is interesting, for it suggests that when important resources (land or cattle) are in short supply, industriousness becomes relevant.

22. Insults.—This variable has only one high correlation, .784 with scale 9, Index of Cattle Concentration, and this correlation is in large measure the consequence of Hehe dominance of the positive pole of this scale. I would conclude that this variable appears to relate more to "cultural" than to "environmental" factors.

23. Jealousy of wealth.—This variable has only one correlation as high as .500, and that is with scale 1, Land Shortage. As mentioned in the earlier discussion of that scale, this correlation does make sense, and may be noteworthy in spite of its relative weakness.

24. *Land.*—Only twice do moderately high correlations emerge. One is .524 with scale 1, Land Shortage; the other is —.634 with scale 4, Dispersion of Homestead Clusters. The variable is, therefore, associated with environmental conditions that exist in farming sites. Overall, however, this variable appears to be rather weakly associated with farming, as it is not found to be very strongly correlated with *any* of the scales.

25. *Litigiousness.*—This variable, too, is weak, having only one correlation over .500; that one correlation is .616 with scale 9, Index of Cattle Concentration. We expected litigiousness to be associated with farming, especially with land shortage, but instead we find it to be associated with cattle shortage. This is not unreasonable, for while litigation can rarely lead to a redistribution of land, it regularly produces a redistribution of cattle. Although the space diagram (figure 6) does link litigiousness with farming, the content analysis showed that, in three of the four tribes, the pastoralists expressed litigiousness more often than did the farmers (table 22).

26. *Physical beauty.*—This variable, too, is only weakly associated with the environmental scales. Although its strongest correlations are pastoral in direction, —.575 with scale 9, Index of Cattle Concentration, and —.571 with scale 2, Crowding within Residences, it is difficult to base inferences upon such weak correlations.

27. *Respect for authority.*—This variable appears again as a pastoral orientation, being consistently correlated with the pastoral end of many of the scales. Its highest correlation is .697 with scale 8, Livestock Ownership. Although this analysis confirms what we concluded earlier concerning the pastoral emphasis upon authority, it does not improve our understanding.

28. *Self-control.*—There are two high correlations between this variable and the environmental scales: .782 with scale 9, Index of Cattle Concentration, and .619 with scale 2, Crowding within Residences. Unfortunately, the high relationship with scale 9 is largely the result, once again, of the strong anchoring of this scale by the Hehe. Thus, scale 2, Crowding within Residences, appears to be the more meaningful environmental variable.

29. *Valuation of cattle.*—This variable is pastoral in orientation, but it is never very highly correlated with any scale. Its highest correlations are of the middle range, for example, .667 with scale 5, Water Management, and —.625 with scale 6, Food Production.

30. *Valuation of independence.*—Like the closely related variable independence, this is a preeminent pastoral variable. It is very

highly correlated with the pastoral pole of most of the scales, and with some scales its correlations are high, for example, .858 with scale 8, Livestock Ownership, and —.825 with scale 10, the Pastoral/Farming Index. It is a dependable pastoral diagnostic.

31. Witchcraft.—This variable is most disappointing. It should have shown an adherence to the farming pole of these many scales, or a negative relationship to the pastoral pole, but instead it showed almost no relationship at all to any of the scales. All correlations were low, the strongest being .310 with scale 2, Crowding within Residences.

THE SEARCH FOR SOURCES

What can be said about this exploratory effort to locate some sources of ecological covariation in attitudes? Let it be clear at the outset that I am not under the illusion that I have discovered the "causes" of pastoral-farming differences. There are too many good reasons this study could not hope to achieve so definitive a solution. First, and at the risk of adding an unnecessary voice to an already deafening chorus, it remains true that correlations do not readily yield causal inferences. It is not impossible to make causal inferences from correlations,[8] but the variables that were correlated in this research do not bear the burden that a cautious investigator in search of causes would have to impose upon them.

In addition to this problem, however, the search for causes ran afoul of difficulties in measurement. For one thing, the environmental variables were always very difficult to quantify; "error variance" was no doubt large, as it must also have been with the interview data. What is more, these measurements were averaged in order to provide scores by which sites could be characterized, and consequently the correlations were, in statistical terms, "ecological." [9] Thus, at several points in the process of constructing environmental scales, precision was lost. Explanatory power was also reduced by the similarity of the ordering of these scales. By virtue of the fact that most environmental variables separated farmers from pastoralists, many of the scales reproduced a relatively similar continuum of sites. Consequently, it was sometimes difficult to discriminate between scales with regard to their explanatory relevance.

Because of such problems of measurement and scaling, I de-

8. See Blalock (1960a) and Borgatta (1969).
9. See Schuessler (1969).

cided not to attempt what was an enticing prospect, that is, to estimate path coefficients from these correlational data by simple
regression procedures. The development of path analysis and causal
inference in recent years has provided sophisticated means for making
causal inferences from correlational data. These techniques, begun as
early as 1921 by the geneticist Sewell Wright, are now appropriate
for many kinds of social analyses.[10] Unfortunately, as Heise has
pointed out, to engage in these analyses, one's data and theory must
meet a number of requirements.[11] In addition to data requirements
of high reliability and validity—points which are, of course, contestable where most social research is involved—Heise tells us that
" . . . theory (1) can postulate only linear relations between data;
(2) can postulate no reciprocal relations between variables or feedback loops; (3) must clearly separate input variables from dependent
variables and must order dependent variables in terms of their causal
priorities over one another; (4) must specify all system inputs so that
they can be considered explicitly in analysis." [12]

Clearly, no ecological theory can meet all of these requirements, and if these requirements are not met, the models that result
are, in Heise's terms and mine, "nonsensical and misleading." It is
for reasons such as these that I have not attempted to go beyond these
correlation coefficients toward formal causal inferences.[13]

CONCLUSION

What general conclusions can be reached? First, we must resist the
temptation to continue constructing scales of environmental variables until all possible combinations of the eight sites have been
exhausted. Fortunately, that point was not reached. Instead, I believe
that in the interview response correlations to several of the ten scales
that were used there are ample and provocative suggestions for future research. However, and I should add that, unfortunately, there
are no available means by which we can determine that the environmental variable we have scaled has indeed produced the response
pattern associated with it. In this regard, I am afraid that multivari-

10. See Borgatta (1969).

11. Heise (1969), p. 68.

12. Ibid.

13. As this was going to press, Boyle (1970) offered a possible solution
by suggesting means of using ordinal data in path analysis.

ate statistical techniques, for example, multiple regression equations, would only serve to impose specious or spurious precision upon matters that our form of measurement has made fundamentally indeterminate. Indeed, it is possible, and in some instances even likely, that the scaling of the eight sites on any one environmental variable might be duplicated by yet another, unsuspected, environmental variable.

What is more, we must be aware that if the environment does exert causal force over attitudes, it most likely does so over a period of years, not overnight. And so attitudes and values as they were expressed in this research interview may well reflect past environments, not present ones, and each site may differ in this regard in unknowable ways. Therefore, we must be content to claim no more than plausibility for the relationships between these scales and their concomitant attitudes and values. Nonetheless, we have seen that several environmental variables are related to an intriguing set of attitudes. In some instances, these linkages between "culture" and the "environment" confirm our basic expectations; in others, they point to unanticipated relationships. I conclude that our search for the "sources" of covariation, while less well designed and far more difficult than the search for covariation itself, has produced some findings that could provide the bases for formal hypotheses.

Still, if there are as yet no grounds for confidence that we have located significant causal dimensions of the environment, we can at least be bolstered in our conviction that we have found further evidence that there are tangible differences in the response patterns of pastoralists and farmers, for throughout this chapter we have found that responses previously associated with farmers or pastoralists have continued to be so associated.

Chapter 11 attempts to review and assess the accumulated evidence concerning these differences between farmers and pastoralists.

Conclusion 11

The time has come to evaluate the findings about farmers and pastoralists, and to consider some general questions about cultural continuity and change. Earlier chapters have discussed the nature of the research design and the strengths and limitations of the data. If the answers to our questions about differences between pastoralists and farmers have not yet been yielded, there is little reason to believe that more or different analyses would provide such answers where all that has gone before has failed to do so. The data have been presented, now we must see what conclusions can be reached.

Before taking up questions of ecological variation, let me be quite clear regarding our views on cultural continuity. Our research always took cultural continuity for granted. At every step in the formulation of this research design, we assumed that each of our four tribes would possess a distinctive culture that would, at least in many of its features, show considerable continuity over time. As I reported in chapter 4, we did find a distinctive core of responses for each tribe, a core that was shared by farmers and pastoralists alike. We assumed that each tribe's cultural core would, in a manner of speaking, be "dominant" over its environment.

We can now conclude that there can be no doubt that if we wished to know how someone in these four tribes would respond to the interview administered in this research, we could best predict that person's responses by knowing the tribe to which he belonged. No other consideration—neither age, nor sex, nor acculturation, nor economic mode of life—tells us as much about a person's responses as tribal affiliation, or "culture." On observational and ethnographic grounds as well, we can be certain that a Pokot pastoralist, for ex-

271

ample, is more like a Pokot farmer than he is like a fellow pastoralist among the Hehe, Kamba, or Sebei. Of this essential fact of cultural identity there can simply be no doubt. What is basic to a person's culture (see chapter 4) remains basic, be that person a farmer or a pastoralist. It is in this sense, then, that we were correct in assuming that a person's tribe, or culture, would be dominant over his economic mode of life. At some levels of analysis, it is appropriate to expect *non*sharing of beliefs, attitudes, motives, values, and feelings within a society. At our level of comparative analysis, however, it was appropriate to expect cultural sharing and cultural continuity. We found both.

The problem and the challenge for us lay in the discovery of ecological differentiation, that is, consistent differences between pastoralists and farmers that could be attributed to ecological variation. As documented in chapters 7, 8, and 9, there were such differences between farmers and pastoralists in all four societies, and these differences were far more numerous than could be expected by chance.

Let me provide a further illustration. When all 31 of the content analysis categories (described in chapter 1 and presented in many of the succeeding chapters) were examined in an effort to determine the relative importance of tribal affiliation (culture) as opposed to economic mode (ecology) in accounting for the responses given in each site, the results were quite impressive. A mere glance at the mean scores of the four tribes on most of these content analysis categories (see chapter 7) is sufficient to indicate that the "culture" of the respondent is an important determinant of his responses. And, when the effect of tribal membership is subjected to statistical test (a two-way analysis of variance for finite populations), for every one of the 31 variables it is possible to reject the null hypothesis of no differences between tribal populations. In all 31 instances, the F-values were so significant that in rejecting the null hypothesis we would be in error many fewer than 5 times out of 10,000.[1] The apparent magnitude of the response differences among tribes is emphatically confirmed by the analysis of variance. As I have said, this is what we expected.

We were a good deal less certain that these same variables would show comparable pastoral-farming differences. This was our central research question, and the answer to it was anything but taken for granted. In fact, however, the same analysis of variance

1. See Appendix X.

indicated that, with one exception (litigiousness), we could also reject the null hypothesis that there were no differences between farmers and patoralists in each tribe on each variable. While it is true, as is reported in Appendix X, that the variance in most of the 31 variables is better accounted for by tribe than by economic mode, it is nevertheless also true that for almost all of these variables we would err in rejecting the null hypothesis that farmers and pastoralists do *not* differ only 5 or fewer times in 10,000. It is the nature of these differences between farmers and pastoralists that constitutes our principal interest.

Given, then, that differences between farmers and pastoralists do exist, what conclusions can we reach about the nature of these differences? I have presented the basic data derived from observation and interview, I have offered tests of statistical significance, and I have made various inferences from these data. I shall now set down my general conclusions about farmers and pastoralists. In doing so, I shall follow my convictions as they are built up out of a long acquaintance with all of these data. I say this not to prepare the reader for my extravagant flights of interpretive fancy, but rather to explain why my conclusions may, at times, be either more or less conservative than the earlier statistical tests of significance might seem to warrant. At times, therefore, I shall be more conservative because it is sometimes possible with samples the size of ours to reject the null hypothesis with deceptive ease. As the psychologist David Bakan has warned, P-values derived from tests on large samples can be comforting, and are often demanded by scientific audiences, but they can also provide a dangerous illusion of proof where an honest skepticism should more properly prevail.[2] At other times, I may appear to go beyond the confidence levels of these data, as for example, when they do not reach the 1 percent or even 5 percent level, but *are* consistently in the expected direction. That is, in this the final analysis I shall rely not only upon my understanding of the magnitude of the differences between farmers and pastoralists, but also upon my sense of the consistency, coherence, and emphasis of these differences.

Proceeding in this manner, I feel confident in saying that farmers and pastoralists can be distinguished by the attributes illustrated in the polar comparison shown in figure 8. This figure attempts to portray diagrammatically both the kinds and the emphases of the differences between farmers and pastoralists. Thus, the attitude clos-

2. Bakan (1968).

est to the farming pole (disrespect for authority) is the most characteristic farming variable. Also highly characteristic, but slightly less
so, are these attributes: anxiety, conflict avoidance, emotional constraint, hatred, impulsive aggression, and indirect action. Somewhat
more weakly related we find friends, then still more distant are
insults, litigiousness, and fatalism. At the periphery, there are two
final, quite weakly associated attributes: fear of poverty and jealousy
of wealth.

At the pastoral pole, we find five fundamental attributes: affection, direct aggression, divination, independence, and self-control.
Almost equally central in importance are these attributes: adultery,
sexuality, guilt-shame, depression, and respect for authority. Somewhat more weakly related are fear, bravery, brutality, and concern
with death. Farther toward the boundary of the pastoral pattern but
still well within it are concern with wrongdoing, cooperation, industriousness, clan, and kinsmen.

Figure 8 is not meant to be a precise map of each attribute in
m-dimensional space. It is simply an illustrative representation of all
those attributes that I feel confident about as farming or pastoral
characteristics. It is also an indication of the relative strength of association between these attributes. The closer a variable lies to either
pole, the greater is my confidence that it serves to characterize that
pole. As variables move toward the central area between poles, I
become less confident about their farming or pastoral affiliation.
Thus, if I were to follow out this illustration, I could place in the
empty center portion of Figure 8 those variables that have *no* farming or pastoral affiliations.

Turning now to the nature of these attributes that best characterize farmers and pastoralists, I believe it possible to note differences in the extent to which each set of attributes is characterized by a
dominant focus. It seems to me that the farming attributes consistently relate to a central core, or theme, that might be called "interpersonal tension." For example, the farmers employ indirect action,
featuring secrecy and caution; their emotions are constrained and
they live with great anxiety. They not only show disrespect for authority, but the prevailing affect between people is hostility or hatred.
They avoid conflict, engaging instead in litigation and witchcraft.
Yet, their hostility, anxiety, and sensitivity to insults sometimes produce impulsive physical attack when open aggression does occur.
There is remarkable coherence in this pattern. What is more, the
pattern contains its own central dilemma, the necessity to avoid overt
conflict. The need of farmers to avoid overt conflict in order to live

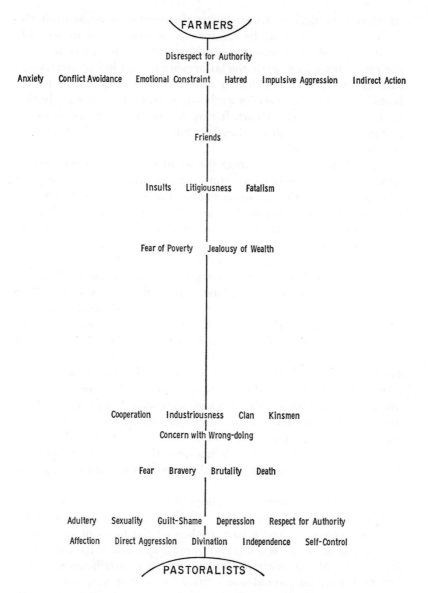

Figure 8. A polar comparison of farmers and pastoralists.

together upon finite, scarce, and usually dwindling land resources was a basic expectation of this research project. I believe that farmers in these four tribes do attempt to avoid overt conflict, and I believe that the other attributes found here to characterize farmers can reasonably be derived from the basic necessity to accomplish this avoidance. The caution, the constraint, the anxiety—all are likely to occur in people who must take care not to provoke incidents with their neighbors. As a result, the farmers are hostile and indirect, often turning to witchcraft, which in turn evokes anxiety and still more hostility. Their disrespect for authority may, in part, be a projection of this hostility, and, in part, it may reflect the failure of litigation and indirect aggression to relieve the anxiety and hostility that these people so keenly feel.

It is not so easy to bring the set of characteristic pastoral attributes under a single focus. However, the farming focus does contrast markedly with one focus among the pastoralists. Where the farmers are constrained in their emotions and indirect in their actions, the pastoralists freely express emotions, both positive emotions such as affection, sexuality, or bravery, and dysphoric emotions such as guilt, depression, brutality, and fear of death. Where the farmers are indirect in their actions, especially in their actions relating to conflict, the pastoralists act independently and aggress openly. Even their concern with divination expresses the individual's effort to predict and control his future. This emphasis on divinatory control contrasts with the farmers' emphasis upon fatalism. There are additional features as well. Despite the open and direct character of pastoral life, pastoralists respect authority, particularly of senior persons and of prophets, and they are self-controlled where the farmers are impulsive. A separable, although somewhat less emphatic, focus among the pastoralists might be called social cohesion. Thus, the pastoralists are concerned with the consequences of wrongdoing, and they value cooperation, industriousness, the clan, and other kinsmen. There is no comparable, socially cohesive focus among the farmers.

I shall have more to say about these basic differences between farmers and pastoralists in a few pages. Now, I would like to turn to a second consideration. I have spoken of the focus of each set of characterizing attributes; it is also possible to speak of its "emphasis." Thus, we find that whereas the farming set of attributes was more tightly integrated around one central focus than were the pastoral attributes, the farming attributes are *less* emphatic. Aside from disrespect for authority, none of the farming attributes was extremely emphatic. The farming variables are coherent; but, taken separately, few are expressed frequently or emphatically enough to permit us great confidence in saying that they typify farmers. On the other hand, many of the pastoral attributes do have this force. They are expressed so frequently and emphatically that many of them can confidently be said to typify pastoralists in these four tribes. The following attributes all carry that degree of force: affection, direct aggression, independence, divination, self-control, adultery, sexuality, guilt-shame, depression, and respect for authority.

We might also compare the "level" of these farming and pastoral characteristics. The many variables that were considered throughout this research, including those that constitute this concluding farming-pastoral comparison, represent different levels of psychological and cultural abstraction. For example, many of these variables clearly represent values (e.g., the desirability or valuation of cattle); others are just as clearly psychological (e.g., anxiety). But most of these variables are more difficult to characterize because they reflect both cultural values and psychological orientations. To oversimplify a complex matter, we might refer to these "mixed" variables as attitudes.

Turning first to values, I would conclude that the characteristic farming variables are rarely expressed as values. Farmers do not say (or, I think, believe) that they *ought* to be anxious, to hate, to aggress impulsively, to disrespect authority, and so on. They do sometimes emphasize the desirability of avoiding conflict, but very seldom do they attach values to the other variables. Conversely, many of the characteristic pastoral variables are regularly expressed as values. All of these variables express pastoral values: direct aggression, independence, divination, self-control, sexuality, respect for authority, bravery, cooperation, industriousness, concern with the consequences of wrongdoing, clan, and kinsmen. On the other hand, both pastoral and farming variables are clearly psychological in that they represent emotions or cognitive orientations which are not normally conceptualized or easily verbalized. I would judge that the farmers and pastoralists are about equal in the psychological level of their characterizing attributes.

There is an important difference here. The pastoralists are characterized by attributes that are expressed as both cultural values and psychological orientations, but the farmers' attributes lack the support of cultural values. In this sense, the core of that which characterizes the farmers is covert, and as such it may exert great influence. Yet, without the corresponding support of values, it lacks cultural recognition and institutionalization as a *proper* way of thinking, feeling, or behaving. The pastoral core of attributes *has* such cultural institutionalization; it is both deeply built into the actors and strongly reinforced by values.

When we take the farming and pastoral cores of characteristic variables together and contrast them with the "cultural" cores (each tribe's distinctive variables as discussed in chapter 4), another difference emerges. These distinctive cultural cores consistently reflect both basic psychological orientations and cultural values. In a few instances, only psychological attributes are expressed (the Hehe, impulsive aggression; the Kamba, need for affection; the Pokot, depression; the Sebei, anxiety); but the great majority of these variables combine both values *and* psychological attributes. Among the characteristic farming and pastoral variables, on the other hand, a far greater proportion are primarily psychological. I would judge, and of course any such judgment must be highly subjective, that of the twenty-six features listed in chapter 4 as distinctive cultural designata, only seven exist on the psychological level alone, without corresponding valuation. These seven include the four listed above plus these three Sebei distinctions: fear of death, fear of the malignant power of women, and jealousy and hostility. (This lack of value support for so much of what was distinctive of Sebei culture led me earlier to speak of the negative, uncommitted character of the Sebei.) In striking contrast, almost all of the farming designata and almost half of the characteristic pastoral variables are primarily or entirely psychological.

In summary, what is distinctive of pastoralists in all four of these societies is a common set of linked values, attitudes, and psychological orientations. Both farmers and pastoralists participate in the distinctive core of their tribe's culture, and in so doing they accept certain values. However, what is distinctive of farmers in these four societies is a nonvalued set of psychological dispositions, most of which are clearly expressive of tension, hostility, and conflict.[3]

To return now to the general question, what finally can be said about the fundamental differences between farmers and pastoralists? I must first make it clear that when I speak of such differences here, these differences, as before, are *relative*. That is, when I

3. If the negativism and hostility characterizing farmers were primarily produced by acculturation or deculturation, it is difficult to see why they should be so selective in their operation, leaving many strong values in place while eroding a few willy-nilly. As Walter Goldschmidt points out in his epilogue, an ecological explanation is a good deal more plausible.

spoke earlier of the farmers being, for example, anxious, I meant that they were substantially more anxious than the pastoralists, not that the pastoralists were completely free of anxiety. Here, too, I am suggesting quantitative contrasts between farmers and pastoralists, not absolute differences.

At the most general level of comparison, I believe that farmers and pastoralists are differentiated on two dimensions: (1) open versus closed emotionality, and (2) direct versus indirect action. These dimensions—themes, perhaps—appear to me to find expression primarily as psychological sets, although they also serve as general orienting principles of the kind sometimes referred to as world view, or value orientation. However, I am far less concerned with the epistemological nature of these themes than I am with how many attitudes and behaviors can be subsumed under them and what predictive utility they might have. I believe that these two summative themes epitomize the differences between farmers and pastoralists and that these themes can account for many of the variables we have previously discussed.

To illustrate what I have in mind in these two dimensions of comparison, let me rephrase what we have already said about the emotionality of farmers. The emotions of farmers may well be strongly felt—indeed, there is every evidence that they are—but they are not openly expressed. Perhaps I should say that they are not readily revealed, for it seems that farmers are actively engaged in conscious concealment of their true feelings. At the same time that they may be unaware of certain emotions (we might presume the presence of certain ego-defense mechanisms), it is my impression that farmers tend to withhold emotional expression because of their calculation that it is in their best interest to do so. For the most part, farmers seem to succeed in closing off their emotions to others, for it is only now and then that suppressed feelings break through in impulsive, uncontrolled fashion. And when this happens, it brings socially disruptive consequences.

In strong contrast, the pastoralists display their feelings easily, openly, and seemingly "naturally." I assume that the emotions of pastoralists, like those of people anywhere, are subject to both conscious concealment and unconscious censorship; nevertheless, in comparison to farmers of the same tribe, pastoralists are remarkably expressive of a wide range of emotion. The good and the bad, the joyous and the sad, the soft and the harsh—all are expressed with far greater freedom. Perhaps because their feelings are so openly expressed, the pastoralists appear to lack those occasional impulsive lapses of control which occur among the farmers.

Similarly, farmers and pastoralists differ with regard to directness of action. The farmers are characteristically indirect. Not only do they avoid direct expression of their feelings, when they do speak and act, it is with a careful eye to obscuring their motives, to veiling their meanings, and to avoiding confrontation over any potentially contestable issue. Compared to farmers, pastoralists strongly value independent and direct action. They make decisions as individuals, openly pursue goals, and typically say and do what they wish—directly. They even aggress openly, abusing or assaulting an adversary, but usually doing so only when appropriate and within sublethal limits. Despite their open, direct, sometimes even brutal approach to other humans and animals, their actions are controlled. When farmers aggress, social cohesion is threatened; when pastoralists do so, social relations continue as before.

As I have argued earlier, there are a number of noteworthy differences between farmers and pastoralists, but these two themes, control of emotion and of action, are to me the most fundamental and the most reliable distinctions of all.

What, then, of the causes of these distinctions? Insofar as we may venture any conclusions regarding how differences between farmers and pastoralists may relate to ecology, we can most confidently begin by pointing to conflict as the pivotal concern. The farmers avoid direct conflict; the pastoralists accept it, sometimes even seek it. This difference is important, but it is a functional distinction, not truly an ecological one until we can specify the conditions that have led to it. Our expectations in this regard have been set forth by Walter Goldschmidt in his introduction to this volume, so I need not repeat them here. I shall, however, reiterate a few of the indications of chapter 10. We should recall that shortage of land appeared to be less efficient as a predictor of farming attributes than was shortage of cattle. Nevertheless, there is reason to conclude that scarcity of major economic resources, land or cattle, *does* relate to farming attitudes and psychological orientations. So, too, does the clustering of households: the closer households are clustered together, the greater is the expression of hatred and the concern with conflict avoidance. Both of these findings support our original expectations.

We anticipated that the pastoral set of distinctive attributes would be related, in large part, to an ecology that set demands, particularly upon a man, to be able, quickly and alone, to take action in order to defend himself and his assets, be these assets his wives, his children, or his herds. We are able to offer no conclusive support for this assumption, but I continue to find it plausible. We did find a strong linkage between the cooperative aspect of the pastoral response pattern and the need to manage water resources; it seems highly likely to me that the pastoral focus upon social cohesion is a direct reflection of this sort of ecological necessity.

But there is a still more basic dimension of the environment to be considered, and this dimension has heretofore been ignored. We had originally postulated that the relative mobility of each population would be a crucial environmental determinant of its members' attitudes, values, and personality. It was not possible to measure this environmental variable with any adequacy, and so it was not discussed in chapter 10; however, if I were now to select the one environmental variable that I believe would explain most about differences between farmers and pastoralists, it would be this one. I believe that Goldschmidt was correct in hypothesizing that farmers must avoid conflict because they cannot move away from it. They are tied to the land, and a neighbor, however angry, will remain a neighbor; given this fact of immobility, it becomes essential to avoid open conflict. The pastoral contrast can be dramatic. Ideally, when a pastoralist quarrels with someone, he can pick up stakes and move away with his family and his animals in tow, all with little difficulty. It is this ability to quarrel directly with, and then move away from, an adversary that so drastically alters the imperatives of social control and conflict avoidance among pastoralists.

Since this surmise is based upon ethnographic observations rather than upon systematic interview responses, and since it is offered as a suggestion for research rather than as a demonstrable finding, I can only illustrate the relevance of such differential mobility for questions of social conflict.

Pastoralists in these four tribes often told me that men who are angry should be allowed to fight, for if anger should not be dispelled, witchcraft would be the likely result. I. M. Lewis, writing of the pastoral Somali, reached a similar conclusion: " . . . where sorcery or witchcraft occur it is usually between people who, for one reason or another, are prevented from fighting." [4] But I was also told by these pastoralists that if a fight were unusually serious or left "bad feelings," then the antagonists should move away from each other. I

4. Lewis (1961), p. 26.

do not know how often combatants actually moved away from one another, but I do know that the option to move away was present and that it was often exercised.

I also know that other East African pastoral societies have recognized the relationship between mobility and the reduction of conflict. For example, Paul Spencer concluded this regarding the pastoral Samburu of Kenya: " . . . the constant need for migration and dispersal *inevitably* dampens local strains (italics mine)." [5] Spencer added this comment: "Moreover, if two people quarreled then they generally moved apart and kept apart throughout the remainder of my stay." [6] As a paradigm example of this same phenomenon, I offer Philip Gulliver's account of the nomadic Turkana of Kenya:

> Another factor leading to the dispersion of a house is the principle that where tensions exist between individuals, for whatever reason, it is best to relieve them by geographical separation, when, if they do not gradually die down, they will at least necessarily be reduced. . . . if two co-wives habitually quarrel, one of them will go to live in the other homestead of the same nuclear family; at another level, if two men quarrel and bad relations persist, then one or both will shift his homestead elsewhere. Such practical arrangements are not difficult in Turkanaland, where on the one hand each family maintains at least two homesteads, and on the other where mobility is high.[7]

Such "practical" arrangements *are* difficult for farmers, and therein lies a major ecological difference between the life conditions of farmers and pastoralists.

Throughout this book, and in Walter Goldschmidt's epilogue, various alternatives to our ecological position have been considered: differential acculturation, deculturation, vagaries of history, and the like. I mention here another alternative, the possibility of selective migration. Might it not be, as some of my academic colleagues have seriously suggested, that the distinctive pastoral response pattern is a product of selective migration from the hills to the plains by those men and women who were already more independent, aggressive, culturally committed, and so forth? Although the histories of these four tribal areas are poorly known, all evidence indicates that no

5. Spencer (1965), p. 207.
6. Ibid., p. xxiv.
7. Gulliver (1966), p. 165.

such migration took place. Past migration patterns were different in all four areas, but none conformed to this putative pattern. Recent migration from the hills to the plains is far from being extensive, and when it does occur, primarily involves land-poor men or young relatives of the rich, not necessarily those with "pastoral" attributes. There is, in short, no evidence whatever to support the idea that the distinctive pastoral-farming differences are the result of past or present selective migration.

But even were we to assume that just such migration took place, or continues to take place, our ecological thesis would in no way be weakened. On the contrary, our position would be just as compelling because such migrants would neither leave their farming areas nor survive in pastoral ones, unless their attitudes, values, and psychological attributes were favored by the pastoral way of life. In a selective migration position, ecology remains sovereign, rendering farming conditions less congenial for these people, and pastoral life more so. Since the facts do not permit us to sustain our thesis by referring to fables about selective migration, however, we have relied upon a more conventional ecological explanation.

This concludes what I have to say about the differences between farmers and pastoralists. My conclusions have been conservative, yet I believe that even these cautious comparisons represent a sizable corpus of farming-pastoral distinctions. Further, I am confident that these distinctions can be verified by independent investigators.

I would like to turn now to more general questions of cultural continuity and change.

PROBLEMS IN THE STUDY OF CULTURAL CHANGE

Those who have studied ecological change, evolution, or adaptation have usually invoked two probabilistic clauses: "Given a sufficient length of time" and "given a sufficient number of instances."[8] Although these two clauses are purposefully vague, they are essential and legitimate for an understanding of the relationship between ecology and culture. The limitations of our research design both with regard to length of time and number of instances have made our task of discovering differences between farmers and pastoralists doubly difficult. Let us look more closely at these difficulties.

8. See Harris (1968).

That it takes time for men's attitudes, beliefs, values, and feelings to adapt to a new environment is a truism. Everything takes time, and adaptation, by definition, is a process occurring over time. Yet, while we agree that attitudinal adaptation "takes time," and can be fully effected only "in the long run," we must ask, how long is long enough? It is possible that some attitudes change the moment a man lays eyes upon a new environment; but some of that same man's attitudes may not change in his lifetime. Although anthropology's long recording of instances in which a people's technology and economy could be more "efficiently" adapted to their environment is no doubt overdrawn and sometimes is frankly in error, we must nonetheless conclude that optimal technological and economic adaptation does not usually take place in a time period as short as a decade, or even a generation, and that attitudes and values may be still slower to change.

Although the four tribes in this research were multigenerational residents of the general tribal areas in which we studied them, their technologies and economies have changed somewhat over time. What is more, when we look at the four pastoral sites within these tribal areas, we cannot be certain how long these low, dry environments have been occupied. In some instances, as among the Sebei, for example, utilization of this low-lying, "pastoral" environment is quite recent in time, taking place at the time of World War I. Among the Pokot, on the other hand, pastoral utilization of the plains areas appears to have been well established by the time of Thomson's visit in 1884.[9]

Thus we must contend with the fact that there are differences in the lengths of time that our four pastoral populations have occupied their environments. We must also admit that we have no idea how long it might take for a population that had previously practiced a mixed farming and pastoral economy to alter its values and attitudes after changing to an exclusively pastoral way of life. We do know, however, from Gulliver's study of the Arusha, that pastoral attitudes and values may endure for many generations among people who are compelled to live by agriculture.[10] Examples from our own research serve to emphasize the point that cultural change may occur rapidly, or very slowly indeed. For an example of rapid change, we offer a Pokot case in point.

9. See Goldschmidt (1967a) and Thomson (1887).
10. Gulliver (1963).

Pokot pastoralist men who were rich in cattle, at least in the area in which this research was conducted, often acquired wives from the cattle-poor mountainous farming areas. As a result, many wives of pastoral men were born and raised in nonpastoral areas. In order to take advantage of this natural comparison, the sample of Pokot women to be interviewed in the pastoral area of Masol was so constructed as to include both Masol-born pastoral women and mountain-born farming-area women now living in Masol. Eighteen pastoral-area women and fourteen mountain-area women were interviewed. Their ages were comparable: the mean age of the pastoral-born women was 38 (S.D. = 14.4), and that of the mountain-raised women was 38.5 (S.D. = 15.5). Each of the mountain women was born and raised in a farming area which she did not leave until she was at least 19 years old, and often older. The amount of time each of these women had spent in the Masol pastoral area before the time of our research varied, but it was estimated that the 14 mountain-raised women had spent an average of 18 years per woman married to a pastoral man and living in a pastoral area.

The obvious question at issue was whether such women would display interview response patterns similar to the Masol-born pastoral women or whether they would maintain a response pattern more like that of the Pokot farming women interviewed at Tamkal. With rare exceptions there were no statistically significant differences between the women born and raised in the farming-mountain areas and those born and raised in the pastoral area. Only four response differentials were noted: (1) the pastoral-born women were more inclined to see humans in the Rorschach (the meaning of a single such finding unsupported by other Rorschach findings is impossible to determine); (2) the farming-raised women more often spoke of wealth as being a central goal in life for a man (P < .01); (3) the farming-raised women were more concerned with avoiding conflict (P < .01); and (4) the pastoral-born women more frequently expressed an acceptance and valuation of direct physical aggression (P < .001). As we have seen, these last two differences reflect fundamental farming-pastoral distinctions.

Although the numbers of women involved in this comparison are too small to permit complete confidence in the findings, it would strongly appear that, in general, farming-raised women who marry pastoral men do *not* express values, attitudes, or personality characteristics that differ markedly from those of women who have spent their entire lives in a pastoral area. The principal exception consists of the tendency for mountain-raised women to maintain "farming" attitudes toward aggression and conflict; that is, more often than their pastoral counterparts, these women attempt to avoid conflict and verbal or physical aggression. It cannot be said that such women do not hold within themselves values or emotions that differ from the Masol-born pastoralists with whom they live, but they do not express them, either in this interview or in everyday life. In this instance, then, as in Chekhov's story, "The Darling," in which the heroine's feelings and beliefs changed to match those of succeeding husbands, attitudinal and psychological change appears to have taken place with remarkable speed.[11]

For a second, and contrasting example, consider the Bumetyek of Uganda. These people, who are a thousand or so in number, call themselves Bumetyek but are apparently a fragment of the Bagwere of the so-called interlacustrine Bantu. They live among the Sebei farmers on the northwestern slopes of Mount Elgon, where they appear to have settled before European contact. They helped the Sebei in their wars against the Bagisu: during these wars and later, some served as blacksmiths, providing weapons for the Sebei, whom the Bumetyek characterized as "warrior people." The Bumetyek acquired land and became farmers among the Sebei, and so complete has the process of intermarriage been between Bumetyek and Sebei that probably no more than a hundred Bumetyek remain whose parents were Bumetyek and who have not themselves married a Sebei. In an effort to please the Sebei who sought Bumetyek women as wives, the Bumetyek accepted the Sebei practice of female circumcision sometime around 1930. Virtually all Bumetyek now speak Sebei well, and in their everyday behavior they are virtually indistinguishable from the Sebei.

Here then is a people who, for several generations, have lived among the Sebei, have adapted to the same physical environment on Mount Elgon, have acquired substantial portions of Sebei culture, and, in a good many instances, have even come to speak of themselves as Sebei rather than Bumetyek. It intrigued us that a Bantu-speaking people should have so dedicatedly come to live among and adopt the culture of a Kalenjin-speaking people. As a consequence, we decided to interview a small number of Bumetyek in the same manner that the Sebei farmers were interviewed. In all, twelve Bumetyek, all men, were interviewed. Although the interviewing was done in the center

---

11. My thanks are due Dr. Miriam Morris for suggesting this analogy.

of the Bumetyek area of settlement, the interpreter was a Sebei (the same man who had interpreted among the Sebei), and the interviews were given in Sebei. What is more, I later learned that at least some of the Bumetyek whom I interviewed believed that I was interested in finding out "how Sebei they really were." Under these circumstances we had every reason to expect that these Bumetyek men would respond to the interview in a manner very similar to Sebei farming men; however, if they attempted to do so, they did not succeed.

Their greatest similarity to the Sebei (see chapter 4) lay in their fear of death; their second most pronounced similarity was their respect for seniority, but here their responses were both fewer and less emphatic than those given by the Sebei. On the four remaining Sebei cultural diagnostics—diffuse anxiety, fear of the malignant power of women, profound jealousy and hostility, and a desire for population increase—the Bumetyek differed noticeably. All four of these foci were absent or nearly so among the Bumetyek. Instead, the Bumetyek protocols were characterized by such non-Sebei emphases as the desirability of female circumcision (perhaps as an effort to emulate the Sebei or convince me of their Sebei-ness), the virtues of their language, the trustworthiness of friends, and the importance of dancing (something the Bumetyek are noted for among the Sebei). The two most emphatic features of the Bumetyek responses were also different from the Sebei, physical violence and overt sexuality. Not only were violence and sexuality mentioned more often than they were among the Sebei, they were often combined in frightening scenes of bloody sexual assault. The prototype of this singular Bumetyek response can be taken from one Bumetyek man's response to values picture 5 (a man either watching or interceding in a fight between two other men): "These are girls—no, one is a girl and one is a boy. The boy has a knife." *What will happen?* "This boy is forcing her to have sexual intercourse with him. If she refuses, he will kill her."

We know far too little about the Bumetyek to comment upon the depth of their understanding of Sebei culture or their commitment to it; but I believe that even at the superficial level of this analysis, it is clear that neither by fear of forcible eviction, by acculturation, nor by ecological adaptation have the Bumetyek "become" Sebei.

These two examples, the Pokot and the Bumetyek, are intended to make the point that to study ecological change we need the "in the long run" clause. We also need to examine a substantial number of cases. Just as we had problems because of our lack of control over time depth, we also had problems because of the small number of societies in our research. Instead of the twenty or so societies we would have preferred in order to give us complete confidence in our analyses, we had only four. As a consequence, we often encountered a set of findings in which pastoralists and farmers varied consistently in three societies, but failed to do so in the fourth society. Our problem, obviously, was what to conclude regarding that single discrepant society. Faced with this problem, there was an immense temptation to engage in what is sometimes called deviant case analysis. I shall illustrate this kind of analysis, and the difficulties inherent in it, by examining our thesis regarding witchcraft.

You will recall that a central hypothesis of the Culture and Ecology Project concerned witchcraft (I use the term "witchcraft" to refer to both witchcraft and sorcery because for my purposes the distinction is not important and because in two of the four tribes no clear distinction was made between the concepts). Following Kluckhohn,[12] Marwick,[13] and many others, we hypothesized that *witchcraft will increase where opportunities for overt aggression are lacking*. Such an hypothesis is based upon a direct rendering of the frustration-aggression model, which is, of course, itself a hypothesis.[14] The argument follows a hydraulic analogy by assuming that man stores frustration in the same manner that steam collects in a boiler, and if there is no opportunity to work off these frustrations in direct aggression, then indirect means must be found, or man, like the boiler, will explode.

Following this line of argument, we anticipated that witchcraft (and other forms of indirect aggression) would occur more often in farming communities than in pastoral ones. We so hypothesized because the opportunities for overt aggression should, in our model, be fewer among farmers and, therefore, the frustrations should be more numerous. That is, in terms of the ecological situation, as we assumed it to exist, we believed that farmers in these four tribes would be subject to crowding together on land that was in short supply, that opportunities to move away from an unpleasant situation (e.g., an aggrieved neighbor or kinsman) would not exist, that the need

12. Kluckhohn (1944).
13. Marwick (1952).
14. Kaufmann (1965).

for cooperation and amicable relations would be great, and consequently, that frustrations would inevitably occur. Yet given the need
to live closely and peaceably together, open aggression could not be
tolerated; therefore, covert aggression in the form of witchcraft (a
phenomenon known and practiced in all four societies) would occur
frequently. On the other hand, the pastoral life-mode with its movement, low population density, and aggressive militarism would have
both fewer frustration-generating conditions (because antagonists
could move away from one another) and greater sanctioned opportunity for a direct, aggressive response to frustration. Therefore, covert aggression in the form of witchcraft would occur less often.
Briefly stated, those were the assumptions.

Let me return to the findings introduced in chapter 7. First, as
we saw in tables 45 and 46, hatred, which I interpret to reflect interpersonal tension and frustration, was mentioned more often by
farmers than by pastoralists in all societies except the Kamba. Similarly, references to insults (see tables 43 and 44) were more frequent
among farmers than among pastoralists in all societies except the
Kamba. This I take to be an indicator of the extent to which persons
give offense to one another. Along with this high level of hatred and
insults we find a corresponding pattern of desire to avoid conflict
(see tables 41 and 42), with farmers—again, except for the Kamba—
expressing this desire more often than pastoralists. To complete the
picture, we find in all four societies that direct aggression (see tables
37 and 38) is lower among farmers. Given this response pattern, we
would expect witchcraft to be higher among farmers than pastoralists.
And so it is, except, once again, for the Kamba (see tables 47 and 48).
To summarize, we found that, with the exception of direct aggression, which met our expectations in all four societies, our frustration-
aggression thesis regarding witchcraft is consistently confirmed
among the Hehe, Pokot, and Sebei, but is consistently disconfirmed
among the Kamba.

What happened among the Kamba? The discrepancy could
simply be ignored if it were but one negative case among a large
number of positive ones. Unfortunately, it is one among only four;
therefore, we feel an obligation to examine this deviant case to see
"what went wrong." We might begin by examining the quality of
witchcraft mention among the Kamba pastoralists. When we do, an
interesting feature comes to light: these mentions are almost entirely
cross-gender. Women use witchcraft against men, and men employ

magic to protect themselves. No comparable degree of sex-linkage was found in any of the other seven sites.[15]

It is a relatively simple matter to explain why the Kamba pastoralists' witchcraft is sex-related; in this sector of the Kamba tribe, antagonism between men and women reaches an unusual intensity. This antagonism was expressed throughout the interviews and, as table 22 indicates, hostility to the opposite sex was substantially greater than anything expressed in any of the other seven communities, even including the Kamba farmers, who themselves expressed this same attitude quite frequently.

But the qualitative differences do not properly convey the depth of these feelings. Here are some typical examples of the sentiment of male dominance that underlies this male-female antagonism. From a man's point of view,

> A man must not show anything to his wife to lead her to believe she is equal. Men must always be superior to women. This is very important. A man can do anything: he can hunt—she cannot hunt; he can clear the bush—she is too weak to do this; he cuts big poles for a granary—she cannot do that either. In the old days, we went to war—women could only stay home with the children. A man comes and goes as he pleases—a woman must always tell her husband where she is going and she must always kneel before him and be very polite. She cannot even look directly at her husband or call him by his name. Women, you see, do not have strong brains: after all, we buy them; we sell them; we give them orders; we beat them. They are not important.

And women also know the rhetoric:

> We are not as good as men. We are inferior. We must only obey. A woman who did not obey would be worse than a wild beast. We know we are inferior—men have stronger brains. Women can only do minor work that is beneath men. We can only cook, or harvest, or milk, or take care of babies. A man is never affectionate to his wife— she is not that important. He would never fondle me or say nice

15. This estimation is approximate. The data do not permit complete tabulation of adversary pairings for each mention of witchcraft; the victim was almost always specified, but the witch was often not identified. However, it is clear that over 70 per cent of Kamba pastoralists' witchcraft mentions involve man versus woman. This percentage is never over 40 per cent in any other site (Kamba farmers and Hehe farmers), and it is usually much lower than that.

things. He only takes me for his own pleasure. That is how things are; men are the ones who do what they want. He orders me; I can never order him.[16]

Beneath this rhetoric, however, there is smoldering antagonism. Women give voice to their discontent in many subtle ways, and when women are alone together they malign men and the male attitude of dominance with an awesome anger. By women's own admission, witchcraft is a principal means by which women even the scales. Men fear female witchcraft, and women admit to directing their witch power against men. As one woman said with surprising candor, "Of course, we bewitch men. Men are too cruel. Mostly we just threaten men with witchcraft so they will not beat us too much, but sometimes we must use our power. I know one woman who is killing her husband right now. I am even thinking of doing so myself."

Of course, to show that the Kamba pastoralists employ more witchcraft than the Kamba farmers because they are riven by excessive male-female conflict is to provide only a very partial, ad hoc sort of explanation.[17] Without more detailed data than it was possible to elicit, I cannot attempt to suggest what it might be about relations between men and women which gives rise to such hostility, except to say that no obvious economic or demographic explanation comes to mind.

Having said all this, what can we conclude about this deviant case? We could say that having so "explained" the Kamba discrepancy, we have brought it within our original expectation. But to argue in that manner would be ecologically vacuous, for while we may have made a plausible case that the high witchcraft concern of the Kamba pastoralists exists alongside an exceptionally great male-female antagonism, we have provided no ecological explanation for the origin of this antagonism. Our original expectations did not call for such antagonism, and we cannot explain it, even after the fact. Furthermore, while it was present to an exceptional degree among the Kamba pastoralists, it was also present, although to a much lesser degree, among the Kamba farmers. It might be argued that male-female antagonism is simply a Kamba cultural emphasis (I have listed it as such in chapter 4) and is quite unrelated to differences in incidence of witchcraft mention. We might also argue that this sort

16. Some of this material was presented as "An Ecological View of Witchcraft in Four East African Societies," at the Annual Meeting of the African Studies Association, in Philadelphia, October, 1965.

17. See Louch (1966).

of witchcraft is quite a different phenomenon from the one we anticipated, and does not run counter to our thesis because we assumed that the lower incidence of witchcraft among pastoralists would be a product of their ability to move away from antagonists, and where the source of antagonism is the spouse (as among the Kamba), this option does not effectively exist.

We might also choose to shift our argument altogether, saying that the Kamba discrepancy is washed away by the effects of the multivariate analyses. As was shown in chapter 9, the smallest space analysis indicated that *even when Kamba respondents are included* in the analysis, there is nonetheless a close association between witchcraft, hatred, conflict avoidance, and land—all of which fell clearly within the farming domain of responses. The factor analysis also linked witchcraft and conflict avoidance; and, therefore, the Kamba pastoralists to the contrary notwithstanding, it is possible to argue that our hypothesis does find support.

We could easily continue to adduce more findings in order to bolster the plausibility of our efforts to bring the Kamba within our explanatory model. And, if the Kamba were but one of twenty cases in our research, we would eventually decide that the Kamba constituted that sort of anomaly that could be ignored even if it could not be explained away. But we had four cases, not twenty, and so we worry about the deviant case. Unfortunately, deviant case analysis can rarely be satisfactory because we are reduced to the position of arguing from a single case, or, if you will, from a single comparison. By any criterion of scientific adequacy, such functional arguments are unsatisfactory, for, strictly speaking, no comparison of a single pair of societies is interpretable.[18]

So we must admit that our small number of cases leaves us at the mercy of deviant cases. We see no reason to apologize for the small number of societies in the research design, however, for even a four-case field comparison is an expensive and complex undertaking for comparative research, and even four cases is an improvement over much that now provides the basis for ecological explanation. Nevertheless, we hope that future investigators can build upon our experience by providing themselves with a larger number of cases and an improved control over history.

18. See Goldschmidt (1966), Hempel (1959), and Louch (1966).

ECOLOGY AND THE INDIVIDUAL

This final chapter has compared farmers and pastoralists in terms of those attributes that most fundamentally yet reliably characterize them. It has also considered some general problems that we faced in this study. Before offering a final evaluation of the findings of this research, I would like to make an important point about the problems that were encountered. These problems have been discussed throughout this volume, so I shall only mention them here. I have in mind the fact that we were not able to locate communities that fitted our ideal pastoral or farming types; instead, our communities were at best approximations of the ideal ecological forms our expectations called for. What is more, within each of the four tribes, there was not only an exchange of information between the pastoral and farming communities, but sometimes there was an exchange of persons as well. In addition, as this chapter has pointed out, we had difficulties in our control over the length of time that each community had existed, as well as in the number of communities in our sample. I return to these difficulties here because their combined effect was to *reduce* the magnitude of the differences that we found between farmers and pastoralists. Our procedures of data collection and analysis did nothing to compensate for this reduction. For example, we sampled respondents on a probability basis: we did not interview only those persons who were most intensively engaged in a pastoral or farming mode of life. Similarly, the analysis of the data attempted to treat the statistical differences between populations quite conservatively, choosing for the most part to err on the side of overlooking rather than enhancing any small differences that might exist.

As a result, the differences that were found to characterize farmers and pastoralists become quite impressive. These differences (open versus closed emotions, direct versus indirect action, social cohesion versus social negativism) seem to be both general and fundamental, general in the sense of including several specific differences, and fundamental in the importance of these differences for an understanding of pastoral and farming life. For example, one is tempted to think of the pastoralists as extraverts with well-developed social consciences and the farmers as angry and fearful introverts. I mention this analogy because many of the basic farming-pastoral differences can be accounted for by this extravert-introvert comparison, but also

293

to point up the fact that the contrasts between the two ecological types are on a similar level of generality.

To summarize, our primary goal was to discover relevant differences in attitudes, values, and personality characteristics between farmers and pastoralists. I believe the differences that we found are valid ones and that they serve effectively to distinguish persons in these two ecological types.

Our second, and more difficult goal, was to relate these human differences to environmental differences. When we attempted to tie particular differences in these personal characteristics to particular features of the environmental and the situational aspects of the two life-modes, we found that we could not demonstrate specific sets of relationships. The relationships we uncovered were at best suggestive. This difficulty may derive from some of the inadequacies of the experimental situation or from our inability to scale some of the more important variables. Another viewpoint is possible, however, namely, that the several environmental and situational features combine as a system, and the attributes of behavior and personality we have found to be relevant to the two modes of economy relate to this generalized system, rather than to this or that specific feature of it.

I believe we can conclude, therefore, that farmers and pastoralists live in significantly differential milieux and that each milieu makes different demands on its human inhabitants and subjects them to different kinds of constraints. As a result, the individual is pressed toward the kind of behavior and attitudes appropriate to the milieu in which he finds himself, and with time he not only takes on attitudes and values that are appropriate to it but some aspects of his personality too come into conformity with that milieu. Individuals of course, vary in their adaptive capacity: some undoubtedly adapt very rapidly to a new environment, perhaps because of their flexibility of character, perhaps because they find it congenial. In other instances, or in other aspects of behavior more recalcitrant to change, the process may be a matter of generations.

But the essential fact is this: we have found significant differences in values, attitudes, and personality attributes where we expected to find them, and of the kind we expected to find, despite the short time span involved and the limited social distance between the communities of farmers and pastoralists, and, we add once more, despite the imperfections of the natural laboratory in which we were testing these ideas. These differences reflect the ecological conditions in which the two types of economy operate. They therefore contribute to an understanding of the processes of cultural adaptation.

Epilogue: The Relation of Intrapsychic Events to Ecological Adaptation

By Walter Goldschmidt

Edgerton's meticulous and detailed analysis of the responses of over 500 East African men and women enables us to say that the attitudes and values of pastoralists and farmers vary significantly, even though they belong to the same set of tribes. Furthermore, in almost every particular these differences conform to those we expected in terms of our theoretical model. If the degree of differentiation is relatively small, this is understandable in terms of the short time and the slight degree of separation between the pastoral and farming communities studied. Furthermore, the East African situation did not afford us that pure contrast in terms of which we formulated our thesis. I want here briefly to relate Edgerton's findings to the actualities of social existence as they differ between farmers and pastoralists, and to draw some general lessons from this phase of our research program.

In the process of analysis, Edgerton evaluated his responses in terms of some 31 categories with demonstrable statistically significant differences between farmers and pastoralists. In his conclusions he examines these differentials in terms of what he calls *focus, emphasis,* and *level. Focus* involves most directly what may be called the manifest content of the responses, or rather, what that content is a manifestation of in terms of action. *Emphasis* has reference to the degree to which these attributes are expressed, either in terms of frequency of expression or in terms of the internal consistency within the relevant category. *Level* involves an entirely different dimension: Is the quality expressed one that deals with culturally valued action; is it one that is intrapsychic and totally unsupported in cultural values; or is it a mixture of the two?

Edgerton finds that the focus of pastoralists differs from that of farmers in two respects: open versus closed emotionality and direct versus indirect action. It seems to me that these are really two facets of the same general phenomenon, the one dealing with emotional states and the other with patterns of action, and that certainly we would expect that persons capable of expressing and handling their emotions would be more likely to meet crises with direct action, while those who cannot handle their feelings would find indirect methods of dealing with the problematic aspects of interpersonal relationships.

According to the general thesis of the Culture and Ecology Project, these differences should be responsive to the recurrent realities of everyday life in the two economies. Therefore these qualities of personality and characteristic forms of activity should relate to these circumstances and needs which pastoralism and farming require or reward. To put the matter another way, why should one form be more appropriate to one situation and another more appropriate to the other?

The pastoralist's economic activities demand and reinforce a pattern of direct action. He cares for animals with wills of their own, and he must restrain their wills and, at the same time, meet their needs. The work of the farmer deals with a passive — though perhaps equally recalcitrant — nature, the control of which requires the constant application of hard work. It is not a conflict of wills.

The pastoralist is involved in constant movement as he takes his stock now to fresh graze, now to water, and occasionally to the salt licks, and in many pastoral areas such movement may be over long distances, require a long period of time, and be accomplished alone or with only his family or one or two other men. The actual daily activity requires little in the form of labor, though it does often cause physical hardship and deprivation; rather, it is characterized by the ever-present threat of danger, either from animals or human marauders. The pastoralist should be constantly alert and ready for action. To this end he goes about armed; he cannot temporize with these elements, and failure to take appropriate action can cost him an animal or even his entire herd. This lesson is learned in early youth, for a goat taken by a hyena can be the source of severe punishment, as more than one informant has reported from painful memory. The farmer has no such demands upon him. His work is drudgery, but not dangerous; he is not in constant movement or away from his community. If a raid comes, it is met more by community action than by personal response.

The care of livestock involves the husbandman in a constant pattern of decision making. His seasonal round of activities is not routinized; he must decide each day where to take his animals, and he may have to include many diverse factors in his computation — the potential quality of the grass, the availability of water, the probability of predators, the competitive action of other herders, and so on. The cumulative quality of such decisions will determine whether the herd prospers or not. The pastoralist must be constantly aware of the condition of each animal and meet its needs. While African pastoralists do not maintain genetic records, the good husbandman does recognize that some animals should be culled, and when the opportunity arises, it is these that are slaughtered, exchanged, or, nowadays, sold. This matter of exchanging and selling animals is of particular importance; the herdsman is engaged in recurrent economic transactions with his neighbors, and the cogency of his decisions and the capacity to arrive at satisfactory bargains are vital to the furtherance of his welfare. I demonstrated in *Kambuya's Cattle* (Goldschmidt, 1969, particularly Appendix E) that the personal acumen of Kambuya and his son Salimu were crucial in building their herds and in available capital.

Decision and action play no similar crucial role in the daily life of the farmer. He must, of course, determine what to plant and at what time, but once that decision has been made, the sequence of events is far more routinized and the action demanded is less urgent. Furthermore, the course of these activities is more clearly set forth by tradition. If there is a market activity, it is relatively unimportant and more often in the hands of women than of the men; it has relatively little influence on the economic well-being and even less on the social position of the farmer.

The pattern of farming life under the conditions prevalent in the four tribes under study and generally throughout tribal Africa also makes demands on the behavior of the individual. Chief among these I would put the insistent need to get along with that community of people whom he finds are his neighbors. The sources of conflict and antagonism in such a community are numerous under the best of conditions, yet the farmer cannot escape them without abandoning his resources. Amicable relationships must be maintained so that the community may stand together for mutual protection and often are desirable for other forms of mutual aid as well. The constant pressure for amiability requires that he develop techniques for hiding his feelings and suppressing his impulses.

These contrasts lead us to realize how different are the actions that lead to social rewards. Universally in pastoral societies, the status

297

of an individual is associated with the size of his herd. The actions he takes have a real and direct bearing on the number of animals he acquires and retains, so that the rewards for appropriate behavior are direct and visible. In farming, the status of an individual may or may not relate to his landholdings. If it does not, then it is dependent on other variant cultural factors; if it does, under conditions of noncommercial farming, it is still not dependent upon the quality of his husbandry, but on other manipulative devices. There was, for instance, one man in the farming community of Sebei who was building his holdings through the use of loans, foreclosures, and purchases. This pattern of action would have been impossible before the introduction of a market economy, yet it still did not depend on the man's capacity as a farmer. I think there is another distinction here that has relevance to the values and attitudes of the people. When a pastoralist acquires animals, his action is not seen to be at the expense of others, for the herdsman does not think in terms of a limited carrying capacity of the land. It is seen, rather, as an expression of his superior abilities. When the farmer acquires land, it is at the direct expense of his neighbors.

I find the following account by Robert Ekvall of Tibetan responses to the threat of hailstorms a kind of parable for his farmer-pastoralist contrast:

> In the case of the farmer we were well protected in the sheltered porch of his house and watched as the storm gathered and churned in white fury at the head of the valley, and then, filling it, moved down toward his field where the crops were almost ready for harvest. His fields were there right in front of him as the storm came on, yet there was nothing for him to do but shout his prayers until his voice was drowned in the roar of the storm that, in little more than minutes, stripped the fields of all harvest and then was gone. All the while, as he said his prayers, he was warm and dry in the shelter of his house porch from which to make any move would have been quite futile.
>
> In the case of the nomad, he and I were sitting on a hilltop beside a noon campfire, and below us hundreds of sheep were scattered across the green slopes as they grazed. When he saw the storm gather, and start to move on a narrow front across the slopes toward those sheep, which were at once his fields and the harvest, he did not waste a second in prayer. In an instant he was gone, shouting to me to pack the kettle and lunch gear, while he rode like one possessed by the "horse necked demon" to round up and drive the sheep into a compact mass, and press them at top speed up a side valley, somewhat out of the course of the storm, where a narrow gorge with high cliffs

promised something of shelter. He rode with utter recklessness across very rough ground; crowding the sheep toward that haven, and pitting his speed against the movement of the grey and white fury that came toward us. We—for I caught up to him as he criss-crossed on the flanks of the flock—won to relative safety, and as it passed only the edge of the storm pelted us and the closely bunched sheep at the foot of the cliffs; but the slope where the sheep had been was pockmarked with hailstones of which some were easily the size of baseballs. By action the nomad had saved both his fields and the harvest, for in his experience, against the storm one must act with immediacy if one would survive [Ekvall, 1964, pp. 28–29].

Edgerton mentions in passing, but does not accord the attention I feel it deserves, a third contrast in focus between pastoralists and farmers. The pastoralists' responses show a sense of community loyalty; the farmers' the negative aspects of community interaction. This cohesion is directly expressed in their preference for clansmen and kinsmen and their more frequent resort to cooperation, as well as in their greater display of respect for authority. It is also expressed indirectly in their stronger sense of guilt and shame, and in their greater concern with wrongdoing. The centrifugal force among farmers stands in sharp contrast. It is revealed directly in their expression of hatred and their disrespect for authority, in their seeking personal ties (friends) rather than formalized ones, in their litigiousness, their verbal aggression, and their greater jealousy of wealth.

In face of the fact that the pastoralist is socialized to independence of action and that his mobility gives him greater freedom from the insistent demands of community life, we may at first view these findings as contrary to expectation or paradoxical in character. I do not think that they are. Though he must be socialized to independence of action, he is not, in fact, independent of his fellows. Depending on local conditions and practices, he may live part of the year in close association with them, but whether or not he does so, he is dependent upon them for mutual assistance and economic interaction. There is thus a continuing need for community and for patterned interaction. Yet significantly, this interdependence tends not to be what one may call person-specific; that is, he does not have to maintain social relationships with persons (other than kindred) from whom for one or another reason he wishes to dissociate himself. This fact enables him to retain his independence of action despite the need for community. The herdsman's ties are, in fact, largely built upon the sentiment of kinship (as noted in the responses) rather than in terms

299

of community. At the same time he does not suffer to like degree the stresses and strains of an enforced and constant interaction with a set of neighbors which, as indicated by the farmers' responses, invoke antisocial sentiments and actions.

This line of thought is also expressed in what Edgerton has called *emphasis,* that is, the relative strength and consistency of responses, which was greater in the pastoralists' protocols than the farmers'. This reflects, I would argue, certain differentials in the forces at work in the two kinds of economy: (1) the narrower range of functionally effective forms of behavior available to pastoralists, and (2) the greater need for a strong commitment to these ways. The two are obviously interrelated. The first has reference to the fact that the pastoral demands on personality and behavior are more insistent and delimiting, that the payoff for conformity and the costs of failure to conform are more direct. The farmers can get by with a greater range of behavior without suffering personal loss. The second relates to the fact that though we are apt to see the pastoral way of life as superior and more desirable because it conforms to our own evaluation of independence, the simple fact of the matter is that, romanticism aside, pastoralism is hard, dangerous, and demanding. We may note that Barth (1964, p. 77) points out that the Bessari tend to settle down as farmers when they can afford to do so. I myself have heard Qashkai pastoralists of Iran bemoan the difficulty and danger of their treks, which have led many of their young men to abandon their pastoralism in modern times. The Sebei farmers view their pastoralist brothers as foolish to suffer the dangers of their way of life. To sustain such a pattern requires a strong commitment: the pastoralist must not only be socialized to independence, he must be strongly indoctrinated with the virtues this life-mode entails.

The matter is carried further when we turn to what Edgerton calls the *level* of responses. This has reference to the fact that the pastoralists' responses were frequently expressions of social values, whereas the farmers' syndrome of responses was constituted largely of personality attributes unsupported by positive expressions of social approval. The former are exemplified by such items as bravery, sexuality, and independence; the latter by anxiety, hatred, and impulsive aggression.

Before I can develop what seems to me to be the meaning of this contrast, it is necessary to consider an alternate explanation that cannot entirely be discounted. The difference in level—and the difference in emphasis, as well—might be attributed not to cultural adaptation but to cultural breakdown. Such an explanation would run as follows: These four tribes had been pastoralists with internally consistent social norms and psychological attitudes; a shift to farming in sectors of each tribe resulted in changed circumstances; the institutions and cultural values therefore were no longer in keeping with the actualities of life and thus were lost, and this in turn undermined the psychological integrity of the personnel. Such a line of argument would have great appeal, except for the important fact that evidence does not support the presumption that the economic shift was in each instance from pastoralism to farming. As best we can reconstruct, the adaptations at each extreme were made from an intermediate mixed pattern of farming and pastoralism. Furthermore, the actual histories, insofar as these can be reconstructed, are quite complex. For example, the Hehe appear to have transformed from an essentially farming people to a state-organized society dependent on cattle as an indirect result of the Ngoni cultural movement through Central Africa, and they subsequently made diverse adaptations to different environments. The Sebei pastoralist community studied by us was settled by people from the farming and mixed-economy escarpment area within the memory of living persons. Pokot pure pastoralism as found in Masol is thought by Conant to have been a recent adaptation. Therefore, though the reasoning of such an explanation may be acceptable, it is based upon a premise that is refuted by such historic data as we have.

There is another reason to doubt this line of argument. When Edgerton analyzed his data by tribal affiliation, he found certain consistencies in response for each tribe without regard to economy. These elements, with but few exceptions, are expressive of cultural values rather than personality attributes, suggesting that there are consistent tribal values in each instance, applying to pastoralists and farmers alike.

The stronger expression of cultural values, just as the greater degree of emphasis on these values, may be viewed as a response to those hardships mentioned above, together with the differential relationship that pastoralists and farmers have to their respective communities. To sustain a pastoral life requires an urgent insistence on the virtues and values of that form of activity, expressed and reiterated. At the same time, the centrifugal forces of the economy not only enable the individual to escape social demands, but might, in the absence of strong ideological supports, result in the loss of a sense of society itself. Finally, the freedom from the daily necessity of getting on with one's neighbors makes it easier to accept an ideal of community solidarity, since it is less fully tested in the crucible of real life. These several forces work together to make it both necessary and easy to accept the formal social ideals. The matter may be stated thus: the farmers must create institutions for the preservation of peaceable relationships among individuals who are forced by economic circumstances to dwell in close communities, while the pastoralists must create ideals that bind together persons who need to preserve a sense of community in the face of the fact that they are forced by economic circumstances to operate as individualists.

There is one further line of thought brought forth by *The Individual in Cultural Adaptation* and, indeed, expressed in its very title. This is the relationships among the intrapsychic character of the individual, the values and norms of the community, and the institutional aspects of social life. It has been characteristic of anthropology to treat these as separate spheres and, more often than not, to consider only one or another of these as the proper subject of anthropological enquiry. The Culture and Ecology Project was built on the opposite assumption, namely, that there is a dynamic interaction among these three kinds of manifestation, and that an understanding of social process involves itself with the interplay among personality, culture, and society.

Ego satisfactions, as well as economic satisfactions, tend to be derived from forms of behavior appropriate to the needs and requirements of a given life-form, for the people will recognize values that are consonant with actions appropriate to the demands of the ecological situation. Through the rewards and punishments, the supports and frustrations that life activities provide, the social and economic conditions also shape the personalities of the personnel involved. While the present volume focuses on the individual—attributes of his personality and his values and attitudes—it shows that these vary significantly with the economic circumstances under which he operates. To understand this relationship requires an appreciation of the normative patterns of interaction and the institutional setting under which such behavior takes place.

Our basic purpose in the Culture and Ecology Project has been to demonstrate the process of adaptation, inspired ultimately by a belief in the evolutionary development of culture. Over the past generation, research has demonstrated certain limited consistencies in the social order for peoples of like economic life. Culture, as a global concept, is not merely a historically developed arbitrary pattern of behavior, nor is society merely responsive to the functional requisites for the maintenance of social order. They are the products of situational adaptation, in which specific cultural forms and patterns of social interaction have greater or lesser viability.

Culture, as such, does not adapt. The process of adaptation can only be studied through the close examination of individual action and specific items of behavior. The present work is an effort to illuminate this process, or a part thereof. It demonstrates that statistically significant differences in expression of personality, in attitudes, and in personal values are found. The members of the eight communities investigated are not homogeneous in these attributes, but they display certain central tendencies. The characteristics of their responses cannot be understood, however, except in the context of the economic circumstances within which they operate, nor without a consideration of the social reinforcements to their action which the community as a whole provides. I stated in my introduction that the grand schemes of cultural evolution must be seen as an epiphenomenon to the process of ecological adaptation; similarly, I think it is reasonable to see ecological adaptation as a generalized statement of the process of individual adaptive acts.

Appendixes

Nine values pictures were finally selected to be used as part of the Culture and Ecology Project interview. Four versions (Hehe, Kamba, Pokot, and Sebei) were drawn of each picture so that the particular respondent being interviewed would readily identify with the house, clothing, or ornaments in the picture and so give an interpretation of the scene.

All four versions of values picture 7 are included in this appendix and are placed on one page such that the Hehe version appears in the upper left-hand corner, the Kamba in the upper right, the Pokot in the lower left, and the Sebei in the lower right-hand corner. For the other pictures, only the Pokot version is shown. The pictures were intended to portray:

1) A father confronted by a misbehaving and disrespectful son
2) Cattle damaging a farmer's maize
3) Armed warriors rushing toward cattle being protected by a few small boys
4) A sick person being treated by a native doctor (diviner) in traditional garb
5) A man either watching or interceding in a fight between two other men
6) A man performing an ambiguous act with a child
7) An attractive woman carrying water along an isolated path while a partially hidden man watches
8) A man viewing what could be construed as a sexual act
9) A man kicking over a beer pot being used by several other men

304

1)

2)

3)

4)

5)

6)

7)

7)

7)

7)

8)

9)

APPENDIX II

CULTURE AND ECOLOGY INTERVIEW SCHEDULE

1. Would the (Hehe, etc.) prefer to have sons or daughters? 2. Why?
3. What is the most important thing for parents to teach a toddler?
4. Is there anything else about as important?
5. What is the first useful task a boy is given?
9. What is the first useful task a girl is given?
13. What is the most important thing for a young man to know before he gets married? 14. What else is important?
15. What is the most important thing for a young woman to know before she gets married? 16. What else is important?
17. What is the best thing that can happen to a man?
18. What is the next best thing?
19. What is the worst thing that can happen to a man?
20. What is the next to the worst thing?
21. What kind of man does a woman want to marry?
22. At what age is a male person most happy? 23. Why?
24. What kind of man do the (Hehe, etc.) respect most?
25. What is the best thing that can happen to a woman?
26. What is the next best thing?
27. What is the worst thing that can happen to a woman?
28. What is the next worst thing?
29. What kind of woman does a man want to marry?
30. At what age is a female person most happy? 31. Why?
32. Does a (Hehe, etc.) girl before marriage usually have sexual intercourse with men? 33. Is this right?
34. How do people feel about an unmarried girl who becomes pregnant?
35. How do people feel about a man who makes an unmarried girl pregnant?
36. Should a young man have sexual intercourse before marriage?
37. Why?
38. After a man is married, should he have intercourse a certain number of times each night?
39. Do men worry that they may not be able to have intercourse with their wives often enough to keep their wives happy?
40. Do women worry that they cannot satisfy their husbands sexually?
41. Do women worry that their husbands do not have intercourse with them often enough?

42. Under what circumstances can a younger brother tell an older brother that he is wrong?
43. Under what circumstances can a young adult man tell a *mzee* that he is wrong?
44. Should a man always obey his father without argument? 45. Why?
46. Do wives ever disobey their husbands? 47. Is this right?
48. If one man says something that makes another man angry, what will happen? 49. Is this right?
50. If your wife (husband) became ill, how would you decide what to do?
51. If someone stole one of your cattle, how would you decide what to do?
52. If someone burned your house down, how would you decide what to do?
53. What should a man do if, suddenly, three of his cattle died?
54. What should a man do if he finds another man having sexual intercourse with his wife?
55. Does this always happen?
56. If a man could have anything he wanted, what should he choose?
57. If a woman could have anything she wanted, what should she choose?
58. In order for a (Hehe, etc.) man to be considered wealthy, what must he own? 59. How can a poor man become wealthy?
60. How do people feel about a rich man?
61. How do people feel about a poor man?
62. How do people feel about a man who loses all his wealth?
63. Which would you rather own (1) good farming land but no cattle (2) good cattle but no farming land?
64. What makes a man a good friend?
65. Is it better to have many friends or many clansmen? 66. Why?
67. Is it better to have many friends or many kinsmen who are not clansmen? 68. Why?
69. Is it better to have many friends or many age-mates? 70. Why?
71. Is it better to have many clansmen or many age-mates? 72. Why?
73. Whom can a person trust? 74. Whom else?
75. Is there one person you can trust beyond all others?
76. What is the worst sickness a person can have? 77. Why?
78. How do mad people behave? 79. How else?
80. Have you actually seen a mad person right here in (name of area)? (If yes) Tell me how this person behaved?
81. Do men or women become mad more often? 82. Why?

83. What causes madness? 84. What should be done with a mad person?
85. Were they cured? 86. Is a person who kills himself mad?
87. Do men or women kill themselves more often?
88. Why do people kill themselves? 89. Why else?
90. Can you tell me about an actual case of suicide you know about?
91. If a person kills himself are the relatives ashamed?

APPENDIX III

RORSCHACH INSTRUCTIONS

I am going to show you some "designs." These "designs" are specially made so that they look like a great many different things. Everyone who looks at these "designs" sees something different. There is nothing here that you are supposed to see or supposed not to see. I just want you to look at the "designs" and tell me what they make you think of. For example, in this one you might say it looks like (1) an elephant doing something, (2) a woman just standing there, (3) a cloud drifting by, (4) a skeleton of an animal, or (5) mountains or hills sticking up off in the distance. Now, what does it look like to you?

APPENDIX IV

SCORING INSTRUCTIONS FOR THE MANIFEST CONTENT ANALYSIS

Instructions: Score each explicit indication of each of the following categories, using the letter in the margin next to the category to indicate its occurrence. Score only manifest content the presence of which is obvious to you. If you must infer the presence of the category and are not completely confident that others would agree with you, then do not score it.

Code	Category	Definition and Additional Instructions
1	Adultery	Any sexual relations involving a married person with anyone other than a spouse (relations between unmarried persons, no matter how illicit, should not be scored).

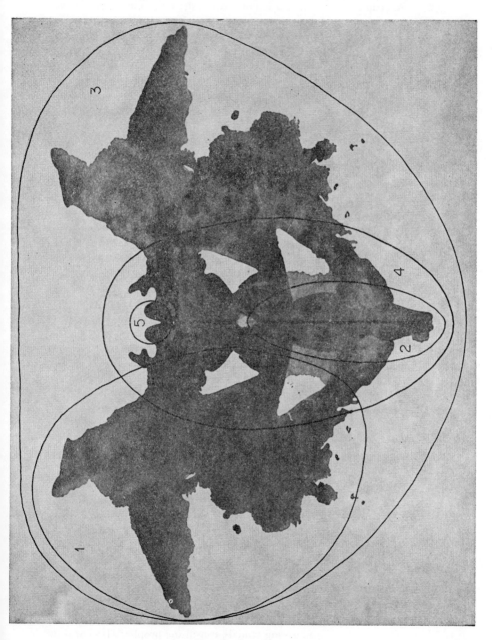

Rorschach card 1.

2	Affection	Any indication of love, tenderness, concern, or the like, of one person for another. Exclude any indication of affection if it is based upon physical sexuality, economic gain, or kinship obligation.
3	Cattle	Any explicit mention of cattle (not goats or other livestock), or any reference to livestock maintenance activities that clearly refer to cattle and not to other livestock (e.g., watering, protecting, marking, selling, etc.)
4	Clan	Score any favorable or neutral mention of the clan (or synonyms such as lineage). If the reference is negative (e.g., "clansmen cannot be trusted"), do *not* score it.
5	Concern with death	Any mention of death, burial, or serious illness which may cause death, where the context clearly indicates a fear or strong concern over death.
6	Conflict avoidance	Score any indication that it is proper or desirable to avoid conflict, dispute, antagonism among members of that society. The society may be defined as the neighborhood, tribe, or other territorial unit; it may not be defined as a kin group.
7	Concern with wrongdoing	Any explicit concern over the consequences of wrongdoing. The wrongdoing may be of any sort as long as it is clearly seen as being wrong and as having unfavorable social (not merely moral) consequences.
8	Cooperation	Any mention that two or more people are or should be in a mutually helpful activity. The activity may be of any kind (except sexual) as long as it is of mutual benefit either in the present or in the future.
9	Depression	Any expression of gloominess, sadness, dejection, discouragement, or the like. Do *not* score concern with death.
10	Desire for friends	Any mention of the personal desire for, or the general desirability of, friends.
11	Direct aggression	Any intrasocietal overt physical action that harms another person, or his immediate interests (economic, familial, etc.). Do *not* score verbal aggression, or any indirect action such as witchcraft.
12	Disrespect for authority	Either disregard for, or disvaluation of, political authority (e.g., elders, chiefs, prophets, tribal courts, etc.), that is, anyone in a formal office or status. If the authority is vested in a European, Indian, or a nontribesman of the society in question, do *not score*.
13	Divination	Score any positive mention of divination in any form (e.g., tossing sandals, consulting prophet). Do not score if the reference is clearly critical of divination.

14	Fatalism	Any mention of a person's inability to overcome or prevent misfortune.
15	Fear	Any expression of fear (or worry or nervousness, etc.) that has a clear cause. Therefore, do score fear of witchcraft, or worry about death, but do *not* score anxiety (e.g., "this man is worried, I don't know why") where no reason for the fear is given or clearly implied by the context. Do *not* score where the fear is explicitly related to poverty.
16	Fear of poverty	Any mention that poverty is or should be feared.
17	Guilt-shame	Any mention that a person is or ought to be guilty or ashamed regarding any activity.
18	Hatred	Any mention of hatred or hostility in any context as long as there is no mention of aggression, either physical or verbal.
19	Hostility to opposite sex	Any criticism of, hostility toward, or aggression toward the opposite sex.
20	Independence	Any mention of a person's taking an action that is described as being an individual decision. Score only major decisions with consequences (economic, jural, marital, etc.).
21	Industriousness	Any mention that a person is, or ought to be, working hard, diligently, regularly, and so on.
22	Insults	Any mention of an explicit public affront between people, whatever the context and whatever the action taken.
23	Jealousy of wealth	Any mention that one person covets or resents another person's wealth.
24	Land	Any neutral or positive mention of cultivated or cultivable land (also score mentions of specific crops in general). Do *not* score negative mentions.
25	Litigiousness	Any mention of litigation, the desire for it, or its desirability.
26	Physical beauty	Any mention by either sex that either is physically attractive. Score any positive mention of obvious physical enhancement such as decoration or clothing as well as direct expression of physical attractiveness.
27	Respect for authority	Any mention that a person respects, or ought to respect, any person in a position of authority (e.g., elder, chief, father, older brother, husband, adult man, etc.).
28	Self-control	Any explicit indication that a person is controlling, or should control, impulses, improper desires, anger, lust, jealousy, and disruptive activities of any kind.

29   Valuation   Any explicit indication that cattle are desirable.
      of cattle
30   Valuation of   Any explicit mention that individual freedom of
      independent   choice in action is desirable.
      action
31   Witchcraft   Any mention of witchcraft or sorcery in any context
                      (do not score divination, any activity involving curing,
                      or "witchdoctor").

APPENDIX V

A SAMPLE PROTOCOL WITH
CONTENT CATEGORY SCORING
(The protocol is that of Sebei farmer no. 11)

	Values Picture
Time	*Number*

0945   1. The cattle [3] owner is wrong. If one lets his *cattle* [3] graze in my *shamba* [24], I will be *annoyed* [18]. (*What should he do?*) Farmer should take a *case* [25] against the cattle owner. Farmer will win.

0947   2. A *case* [25] is taking place—this is the plaintiff, these are the defendants. (*What will happen?*) He will win because he is the previous farmer. The others are responsible for their *cattle* [3] ruining the *crops* [24].

0949   3. I see *cattle* [3]—and people with spears. One with a bow and arrow. Someone here has a stick. (*What will happen?*) Ones with spears are defending themselves and their *cattle* [3]—the enemy may be nearby.

0951   4. This is a woman—this is a man. Shoes. A pot. (*What will happen?*) The woman is sitting down—the man looks like one who wants to *attack* [11, 19] the wife. He *hates* [18, 19] her.

0954   5. A person with a knife. One with a stick. Someone is looking at them. (*What will happen?*) Looks like they will *kill* [11] each other. Not a stick—it is a spear. They will *kill* [11] each other. This man wants to stop the spear man from spearing the *other* [6].

0956   6. A woman carrying something on her head—she has good clothes on. A debbie containing water. A man there. He is holding something in his hand. (*What will happen?*) He will try to *rape* [11] her. (*What should she do?*) She has a stick to *hit* [11] him with. She should defend herself with the stick.

Values Picture

Time	*Number*	

0959   7. One woman near the house with her child—husband is there with another child. Hens, too. House is very good. The wife has a stick in her hand. The child is holding her clothes—child has its left eye closed. The father sits and holds the other child—the child is raising his hands. All are *happy* [2].

1001   8. A man standing in the door of his house—a very good house. Tea pots and sticks. I see a woman and a man; they are holding each other. They were sleeping—just sleeping. They are *happy* [2].

1003   9. A pot of beer. They are drinking—they all sit properly [6] around the pot—big beer straws. One is holding a bottle of beer—she is drinking it. These people are all *happy* [2]. A child is there, too. Seven in all. All are happy—that's all.

Questions

1005   1. Both.   2. (long delays) Because then all can go to school.
       3. (long delay—60 seconds) School and how to *work* [21].
       5. Learn to herd.   9. Hoe in the *shambas* [24].
    13. *Farming* [24].

1010   14. After having property he must find a wife.
    15. All housework.   16. Look for husband.

Rorschach

1014   I. lt– 5
      1. Elephant on this side.
      2. Looks like a woman.
      3. Looks like tusks of an elephant.
      4. Looks like breasts.
      5. Looks like legs but they are not right.
      6. All of it at once looks like a cloud.
      7. Looks like a skeleton of an animal that *died* [5] long ago.
      8. Also looks like hill with some stones balanced on top.

    II. lt– 45
      1. Difficult! (. . . . 35). An animal with testicles hanging there (lower red).
      2. All of it is a cloud.
      3. A skeleton of something long *dead* [5].
      4. Looks like a body of a person who has been *buried* [5] and is rotting.
      5 Looks like a lion (up. red); they are standing on a hill.

(two-minute interruption)

	Values	*Picture*
Time		*Number*
1022	III.	lt– 25

      1. People—they have eyes. These red things on their backs look like cocks (chickens), red comb. It might also be some animal. Don't know what is in the middle.

         IV. lt.– 45

1025

      1. Looks like a bat. It is hanging on a tree or a stone. (. . . . 60) Two feet and two tails. (. . . . 45) Looks like an animal.

         V. lt– 30

1028

      1. This has ears—eyes—feet—wings, too. Looks like a bat. It was in a cave.

         VI. lt– 70

1030

      1. Looks like a countryside—looking down from the mountain onto the plains. At the top is a tree.

         VII. lt– 30

1032

      1. Looks like clouds. Very difficult. (. . . . 45) Clouds.

         VIII. lt– 35

      1. Two animals, climbing on a tree. Looks like baboons—climbing a tree looking for food.

         IX. lt– 20

1035

      1. Green! On the bottom looks like people—they have eyes. I can see eyes—they have tails. Hips. They were hiding in the green thing. It is brown and green, and the top looks like a tree.

         X. lt– 35

1038

      1. Looks like animals (red).
Looks like a partridge—also they look like people—people with horns.
Looks like flower (out. blue).
Looks like people without heads (in. blue).

1042 *Questions*

      17. If he *works hard* [21] and becomes rich.

      18. (. . . . 45) Let me think (. . . .) get married.

      19. *Theft* [7].

      20. No.

1045

      21. One who is educated and has a good job and is *handsome* [26].

      22. (. . . . 60) Stay alive a long time.

      23. Don't know—want to live.   24. Polite.

      Slides (*Does all the outside noise bother you?* No, they are far away.)

<table>
<tr><td>Time</td><td>Values Picture
Number</td><td></td></tr>
</table>

Values Picture
Time   *Number*

1049   1. People—spears—*well decorated* [26]—red clothes—heads and ears decorated. Masai—look very good. (Smiles delightedly.)

2. One person—colobus monkey on the head—beads. Cloth. Scars on chest—chest decorated—also stomach—letters *O* and *B* on his stomach—also letter *K*. Leader of Masai warriors—*dressed very well* [26].

3. Bow and arrow—three of them. Cloth around his head. Another around his waist. Skin bag. This man is sick. His nose is closed. He is naked. Rope around his head—a brown and short man. Old—has a disease on his stomach.

4. So many people—one with a shield—monkey skin, pipe. Spear. Very many people, also girls far away behind. *Well decorated* [26]. It is pleasing. Masai.

1055

Questions

25. Married or unmarried? *Married! Dress well* [26].

26. No.   27. (. . . . 60) Don't know.   28. Don't know.

29. One who is *good appearing* [26].

1100   30. Always happy—women are happy,

31. Don't know.

32. a. Yes.   b. Yes—nowadays they do.   c. No—only one.

33. No—only pet.

34. If she is uncircumcised, she must be circumcised; if already circumcised, should be married.

35. Forced to marry her.   36. (laughs) Yes.

37. Because it is good to please a girl and make her want to marry him.

1105   38. I don't know—depends on his strength.

39. Yes [*worry*, 15].

40. Yes [*worry*, 15].

41. Yes [*worry*, 15].

1107 *Slides*

5. I love her—she *dresses well* [26]. Small cuts on her face look very nice. Good cloth. Very good woman.

6. Three women—*well decorated—clothes* [26]—breasts can be seen—earrings. They stand very well.

7. A young girl—cloth around her waist—breasts uncovered. She is unmarried. *Pretty* [26].

8. An old woman—she is laughing—*happy* [2]—has a key around her neck—head tied properly. Skin clothes like we had in old days.

Values Picture

Time *Number*

1110   (*Which slide did you like best?*) Can't recall—must see again! No. 5 is best.

Questions

42. Yes—if *land* [24] is not properly divided.
43. I hear from the *old men* [27] that during olden days they should not, but nowadays they do.   44. Yes.
45. If father teaches the son well, he will *respect the father* [27].
46. Yes. Some respect their husbands, some do not.
47. No. Should *respect* [27].
48. *Fight* [11].   49. No *conflict avoidance* [6].
50. Report to *the chief* [27] as soon as possible.

1115
53. Go to vet staff. (*What about the old days?*) Used to burn the beasts.
54. *Arrest* [25] him.

Slides

9. A table.   10. Looks like a house.   11. House built of stones.   12. Looks like a bush.   13 Looks like cloth.

1120 *Questions*

56. Wife.   57. Husband.   58. *Cattle* [3].
59. *Farm* [24] and trade.
60. Like him because he is rich.
61. If uneducated they *disrespect* [23] him. They should help him to find a wife to *farm* [24] for him.
62. They still *respect* [27] him.
63. *Cattle* [3], because then I can be married.

1125 *Slides*

14. I like these *cattle* [3]—a man is herding—a *shamba* [24] there, too. Very good *land* [24].
15. These *cows* [3] are good, too—eating salt.
16. White *cows* [3]—sandy country. One likes the hill. I can see hills far away.
17. Near the road—*herdsman* [3]. Sheep too. Good country. Some hills.

Questions

64. Feed people.   65. *Friends* [10].
66. If they live far away then they can feed me.
67. Both *friends* [10].   68. They both feed me.   69. Both.

1130
70. Both welcome you and give you food and beer. According to our custom an age-mate brews beer and if you go to him and are the first person there, you have the right to drink without paying anything.

Time	Values Picture Number		
	71. Both.	72. Both.	
	73. God.	74. Father.	75. No.

Slides

18. Dog—green country.

19. A leopard in a tree—feet are hanging.

1135   20. Elephant—dry country. Very big elephant.

21. Long hairs—teeth. Four teeth. Mouth is open. I think it is a lion. It wants to eat something.

22. What a snake! Very big eye—very big snake. Lion is worst animal, then snake.

Questions

76. Don't know—worst is *leprosy* [5].   77. It is bad—fingers and toes fall off.

78. Make noise, jump about, wave hands about—speak nonsense. You can't understand them.

79 Will *beat* [11] someone for nothing.

80. Yes, I saw one—took off all his clothes and walked naked. And he abused people.

81. Men.   82. People are jealous of you and *bewitch* [31] you.

83. Sickness.   84. Nothing could be done.

86. No.   87. Both.

88. One may be drunk and *beat his wife* [11, 19], and she runs away and *hangs herself* [7].

89. Same [7]—she feels ashamed [11, 19].

90. No—have never seen one.

91. No.

APPENDIX VI

RESPONSE VARIABILITY AMONG THE HEHE, KAMBA, POKOT, AND SEBEI

The questions used as titles for the following ten tables (A through J) were chosen from the 85 interview questions. Simple inspection of these ten sets of answers (selected at random from all answers given) should be sufficient to indicate that the Sebei tended to give a greater variety of answers to the questions than did members of the other tribes. Taking even the crudest index of variability, the average number of different answers given, the Sebei answers are impressively more varied. The Sebei averaged 8.2 answers per question, compared with 5.5 for the Hehe, 4.3 for the Kamba, and 5.1 for the Pokot.

TABLE A
Do the Hehe [etc.] Prefer Sons or Daughters, and Why?

Answer	Hehe	Kamba	Pokot	Sebei
Both—to produce children	0	0	0	58
Both—to inherit property	0	0	0	15
Son—to help at home	20	81	8	16
Son—to inherit property	2	29	5	9
Son—to continue clan name	52	2	0	4
Son—to be a warrior	0	0	0	7
Daughter—polygyny	0	0	0	2
Daughter—to bring in cattle	0	0	0	4
Just custom	48	14	115	6
No answer, or don't know	1	0	0	7

TABLE B
What Is the Most Important Thing for Parents to Teach a Toddler?

Answer	Hehe	Kamba	Pokot	Sebei
To walk	58	1	3	18
To obey, be polite, be responsible	2	10	54	15
Not to steal	0	2	3	0
To eat	0	1	1	20
To avoid harm	10	0	0	6
To work	1	6	67	28
To talk	34	1	0	28
To say "father"	0	105	0	0
To be clean	3	0	0	0
No answer, or don't know	15	0	0	13

TABLE C
What Is the Worst Thing That Can Happen to A Man?

Answer	Hehe	Kamba	Pokot	Sebei
Death	2	4	4	34
Disease	20	6	4	18
Poverty	42	93	30	11
No wife or wife dies	12	1	47	6
Barren or child dies	18	9	10	19
Major moral violations	5	8	15	6
To be a witch	0	0	1	2
To be quarrelsome	7	5	2	17
Adultery	3	0	8	·1
No answer, or don't know	14	0	7	14

TABLE D

DO UNMARRIED FEMALES HAVE SEXUAL RELATIONS AND IS IT RIGHT?

Answer	Hehe	Kamba	Pokot	Sebei
No—wrong	89	0	28	7
Pet with boys—is OK	0	2	0	42
Pet with boys—is wrong	0	0	0	3
Intercourse with one is OK	1	0	0	38
Intercourse with one is wrong	1	24	0	13
Intercourse with several is OK	3	75	98	10
Intercourse with several is wrong	0	2	0	4
Intercourse is OK only after circumcision	0	1	0	1
Other	0	0	0	0
No answer, or don't know	29	22	2	10

TABLE E

WHAT SHOULD A MAN DO IF THREE OF HIS CATTLE SUDDENLY DIE?

Answer	Hehe	Kamba	Pokot	Sebei
Nothing	71	0	17	39
Commit suicide	0	0	6	2
Report to authorities	4	0	0	29
Get more cattle	0	0	20	2
Move away	0	1	2	23
Find out who bewitched them	36	42	28	11
Divine	10	82	54	3
Cry and feel sad	1	1	0	11
Other	0	0	1	8
No answer, or don't know	1	0	0	0

TABLE F

IF A MAN COULD HAVE ANYTHING HE WANTED, WHAT WOULD HE CHOOSE?

Answer	Hehe	Kamba	Pokot	Sebei
Wealth	51	68	0	2
Cattle	19	32	101	40
Land	5	12	0	34
Money	9	0	0	8
Wife	20	7	24	32
Children	5	7	0	4
Feathers	0	0	1	0
Spear	0	0	1	1
Other	2	0	0	5
No answer, or don't know	12	0	1	2

TABLE G

To Be Considered Wealthy, What Must a Hehe [etc.] Man Own?

Answer	Hehe	Kamba	Pokot	Sebei
Cattle	111	49	123	43
Land	3	33	3	39
Money	5	1	0	2
Other livestock	0	0	0	0
Wives	0	8	1	22
Children	1	35	1	14
Food	1	0	0	5
Special	1	0	0	2
Other	1	0	0	1
No answer, or don't know	0	0	0	1

TABLE H

Whom Can a Person Trust?

Answer	Hehe	Kamba	Pokot	Sebei
Mother	2	8	11	8
Father	5	57	58	23
Spouse	0	43	16	8
Friend	13	0	9	6
Brother	8	1	18	34
In-laws	0	15	9	0
Son	0	1	1	7
Chief, leader	16	0	0	1
Other	72	1	5	39
No answer, or don't know	7	1	1	2

TABLE I

IS THERE ONE PERSON YOU CAN TRUST BEYOND ALL OTHERS?

Answer	Hehe	Kamba	Pokot	Sebei
No	104	3	2	21
Mother	0	7	21	3
Father	2	57	47	33
Spouse	1	43	14	15
Friend	1	0	18	11
In-laws	0	15	18	0
God	1	1	0	9
Brother	0	0	6	27
Chief or leader	8	0	1	2
No answer, or don't know	6	0	1	7

TABLE J

WHY DO PEOPLE KILL THEMSELVES?

Answer	Hehe	Kamba	Pokot	Sebei
Poverty, debts	1	28	6	24
Marital quarrels	21	28	2	18
Caught in wrong	2	1	2	16
Grief	0	0	41	5
Forced to marry	0	10	3	10
Bewitched, mad	49	52	42	12
God	14	0	0	4
Annoyed	17	7	1	25
Other	0	0	8	6
No answer, or don't know	19	0	23	8

APPENDIX VII
MEANS AND STANDARD DEVIATIONS FOR ALL CONTENT CATEGORIES

	Hehe Farmers		Hehe Pastoralists		Kamba Farmers		Kamba Pastoralists		Pokot Farmers		Pokot Pastoralists		Sebei Farmers		Sebei Pastoralists	
	X̄	S	X̄	S	X̄	S	X̄	S	X̄	S	X̄	S	X̄	S	X̄	S
1. Adultery	1.83	0.49	4.11	1.62	0.46	0.11	2.08	0.73	0.90	0.24	1.34	0.41	1.54	0.60	1.76	0.53
2. Affection	2.36	0.82	5.14	1.41	0.80	0.26	1.85	0.66	6.60	2.71	9.20	4.00	1.90	0.94	2.78	1.38
3. Cattle	14.51	6.26	19.92	8.13	18.39	7.41	18.33	6.39	25.71	9.64	25.69	8.02	14.90	5.37	16.90	5.52
4. Clan	2.77	0.90	3.08	1.14	5.78	1.62	3.47	0.97	1.87	0.88	2.88	1.20	3.20	1.51	3.20	1.36
5. Concern with death	12.86	5.34	15.55	7.89	8.58	3.22	13.74	6.04	14.18	4.10	15.40	3.72	19.97	8.72	22.88	9.46
6. Concern with wrongdoing	24.04	6.41	28.74	9.04	18.59	4.77	23.82	6.24	21.94	7.02	12.94	3.21	10.55	3.94	16.83	6.18
7. Conflict avoidance	2.85	0.87	2.44	0.62	2.87	0.77	3.08	1.08	2.98	0.92	1.60	0.46	1.98	0.60	1.51	0.38
8. Cooperation	9.86	2.15	17.60	5.91	8.41	2.11	9.70	2.89	17.34	8.19	11.20	4.04	7.85	3.70	8.06	3.27
9. Depression	0.99	0.21	1.44	0.50	1.35	0.47	1.83	0.68	2.01	1.11	2.87	1.27	0.98	0.43	1.54	0.76
10. Desire for friends	1.26	0.76	0.90	0.40	2.19	0.80	2.79	0.96	7.14	2.24	0.76	0.26	2.35	1.02	4.23	2.43
11. Direct aggression	23.64	5.65	32.13	8.79	21.64	4.82	26.95	4.61	24.21	7.83	28.56	6.75	17.50	6.21	19.46	5.11
12. Disrespect for authority	4.12	2.08	0.42	0.17	3.17	1.62	0.29	0.11	4.20	1.12	0.16	0.08	3.32	1.09	1.03	0.42
13. Divination	0.00	0.00	0.49	0.16	1.04	0.27	1.69	1.04	0.22	0.04	1.59	1.12	0.06	0.01	1.82	1.03
14. Fatalism	1.68	0.41	2.65	0.76	0.17	0.04	0.08	0.02	1.34	0.37	0.90	0.21	1.65	0.79	2.13	1.35
15. Fear	5.62	2.11	7.20	3.29	6.32	2.32	5.70	2.09	8.96	3.47	8.06	3.54	6.20	3.61	8.55	4.52
16. Fear of poverty	1.87	0.29	4.75	1.25	4.00	0.94	4.05	0.71	3.48	1.12	1.24	0.48	0.98	0.41	3.07	1.56
17. Guilt-shame	0.21	0.06	0.41	0.11	1.62	0.42	0.80	0.22	1.81	0.67	1.32	0.43	0.77	0.28	1.58	0.60
18. Hatred	12.47	5.41	11.05	3.96	10.03	3.39	13.01	5.42	9.26	4.18	5.06	2.06	9.59	3.67	6.25	4.58
19. Hostility to opposite sex	1.50	0.37	2.72	0.57	2.11	0.68	3.28	1.03	1.14	0.31	0.81	0.16	0.92	0.25	0.88	0.31
20. Independence	1.80	0.88	2.71	1.42	1.23	0.65	3.00	1.16	2.58	1.19	3.05	1.31	1.55	0.74	2.36	1.06
21. Industriousness	1.96	0.73	3.21	1.40	1.39	0.56	1.93	0.67	0.89	0.33	0.51	0.19	0.90	0.44	0.80	0.41
22. Insults	20.19	7.89	17.71	7.19	6.67	2.11	7.77	3.14	8.18	3.65	4.86	1.72	6.60	2.07	4.15	2.50
23. Jealousy of wealth	1.92	0.50	1.34	0.39	0.82	0.26	2.74	1.57	1.32	0.40	0.10	0.01	0.97	0.33	2.28	1.42
24. Land	6.19	3.03	14.52	6.17	12.76	3.81	10.24	4.29	8.77	3.70	2.18	0.73	8.60	4.57	8.13	4.24
25. Litigiousness	5.98	1.41	10.97	3.22	1.22	0.40	2.22	0.68	8.40	3.09	2.25	0.82	2.74	1.16	3.30	1.53
26. Physical beauty	0.65	0.16	0.75	0.32	0.39	0.09	1.46	0.38	7.49	2.06	4.74	1.24	4.85	1.55	1.67	0.61
27. Respect for authority	3.47	1.61	5.94	2.14	4.25	1.67	5.74	1.98	4.86	2.20	5.12	2.13	4.63	2.41	7.03	3.58
28. Self-control	15.91	6.69	16.47	6.24	9.06	4.07	5.40	5.40	6.66	2.85	8.42	3.36	5.91	2.33	6.17	3.18
29. Valuation of cattle	3.93	1.26	6.19	2.11	7.65	3.10	6.36	2.73	12.15	6.11	12.93	5.24	2.37	1.02	4.41	1.27
30. Valuation of independence	0.43	0.07	2.40	1.40	0.46	0.12	2.78	1.57	1.02	0.28	2.99	1.37	0.81	0.16	1.94	1.04
31. Witchcraft	5.87	2.21	2.57	0.91	0.50	0.09	7.16	1.29	1.62	0.40	0.95	0.19	1.88	0.56	1.01	0.25

APPENDIX VIIIA

COORDINATES IN THE BEST THREE-SPACE FOR EACH CATEGORY OF
43 VARIABLES OBTAINED FROM SSA-I

	Smallest space coordinates		
Variable	First	Second	Third
1 (1)	−120.321	363.736	−7.115
2 (2)	169.415	113.950	424.230
3 (3)	280.570	245.393	261.637
4 (4)	144.271	−211.197	−431.744
5 (5)	−342.697	142.118	−36.045
6 (6)	244.807	−232.391	−161.092
7 (7)	507.834	190.933	−52.101
8 (8)	−280.010	−29.716	100.787
9 (9)	59.750	−22.619	−375.151
10 (0)	−289.386	66.065	−181.330
11 (A)	−101.463	−17.959	232.516
12 (B)	41.215	138.145	−188.863
13 (C)	−160.131	−272.331	−54.698
14 (D)	284.075	221.733	383.353
15 (E)	−240.618	−251.344	117.504
16 (F)	175.230	5.229	−313.233
17 (G)	−120.592	−179.544	230.926
18 (H)	−306.463	−17.144	49.059
19 (I)	−40.089	−343.728	−67.301
20 (J)	−229.142	47.644	174.165
21 (K)	−343.839	−63.111	−162.839
22 (L)	−40.164	−272.744	−238.742
23 (M)	589.504	3.799	44.907
24 (N)	−335.677	1.755	−163.072
25 (O)	−238.884	−88.294	−145.225
26 (P)	316.070	162.159	−99.693
27 (Q)	225.413	296.593	61.599
28 (R)	235.500	−23.578	147.042
29 (S)	122.294	−422.838	92.475
30 (T)	−150.664	81.209	−267.291
31 (U)	−180.745	−76.581	273.059
32 (V)	258.229	221.703	−315.777
33 (W)	130.625	−238.744	213.982
34 (X)	7.333	−197.270	305.871
35 (Y)	−94.781	−104.845	−36.876
36 (Z)	−175.421	171.800	−87.777
37 ($)	−63.881	256.100	46.812
38 (.)	−147.058	−16.118	−25.063
39 (,)	7.082	248.217	265.108
40 (=)	22.398	233.846	104.289
41 (')	−151.797	131.181	166.499
42 (()	224.162	−154.984	−191.256
43 ())	108.073	−106.193	−93.516

NOTE: Normalized PHI = 0.02720 for 26 iterations; coefficient of alienation = 0.2316.

APPENDIX VIIIB

COORDINATES IN THE BEST FOUR-SPACE FOR EACH CATEGORY OF
43 VARIABLES OBTAINED FROM SSA-I

Variable	Smallest space coordinates			
	First	Second	Third	Fourth
1 (1)	−23.014	193.990	13.935	375.864
2 (2)	174.649	147.096	444.447	88.952
3 (3)	275.853	299.602	233.302	158.809
4 (4)	171.643	−252.983	−405.410	−193.658
5 (5)	−352.194	160.995	−63.806	123.016
6 (6)	265.492	−250.776	−188.329	31.889
7 (7)	531.417	178.928	−53.736	102.181
8 (8)	−206.669	−57.902	19.192	270.592
9 (9)	90.235	−46.563	−406.880	−68.729
10 (0)	−273.534	31.887	−218.238	187.726
11 (A)	−141.433	−56.952	274.707	−111.545
12 (B)	−13.180	190.198	−215.403	−225.094
13 (C)	−133.668	−310.008	−99.696	108.489
14 (D)	334.031	172.537	393.431	109.915
15 (E)	−251.677	−294.597	148.004	−58.840
16 (F)	218.770	−45.862	−332.694	21.776
17 (G)	−110.790	−228.778	253.601	48.480
18 (H)	−310.062	−63.287	28.844	154.164
19 (I)	−37.049	−393.585	−22.691	−84.268
20 (J)	−226.339	94.377	155.078	163.402
21 (K)	−372.274	29.194	−180.639	−135.285
22 (L)	4.071	−329.407	−165.163	−197.703
23 (M)	599.829	−53.727	69.537	134.008
24 (N)	−353.505	92.001	−188.369	−106.880
25 (O)	−276.238	−102.689	−144.469	−89.730
26 (P)	281.499	267.201	−144.808	−191.266
27 (Q)	276.025	245.784	127.983	−188.536
28 (R)	62.568	328.453	−121.471	189.117
29 (S)	34.934	−210.119	−55.891	449.137
30 (T)	−111.608	79.949	−291.578	165.565
31 (U)	−173.741	−64.428	290.416	137.429
32 (V)	334.790	28.490	−261.692	256.497
33 (W)	171.722	−285.733	206.930	43.128
34 (X)	42.610	−244.092	331.552	−0.475
35 (Y)	−109.247	−110.557	−72.479	24.240
36 (Z)	−231.569	178.723	−19.266	−181.583
37 ($)	−88.184	320.484	62.224	−71.962
38 (.)	−164.360	−23.792	49.792	−260.123
39 (,)	10.515	223.008	315.642	−185.826
40 (=)	8.070	172.621	163.348	−268.398
41 (')	−184.568	143.800	202.817	−59.903
42 (()	213.832	−120.122	−102.065	−320.028
43 ())	42.367	−33.319	−29.943	−344.657

NOTE: Normalized PHI = 0.01373 for 43 iterations; coefficient of alienation = 0.165.

APPENDIX IX

	Scale 9	Scale 3	Scale 4	Scale 6	Scale 8	Scale 7	Scale 10
Scale 9 (cattle concentration)	1.000						
Scale 3 (population density)	−.187	1.000					
Scale 4 (homestead clusters)	−.306	−.628	1.000				
Scale 6 (food production)	.187	.873	−.762	1.000			
Scale 8 (livestock ownership)	.314	−.806	.454	−.781	1.000		
Scale 7 (farming feasibility)	.073	.842	−.504	.885	−.831	1.000	
Scale 10 (pastoral/farming index)	−.287	.909	−.506	.775	−.742	.633	1.000

APPENDIX X

ANALYSIS OF VARIANCE OF
31 CONTENT ANALYSIS VARIABLES

Means and standard deviations were computed for the four tribes (two economic modes per tribe) with respect to each of 31 content analysis categories. It was decided to test the equality of mean responses by Analysis of Variance, for we wished to examine both the row (tribal) and column (economic) effects; it was suspected that interaction between the two would be high. The test felt to be most applicable was the Two-Way Analysis of Variance for finite populations (Brownlee, 1965, pp. 489–499; Dixon and Massey, 1969, pp. 175–181). Calculations were performed using the mean (Y^{ijk}) and standard deviation values for all eight sites. The variation among the individual n^i's was felt to be of a small enough range (61–65) to permit an average $n^i = 63$ to be used for the calculation of row and column sums of squares, however the individual n^i's were used to calculate the interaction and within sums of squares. No test was made of equality of variances prior to the Analysis of Variance test.

This analysis was conducted by Fred Prinz. We are grateful for the assistance provided by Professor Virginia A. Clark, Department of Biostatistics, School of Public Health, University of California, Los Angeles.

RESULTS OF THE TEST

The F-values of all row effects (tribes) were significant at the $P < .0005$ level (F (3,496) df), thus the effect of the tribal membership was uniformly great. The F-values of the column effects (economic mode) varied between $P < .50$ and $P < .0005$ (F (1,496) df) and are summarized below. All values not listed below are $p < .0005$.

$P < .50$ Litigiousness
$P < .05$ Land, cooperation
$P < .025$ Guilt-shame, fear
$P < .01$ Clan
$P < .001$ Hostility to opposite sex, self-control, cattle, and hatred

A surprising result of this test was the large values that appeared in the interaction mean square column. This interaction is all that variance not accounted for by row, column, or error variance. When tested, all were found to have F-values in excess of $P < .0005$ (F (3,496) df). Thus, it would appear that the data do not follow a linear model. This may be attributable to any of the following factors: (1) the variances for each tribes may not be equal; (2) there are other effects that are interacting with our row and column effects; (3) the most useful model for these data may be of a different order than a linear model; or (4) the data may not be normally distributed. There is reason to believe that all four may apply.

Bibliography

AINSWORTH, L. H.
1959 Rigidity, stress, and acculturation: (Uganda). The Journal of Social Psychology 49:131–136.

AINSWORTH, L. H., AND MARY D. AINSWORTH
1962a Acculturation in East Africa, I: Political awareness and attitudes toward authority. Journal of Social Psychology 57:391–399.
1962b Acculturation in East Africa, II: Frustration and aggression. Journal of Social Psychology 57:401–407.
1962c Acculturation in East Africa, III: Attitudes toward parents, teachers, and education. Journal of Social Psychology 57:409–415.
1962d Acculturation in East Africa, IV: Summary and discussion. Journal of Social Psychology 57:417–432.

AMES, LOUISE, RUTH METRAUX, AND R. N. WALKER
1959 Adolescent Rorschach responses. New York: Paul B. Heber, Inc.

ANDERSON, B. G., AND M. CLARK
1967 Culture and aging: an anthropological study of older Americans. Springfield, Ill.: Charles C. Thomas, Publisher.

ANDERSON, HAROLD H., AND GLADYS L. ANDERSON, EDS.
1956 An introduction to projective techniques and other devices for understanding the dynamics of human behavior. Englewood Cliffs, N.J.: Prentice-Hall.

ARTH, M. J.
1965 The role of the aged in a West African village. Paper read at the annual meeting of the Gerontological Society, Los Angeles, November 13.

BACON, ELIZABETH
1958 Obok: a study of social structure in Eurasia. Viking Fund Publications in Anthropology, no. 25.

BAKAN, DAVID
1968 On method: toward a reconstruction of psychological theory. San Francisco: Jossey-Bass.

BALES, R. F.
1950 Interaction process analysis: a method for the study of small groups. Cambridge, Mass.: Addison-Wesley Publishing Company.

BARKER, ROGER C., AND HERBERT F. WRIGHT
1954 Midwest and its children. Evanston, Ill.: Row, Peterson.

BARNETT, H. G.
1953 Innovation: the basis of cultural change. New York: McGraw Hill.

BARTH, FREDRIK

1961　Nomads of South Persia: the Basseri tribe of the Khamesh Confederacy. Oslo: Oslo University Press; London: George Allen & Unwin.

1964　Capital, investment and the social structure of a pastoral nomad group in south Persia. *In* Capital, savings and credit in peasant societies, ed. Raymond Firth and B. S. Yamey. London: George Allen & Unwin; Chicago: Aldine Publishing Company.

BARTON, J.

1921　Notes on the Suk tribe. Journal of the Royal Anthropological Institute 51:82–100.

BAVELAS, A.

1942　A method of investigating individual and group ideology. Sociometry 5:371–377.

BECK, AARON T.

1967　Depression. Clinical, experimental and theoretical aspects. New York: Hoeber, Harper & Row.

BEECH, M. W. H.

1911　The Suk, their language and folklore. Oxford: Clarendon Press.

BENNETT, J. W., AND G. THAISS

1967　Sociocultural anthropology and survey research. *In* Survey research in the social sciences, ed. C. Y. Glock, pp. 269–314. New York: Russell Sage Foundation.

BERELSON, B.

1954　Content analysis. *In* Handbook of social psychology, ed. Gardner Lindzey, Vol. I, pp. 488–522. Cambridge, Mass.: Addison-Wesley Publishing Company.

BIDNEY, DAVID, ED.

1963　The concept of freedom in anthropology. The Hague: Mouton and Company.

BIESHEUVEL, S.

1958　Methodology in the study of attitudes of Africans. Journal of Social Psychology 47:169–184.

BIRREN, J. E.

1968　Aging: psychological aspects. International Encyclopedia of the Social Sciences 1:176–186.

BLALOCK, H. M., JR.

1960a　Social statistics. New York: McGraw-Hill.

1960b　Correlational analysis and causal inferences. American Anthropologist 62:624–631.

BLOOMBAUM, MILTON

1968　Tribes and traits: a smallest space analysis of cross-cultural data. American Anthropologist 70:328–333.

BORGATTA, E., ED.

1969　Sociological methodology. San Francisco: Jossey-Bass.

BOYER, L. BRYCE, B. KLOPFER, F. B. BRAWER, AND H. KAWAI
1964 Comparisons of the shamans and pseudoshamans of the Apaches of the Mescalero Indian Reservation: a Rorschach study. Journal of Projective Techniques and Personality Assessment 28(2):173–180.

BOYLE, RICHARD P.
1970 Path analysis and ordinal data. American Journal of Sociology 75:461–480.

BRASS, W., ed.
1968 The demography of tropical Africa. Princeton: Princeton University Press.

BREHM, H. P.
1968 Sociology and aging: orientation and research. The Gerontologist 8(2):24–31.

BRIDGMAN, P. W.
1927 The logic of modern psysics. New York: The Macmillan Company.

BROWN, G. G., AND A. McD. HUTT
1935 Anthropology in action. London: Oxford University Press.

BROWNLEE, K. A.
1965 Statistical theory and methodology in science and engineering. 2d ed. New York: John Wiley & Sons.

BURKE, F. G.
1966 Political evolution in Kenya. In The Transformation of East Africa, ed. S. Diamond and F. G. Burke, pp. 185–240. New York: Basic Books.

CAMPBELL, D. T.
1955 The informant in quantitative research. American Journal of Sociology 60(4):339–353.
1961 The mutual methodological relevance of anthropology and psychology. In Psychological anthropology, ed. F. L. K. Hsu, pp. 333–352. Homewood, Ill.: Dorsey.

CATTELL, R. B.
1952 Factor analysis: an introduction and manual for the psychologist and social scientist. New York: Harper and Brothers.

CHAPPLE, ELIOT D.
1953 The standard experimental (stress) interview as used in interaction chronograph investigations. Human Organization 12(2):23–32.

CHAPPLE, ELIOT D., AND CARLETON S. COON
1942 Principles of anthropology. New York: H. Holt and Company.

CICOUREL, A. V.
1964 Method and measurement in sociology. New York: Free Press of Glencoe.

CLARK, MARGARET
1967 The anthropology of aging, a new area for studies of culture and personality. The Gerontologist 7(1):55–64.

COHEN, YEHUDI A.
1961   The sociological relevance of schizophrenia and depression. *In* Social structure and personality: a casebook, ed. Y. A. Cohen, pp. 477–484. New York: Holt, Rinehart and Winston.
1968   Man in adaptation, Vol. II: the cultural present. Chicago: Aldine Publishing Company.

CONANT, FRANCIS P.
1965   Korok: a variable unit of physical and social space among the Pokot of East Africa. American Anthropologist 67:429–434.
1966   The external coherence of Pokot ritual behavior. Philosophical Transactions of the Royal Society of London, B., no. 772, vol. 251, pp. 505–519.

COOMBS, C. H.
1964   A theory of data. New York: John Wiley & Sons.

CRESPI, I.
1965   Attitude research. Marketing Research Techniques Series, 7. Chicago: American Marketing Association.

CRIJNS, A. G.
1966   African personality structure: a critical review of bibliographical sources and of principal findings. Gawein 14(4):239–248.

DE SOLA POOL, ITHIEL, ED.
1959   Trends in content analysis. Urbana: University of Illinois Press.

DEUTSCHER, IRWIN
1966   Words and deeds: social science and social policy. Social Problems 13:235–254.

DIXON, WILFRID J., AND FRANK J. MASSEY, JR.
1957   Introduction to statistical analysis. New York: McGraw-Hill.

DIXON, W. J., AND F. J. MASSEY, JR.
1969   Introduction to statistical analysis. 3d ed. New York: McGraw-Hill.

DOLLARD, J.
1948   Under what conditions do opinions predict behavior? Public Opinion Quarterly 12(4):623–632.

DOOB, L.
1960   Becoming more civilized, a psychological exploration. New Haven: Yale University Press.

DRIVER, H. E., AND K. F. SCHUESSLER
1957   Factor analysis of ethnographic data. American Anthropologist 59:655–663.

DUNDAS, CHARLES
1913   History of Kitui. Journal of the Royal Anthropological Institute 43:480–549.

EDGERTON, ROBERT B.
1960   An initial experiment toward the development of a picture test of values. Ph.D. dissertation, University of California, Los Angeles.

1965 Some dimensions of disillusionment in culture contact. Southwestern Journal of Anthropology 21:231–243.

1966 Conceptions of psychosis in four East African societies. American Anthropologist 68:408–425.

EDGERTON, ROBERT B., AND FRANCIS P. CONANT

1964 Kilapat: the "shaming party" among the Pokot of East Africa. Southwestern Journal of Anthropology 20:404–418.

EISENSTADT, S. N.

1954 The absorption of immigrants. London: Routledge and Kegan Paul.

EKVALL, ROBERT B.

1964 The Tibetan nomadic pastoralist: structuring of personality and consequences. Burg-Wartenstein, Austria: Wenner-Gren Foundation for Anthropological Research. Symposium no. 24. Lithographed.

ELKAN, WALTER

1958 The East African trade in woodcarvings. Africa 28:314–323.

FLANAGAN, JOHN C.

1954 The critical incident technique. Psychological Bulletin 51:327–358.

FLEMING, H. C.

1969 Asa and Aramanik: Cushitic hunters in Masai-Land. Ethnology 8:1–36.

GALTUNG, J.

1967 Theory and methods of social research. Oslo: Universitets-forlaget.

GELLERT, ELIZABETH

1955 Systematic observation: a method in child study. Harvard Educational Review 25:179–195.

GLOCK, CHARLES Y., ED.

1967 Survey research in the social sciences. New York: Russell Sage Foundation.

GOLDSCHMIDT, WALTER

1946 Small business and the community: A study in Central Valley of California on effects of scale of farm operations. Washington, D.C.: U.S. Government Printing Office. (Report of the Special Committee to Study Problems of American Small Business. U.S. Senate. Seventy-ninth Congress, Second Session. Print No. 13.)

1959 Man's way: a preface to the understanding of human society. Cleveland, Ohio: The World Publishing Company; New York: Holt, Rinehart and Winston.

1965 Theory and strategy in the study of cultural adaptability. American Anthropologist 67:402–408.

1966 Comparative functionalism: an essay in anthropological theory. Berkeley and Los Angeles: University of California Press.

1967a Sebei law. Berkeley and Los Angeles: University of California Press.

1967*b* On the accommodation of pastoralists to modern life: a reply to McLoughlin. American Anthropologist 69–223.

1969 Kambuya's cattle. The legacy of an African herdsman. Berkeley and Los Angeles: University of California Press.

GOLDSCHMIDT, WALTER, AND ROBERT B. EDGERTON

1961 A picture technique for the study of values. American Anthropologist 63:26–47.

GOODMAN, M. E.

1967 The individual and culture. Homewood, Ill.: Dorsey Press.

GOULDNER, A. W., AND R. A. PETERSON

1962 Notes on technology and the moral order. Indianapolis, Ind.: Bobbs-Merrill.

GRAVES, T. D.

1967 Psychological acculturation in a tri-ethnic community. Southwestern Journal of Anthropology 23(4):337–350.

GREENBERG, J. H.

1963 The languages of Africa. International Journal of American Linguistics 29(1):part ii.

GUILFORD, J. P.

1956 Fundamental statistics in psychology and education. 3d ed. New York: McGraw-Hill.

GULLIVER, P. H.

1961 Land shortage, social change, and social conflict in East Africa. Journal of Conflict Resolution 5:16–26.

1963 Social control in an African society: a study of the Arusha agricultural Masai of northern Tanganyika. Boston: Boston University Press.

1966 The family herds. 2d ed. London: Routledge and Kegan Paul.

GUTTMAN, LOUIS

1968 A general nonmetric technique for finding the smallest Euclidian space for a configuration of points. Psychometrika 33:469–506.

GUTTMAN, RUTH, L. GUTTMAN, AND K. A. ROSENZWEIG

1967 Cross-ethnic variation in dental, sensory, and perceptual traits: a non-metric multibivariate derivation of distances for ethnic groups and traits. American Journal of Physical Anthropology 27:259–276.

HALLOWELL, A. I.

1956 The Rorschach technique in personality and culture studies. *In* Developments in the Rorschach technique, ed. Bruno Klopfer et al., Vol. II, pp. 458–544. Yonkers-on-Hudson: World Book Company.

HARRIS, MARVIN

1964 The nature of cultural things. New York: Random House.

1968 The rise of anthropological theory: a history of theories of culture. New York: Thomas Y. Crowell.

HAUCK, M., AND S. STEINKAMP

1964 Survey reliability and interview competence. Studies in consumer savings, no. 4. Consumer Savings Project Inter-University Committee for

Research on Consumer Behavior. Urbana: Bureau of Economic and Business Research, University of Illinois.

HAVIGHURST, R. J.

1968 Personality and patterns of aging. The Gerontologist 8(2):20–23.

HAYS, W. L.

1963 Statistics for psychologists. New York: Holt, Rinehart and Winston.

HEISE, D. R.

1969 Problems in path analysis and causal inference. *In* Sociological methodology, ed. E. Borgatta, pp. 38–73. San Francisco: Jossey-Bass.

HEMPEL, CARL G.

1959 The logic of functional analysis. *In* Symposium on sociological theory, ed. Llewellyn Gross, pp. 271–310. Evanston, Ill.: Row, Peterson.

HENRY, F.

1967 The survey research design in anthropological field work: some practical problems. Anthropologica 9(1):51–58.

HENRY, J., AND SPIRO, M. E.

1953 Psychological techniques: projective tests in fieldwork. *In* Anthropology today, ed. A. L. Kroeber, pp. 417–429. Chicago: University of Chicago Press.

HEYNS, ROGER W., AND RONALD LIPPIT

1954 Systematic observational techniques. *In* Handbook of social psychology, ed. Gardner Lindzey, pp. 370–404. Cambridge, Mass.: Addison-Wesley Publishing Company.

HOBLEY, CHARLES WILLIAM

1910 Ethnology of A-Kamba and other East African tribes. Cambridge, England: The University Press.

HOLTZMAN, WAYNE H.

1961 Inkblot perception and personality. Austin: The University of Texas Press.

HUMPHREY, N. D.

1944 The changing structure of the Detroit Mexican family: an index of acculturation. American Sociological Review 9:622–626.

HUNTINGFORD, G. W. B.

1953 The southern Nilo-Hamites. London: International African Institute.

HYMAN, H. H.

1954 Interviewing in social research. Chicago: University of Chicago Press.

1955 Survey design and analysis. Glencoe, Ill.: Free Press.

JACOBS, DONALD R.

1961 The culture themes and puberty rites of the Akamba, a Bantu tribe of East Africa. Ph.D. dissertation, New York University.

JAHODA, GUSTAV

1958 Boys' images of marriage partners and girls' self-images in Ghana. Sociologus 8:155–169.

KAISER, H. F.

1960   The application of electronic computers to factor analysis. Educational and Psychological Measurement 20:141–151.

KAPLAN, ABRAHAM

1964   The conduct of inquiry. San Francisco: Chandler Publishing Company.

KAPLAN, B.

1961   Studying personality cross-culturally. Evanston, Ill.: Row, Peterson.

KAPLAN, B., AND R. LAWLESS

1965   Culture and visual imagery: a comparison of Rorschach responses in eleven societies. In Context and meaning in cultural anthropology, ed. M. E. Spiro. New York: Free Press.

KAUFMANN, HARRY

1965   Definitions and methodology in the study of aggression. Psychological Bulletin 64:351–364.

KISH, LESLIE

1965   Survey sampling. New York: John Wiley & Sons.

KLOPFER, B., M. D. AINSWORTH, W. G. KLOPFER, AND R. R. HOLT

1954   Developments in the Rorschach technique. Vol. I: Technique and theory. New York: Harcourt, Brace, & World.

1956   Developments in the Rorschach technique. Vol. II: Fields of application. New York: Harcourt, Brace, & World.

KLUCKHOHN, CLYDE

1944   Navajo witchcraft. Papers of the Peabody Museum of American Archaeology and Ethnology, Harvard University, no. 22. Cambridge, Mass.: Harvard University Press.

KROEBER, A. L.

1919   On the principle of order in civilization as exemplified by changes in fashion. American Anthropologist 21:235–263.

1963   An anthropologist looks at history. Berkeley and Los Angeles: University of California Press.

LA FONTAINE, J. S.

1967   Parricide in Bugisu: a study in intergenerational conflict. Man 2(2):249–259.

LAUMANN, E. O., AND L. GUTTMAN

1966   The relative associational contiguity of occupations in an urban setting. American Sociological Review 31:169–178.

LEBLANC, MARIA

1960   Personnalité de la femme Katangaise. Contribution à l'étude de son acculturation. Louvain: Editions Nauwelaerts.

LEE, DOROTHY

1959   Freedom and culture: essays. Englewood Cliffs, N.J.: Prentice-Hall.

LEE, S. G.

1950   Some Zulu concepts of psychogenic disorder. Journal for Social Research 1:9–18.

1953   Manual of a Thematic Apperception Test for African subjects: set of 22 pictures. Pietermaritzburg, South Africa: University of Natal Press.

LEIGHTON, ALEXANDER, ET AL.

1963   Psychiatric disorder among the Yoruba: a report from the Cornell-Aro Mental Health Research Project in the Western Region of Nigeria. Ithaca, New York: Cornell University Press.

LEVINE, ROBERT A.

1960   The internalization of political values in stateless societies. Human Organization 19:51–58.

1961   Africa. *In* Psychological anthropology: approaches to culture and personality, ed. F. L. K. Hsu, pp. 48–92. Homewood, Ill.: Dorsey Press.

1962   Witchcraft and co-wife proximity in southwestern Kenya. Ethnology 1:39–45.

1965   Intergenerational tensions and extended family structures in Africa. *In* Social structure and the family, ed. E. Shanas and G. F. Streib, pp. 188–204. Englewood Cliffs, N. J.; Prentice-Hall.

1966a   Outsider's judgments: an ethnographic approach to group differences in personality. Southwestern Journal of Anthropology 22:101–116.

1966b   Sex roles and economic change in Africa. Ethnology 5:186–193.

LEWIS, I. M.

1961   A pastoral democracy. London: Oxford University Press.

LINDBLOM, GERHARD

1920   The Akamba in British East Africa, vol. 17. 2d ed. Uppsala: Archives D'Études Orientales.

LINDZEY, GARDNER

1961   Projective techniques and cross-cultural research. New York: Appleton-Century-Crofts.

LINGOES, J. C.

1965   An IBM-7090 program for Guttman-Lingoes Smallest Space Analysis-I. Behavioral Science 10:183–184, 487.

1966   Recent computational advances in nonmetric methodology for the behavioral sciences. Proceedings of the International Symposium in Mathematical Computational Methods in the Social Sciences. Rome.

LOUCH, A. R.

1966   Explanation and human action. Berkeley and Los Angeles: University of California Press.

LYNN, D. B., AND ROSALIE LYNN

1959   The structured doll play test as a projective technique for use with children. Journal of Projective Techniques and Personality Assessment 23:335–344.

LYSTAD, MARY

1960   Traditional values of Ghanaian children. American Anthropologist 62:454–464.

MACANDREW, CRAIG, AND ROBERT B. EDGERTON

1969   Drunken comportment: a social explanation. Chicago: Aldine Publishing Company; London: Thomas Nelson & Sons.

McLoughlin, P. F. M.
1966 Some observations on the preliminary report of the Culture and Ecology in East Africa project. American Anthropologist 68:1004–1009.

Malcolm, D. W.
1953 Sukumaland: an African people and their country. London: Oxford University Press.

Mandell, Arnold J.
1970 Neurochemical considerations relevant to human affective states. *In* Science and Psychoanalysis, ed. W. Muensterberger, vol. 17. New York: Grune and Stratton.

Marwick, M. G.
1952 The social context of Cewa witch beliefs. Africa 22:120–135, 215–233.

Matarazzo, Joseph D., et al.
1956 The interaction chronograph as an instrument for objective measurement of interaction patterns during interviews. Journal of Psychology 41:347–367.

Mbiti, J.
1966 Akamba stories. London: Oxford University Press.

Middleton, John
1953 The central tribes of the northeastern Bantu; the Kikuyu, including Embu, Meru, Mbere, Chuka, Mwimbi, Tharaka and the Kamba of Kenya. London: International African Institute.

Miller, J. G.
1965 Living systems: basic concepts. Behavioral Science 10:193–237.

Minturn, L., and W. W. Lambert
1964 Mothers of six cultures: antecedents of child rearing. New York: John Wiley & Sons.

Mitchell, R. E.
1967 The use of content analysis for explanatory studies. Public Opinion Quarterly 31(2)230–241.

Murdock, George P.
1959 Africa: its peoples and their culture history. New York: McGraw-Hill.

Naroll, R.
1962 Data quality control. New York: Free Press.
1969 Cultural determinants and the concept of the sick society. *In* Changing perspectives in mental illness, ed. S. C. Plog and R. B. Edgerton, pp. 128–155. New York: Holt, Rinehart and Winston.

Ndeti, Kivuto
1967 Elements of Akamba life. Order No. 68-7776. Syracuse University. Dissertation Abstracts 28 (12):4855–B.

Nigmann, E.
1908 Die wahehe. Ihre geschichte, kult-, rechts-, kriegs-, jadg-gebrauche. Berlin: Ernst Siegfried Mittler und Sohn.

NORTH, R. C.

1963 Content analysis: a handbook with applications for the study of international crisis. Evanston, Ill.: Northwestern University Press.

NUTCH, F. J., AND M. BLOOMBAUM

1968 A smallest space analysis of gang boys' behaviors. Pacific Sociological Review 11:116–112.

OLIVER, SYMMES C.

1962 Ecology and cultural continuity as contributing factors in the social organization of the Plains Indians. University of California Publications in American Archaeology and Ethnology 48(1):1–90.

1965 Individuality, freedom of choice, and cultural flexibility of the Kamba. American Anthropologist 67:421–428.

OMBREDANE, A.

1954 L'exploration de la mentalite des Noirs Congolais au moyen d'une epreuve projective: le Congo TAT. In Mem. in 8 de l'Inst. Royal Colon. Belge, Sect. Soc. Mor. et Pol. (37), 5.

PAUL, B. D.

1953 Interviewer techniques and field relationships. In Anthropology today, ed. A. L. Kroeber, pp. 430–439. Chicago: University of Chicago Press.

PAULME, D.

1963 Women of tropical Africa. Berkeley and Los Angeles: University of California Press.

PERISTIANY, J. G.

1951 The age set system of the pastoral Pokot. Africa 21:188–206, 279–302.

1954 Pokot sanctions and structure. Africa 24:17–25.

PETERSON, CLAIRE L., AND T. J. SCHEFF

1965 Theory, method, and findings in the study of acculturation: a review. International Review of Community Development 13–14:155–176.

PFEIFFER, E.

1959 Données obtenus au test de Rorschach chez noirs d'Afrique occidentale française. Bulletin de L'Institut Français D'Afrique Noire 21:20–60.

PFEIFFER, E., S. PELAGE, AND MME. PELAGE

1963 Quelques résultats obtenus au test de Rorschach chez les Bamilékés du Cameroun. Bulletin de L'Institut Français d'Afrique Noire 25:454–456.

PHILLIPS, B. S.

1966 Social research: strategy and tactics. New York: Macmillan.

PORTER, P. W.

1966 East Africa—population distribution (August, 1962). Map Supplement No. 6, Annals of the Association of American Geographers, 56.

RICHARDSON, STEPHEN A., ET AL.

1965 Interviewing, its forms and functions. New York: Basic Books.

ROCHEBLAVE-SPENLÉ, ANNE-MARIE

1964 Les roles masculins et féminins. Paris: Presses Universitaires de France.

RODGERS, W. B.

1969 Environment and change. Anthropology U.C.L.A. 1:1–13.

ROKEACH, M.

1968 Beliefs, attitudes, and values: a theory of organization and change. San Francisco: Jossey-Bass.

ROSCOE, JOHN

1924 The Bagesu and other tribes of the Uganda Protectorate: the third part of the Mackie Ethnological Expedition to Central Africa. Cambridge: The University Press.

ROY, P.

1962 The measurement of assimilation: the Spokane Indians. American Journal of Sociology 67(5):541–551.

SAHLINS, MARSHALL D., AND ELMAN R. SERVICE, EDS.

1960 Evolution and culture. Ann Arbor: University of Michigan Press.

SCHNEIDER, H. K.

1953 The Pakot of Kenya with special reference to the role of livestock in their subsistence economy. Ann Arbor: University Microfilms.

1956 The moral system of the Pakot. In Encyclopedia of morals, ed. V. Ferm, pp. 403–409. New York: Philosophical Library.

1957 The subsistence role of cattle among the Pakot in East Africa. American Anthropologist 59:278–300.

1959 Pakot resistance to change. In Continuity and change in African cultures, ed. W. R. Bascom and M. J. Herskovits, pp. 144–167. Chicago: University of Chicago Press.

1967 Pokot folktales, humor, and values. Journal of the Folklore Institute 4:265–318.

SCHREIER, F. T.

1963 Modern marketing research: a behavioral science approach. Belmont, Calif.: Wadsworth Publishing Company.

SCHUBERT, GLENDON

1967 Academic ideology and the study of adjudication. American Political Science Revue 61:106–129.

SCHUESSLER, KARL

1969 Covariance analysis in sociological research. In Sociological methodology, ed. E. F. Borgatta and G. W. Bohrnstedt, pp. 219–244. San Francisco: Jossey-Bass.

SECOY, FRANK RAYMOND

1953 Changing military patterns on the Great Plains. New York: American Ethnological Society. Monograph 21.

SHANAS, E.

1963 Some observation on cross-national surveys of aging. The Gerontologist 3:7–9.

SHANAS, E., AND G. F. STREIB, EDS.
1965   Social structure and the family: generational relations. Englewood Cliffs, N. J.: Prentice-Hall.

SHELTON, A. J.
1965   Ibo aging and eldership: notes for gerontologists and others. The Gerontologist 5:20–23.

SHERWOOD, EDWARD T.
1957   On the designing of TAT pictures, with special reference to a set for an African people assimilating Western culture. Journal of Social Psychology 45:161–190.

SHNEIDMAN, E. S.
1947   The Make a Picture Story (MAPS) Projective Personality Test: a preliminary report. Journal of Consulting Psychology 11:315–325.

SIMMONS, L. W.
1945   The role of the aged in primitive society. New Haven: Yale University Press.
1946   Attitudes towards aging and the aged: primitive societies. Journal of Gerontology 1:72–95.
1960   Aging in preindustrial societies. In Handbook of social gerontology, ed. C. Tibbitts, pp. 62–91. Chicago: University of Chicago Press.

SPENCER, PAUL
1965   The Samburu: a study of gerontocracy in a nomadic tribe. Berkeley and Los Angeles: University of California Press.

SPINDLER, G.
1955   Sociocultural and psychological processes in Menomini acculturation. University of California Publications in Culture and Society, vol. 5. Berkeley and Los Angeles: University of California Press.

SPINDLER, G., AND L. SPINDLER
1965   Instrumental Activities Inventory: a technique for the study of the psychology of acculturation. Southwestern Journal of Anthropology 21:1–23.

SPINDLER, L.
1962   Menomini women and culture change. American Anthropological Association, Memoir 91. American Anthropologist 64(1): part 2.

SPUHLER, J. N., ED.
1967   Genetic diversity and human behavior. Chicago: Aldine Publishing Company.

STONE, P. J., D. C. DUNPHY, M. S. SMITH, AND D. M. OGILVIE
1966   General inquirer: a computer approach to content analysis. Cambridge: M.I.T. Press.

STREIB, GORDON F.
1952   An attempt to unionize a semi-literate Navaho group. Human Organization 11(1):23–31.

TALLAND, G. A.
1968   Human aging and behavior. New York: Academic Press.

TALMON, YONINA
1968   Aging: social aspects. International Encyclopedia of the Social Sciences 1:186–196.

THOMAS, L. V.
1959   Remarques sur la mentalité du Diola. Revue de Psychologie des Peuples 14:253–276.
1963   Le test de Rorschach comme mode d'approche de la psychologie noire: aperçus sur la personnalité diola. Institut Français D'Afrique Noire, Bulletin 25:288–350.

THOMSON, JOSEPH
1887   Through Masai land: a journey of exploration among the snow-clad volcanic mountains and strange tribes of Eastern Equatorial Africa. London: Sampson Low, Marston, Searle, and Rivington.

THURSTONE, L. L.
1947   Multiple-factor analysis. Chicago: University of Chicago Press.

WALLACE, A. F. C.
1961   Culture and personality. New York: Random House.

WATT, KENNETH E. F.
1966   Systems analysis in ecology. New York: Academic Press.

WEATHERBY, J. M.
1963   Discussion on "Nandi speaking groups." Kampala, Uganda: Makerere College, East African Institute of Social Research.
1966   A preliminary note on the structure of clan and bororiet among the southern groups of the Sebei-speaking peoples. Uganda Journal 30:93–97.

WHITE, R. K.
1951   Value Analysis: the nature and use of the method. Glen Gardner, N. J.: Society for the Psychological Study of Social Issues.

WHITING, JOHN W. M.
1961   Socialization process and personality. In Psychological Anthropology, ed. F. L. K. Hsu, pp. 355–380. Homewood, Ill.: Dorsey Press.

WHITING, JOHN W. M., AND BEATRICE B. WHITING
1960   Contributions of anthropology to the methods of studying child rearing. In Handbook of research methods in child development, ed. P. H. Mussen, pp. 918–944. New York: John Wiley & Sons.

WHITTAKER, J.
1967   Sex and age as variables in persuasibility. Journal of Social Psychology 73:47–52.

WINANS, EDGAR V.
1965   The political context of economic adaptation in the southern highlands of Tanganyika. America Anthropologist 67(2):435–441.

WINANS, EDGAR V., AND ROBERT B. EDGERTON
1964   Hehe magical justice. American Anthropologist 66:745–764.

ZELDITCH, MORRIS, JR.

1962   Some methodological problems of field studies. American Journal of Sociology 67:566–576.

ZUBIN, JOSEPH

1954   Failures of the Rorschach technique. Journal of Projective Techniques and Personality Assessment 18:303–315.

Index